# Early Intervention with High-Risk Children

# Early Intervention with High-Risk Children
## Freeing Prisoners of Circumstance

edited by

**Arthur B. Zelman, M.D.**

JASON ARONSON INC.
*Northvale, New Jersey*
*London*

The authors gratefully acknowledge permission to reprint excerpts from "The Cornerstone Treatment of a Preschool Boy from an Extremely Impoverished Environment" by T. Lopez and G. W. Kliman, in *The Psychoanalytic Study of the Child*, 1980, vol. 35, pp. 346–348. Copyright © 1980 by Yale University Press, New Haven, CT.

Production Editor: Elaine Lindenblatt

This book was set in 10 pt. New Baskerville by Alpha Graphics of Pittsfield, New Hampshire, and printed and bound by Book-mart Press of North Bergen, New Jersey.

**Library of Congress Cataloging-in-Publication Data**

Early intervention with high-risk children : freeing prisoners of circumstance
    edited by Arthur B. Zelman.
        p.   cm.
    Includes bibliographical references and index.
    ISBN 0-7657-0008-5 (alk. paper)
    1. Child psychopathology—Prevention.   2. Socially handicapped
children—Mental health services.   3. Psychologically abused
children—Mental health services.   4. Child psychotherapy.
    I. Zelman, Arthur B.
    RJ499.E23   1996
    618.92'89—dc20                                                    96-16403

Manufactured in the United States of America. Jason Aronson Inc. offers books and cassettes. For information and catalog write to Jason Aronson Inc., 230 Livingston Street, Northvale, New Jersey 07647.

*To my own links in the great chain of being:*
*Rae, Irving, Diane,*
*David, Daniel,*
*Aaron, and Virginia*

# Contents

# V
# CHILDREN OF SYMBIOTIC AND PSYCHOTIC PARENTS

# VI
# CHILDREN OF NEGLECT

# VII
# HELPING INSTITUTIONS TO ASSIST HIGH-RISK CHILDREN

# VIII
# FOLLOW-UP STUDIES OF INTERVENTION FOR
# MULTIPLY STRESSED CHILDREN

# Foreword

Having identified with The Center for Preventive Psychiatry for more than thirty years, it is a special pleasure and privilege to write a foreword to this superb volume that documents in a scholarly and timely fashion how well the Center has kept its promises over the years. In the Introduction and unfolding throughout its chapters, the book demonstrates how the uniqueness of each child and the public mental health needs of the community can be brought together for high-risk children and their parents in a mutually enhancing manner. This is no small feat since most previous efforts to bring these two perspectives together have failed to do justice to either. Thus, this book is essential reading for all child experts concerned with children born into and growing up in high-risk environments.

The clinical programs described in this volume are framed by the predictably traumatic experiences to which these children and their families have been exposed. Homelessness, physical and sexual abuse, drug-abusing and psychotic parents, inappropriate foster home placements, and chronic, life-threatening illnesses (including HIV/AIDS) are the high-risk environments in which these services and studies have taken place. Such environments and experiences are all too frequently associated with a troubled, disrupted, depriving, damaging childhood and adolescence. The underlying assumption of the studies reported in this vital book is that each such child is entitled to the opportunity to mitigate and overcome the risks of a severely disadvantaged advent and life experience.

The chapters of this volume are more than the sum of their parts as they move from individual, family, group, and milieu interventions to school and community interventions. The authors describe how they have applied our best dynamic, clinical, and epidemiological knowledge in the service of fostering each child's and family's development. Such programs emphasize the child's strengths, minimizing weaknesses or transforming them into useful personal resources.

Demonstrating action research in the 1990s, this book vividly describes how model prevention-intervention services have provided the culture for relevant evaluation research and training programs. The Center's teams have documented the impact of their interventions on the emotional and cognitive developments of the children they have served, as well as on the competence of their parents. In this manner, these scholarly reports move our practices and theory significantly forward. Thus, *Early Intervention with High-Risk Children* responds productively and appropriately to our central public mental health challenge, that is, to meet the needs of that large group of children whose early development is going off-track.

Historically, this 1996 report is a creative, scholarly elaboration and updating of Anna Freud's, Dorothy Burlingham's, and Edith Jackson's pioneering venture of the first day-care program for infants and toddlers of poor families in Vienna in 1926. The initial model was succeeded during the war years by The Hampstead Nursery for children removed from their blitz-threatened families in inner London. Later this became The Hampstead Child-Therapy Course and Clinic, now known as The Anna Freud Centre. This new volume has an integrative historical and scholarly impact as it brings the legacy of Anna Freud and Marianne Kris together with the evolved creative vision of the founders of this unique prevention/early intervention clinic.

*Albert J. Solnit, M.D.*
Sterling Professor Emeritus,
Yale University Child Study Center
July 1996

# Preface
## The Center for Preventive Psychiatry: Evolution of an Early Intervention Clinic

*Arthur B. Zelman*

The work described in this book was performed or originated at The Center for Preventive Psychiatry (CPP), located in White Plains and Yonkers, New York. Following is a brief history of The Center.

In the early 1960s, Dr. Gilbert Kliman, a community-oriented psychiatrist and child psychoanalyst, working at the Albert Einstein College of Medicine in New York initiated a project entitled "Children's Reactions to the Loss of a Parent."* Kliman's interest in preventive intervention had been spurred by findings associating childhood bereavement with later depression (Beck et al. 1963, Brown 1961) and psychiatric hospitalization, as well as findings (Glueck and Glueck 1950) associating sociopathy with parental loss in childhood (Kliman 1968).

Since the project was preventive rather than treatment-focused, the Department of Psychiatry felt it could not support it with the city hospital funds then at its disposal. Having co-authored, with Dr. Martha Wolfenstein (1965), a study entitled Children and the Death of a President, based on children's reactions to the assassination of President Kennedy, and hoping to continue his work on children's reactions to parental loss, Kliman set up a private clinic called The Center for Preventive Psychiatry. Its initial focus was intended to be on preventive intervention and research with bereaved children.

---

*The issue of bereavement had been critical to psychodynamic thinking at least since the publication in 1917 of Freud's *Mourning and Melancholia*, in which emerged the idea of "depression" as resulting from identification with the lost object. A few years later in *The Ego and The Id* (1923) the subject of object loss took on greater importance when Freud proposed that "the character of the ego is a precipitate of abandoned object-cathexis." Hence, not only specific illnesses like depression but the structure and health of the ego itself depended in large measure on earlier losses, both real (bereavement) and felt (quality of relationship) (Zelman 1989).

Kliman invited Doris Ronald, an early childhood educator, to organize a therapeutic nursery (Cornerstone) for bereaved children, the first operating unit of the clinic. Kliman's interest in preventive intervention was not limited to childhood bereavement, however. Shortly after The Center was created, Ann Kliman, a clinical psychologist who had also performed research in childhood bereavement, established a service for persons of all ages suffering from bereavement as well as other situational crises. Based on work such as that of Lindemann (1944) on acute reactions to severe stress, as well as Caplan's (1964) on crisis theory, situational intervention was designed to prevent maladaptive responses to crisis, and promote coping and resiliency.

In 1968, the psychoanalysts Marianne Kris, M.D., Mary O'Neal Hawkins, M.D., and Peter Neubauer, M.D. formed a research trust entitled The Foundation for Research in Preventive Psychiatry, to help support the Cornerstone Therapeutic Nursery. With the help of Albert Solnit, M.D., of the Yale Child Study Center, the W. T. Grant Foundation was persuaded to provide the Foundation's first major grant.

In spite of efforts to inform the community of the availability of services for bereaved children, the nursery received relatively few referrals of this kind. Instead, preschool children with a variety of problems were referred to the nursery, while a growing number of older children, adolescents, and adults began to be seen for crises other than bereavement. By 1970 the clinic was treating almost 300 patients annually, a significant but still relatively small portion of whom had experienced childhood bereavement. What had started out as a preventive demonstrations project was developing into a mental health clinic with two seemingly unrelated services: a therapeutic nursery for preschool children and a situational crisis service for people of all ages (Kliman 1978).

Underlying these two disparate modalities, however, remained the idea of prevention. In the instance of young children, whether already symptomatic or not, the goal remained the prevention of later illness. In the case of the situational crisis service, the goal was to promote optimal adaptation to the stressful event or circumstances in order to prevent deterioration of individual or family functioning. Such events, in addition to bereavement, included diagnosis of a serious illness, debilitation accidents, crime victimization, separation and divorce, and loss of a home or a job.

In 1970 The Foundation for Research in Preventive Psychiatry and The Center for Preventive Psychiatry merged and a nonprofit community mental health center was formed. This was done partly in recognition of the reality that the community's perceived need went beyond bereavement and beyond purely preventive intervention. By the late 1960s, the flood of referrals of symptomatic preschool children to the clinic inspired the development by Dr. Stein and Doris Ronald (1974) of a training program in "educational psychotherapy" for early childhood teachers. Initiated as a purely supportive modality, the graduates of this program learned to make reality based interpretations and work with older children as well (see Chapter 12).

Simultaneously, The Center developed a four-year training program in child psychoanalysis and psychoanalytic psychotherapy, with the primary objective of training therapists to apply psychoanalytic insights and treatment to children from disadvantaged families. Similarly, the Cornerstone Therapeutic Nursery (Kliman 1975) evolved into a modality in which a child analyst could attempt to apply psychoanalytic methods to community psychiatry (see Chapter 1).

By the early 1970s The Center had an Early Childhood Program, staffed in large part by participants of these two programs, which, in addition to the therapeutic nursery, provided supportive and psychodynamically oriented treatment to preschool children and their caretakers.

In 1970, The Center sent a clinical team to a local daycare center to provide treatment on site to children already identified as emotionally disturbed. This was the first of many collaborations with day care, Head Start, prekindergarten and other community programs, including a spouse abuse shelter (see Chapters 13 and 14) and a program for teenage mothers. This ongoing outreach service continues to provide various combinations of consultation and staff training on the one hand, and on-site direct services, including parent and child groups and therapeutic nurseries (See Chapter 7), on the other.

Led by Ann Kliman, The Center also began providing crisis intervention consultation to various community agencies, modeled on the work of Caplan (1961), including other clinics but especially emphasizing school systems. Initially these interventions were incident based, for example postvention for a death of a member of the school community. Later they involved helping school systems to set up procedures and training enabling the school staff itself to handle crises.

Crisis consultation was also provided by The Center to whole communities—in 1972 to the Town of Corning, New York, which had experienced catastrophic flooding (Kliman 1973), and in 1974 to the Town of Xenia, Ohio, following a tornado. More recently (1992), The Center provided consultation in Coral Gables, Florida, following Hurricane Andrew. These efforts were similar to the widely reported intervention provided by Kai Ericson (1976) following the Buffalo Creek flood in 1972.

In 1985, The Center's Crisis Service and Early Childhood Service combined to provide its most extensive and difficult community consultation effort to date. This involved an unlicensed daycare center in Mt. Vernon, against which allegations of massive sexual abuse had been made (see Chapter 15).

Between 1970 and 1975, The Center almost doubled in size, the number of treatment visits having increased from 7,600 to 14,000 annually. Both the Early Childhood Service and Situational Crisis Service had been augmented by group psychotherapy so that individual, group, and family modalities were being provided, as in a traditional clinic. While the Situational Crisis Service continued to see a stream of relatively intact individuals and families for whom "psychological first aid" (Kliman 1978) was sufficient, for an increasing number of patients "situational crises" were superimposed on a pattern of chronic stress that required more intensive intervention. The Therapeutic Nursery, meanwhile, was increasingly being utilized for the children of severely disrupted families (see Chapter 2). In short, the "primary" preventive focus of The Center was evolving into something else, based on the perceived needs of the community it served.

In 1978, The Center was awarded a four-year NIMH grant to assess the effectiveness of mental health services on children about to be placed on foster care. This project served to bring into relief and hasten the shift from The Center's original focus on children living in intact environments who had suffered a loss through bereavement to children whose environments had been chronically stressful. These latter children were placed at high risk by virtue of their previous environments and current situations rather than by a single event.

A variety of projects followed in this vein. For example, in the 1980s The Center began to work with homeless children. Three separate outreach projects were designed (one of which is described in Chapter 7) to assist this population. Another group of young children living in a high risk situation are children of mentally ill parents. In 1987 The Center received a grant from New York State to establish a therapeutic nursery for these children and their families (see Chapter 11).

Similarly, experience accumulated at The Center with children of HIV-afflicted families led in 1994 to an ongoing collaboration between The Center and a local community agency, the Sharing Community in Yonkers, New York, in which the children of HIV-afflicted families receive mental health as well as concrete and case management services. The high-risk status of children of incarcerated parents has similarly led, during the past decade, to an ongoing consultation with the local County Woman's Prison. Finally, The Center received funding in 1994 to collaborate with another community agency (Westchester Jewish Community Services) in the provision of integrated services for severely disrupted and multiproblem families, in an effort to prevent the hospitalization and out-of-home placement of children.

In 1995, The Center provided over 30,000 visits, the majority for children (and their families) living in high-risk situations. It is a sobering fact that the need for those services exists in New York's Westchester County, one of the wealthiest (based on per capita income) in our country. This would suggest a pervasive need for early intervention clinics providing the kind of services described in this volume.

The Center's expanded focus on children living in these high-risk environments and situations has resulted in a shift of perspective from primary prevention to early intervention. This shift has not occurred by choice but through necessity. The unfortunate fact is that there are hundreds of thousands of young children living in circumstances that have already compromised their development and have placed in jeopardy their potential to become contributing members of our society. It is our impression that the history of our clinic accurately reflects not only the bad news of a growing need for early intervention but also the good news of a growing awareness of the need. This book describes various interventions that we have found useful in our attempt to meet this need. We hope it will encourage others to attempt and refine this work.

## REFERENCES

Beck, A. T., et al. (1963). Childhood bereavement and adult depression. *Archives of General Psychiatry* 9:295–302.

Brown, F. (1961). Depression and childhood bereavement. *Journal of Mental Science* 107:754–777.

Caplan, G. (1961). *An Approach to Community Mental Health*. New York: Grune & Stratton.

——— (1964). Principles of Preventive Psychiatry. New York: Basic Books.

Erikson, K. T. (1976). *Everything in Its Path*. New York: Simon & Schuster.

Glueck, S., and Glueck, E. (1950). *Unraveling Juvenile Delinquency*. Cambridge, MA: Harvard University Press.

Kliman, A. S. (1973). *The Corning Flood Project: Psychological First Aid Following a Natural Disaster*. Presented at hearings before the Subcommittee on Disaster Relief of the Committee on Public Works, U.S. Senate. Washington, DC: Center for Preventive Psychiatry.

——— (1978). *Crisis: Psychological First Aid for Recovery and Growth*. New York: Holt, Rinehart & Winston.

Kliman, G. W. (1968). *Psychological Emergencies of Childhood*. New York: Grune & Stratton.

———— (1975). Analyst in the nursery: experimental application of child analytic techniques—the Cornerstone method. *Psychoanalytic Study of the Child* 30: 477–510. New Haven, CT: Yale University Press.

Lindemann, E. (1944). Symptomatology and management of acute grief. *American Journal of Psychiatry* 101:141–148.

Stein, M., and Ronald, D. (1974). Educational psychotherapy of preschoolers. *Journal of the American Academy of Child Psychiatry* 13(4):618–634.

Wolfenstein, M., and Kliman, G. W. (1965). *Children and the Death of a President.* New York: Doubleday.

Zelman, A. B. (1989). Preventive psychiatry and object loss: development of a preventive clinic. In *Preventive Psychiatry: Early Intervention and Situational Crisis Management,* ed. S. Klagsbrun et al., pp. 3–9. Philadelphia: Charles Press.

# Acknowledgments

I would like to thank the following individuals whose efforts contributed, in various ways, to the existence of this book:

David Abrams, Ph.D., on whose keen interest and scholarly enthusiasm I depended for inspiration; Alyson Aurelio, for her stalwart secretarial assistance rendered under difficult conditions; Susanne French, for additional secretarial assistance; Marc Galanter, M.D., for his encouragement and suggestions concerning data collection; Gilbert Kliman, M.D., who, in his successive roles as my supervisor, mentor, Medical Director, and collaborator, taught me much while giving me wide berth; Elaine Lindenblatt, production editor, for keeping things moving; Helen Marsh, for her special assistance; Marcia Miller of New York Hospital, for invaluable bibliographical assistance; Landrum Tucker, M.D., for his clinical wisdom and the model he provided of good-humored persistence in the face of adversity; and my wife, Virginia, whose assistance covered the gamut from psychological support to clarification of ideas to editorial work.

I also wish to thank the Archaeus Foundation for their financial support and the Board of The Center of Preventive Psychiatry for giving me much of the time needed to complete this project.

Finally, I thank the staff of The Center for Preventive Psychiatry, past and present, unnamed as well as named contributors to this book, for the work done over the years (only a small amount of which is presented here) and for creating an environment of mutual support, caring, and openness, without which this kind of project cannot be realized.

# Contributors

**David Abrams, Ph.D.**
Clinic Director, East New York Diagnostic and Treatment Center, Child and Adolescent Clinic, Brooklyn, NY

**Norma Balter, C.S.W.**
Supervising Psychotherapist, The Center for Preventive Psychiatry

**Susan Berenzweig, Psy.D.**
Staff Psychologist, The Center for Preventive Psychiatry

**Nancy Berlin, Ph.D.**
Staff Psychologist, The Center for Preventive Psychiatry

**Elissa Burian, M.A.**
Clinical Consultant, The Center for Preventive Psychiatry

**Paul J. Donahue, Ph.D.**
Staff Psychologist, Coordinator of Homeless Services, and Director of Early Childhood Consultation, The Center for Preventive Psychiatry

**Richard Evans, M.D.**
Senior Child Psychiatrist, The Center for Preventive Psychiatry

**Murray J. Friedman, Ph.D.**
Former Research Psychologist, The Center for Preventive Psychiatry

**Judith Brown Gordon, D.S.W.**
Associate Professor, College of New Rochelle

**Susan Howard, C.S.W.**
Director, Cornerstone Therapeutic Nursery, Yonkers, The Center for Preventive Psychiatry

**Elizabeth Jacobson, C.S.W.**
Supervising Psychotherapist, The Center for Preventive Psychiatry

**Ann S. Kliman, M.A.**
Director, Situational Crisis Service, The Center for Preventive Psychiatry

**Gilbert W. Kliman, M.D.**
Medical Director, The Psychological Trauma Center, San Francisco, California

**Aviva Levy, M.A.**
Supervising Psychotherapist, Coordinator of The Learning Center and Groups, The Center for Preventive Psychiatry

**Janet Brown Lobel, M.A.**
Associate Psychotherapist, The Center for Preventive Psychiatry

**Thomas Lopez, Ph.D.**
Clinical Supervisor and Director, Cornerstone Nursery, White Plains, The Center for Preventive Psychiatry

**Laurie Mendik, M.A., C.S.W.**
Senior Psychotherapist, The Center for Preventive Psychiatry

**Bernard G. Pasquariella, M.A.**
Senior Psychotherapist, Clinical Coordinator of P.A.C.T. Therapeutic Unit, The Center for Preventive Psychiatry

**Rosetta M. Rhodes, A.C.S.W.**
Clinic Director, Yonkers, The Center for Preventive Psychiatry

**Shirley C. Samuels, Ed.D.**
Assistant Clinic Director, White Plains, The Center for Preventive Psychiatry

**Rita Stewart, M.S.**
Supervising Psychotherapist, The Center for Preventive Psychiatry

**Arthur B. Zelman, M.D.**
Medical Director, The Center for Preventive Psychiatry

# 1

# Introduction: Prevention, the Medical Model, and Early Intervention

*Arthur B. Zelman*

The concept of prevention was borrowed from the field of physical medicine. In this model, three kinds of prevention are specified: primary, secondary, and tertiary. Primary prevention precedes the onset of an illness and reduces its incidence; secondary prevention reduces its severity and duration; tertiary prevention reduces impairment and promotes compensation for loss of function due to the illness.

Primary prevention has perhaps had its greatest success in the field of infectious disease. A pathogenic organism is identified, measures are taken to eliminate it from the environment, or to create host resistance to it, before it can cause illness. In the case of the yellow fever virus, for example, the draining of swamps eliminated the vector (the aedes mosquito) through which the virus was introduced, and vaccination provided protection of the human host. Since the onset and presence of the illness caused by the pathogen is readily detectible, the effectiveness of the preventive measure is readily demonstrated.

The onset and presence of "mental illness," however, is not as easily determined. Therefore, it is not so clear at what level of prevention, or even whether, the preventive measure has succeeded.

This is an important question because an ounce of primary prevention is usually worth a pound of cure. The benefit of diet and exercise is high compared to the cost of the symptoms and treatment of heart disease. Similarly, if a parentally bereaved 5- year-old child can, with a few hours of psychological "first aid," be spared years (if not a lifetime) of depression, the argument for crisis intervention is irrefutable.

Indeed, although the relationship between adult and childhood depression is not altogether clear, and even if, for this and other reasons, the effi-

1

cacy of crisis intervention with bereaved children in preventing adult depression has not been proven, the cost compared to the potential benefit of the intervention is so low that it is hard to argue against it. (Notwithstanding, most third party payers will not reimburse intervention for an "uncomplicated bereavement.") This is one reason we, along with an increasing number of practitioners and clinics during the past twenty-five years or so, continue to provide and advocate for routine early intervention for bereaved children.

However, for many children, bereaved or not, neither their environments nor their previous development may be described as "uncomplicated." For these children, psychological first aid will not suffice and the cost–benefit ratio of a given preventive or early intervention is not so easy to determine. Even if it were determined that it was relatively low, support for the intervention would depend on the question of cost and benefit to whom. There is evidence that early intervention with aggressive young boys can prevent the onset of conduct disorder (discussed below) and later juvenile delinquency. The beneficiaries of intervention, therefore, would include society as a whole. However, a major transfer of financial responsibility from public funding such as Medicaid to for-profit institutions such as insurance and managed care companies is now occurring. There is no reason to expect private companies to shoulder these profit reducing costs, the benefits of which go to society at large.

A further problem with the application of a physical illness model to mental illness is its lack of fit with a developmental model of behavior. The latter model implies continuity and relativism, while the physical illness model presupposes an "on-off" situation: either an illness exists or it doesn't.

Recognizing these limitations of the application of the traditional preventive model to mental illness, the Committee on Prevention of Mental Disorders of the Institute of Medicine (1994) discards classification of mental health interventions as primary, secondary, and tertiary in favor of Gordon's (1993) system, also derived from physical medicine, in which preventive measures are classified as universal, selected, or indicated. In this system a *universal* measure is defined as one that is good for all members of a population, for example, immunization for *all* children; a *selected* measure is one used for a member of a subpopulation that is viewed as high risk, for example, the provision of home counseling and a center-based child development program for the families of low-birth-weight children (Infant Health and Development Program 1990); and *indicated* measures are taken for individuals who may already be exhibiting a symptom or other risk factor for a disorder that has not yet been diagnosed, for example, Parent–Child Interaction remediation for pre-school children who have already manifested behavioral symptoms (Strayhorn and Weidman 1991), in order to prevent conduct and other disorders.

Gordon's focus on risk factors in addition to the presence or absence of a particular disease fits better with a developmental model of mental health and illness. It allows for the fact that a variable constituting a risk factor for one population may be an outcome measure for another. For example, the presence of high aggressivity in a group of 5-year-olds may be viewed as a risk factor requiring intervention to prevent the onset of a conduct disorder, or as an outcome measure of earlier interventions for pre-school children with dysfunctional parents.

Gordon's classification system, however, insofar as its use reinforces the assumption of the existence of discrete mental "illnesses," continues to support a medical model of prevention. This model may be useful in adult psychiatry, with its focus on such conditions as schizophrenia or bipolar affective disorder, but it has less applicability to dysfunctions of childhood (and therefore prevention and early intervention) due to its lack of diagnostic clarity.

The medical model leads to an emphasis on medical science and technology in a search for improved interventions. The notion is: even if we don't yet have a cure, we will soon find one as we did for smallpox and polio, if not with vaccines then with better drugs. The medical model also lends itself to a focus on the individual at the expense of scrutiny of his environment. In keeping with this focus, concepts like resilience are emphasized, which highlight the exceptional "survivor" while underestimating the powerful effects of the noxious environments on the many. Reinforcing the medical model is the fact that medical solutions are simpler and more definitive than are social solutions, in addition to being cheaper in the short if not the long run. The wish for simple solutions, to which professionals are not immune, leads to prematurely optimistic beliefs that these solutions have been found. For example, the efficacy of Ritalin in altering disturbing behavior of children with so-called attention deficit disorder has obscured the fact that the drug does not necessarily alter attention and has not been demonstrated to affect long-term academic achievement and learning (Barkley 1990).

When drugs do have a beneficial effect, this is seen as proof that a biological defect, such as a "chemical imbalance," is present (the application of this same logic to the social use of alcohol in reducing social anxiety would lead to the conclusion that most of us suffer from faulty chemistry).

In part, this book is intended as a corrective to the seductiveness of the medical model as it relates to the idea of prevention and early intervention in the area of mental health and "illness." It thus represents an attempt to ensure that we don't forget the psychosocial component of the biopsychosocial model to which much lip service is given.

With the above consideration in mind, we have come to doubt the usefulness of the idea of primary prevention at least in the clinical arena. Feeling, fantasy, perception, and behavior—the raw material of the mental health or illness of the individual—are so intertwined with individual, family, and cultural history on the one hand, and current family, community, and cultural context on the other, that it is impossible to conceive of a time before which the seeds of dysfunction were not present or were not being watered by forces outside as well as inside the individual.

From this point of view, the distinction between situation crisis intervention after a stressful event constituting primary prevention on the one hand and intervention for young children living in chronically stressful conditions constituting secondary prevention on the other becomes blurred. We have come to prefer, as an alternative, the concept of early intervention, whether it signifies early in the life of a child or early after an event such as a bereavement. No matter how early an intervention, antecedent as well as current individual, historical, and social processes are shaping the person's behavior. There is, of course, no such thing as an uncomplicated bereavement. Instead, there are bereavements, following which the interplay of complex forces at work will result in a more or less adaptive set of responses of the individual to the event. The purpose of intervention is to facilitate or reinforce adaptive responses and counter or reduce maladaptive ones. With chronically environmentally stressed young children, the forces acting upon them may constitute more salient criteria for preventive intervention than the presence or absence of a diagnosis.

Whatever the limitations of the application of the public health model of prevention to psychiatry, the model has generated two concepts that do seem to be of great value: (1) the idea of risk, and (2) the idea of protective factors. The quality of a child's ongoing development will depend on the balance of risk factors and protective factors to which he is exposed. Preventive or early interventive measures are designed to reduce risk factors or enhance protective factors.

## RISK FACTORS

Using a biopsychosocial model, the Institute of Medicine (1994) categorizes as *biological, psychosocial,* or *community* the following risk factors for the development of conduct disorders as identified by research. In the biological sphere are genetic vulnerability, physiological variables (e. g., low reactivity of the autonomic nervous system), gender, temperament, hyperactivity, cognitive and neuropsychological deficits including academic underachievement, and chronic ill health. Among risk factors in the psychosocial sphere are precursor symptoms such as aggression, antisocial behavior of family members, parental psychopathology, marital discord, and dysfunctional parenting practices such as especially harsh and abusive forms of discipline (the authors here refer to one study [Patterson et al. 1982] that found a specific correlation between a combination of poor supervision, parental criticism, harsh and erratic discipline, and rejecting stances toward the child on the one hand, and antisocial behavior in children on the other). Community risk factors, including poverty, overcrowding, and high crime rate neighborhoods, are also included in the list of psychosocial risk factors.

Most of the factors listed above that put the child at risk for the development of a conduct disorder will also put him at risk for a variety of other disorders. Closer scrutiny, however, reveals that not much can be done for the child who needs early intervention to reduce either the biological or the community risk factors. What remains are intrapsychic and intrafamilial variables that are closely intertwined. These include aggression, antisocial behavior of a family member, parental psychopathology, marital discord, and dysfunctional parenting. It is these risk factors that are, in principle, amenable to intervention.

This book is loosely organized according to situations or environmental circumstances that are associated with these psychosocial risk factors. They are therefore conceptualized as high-risk situations in proportion to the number and intensity of risk factors with which they are associated.

Sometimes these situations refer to concrete circumstances such as homelessness, placement in foster care, or living in severely disrupted or chaotic families (Chapters 2–7). Sometimes they are more focused on factors that directly involve the quality or loss of a primary caretaking relationship, for example, children of mentally ill parents, children of symbiotic parents, or bereaved children (Chapters 8–12). In Chapter 4, on ADD, the risk factor is located "in" the child, albeit interacting with, if not induced by, stressful external circumstances.

The different situations in which these children find themselves could be ranked by the number and intensity of risk factors. Homelessness, for example, might head the list since it is probably associated with the most risk factors, including developmental delays, marital discord, family dysfunction, parental psychopathology, poor parent–child relationships, parental neglect and/or abuse, and exposure to violence and poverty.

This multiplicity of psychosocial threats to the young child's development may have a common denominator. If we view the situation of homelessness from a systems point of view, we might say that lack of a secure shelter, poverty, high-crime neighborhoods, and chronic exposure to violence leads to parental psychopathology, poor parenting and parent–child relationships, abuse, and neglect, all of which, in turn, lead to, and intensify, the insecurity, cognitive impairment, developmental delays, poor self-esteem, lack of impulse control, and poor object relations of severely stressed children. The final common pathway of risk to the young child, in this analysis, appears to involve the state of mind and functioning of the child's primary caretakers and the quality of their relationship to the child.

## PROTECTIVE FACTORS

Factors that appear to protect at risk young children from developing conduct disorders according to the Institute of Medicine (1994) review include "good intelligence, easy disposition, an ability to get along well with parents, siblings, teachers, and peers;" and, for older children, "an ability to do well in school, having friends, competence in non-school skill areas, and a good relationship with at least one parent and with other important adults" (p. 180).

As with risk factors, most of the factors found to be protective against the development of conduct disorders are protective against both biological and psychosocial risk factors during childhood. These include "positive temperament, above-average intelligence and social competence" (p. 184). Especially salient, however, is the "quality of interaction with parents. . . . There is consistent evidence that the nature and quality of children's interaction with their parents affect school performance, social competence, interpersonal behaviors" and the presence or absence of behavior problems (p. 185).

Werner and Smith (1992) described three clusters of protective factors obtained from the Kauai Longitudinal Study: (1) at least average intelligence and temperamental attitudes that elicit positive responses from family members and strangers; (2) good relationships with parents or parent substitutes that encourage trust, autonomy, and initiative; and (3) an external support system that rewards competence and provides a sense of coherence.

A common denominator of all these variables is the protective function of the human relationship, initially provided by parents and revolving around nurturing, attachment, and the provision of security, later increasingly located outside the family and focused on issues of competency. These findings from the epidemiological literature converge with clinical theory and practice, as elucidated and described in this book.

## SELECTED FINDINGS FROM THE LITERATURE ON EARLY INTERVENTION FOR HIGH RISK CHILDREN

Two early intervention projects have been reported that yielded disappointing results. Egeland and Erickson (1993) worked with a group of expectant mothers viewed as at high risk due to poverty, lack of education, age (17 to 25), single status, social isolation, and unstable life circumstances. Coming from the perspective of attachment theory, their overriding goal was to optimize the quality of attachment between mother and child as measured by Ainsworth's Strange Situation. This and other assessments were administered when the children were 13 months and again at 19 and 24 months.

The intervention had two major components. First regular home visits were made by a facilitator starting at the beginning of the second trimester. Second, three hour-long group meetings of eight mothers were held every other week (alternating with the home visits) until one year after the birth of the child. Group sessions were divided between baby-centered and mother-centered activities. The leader of each mother's group was the same person who made the home visits. Facilitators were selected mothers who had had experience working with low-income families.

The program yielded mixed results that disappointed the investigators. On the positive side, the experimental group showed increased maternal sensitivity, a willingness to seek further treatment, enhanced building of relationships, better coping with stress and less depression and anxiety (compared with controls), and increased competence in daily life. On the negative side, there were no differences between the control and experimental children in quality of attachment.

Galenson (1993) also reported disappointing results with a similar population of high-risk mothers of infants and toddlers. In her program, mother–child pairs were seen three times per week for two hours, from 1 to 3 years, using intervention models suggested by Fraïberg and Mahler.

Galenson concluded that this population needed "a full-day therapeutic experience in which the young child spends the greater part of his early years within a structured program carried out under the supervision of trained mental health professionals" (p. 82). According to Galenson, more time and expertise were required.

The Institute for Medicine (1994) reviewed several preventive programs for infants and young children. All but one of these programs were classified as *selective* interventions. These programs were thus aimed at high-risk populations characterized by such factors as economic deprivation, poor maternal mental health maintenance, poor family management practices, pre-term delivery, low birth weight, teenage parenthood, low socioeconomic status, academic failure, early behavior problems, and maternal depression.

Intervention strategies utilized in these programs included increased tactile stimulation of low-birth-weight babies, home-based parenting skills education, high quality of health care and community services, a center-based child development program, full daycare from the first two months through kindergarten entry, parent group meetings, weekend workshops for fathers, intensive classes for mothers with concurrent nursery school for children, and specialized pre-school curricula including programmed learning.

Evaluations of these programs showed promising results. For example, the interventions for infants suggested that "infants born to high-risk mothers . . . could benefit from preventive interventions that reduce financial, institutional and other access barriers. Home nurse visitation can be an effective means (with high risk mothers) of influencing maternal and child outcomes . . . and the provision of intensive and prolonged center-based early childhood education, combined with home visitation to families, can prevent cognitive developmental delays and academic failure in children at risk" (Institute of Medicine 1994, pp. 240–241).

Similarly, their review of interventions for older children showed that

> multicomponent interventions that address multiple risk factors have proved effective in improving the family management practices of low-income parents and in facilitating the cognitive and social development of children of low-income, low birth weight, and low education backgrounds. . . . There is also some evidence showing that multicomponent interventions have shown effects in . . . preventing behavior problems.
>
> Preventive interventions designed to enhance social competence through teaching interpersonal problem-solving skills at ages four and five in urban day care and school settings and through parents training their children in these skills at home have produced durable effects on conduct problems in children. Early childhood interventions can have positive long-term effects on academic performance and social adjustment. [Institute of Medicine 1994, p. 248]

The NIH Committee goes on to identify common elements in successful programs. "All of these [programs] are characterized by intensity. In most, services were provided daily over periods of several years" (p. 248). All of the successful programs also worked with parents, whether at home or in a center, to enhance the cognitive or behavioral development of their children. Finally the successful programs "typically involved multiple intervention components focused on multiple risk factors for later disorders" (p. 248). The authors conclude that "early childhood interventions, delivered with fidelity and quality, clearly can reduce risks for later disorders in children from at-risk families" (p. 249).

Similarly, Schorr and Schorr(1988) has marshaled evidence from programs that have achieved some success, which suggests that we already have the knowledge and ability to decrease teenage pregnancy, reduce child abuse and neglect, decrease school dropout rates, decrease violent crimes, and decrease adult criminality, most of which behaviors are associated with antecedent childhood and adolescent conduct disorders (p. 155).

She adduces three principles underlying successful programs: they must be intensive, individualized, and comprehensive. They also require skilled and committed staff and enforcement of the functioning of primary caretakers (p. 155). Obviously such programs require considerable resources and long-term commitment.

## THE REAL OBJECT AND EARLY INTERVENTION

In recent years, object relations theory has recogized the importance of the actual behavior of the child's early caretakers as a key determinant of the child's self and object representations. Underlying most disturbed emotional states (including anxiety and depression), as well as dysfunctional or destructive behavior, is the quality of these self and object representations.

Most of the therapeutic interventions described in this book are designed both to provide the high-risk child with real nurturing and competence-inducing experiences and to facilitate their internalization. To the maximum extent possible this is attempted through the enhancement of the primary caretaker's functioning and the parent–child relationship itself. To the extent that the primary caretaker is not accessible, the intervention is designed to compensate for this limitation.

In the pursuit of this goal, concepts provided by object relations theories are especially useful. They include the holding environment (Winnicott), attachment (Bowlby), separation-individuation (Mahler), and the selfobject (Kohut). The nature and applicability of each therapeutic approach is determined in large part by the nature and intensity of the threat of the situational factors that are putting in jeopardy the satisfaction of the child's need for, or ability to internalize, an adequate selfobject.

## THE EARLY INTERVENTIONS

Five kinds of therapeutic approaches or modalities are described: (1) therapeutic nurseries, (2) non-milieu multimodality, (3) three kinds of individual child psychotherapy, (4) group psychotherapy, and (5) "tripartite" psychotherapy.

Three therapeutic nurseries are included: the Cornerstone Nursery (CNS) for severely dysfunctional or disrupted families, (Chapter 2), a nursery located in a Head Start program for homeless children (Chapter 7) and a nursery for the children of mentally ill parents (PACT, Chapter 11). All three nurseries constitute intensive modalities and milieus designed to provide support and intervention at various levels. The first two are more intensive, meeting five half-days per week, compared with three 2-hour sessions per week. This different level of intensity in part reflects the greater number of situational risk factors (discussed above) to which the children of homeless and disrupted families are exposed. All three nurseries encourage parents to attend. It is only the PACT nursery, however, that requires it. In part, this reflects the fact that parents in the first two groups are not always available or cannot tolerate attendance, especially at first. An ongoing goal of both of these nurseries is to facilitate greater parental involvement. The PACT program's requirement of parental attendance is based on the effect of parental illness on the parent–child relationship and because the program has as a primary objective the amelioration of the parents' illness.

A multimodal approach appears to be especially indicated when ADD-diagnosed children are faced with multiple situational stressors (Chapter 4). Such children generally have a high rate of comorbidity. In the illustrative case, the son of an incarcerated father and a guarded mother required a combination of individual, parent–child, and group modalities, along with medication and intensive school consultation. Over the course of treatment, the mother's initial passive and punitive attitude toward her son's difficulties shifted to an actively supportive one.

Three variations of individual treatment with children at high situational risk are included here. The first, a traditional intensive, psychodynamically based modality is used to assist foster children to resolve past object losses and in so doing rework the internalization of the lost objects, and be freed up to internalize new and benign ones (Chapter 6).

The second individual approach, which we call *sustaining* psychotherapy, is utilized for children whose ongoing parenting or caretaking situation is clearly inadequate and/or the child is exposed to ongoing losses (Chapter

12). Hence, in the illustrative case, during the course of treatment, Sam is transferred from one foster home to another and repeatedly disappointed by his biological mother. The treatment is designed to provide a corrective object relationship, bridge the emotional gap created by a change of care-takers, and to help detoxify the effects of his mother's behavior. In the case presented here the maintenance of a therapeutic relationship with Sam over many years ultimately resulted in Sam's return to his biological family.

The third individual approach (Chapter 5), like that described by Samuels in Chapter 6, is designed to help foster children mourn their previous losses. It is a psychodynamically informed, supportive-expressive, time-limited in-tervention (30 sessions), which is organized around a personal life history book (PLHB). This approach has as its primary objective the prevention or reduction of transfer rate from one foster home to another. Data is presented to suggest that the approach can achieve this goal by reducing the child's symptomatology and enhancing the foster parent's positive perception of the child. It is also designed to be used by relatively inexperienced thera-pists and when therapeutic time is limited. However, the use of the PLHB itself would seem to have applicability to more intensive and long-term treat-ment of high-risk children who may be hard to reach.

Chapter 8 contains a group approach to the risk situation of parental be-reavement. Parentally bereaved children tend to view themselves as excep-tional and different from others. They feel ashamed of their loss and may avoid bereavement-related issues. Group treatment with bereaved peers would appear to be especially useful in countering this resistance. The ad-dition of bereaved adolescents as therapeutic assistants can further help to make communication about bereavement a normative experience. At the same time, their role, in relation to the children, as experts on bereavement can help reduce its stigma and turn it into a source of competence for the adolescents themselves.

*Tripartite psychotherapy* was the name given by Margaret Mahler and co-workers to a therapeutic modality designed to provide a "corrective symbi-otic experience" for very young children suffering from symbiotic psycho-sis. In this modality, the therapist works with the mother–child pair to help renegotiate the symbiotic share of the separation–individuation process. This approach is employed as one of the major therapeutic components of the PACT nursery. Its usefulness for older children whose development is put at risk by virtue of a faulty earlier separation–individuation process is illus-trated in the successful treatment and resolution of a school phobia in an 8-year-old girl (Chapter 10). The technique was also effective in reinforcing attachment in a mother–child pair with an AIDS-afflicted mother (Chapter 11). The tripartite approach holds promise for the many childhood disturbances in which preoedipal pathology is central.

## EARLY INTERVENTION, BRIEF INTERVENTION, AND THE HUMAN RELATIONSHIP

We have seen that early intervention in the lives of young children does not necessarily constitute a primary preventive intervention. The greater the number and intensity of risk factors, the less likely that "psychological first aid" or brief intervention will suffice.

Terr (1991) has distinguished between two types of traumatic conditions of childhood: acute reactions following an unanticipated event (a situational crisis), and disorders resulting from longstanding or repeated exposure to extreme external events. The latter disorders are characterized by such reactions as extreme use of denial, psychic numbing (lack of emotional responsiveness), and negative attitudes about people, the world, and the future. Such reactions make these children hard to reach.

Beutler and colleagues (1994) have stressed the importance of the "pre-existing and coexisting conditions in the victim's environment and family life" (p. 161) that will influence the type and cause of treatment that will be effective. Similarly, Briere (1993) has identified parental support and social isolation (and presumably treatment as well) as variables that may mediate the long term effects of sexual abuse. We see once again the importance of the human relationship as a potential protective factor.

Structured and focused techniques associated with time-limited approaches, such as those described by Kliman, can be enormously useful in early intervention work with high-risk children. In relatively simple situations they may even suffice. Invariably, when they do, it is because the human support system on which the child depends is adequate. Whether, for example, the encouraging results obtained by Kliman's focused, time-limited PLHB approach can be obtained in any individual case would largely depend on the quality of ongoing support and consistency the child experiences in his foster care environment. Indeed, the recognition of this fact in large part determines the emphasis on rate of transfer as an outcome variable.

Even when the complexity of situational risks to which a child is exposed is such that brief intervention will not be enough, techniques and strategies usually associated with brief treatment are likely to be helpful. For example, the PLHB is an effective means of breaking through the barriers to memory and affect erected by high risk children. Similarly, cognitive-behavioral approaches, building on the child's wish to succeed, can facilitate areas of competence that in turn can lead to self-reinforcing and broadening areas of adaptive behavior. Such techniques are deliberately incorporated into the milieu therapies described in this book. However, the impact of these and other techniques and strategies will vary according to the degree to which the human environment in which they are employed can reduce the high-risk child's resistance and enhance his receptivity.

Psychodynamic, attachment, object relations, developmental, and social learning theories, as well as observational, epidemiological, and risk prevention research, all point to the centrality of the human relationship as the key to protection and intervention as well as to risk. The identification of biological risk factors is essential for primary intervention. For example, identification of low birth weight, high lead levels, or, more recently, in utero exposure to addictive drugs, as high risk factors associated with later dysfunction, can result in cost-effective public health measures to reduce risk. It is possible that biological research may also have something to offer in the area of secondary prevention. For example, studies on the biological effects of trauma may ultimately help us to reduce, if not prevent, its long-term sequelae. For the present, however, biological understanding and remedies (e. g., drugs) for children already intensively exposed to high-risk environments, must remain adjunctive to psychosocial approaches.

It is the essence of high-risk environments that they reflect the inadequacy of the social, that is, the human, environment on which children depend. Trust is the basic building block of the human personality. It is the social world that must provide for the infant and young child the conditions of trust. Only the social world can restore the conditions of trust if they have been lacking. This is a guiding principle of early intervention with high-risk children.

The greater the severity and duration of situational risk factors to which the child has been exposed, the more difficult it will be and the more time and effort required, to compensate for them.

Hence Stewart and Mendik (Chapter 3) describe an intensive triphasic long-term approach of gradually decreasing intensity. The program combines individual, milieu, and group psychotherapy, family therapy, parent/foster parent guidance, case management, and collateral work with schools, legal, and welfare systems. The first phase consists of the CNS therapeutic nursery described in Chapter 2. The second phase revolves around, but is not limited to, a twice-weekly two-hour children's group in which family members participate.

The third phase involves a weekly two-hour group for the children. Additional interventions (e. g., individual family, parent guidance, case management), are provided as needed, outside the group. The effectiveness of this program is suggested by post-treatment data that indicate enhanced family interactions, an increasing number of parents able to work, stabilization of family environment, and enhanced ability of the children to function in a normative school environment.

These encouraging findings are buttressed by the two studies of IQ change following intensive and long-term treatment, presented in Chapters 16 and 17.* The first study involved a selected sample of ten children who were thought by their therapists to have benefited from treatment. It showed an average IQ gain of 27.9 points.

The second study added to the original cohort all the cases at the clinic for which there was both pre-treatment and post-treatment data. This consecutive series of 52 children who had received long-term treatment revealed an average IQ gain of 10.1 points, a finding of high statistical significance.

## MENTAL HEALTH CONSULTATION
## TO COMMUNITY AGENCIES

The high numbers of high-risk children growing up in our communities preclude treatment for them all. Mental health consultation to institutions who are themselves providing intensive services to this population is a way of leveraging the impact of an early intervention clinic. In the course of our work with community daycare centers, Head Start, and other such programs, particularly those serving minority populations, we became aware of impediments to communication that were limiting our effectiveness. In an effort to reduce this problem, a study was done comparing the perceptions of the needs of young children held by mental health consultants with the perceptions of the consultees (Chapter 13). Among the findings was the greater importance attributed to dependency needs and the lesser emphasis placed on punishment by the mental health workers relative to the daycare workers. This data formed the basis of discussions which strengthened the alliance between the clinic and daycare centers then being served. It also in-

---

* This study was stimulated in part by Dr. Gilbert Kliman's finding of a dramatic IQ rise in one child and significant increases in several others he had treated in the CNS therapeutic nursery.

formed subsequent consultations, adding to the sophistication with which the consultants approached their consultees.

One of the ultimate goals of mental health (or perhaps any) consultation is to attempt to transfer the knowledge and expertise of the consultant to the consultee. In the early 1980s the Center was asked to provide consultations to a spouse abuse shelter which provided shelter to domestically abused women and their children. The request for consultation was precipitated by increasing feelings of demoralization of the staff of the shelter. Many staff had been attracted to the job because of sympathy with the victimized spouses. They were not prepared for the disturbed behavior, especially with respect to their children, exhibited by many of the mothers. At the same time, the staff was at a loss as to how to make constructive use of the considerable time spent by the children and mothers at The Center.

The paper describes strategies and programs that were set up in the shelter which reduced the frustration of the staff and enhanced the quality of services offered through collaboration with the consultant (Chapter 14). Eventually the shelter created a position for a mental health worker to help maintain these programs.

The discovery of endemic sexual abuse allegedly involving over 100 children at a local unlicensed daycare center resulted in a multimodal consultation effort aimed at different layers of the community, in addition to direct services to the child victims and their families. It was necessary to mobilize and integrate the efforts of several community groups and agencies. These included the Department of Social Services, the District Attorney's office, local government officials, and community activist organizations.

The focal point of this work was a group of parents and relatives of some of the abused children. This group was formed, against great resistance, as a result of a close and ongoing collaboration between senior personnel of the mental health agency and the Department of Child Protective Services. This group served to establish and maintain sufficient cohesiveness among the parents, and collaboration between parents and governmental agencies, that the perpetrators were successfully prosecuted. This was achieved over and against active efforts at intimidation by allies of the perpetrators, on the one hand, and the passivity of influential segments of the community (due in part to denial and avoidance), on the other. The consultation thus succeeded in facilitating a desired shift from passive victimization to active mastery on the part of the participatory families. Simultaneously the community's consciousness was raised as to the needs of its children for greater protection.

## THE NEED FOR EARLY INTERVENTION

The number of children living in high-risk situations, and consequently the need for early intervention, is great. Approximately one-quarter of children in our country live in poverty, 25 percent are being raised by a single parent (over 50 percent of black children), over one million are abused each year, hundreds of thousands are homeless, over 300,000 live in foster care, tens of thousands have been left motherless by the HIV/AIDS epidemic, at least seven million live with an alcoholic parent, and 10 to 20 percent live with a mentally ill parent (Institute of Medicine 1994, Wright and Devine 1993, Zeanah 1993). Furthermore, most of these statistics have been increasing in recent years, some dramatically.

For example, the number of children living in poverty (Miringoff 1995), the incidence of child abuse, the number of children exposed to violence (Osofsky 1995), and the number of children of HIV-infected parents are all increasing. Therefore, the need for early intervention is increasing as well. If this need is not met we can expect the incidence of substance abuse, crime, and mental illness in the next generation to increase as well.

Obviously the more that risk factors such as poverty and social disorganization are addressed, the less need for early intervention. The reduction of such risks is the responsibility of society at large. In the meantime early intervention remains a necessary and potentially cost-effective application of clinical resources.

## THE PRINCIPLES OF EARLY INTERVENTION

Experience with the provision of early intervention for children living in high-risk situations, both that of others and our own, suggests a few basic principles which need to be invoked in proportion to the intensity of situational risk:

- it needs to be intensive
- it needs to be long term
- it may need to be multifaceted
- it needs to be flexible, according to the circumstances of the child and family
- to the maximum extent possible it needs to involve the child's primary caretaker(s)

- it needs to be conceptualized around the child's need for adequate relationships
- it needs to be embedded in a supportive milieu
- it needs to be collaborative, and should promote simultaneous attention to "health, family, education and child care." (Zigler et al. 1993, p. 487).

At this juncture, much is already known about situational risks to children. While the effects of intervention have not been as well studied or are not as clear, there is an emerging consensus regarding its basic elements. Recent federal law concerning children under 6 years of age reflects a growing awareness of this need for early intervention. For example, Federal Public Law 99–457, Education for all Handicapped Children Act, Amendments of 1986, encourages "statewide comprehensive coordinated multi-disciplinary inter-agency programs of early intervention services for all handicapped children and their families" (Meisels and Shonkoff 1990). Implementation of this law has been inadequate.

What is lacking is the will to act on what we know. It is ironic that at a time of increasing public awareness of the need for and potential benefits of early intervention, the prevailing political and economic climate is leading to a reduction of the resources needed to make it happen.

## THE DEVELOPMENTAL MODEL AND THE SCHOOL AS AN ONGOING THERAPEUTIC MILIEU FOR SEVERELY-AT-RISK CHILDREN

We have already discussed conceptual and funding limitations of a medical model in the field of mental health prevention and early intervention.

In contrast, the more suitable developmental model focuses on continuity, both vertical (over time) and horizontal (across settings and functions). For example, it blurs the distinction between psychological and educational issues, institutions and functioning. Accordingly, it predicts poor school functioning following earlier psychological trauma, as well as the mutually reinforcing relationship of cognitive and emotional impairment.

The developmental model similarly leads in the direction of an integrative and collaborative approach to intervention, especially betwen clinic and school. The more stressors or risk factors, the more this collaboration is needed to maximize the efforts at intervention. In this developmental model the school is seen as an ongoing co-provider of early intervention. One can envision a continuous series of increasingly intimate collaborations between school and clinic with the end point being a therapeutic milieu that would constitute an extension into elementary school of the milieu of the therapeutic nursery. This milieu would be characterized by intensive parental participation (Comer 1980), case management, a spectrum of clinical interventions such as those described in this book, case management and pediatric liaison all school-based. Zigler and Lang (1991) propose a similar comprehensive model in their school for the 21st century.

This multimodal milieu, by addressing and reducing impediments to learning, could reduce the expense of predictably fruitless efforts to teach children who are not yet able to learn. Its chances of being effective should further enhance its long-term cost effectiveness compared to traditional and noncollaborative approaches to children exposed to severe situational risk.

## REFERENCES

Barkley, R. A. (1990). *Attention Deficit Hyperactivity Disorder. A Handbook for Diagnosis and Treatment.* New York: Guilford.

Beutler, L. E., Williams, R. E., and Zetzer, H. (1994). Efficacy of treatment for victims of sexual abuse. *The Future of Children,* vol. 4, no. 2, pp. 156–175. Los Altos, CA: David and Lucille Packard Foundation.

Briere, J. (1993). Long-term sequelae of childhood sexual abuse: perceived family environment, psychopathology, and dissociation. *Journal of Consulting and Clinical Psychology* 61:1–8.

Comer, J. P. (1980). *School Power—Implications of an Intervention.* New York: Free Press.

——— (1988). Educating poor minority children. *Scientific American* 259(5):42–48.

Egeland, B., and Erickson, M. (1993). Implications of attachment theory for prevention and intervention. In *Prevention in Mental Health,* ed. H. Parens and S. Kramer, pp. 21–50. Northvale, NJ: Jason Aronson.

Galenson, E. (1993). Infant psychiatry with high-income and low-income multi-risk families, 1980–1990. In *Prevention in Mental Health,* ed. H. Parens and S. Kramer, pp. 61–84. Northvale, NJ: Jason Aronson.

Gordon, R. (1983). An operational classification of disease prevention. *Public Health Reports* 98:107–109.

Infant Health and Development Program (1990). Enhancing the outcomes of low birthweight premature infants: a multi-site randomized trial. *Journal of the American Medical Association* 263:3035–3042.

Institute of Medicine (1994). *Reducing Risks for Mental Disorders.* Washington, DC: National Academy Press.

Meisels, S. J., and Shonkoff, J. P. (1990). *Handbook of Early Child Intervention.* New York: Cambridge University Press.

Miringoff, M. (1995). Toward a national standard of social health: the need for progress in social indicators. *American Journal of Orthopsychiatry* 65(4):462–467.

Osofsky, J. D. (1995). The effects of exposure to violence on young children. *American Psychologist.* 50(9):782–788.

Patterson, G. R., Chamberlin, P., and Reid, J. B. (1982). A comparative evaluation of a parent training program. *Behavior Therapy* 13:638–650.

Schorr, L. B., with Schorr, D. (1988). *Within Our Reach.* New York: Anchor/ Doubleday.

Strayhorn, J. M., and Weidman, C. S. (1991). Follow-up one year after parent–child interaction training: effects on behavior of pre-school children. *Journal of the American Academy of Child and Adolescent Psychiatry* 30:138–143.

Terr, L. C. (1991). Childhood traumas: an outline and overview. *American Journal of Psychiatry* 148(1):10–20.

Werner, E. E., and Smith, R. S. (1992). *Overcoming the Odds: High-Risk Children from Birth to Adulthood.* New York, NY: Cornell University Press.

Wright, J. D., and Devine, J. A. (1993). Housing dynamics of the homeless: implications for a count. *American Journal Of Orthopsychiatry* 65(3):320–329.

Zeanah, C. (1993). *Handbook of Infant Mental Health.* New York: Guilford.

Zigler, E., Hopper, P., and Hall, N. W. (1993). Infant mental health and social policy. In *Handbook of Infant Mental Health,* ed. C. H. Zeanah, Jr., pp. 480–492. New York: Guilford.

Zigler, E., and Lang, M. (1991). *Child Care Choices: Balancing the Needs of Children, Families, and Society.* New York: Free Press.

# I

# CHILDREN OF DISRUPTED FAMILIES

# 2

# Cornerstone: A Therapeutic Nursery for Severely Disadvantaged Children

*Thomas Lopez*
*Norma Balter*
*Susan Howard*
*Rita Stewart*
*Arthur B. Zelman*

The Cornerstone Therapeutic Nursery (CNS) is a five-morning, fifteen-hour-per-week, multimodal therapeutic milieu whose principal aim is to address the psychological needs of disturbed pre-school children from impoverished, highly disadvantaged, multiproblem backgrounds. It attempts to create within its setting, a microcommunity of children, parents, and nursery staff, working to counter the effects of shattered family and community ties in the lives of these children and their parents. In this chapter we will describe the evolution of the program and its four major components: (1) individual therapy within the nursery setting, (2) group discussions with the children, (3) work with parents, and (4) education. A common theme running through the discussions concerns the contribution of each component to the establishment of therapeutic alliances and emotional contact with the children and their caretakers.

## EVOLUTION OF THE CORNERSTONE NURSERY

From its beginnings in 1965, when it was started by Gilbert Kliman, M.D., Cornerstone has been distinguished by the unusual practice of treating children in daily individual psychotherapy within the nursery setting itself. The approach has gone roughly through three phases, in parallel with the changing nature of the population served.

23

*Phase 1.* Initially, Cornerstone was thought of along traditional lines (Brenner 1988, Colonna and Friedman 1984, Edgcumbe 1975, A. Freud 1975, 1979, Friedman 1988, Furman and Katan 1969, Miller 1988, Salo and Friedman 1988, Weise 1995, Wilson 1977, 1988, Woods 1988), with emphasis on offering patients a sensitive, psychoanalytically informed milieu, supportive of their coping capacities and development. Patients were typically from intact or recently disrupted middle-class families and were either emotionally disturbed or basically healthy but suffering from an acute trauma or crisis, such as bereavement. However, Kliman, whose practice it was to spend one hour daily in the nursery, was soon prompted to take an innovative path. He found that "several children talked to me regularly about their symptoms. Several had marked reactions to my arrival and departure. They spoke of me after I had left, both in the nursery and at home. Some children told me their dreams in the classroom. Soon a marked thematic continuity in each child's communications became evident. After a few weeks I cautiously began to respond with interpretive comments akin to my usual analytic work with young children. The experiment was then pursued not only for its clinical value, but also for the scientific value of learning what phenomena would occur" (Kliman 1975, p. 478).

This "experiment," the first version of Cornerstone, came to have the following characteristics: (1) two teachers conducting a full-scale nursery program for six to eight children, three hours daily, five days per week; (2) a psychotherapist carrying out individual therapy within the nursery setting, four or five of those days, 90 minutes per day; (3) parents given weekly guidance by the head teacher, except for once monthly when the therapist would meet with each parent; (4) the roles of teachers and therapist kept sharply distinct.

The therapist, relieved by the teachers of the need to employ educational, limit-setting or other caretaking measures, functioned in an even more "purely analytic" manner than when treating a pre-schooler in the more conventional one-on-one setting. However, in contrast to psychotherapy in the more usual setting, children in Cornerstone were free not only to make use of toys and dolls in order to communicate, but also of other children and staff. Only the therapist made interpretations to the children. Whatever insights teachers might have into the unconscious roots of a child's behavior were conveyed to the therapist who, in turn, used them to enhance his or her understanding.

*Phase 2.* By the early 1970s—as the Center had increasingly become an agency responding to the needs of the community as a whole—Cornerstone's population had changed dramatically. The majority were no longer children of the middle class, but rather of impoverished, or marginally adaptive inner-city parents, (usually either single mothers on public assistance or foster parents). Typically, these were children who had been subjected to major developmental interferences and manifested unmistakable arrests and deviations in development. Although they were usually hungry to form ties with adults, their relationships with people and with the world about them tended to be dilute and erratic. Their emotional experience was impoverished, their cognitive functioning and ability to communicate symbolically— either verbally or through play—well below age level and their own potential. Impulsive, destructive behavior among them was common. Especially deficient was their sense of being worthwhile and of having a meaningful place in the scheme of things. Many had failed to benefit from prior individual therapy or daycare. Almost all were close to needing hospitalization or placement in other forms of residential care.

With the change in patient population came a corresponding change in the way the therapist in the nursery functioned. The new crop of children would regularly disrupt group activities with their "misbehavior," loss of control, fits of rage, hurling of objects. Often they would pose a danger to others and themselves, requiring physical restraint. At other times, desperate for affection, they would plead to be held and comforted. It became apparent that for the therapist, in these instances, to step aside and call upon a teacher to provide restraint or comfort would be artificial, rejecting of the child and destructive to the treatment. No longer could the therapist take as strict an analytic stance as Kliman (now a supervisor) had advocated for the population he had treated. Greater flexibility became key. Consistent awareness on the part of the therapist as to how the child was trying to use him or her therapeutically was especially required, as was ability to move intelligently between an analytic and an essentially parental, caretaking role. The therapist, who now often functioned as the teachers had in the past, no longer was a person apart but one who aimed to be more richly experienced by and more "real" to the child (A. Freud 1965).

Also during this phase, staff having prior experience with the Cornerstone population began making two exciting observations. Children who had had prior individual therapy were consistently benefitting more from such therapy within the nursery setting than they had within the one-on-one setting, and the children generally were benefitting from the nursery setting itself, as one withdrawn child after another—often after having failed to be helped by other approaches—would in amazingly short periods of time come emotionally to life and begin interacting positively with other people.

*Phase 3.* The current phase of Cornerstone involves a further shift in the functioning of staff in the direction of de-differentiation. Instead of one therapist and two teachers, the nursery is now staffed by four therapists and one assistant. The program now accommodates twelve or thirteen children, each therapist being responsible for the individual therapy of three or four children. As in previous phases, only a given child's therapist makes interpretive interventions with that child, while for that child the other three therapists and assistant function as the teachers formerly did—teaching, nurturing, limit setting, and relating spontaneously.

Reasons for this new arrangement are instructive. As financial pressures required that more children be treated in the nursery, the team initially was to consist of two therapists to work therapeutically with the children, another therapist to work with parents and other professionals, and a pre-school education specialist to be responsible for activities and learning. However, within a year the differentiation of roles had been eliminated and the four team members were performing identical functions—an outcome made possible by the fact of all of them having been trained as child therapists. One result of this arrangement was that the same therapist treated and worked with the child and his or her parent(s). This outcome, we believe, was dictated primarily by the nature of the work itself. First, given the parents' typical difficulties in trusting, working with a therapist other than their own child's therapist created an unnecessary and harmful distance between the parent and the child's therapist. Second, educational efforts with our children in the absence of close personal involvement between teacher and child have proven ineffective. However, for workers trained as child therapists, personal helping involvements with children inevitably tend toward psychotherapy with these children. For this team, therefore, the best approach seemed for each member to function as a therapist, to also work with his or her patients' parents, and to function as a teacher and parent substitute as well.

## THE TEAM AND LIMIT SETTING

This arrangement of one all-purpose primary therapist per family might be construed as precluding or de-emphasizing a team approach. Such is not the case. If we view each therapist as in part representing a substitute parent for the individual children (and often their parents as well), then the nonprimary therapists may be viewed as extended family members who play an important auxiliary role in supporting, educating, and setting limits for the child.

The importance of this "teamness" is perhaps most easily seen in relation to the issue of limit setting. Most children treated in the Nursery have been living in environments in which their caretakers are overwhelmed by their own and their children's needs. Their responses to the latter therefore include admixtures of sadism (attacks on the children), masochism (victimization by the children), and avoidance (neglect and abandonment of the children). The result is that the children bring to the Nursery high states of anxiety, which frequently translate into out-of-control behavior. Such behavior, fueled as it is by sadomasochistic fantasies and impulses, sorely tests the CNS staff. At the same time, these behavioral and emotional displays present special therapeutic opportunities for at least two reasons. First, insofar as they replicate disturbed relationship patterns in their lives, an appropriate response from the staff will help counter these patterns. Second, these displays often signify that the child has been reached emotionally and may be especially receptive to empathic handling.

The degree to which therapeutic advantage can be taken of these episodes, however, depends to a large degree on the capacity of the team members to help each other contain sadomasochistic impulses. Such containment is a precondition for therapeutic limit setting that is neither excessively harsh, permissive, nor avoidant. This issue is discussed in greater detail later.

## INDIVIDUAL PSYCHOTHERAPY WITHIN THE NURSERY SETTING

Two examples follow of individual psychotherapy of severely disadvantaged children within the nursery setting. The first, excerpted from a published account (Lopez and Kliman 1980), focuses on a relatively short time span in the child's treatment. The second is an overview of two years of a child's therapy. In each there occurred a dramatic revival and considerable working through within the transference of overwhelmingly painful affect associated with the failure and loss of their caretakers. Never in our experience with this population (including indirect experience with The Center's substantial caseload) have we observed expressions of transference as intense as those expressed by these two (and a small but substantial number of other children treated in Cornerstone) in the more usual one-on-one setting for individual psychotherapy. We believe that the nursery setting provides a "holding environment" (Winnicott 1965), for the child and for the therapist, that is central in permitting and sustaining this deeply valuable therapeutic process (Lopez and Kliman 1980). For the child the nursery setting provides a safe context (Sandler 1987) in which to express intense pain and rage; the setting provides reassurance against fear of destroying the therapist, of being retaliated against and, likely, of total disintegration. For the therapist—in addition to the more obvious emotional and physical supports—the setting provides "witnesses," that is, confirmation that matters have not gotten dangerously out of control but that he or she is engaged in a profound therapeutic process *dictated* by the child's struggle to become psychologically healthier.

## Example 1[1]

Monroe began what was to be two years of treatment in Cornerstone at age 4 (Lopez and Kliman 1980). The second of three sons born to an impoverished inner-city black couple, when he was 2½ years old his mother suffered a psychosis following the birth of her third child. She was hospitalized for nine months and treated with drugs, the high dosage level of which induced her face to take on a masklike appearance and caused her to become grossly obese and slow in her movements—a condition which persisted throughout Monroe's treatment. While she was in the hospital, Monroe and his brother, older by two years, were cared for by their father and paternal grandmother. The baby was placed in permanent foster care. When the mother returned home, the father moved out permanently, and remained out of contact with the family except for occasional visits.

Monroe was referred by a daycare center as a result of his obvious profound developmental lags and grossly atypical behavior, including sparse use of language (limited to occasional phrases such as, "I don't know" or "John hit me"), poor capacity for learning, a withdrawn, detached appearance interrupted primarily by outbursts of obstreperousness, and a joyless lack of vitality. On intake, he was described as having a wandering gaze, lax facial musculature, paucity of expressive interchange, and impoverished affect. On testing, he obtained an IQ (WISC) score of 53. However, the examining psychiatrist noted some positive features. Monroe's receptive comprehension of verbal communication was at a higher level than his active linguistic expression. For example, he readily brought a toy elephant and a yellow truck when asked to find them in the middle of a cluttered floor. On

---

[1]The therapist was Thomas Lopez, Ph.D. Other published examples of individual therapy in the Cornerstone Nursery are Kliman (1975) and Balter and Lopez (1990).

request he built a tower of blocks with some 25 pieces. He also seemed pleased at the examiner's admiration and encouragement.

By the middle of the fourth month of treatment, Monroe's demeanor and behavior—the sound of his crying; the clinging torturing manner by which he related; his preference for drinking from a baby bottle; his occasionally becoming incontinent with regard to urine; the manner in which he sought adults' laps for "refueling"—increasingly had taken on the qualities of a desperately grieved toddler. Time and again, on little or no pretext, or on one he had largely manufactured himself, he spent long periods crying pitiably on a teacher's lap. In one session . . . Monroe clawed and hit at my watch. When I verbalized how terrible it was that good things, like our playing, come to an end, Monroe became desperate, pleaded to be given a baby bottle, and calmed only after he had received it. But when I verbalized the hurt "baby feelings" that had been stirred in him, Monroe again broke down into desperate crying and continued uninterruptedly for some 20 minutes. During this time Monroe repeatedly called for his mother and cuddled close to me while sitting on my lap. Presently, he picked up a plastic shell shaped like an egg split in half (a container for pantyhose), placed it on my chest, and mouthed and sucked it as a baby would a breast. At that time I attempted an interpretation that related his behavior to his mother's current psychically impoverished condition and past breakdown. I reconstructed: Long ago, his mother became sick, and had to leave him to go to a hospital. He could not be with her, sit on her lap, or get "good feelings" from her. She still was very sad, slow, and difficult to feel close to. Now, when he is unable to get something he wants, the terrible pain of being unable to feel close to his mother comes up.

For the next four months this was the main line of interpretation. The results were dramatic. A way had become available for making sense of Monroe's internal chaos and desperation. Although the reconstruction may have been valid only in a "hazy way" (Valenstein 1975, p. 63), and though it surely made use of much that Monroe had since pieced together from discussions with his mother and perhaps from other sources, dialogue became possible where previously only comforting and restraint could be resorted to. Material became accessible for understanding and mastery which otherwise almost surely would have remained out of reach.[2] In one session, after having become furious with me for working with other children before working with him, Monroe ostentatiously ignored me when his own turn came. I verbalized his rejecting me as a retaliation, and said how difficult it was to wait for someone one wanted to be close to and how often he must have felt and still feel rejected at home by his mother. He continued to ignore me. I then became more concrete. I first enacted Monroe's feeling rejected when I worked with other children, playing both Monroe's and my own role, and verbalizing his

---

[2]Settlage and Spielman (1975) offer a similar formulation.

pain and anger. Then I enacted Monroe's trying to gain his mother's attention, imitating Monroe's and his mother's mannerisms and vocal qualities. Monroe abandoned his withdrawal. He alternated between furiously attacking me with spit, bites, kicks, and punches, on the one hand, and desperate crying, on the other. Finally, with great venom, he loudly accused me of being "crazy." I pointed out to him that Monroe's mother had been "crazy" when he lost her, and might still seem "crazy" to him. Moreover, her withdrawn state might often make Monroe feel "crazy." He sobered, went to a doll representing a woman, undressed it and caressed it. Then he twisted its movable limbs so that they became hopelessly tangled. I interjected that Monroe's mother had become all messed up. Monroe dressed the doll and again caressed it. "How you love your mother and want to care for her," I commented. Again Monroe began to cry, but this time, instead of hitting out he hugged and kissed me. [Lopez and Kliman 1980, pp. 346–348]

After the two years of treatment Monroe moved to the South with his mother and brother to live with his grandmother. Phone calls to mother and school three and one-half years after treatment yielded reports that he was at the appropriate grade-level for his age, enthusiastic about learning and, overall, doing well.

## Example 2[3]

Shaniqua also was 4 when she began treatment in Cornerstone. Her father's whereabouts unknown, her substance-abusing addicted mother four months prior had left her and her two younger brothers (3 and 2 years old respectively) alone in the homeless family's motel room for a night and a good part of the next day, until neighbors, hearing the children crying, contacted Child Protective Services (CPS). The children were placed in emergency foster care and then transferred to a long-term foster home. Shaniqua was referred by CPS because her behavior both in her foster home and in daycare had been extremely difficult to manage. Indeed, just prior to intake Shaniqua had been expelled from daycare for screaming, hitting, spitting, not following instructions, and repeatedly running out of the classroom.

After gathering what background information she could from the caseworker and foster mother—but not her biological mother, whose whereabouts were unknown—the therapist introduced Shaniqua, accompanied by her foster mother, to the nursery. Shaniqua, obviously frightened, entered silently, avoiding eye contact, her body stiff, her expression glazed. The foster mother, seemingly fearing her charge would become overwhelmed,

---

[3]The therapist was Susan Howard, C.S.W.

anxiously tried diverting her with toys. The therapist told them that this was a safe place in which we try to understand and deal directly with feelings and that there was no need to push them aside. Shaniqua's attention was soon caught by a child who was crying. Looking even more frightened than she had, she abruptly stood up as though about to try to escape. The foster mother, quickly taking her on her lap, related that once during the previous week Shaniqua had run out into the street in the middle of the night, terrifying her that Shaniqua would be hit by a car. The foster mother went on to report that at home Shaniqua was generally fearful, often cried for long periods, and interacted very little with anyone on a friendly basis. She was, however, awakening nightly with nightmares of monsters biting her and regularly hit the other children in the home (her own two grandchildren as well as Shaniqua's younger brothers) and even the foster mother herself. Shaniqua, silent and stiffly immobile in the midst of the nursery's noisy activity, relaxed enough to sip from a cup of juice the therapist had offered her. After being told that we would like her to attend the nursery, she whispered to the therapist that she would like to go down the slide.

Shaniqua's nearly two years of treatment—the first 16 months of which her biological mother remained unavailable—began two days later. Almost immediately Shaniqua became attached to a baby doll, which for several months, while in the nursery, she almost always carried with her. At first she seldom talked or played with any of the other children or adults and would tune out when efforts were made to reach her. Shaniqua did, however, eat snacks voraciously and—in response to persistent efforts to engage her—assigned to the therapist the role of her "older daughter" while she (mostly silently) ministered to her baby doll. The therapist (S. H.) verbalized how caring of her baby she was. Apparently because Shaniqua found relating to the group less threatening than relating to individual people, she was at her most spontaneous and free in response to playfulness among staff, children, and often parents in the nursery. She would join in chasing games, dance during music time, and display what was to prove to be a talent of hers, mimicking the voices and gestures of various staff and children.

Gradually Shaniqua began taking the initiative to make contact with the therapist. She would ask to sit on the therapist's lap—putting her face inches from hers—gaze intently into her eyes and tenderly touch, explore, and caress her eyes, earrings, sweater, and nails. When she whispered, "Will you paint my nails like yours?" the therapist obtained permission from her foster mother and, using children's nail polish, did so. While sitting on her therapist's lap she would often continue holding her baby doll on her own, simultaneously playing Baby and Mommy. During one of our daily group meetings—listening to other children relate their stories and in the context of the discussion—she volunteered her first statement concerning her loss of her mother: "The police came to my house to take me."

After some five months of treatment, Shaniqua was expressing a range of ideas and affect—including intense anger, even rage—and could no longer be described as detached. Following a one-week winter vacation, Shaniqua greeted the therapist—as had become her custom—by affectionately placing herself on her lap. When other children began talking to the therapist, Shaniqua became angry. She ordered the therapist to "shut up" and ran from her. She then pushed to the ground another child who had just embraced the therapist. When the latter reprimanded her, insisting that she was not to hurt other children, Shaniqua spat in her face. Taking firm hold of her, turning her so that she faced away from her, restating her position with even greater firmness, the therapist added that spitting in another's face also was prohibited. The therapist maintained her hold until—after a good while—seeing that Shaniqua's anger was giving way to tears, she relaxed, hugged her, and verbalized that their time away from one another during vacation must have been deeply painful. Shaniqua dissolved into convulsive sobbing, after which she asked to wear the therapist's lipstick.

Shaniqua's expressions of rage became more frequent and intense. At the same time, she exhibited increasing interest and pleasure in her interactions with peers and other staff. She also began verbalizing memories. Often they were of nightmares she had had, of monsters and snakes climbing into her bedroom to bite her. At other times, she dreamed of being alone, hungry, and unsuccessfully searching for food. She talked of times when, however much she cried for her mother, she wouldn't wake up. Strikingly, while in the nursery setting her diminished detachment was accompanied by intense anger and difficult behavior, at home she became calmer and easier to manage. Her night terrors ceased. She stopped running away and rarely did she hit out at others.

Over the next six months of treatment—Shaniqua's biological mother still not heard from, her foster mother, troubled by a heart ailment, increasingly experiencing her as burdensome—Shaniqua's affect in individual therapy became even more intense. The following is illustrative: in a corner set up for playing house, Shaniqua assigned to the therapist the role of her daughter. The therapist was to be totally silent and clean up after her "mother." As mother, Shaniqua went about her household duties, cooking, tidying up, and so on, all the while spilling water and dropping things to keep her therapist busy wiping and picking up. Presently, however, her hostility spilled over the limits of play. When another child tried to join the play Shaniqua struck her. When the therapist intervened, insisting that such behavior was prohibited, Shaniqua hit and kicked her. The therapist was forced to restrain her to prevent her from hurting anyone. Crying and trying to free herself, Shaniqua repeatedly screamed, "I hate you!"—with matching intense affect the therapist responded with an interpretation of Shaniqua's feelings: "I'm afraid! My mommy and daddy have left me! My foster mother is sick! Who's going to take care of me? I want to hurt other people because I'm hurt! I'm so, so hurt!" The violence of Shaniqua's sobbing was such that, before it subsided, she had soaked a good part of herself and her therapist with tears and saliva. Similar scenes recurred during the next six months, sometimes with such intensity that child and therapist would end up exhausted and drenched, at times with the former's urine and vomit.

Toward the latter part of this period, Shaniqua was dealt what had the potential to be a devastating blow. Her foster mother "retired" and Shaniqua was placed in a new foster home, one different from that in which her brothers were placed—the first time she had been separated from them. Despite her loss, she not only did not regress but continued to make progress, perhaps related to an intensification of her positive identification with the therapist. She would use her talent as a mimic to charmingly pretend to be her therapist. The therapist would refer to her as "Ms. H.," she to the therapist as "Shaniqua." As "Ms. H." she would play at being therapist to other children, and did so skillfully enough that they readily joined her in her game. Her adversarial, bullying attitudes faded. In their place emerged a striking degree of kindness and empathy in her relationships. She also became a regular advocate of the younger children. Though she still frequently expressed emotional pain and rage, increasingly these feelings were verbalized. No longer were they all-consuming and undermining of her functioning. Shaniqua also made a good adjustment to her new foster home, developing a warm, easy relationship with her foster mother. The only child in the home, she seemed to benefit from this exclusivity.

With some six months remaining before Shaniqua was to leave Cornerstone to move onto kindergarten, her biological mother reappeared. She had entered a drug rehabilitation program and declared her wish to reunite with her children. Weekly sessions in the nursery were set up for her. An intelligent, articulate woman who appeared motivated (although depressed), she filled in some of Shaniqua's early history. She had been addicted throughout her children's lives and had been only inconsistently available to them. She acknowledged that she had left her children alone on occasions other than the one that had precipitated the children's removal. Mother described having herself been deprived and neglected as a child, having been raised by several relatives, none of whom had been invested in her.

At first Shaniqua defensively exaggerated her affection toward her mother, but after a few sessions with her in the nursery setting and in joint therapy she became able to tell her mother how pained and angry she felt at having been abandoned as well as her own need to, in turn, reject and hurt her mother. Mother responded in an impressively sensitive and understanding way, and by the end of Shaniqua's time in Cornerstone the beginnings of reconciliation were well underway. Indeed, during the last two months, Shaniqua, decked out in high heels and pocketbook, portraying an image of an attractive, competent, admirable woman, regularly played at being her mother. As a graduation gift from her therapist she was adamant about wanting a ring "she could always wear."

Following graduation, Shaniqua was placed in regular kindergarten and joined the Steppingstone program at the clinic. Her further treatment and progress is described in Chapter 3.

## GROUP DISCUSSIONS WITH THE CHILDREN

At about midmorning one of the therapists will call the discussion meeting to order. Then for about a half-hour, children, staff, and parents sit side by side on mats, backs resting against the wall. On one adult's lap sits a child, on another's two or even three. Some children choose to sit by themselves. Directly in front of the group is found a timeworn orange chair, fondly called the "news chair." From it speaks the child whose turn it is to tell "news." News is usually communicated verbally, but for less verbal children it might involve receiving praise for having used the toilet or for block building or painting. Topics range from here-and-now interaction in the Nursery to the most devastating events in the children's lives.

The meetings were initially intended only as a means of planning morning activities and pulling things together. What emerged, however, was a surprising eagerness on the children's part to speak, a striking ability to listen to and identify with peers and their problems, and an equally striking enhancement of their verbal abilities. In part because so many Cornerstone children are verbally deficient, group discussion was soon instituted as a daily feature of group life.

Six examples follow. In the first, a child tells of having visited her father in prison. The second illustrates a discussion of a quarrel between two children in the nursery setting. In the third, a conflict between children in the nursery uncovers conflict at home. The fourth concerns helping a child with having been removed from his parents. The fifth has to do with helping a child, over a period of several weeks, deal with her mother's having committed a murder. The sixth example is of a nearly nonverbal foster child helped to communicate with her biological mother.

## A Child Tells of Visiting Her Father in Prison

"I'd like Tania to be the first to tell news," Ms. S., Tania's therapist, announced soberly. "She's got big news."

"Big, big, big news," Tania echoed loudly as she rose from the mat, went to the news chair and settled into it. She was an attractive black 3-year-old, elegantly dressed in light blue blouse and dark blue jeans—both seeming brand new—and her hair was tastefully arranged in bunches. She hesitated, then, smiling mischievously, popped out of the chair and whispered into the ear of one child and then another. The first understood immediately what she had said. But the second, a pale blond boy, after listening intently shouted, "What!?" Again, Tania whispered in his ear, and again the same response. Before she could make a third attempt, Ms. S. intervened, instructing Tania to speak to the group as a whole—speaking to each child individually would take too long. Reluctantly, Tania went back to the news chair, took a deep breath, and in staccato rhythm conveyed her news: "I-went-to-see-my-Daddy." Where had Tania seen him, asked Ms. H. "Jail," Tania replied, her voice barely above a whisper. "You went to jail to see Daddy?" Ms. H. asked, surprised. "Yeah," Tania answered, her voice loud but tired and sad. "What was it like?" Ms. H. pursued. "Doo doo," Tania replied, generating laughter and shouts of "doo doo," from some of the children, although a firm request from the staff for quiet and attention was quickly complied with.

"In what way was jail like 'doo doo'?" Ms. H. asked. "It smelled like it. . . . The police got AIDS," Tania answered. More nervous laughter from the children and another effective call for quiet from the therapists. Could Tania tell us more about it, Ms. H. pursued softly. The little girl remained silent. Her feistiness had given way to a depressed sagging of her body. Had she been allowed to touch her father? Ms. H. asked gently. "No-girl," Tania replied, reverting to staccato, now infused with bitterness. "With-them-po-lice-in-there-I-don't-sit-on-no-Daddy's-lap."

The group reacted with total silence. After a short while Ms. H. pointed out that other children in the group also had fathers missing from their lives. Speaking directly to each child in turn she elaborated: Coreen's father was in jail for having killed his brother in a fight; Laura's has been in jail since her infancy; Torrel's father was in jail for having mistreated him (omitting the fact that his father had abused him sexually); the whereabouts of Andrew's father were unknown; Sam's father was living at home, but chronically ill; Godfrey's father was in a psychiatric hospital.

"My Dad's in jail too," interjected Sara, a pale thin blond girl in foster care for the past two years, having been removed from her parents because of gross neglect. For a long moment no one spoke. Everyone present knew that Sara's father was not in jail. "Maybe you wish Daddy were in jail," Ms. B. suggested gently. "At least you would know where he is, and why he hasn't been visiting." Sara, near tears, only stared at Ms. B., who reached out to her, hugged her, and held her on her lap.

Ms. S. directed the group's attention back to Tania. She related that during Tania's visit with her father he had apologized to her for having stolen her radio to buy drugs. But this was beyond Tania's tolerance as she blurted out, "No, no, no!" Startled, Ms. S. was momentarily at a loss for words. Then gently lifting Tania, slumped in dejection, she herself sat on the news chair and held the little girl on her lap. "You did tell me he apologized," Ms. S. said softly. "I called him a fuckin' peanut head!" Tania shot back, her body tense with rage.

For a moment no one spoke. "Please tell us more," Dr. L. urged. "What was it like visiting Daddy in jail?" No answer. "Were you allowed to touch Daddy?" "Yes . . . I don't wanna talk. I don't wanna say no more."

"There are lots of feelings here," Ms. H. interjected. "Shut up!" Tania shot back. But Ms. H. persisted. "No. Don't say shut up. How did he look? Tired? Sad?" "I said shut up!" Tania reiterated. "I said 'fuckin' peanut head' to him. That's all, la, la la," she chanted defiantly.

At this, another child tauntingly shouted out his own "la, la," and began nervously wriggling about. "Stop that, you ugly pig!" Tania shouted at him. "You're dumb and stupid. Everybody's dumb and stupid. I'm not comin' tomorrow!"

But now Tania's voice cracked. Burying her face in Ms. S.'s chest, her fury gave way to convulsive sobbing. A good five minutes passed before she had cried herself out, through all of which the group remained silent. Then Ms. S., holding Tania gently, said, "I have some more news about Tania. When she came in this morning she got herself pencil and paper and said to me, 'I'm smart. I'm going to do some brain work.' I think Tania was saying, 'Even though my Daddy's messed up, I'm going to learn and be smart.'"

Tania, her face puffy and wet, looked up and whispered, "Later I'm gonna do more brain work."

## COMMENT

Consistent with the circumstances in which the great majority of the children live, endemic stress rooted in the inadequacy of their caretaking environments is a frequent focus of group discussion. Though it is rare for a child to refuse to "tell news," the painful nature of what emerges often causes him or her to balk at speaking further. Most often, however, with encouragement, the reticence gives way. While it is common for the children to become sporadically inattentive or act disruptively both tendencies are greatly diminished by their feeling themselves to be part of a benign group oriented to taking seriously what is being discussed.

## A Conflict between Two Children

Ms. H. is sitting on the news chair, on her lap Shaniqua, a 4-year-old girl (described earlier) in foster care as a result of neglect by her substance-abusing parents. Ms. H. tells the group, "Shaniqua was very angry. She threw a chair at Lendal when he wouldn't play with her." Shaniqua began to get tense and try to get off Ms. H.'s lap. The therapist held her firmly and continued. "When I stopped her from hurting Lendal she tried scratching and spitting at me." By now Shaniqua's efforts to get away had become halfhearted. "We have to deal with this," Ms. H. insisted to her. "You hurt Lendal and you tried to hurt me!" "I hate you!" Shaniqua blurted out.

"Why do you hate me?" Ms. H. asked, trying to convey that she truly wanted to know. "Because you hurt me! You don't play with me!" she screamed. "Who doesn't play with you, Shaniqua?" Ms. S. asked gently. "Who hurts you when she doesn't come to see you?" Ms. H. added. Tears welling, Shaniqua tightened her lips. "Nobody! Nobody!" she shouted. "I'm nobody." she continued. "I'm doo doo."

The children stared at therapist and child. One, speaking barely above a whisper, said, "I think she misses her mommy." Another began rolling about, grinning all the while.

"Kevin doesn't see his mommy either," Ms. B. interjected. "Maybe that's why he's rolling around." Ms. H. interjected gently, "Maybe he is trying to get away from his feelings."

Ms. Keeler, a young mother, usually quiet, spoke, causing the group's attention to turn to her. "I know how you feel, Shaniqua. I lost my mother, too, when I was little. I never had anyone to help me with my feelings."

Ms. Keeler herself had been abandoned at 4 by her own drug-abusing mother, and was now struggling to relate positively to her own two young children.

"Moms have problems and hurt feelings, too," Ms. H. said softly to Shaniqua. "I think Ms. Keeler understands how you feel. Sometimes moms' problems become so big that like your mom, they're not able to take care of their kids." Shaniqua gazed intently at Ms. Keeler.

"Lendal has hurt feelings, too," Dr. L. interjected. "He's lost important people in his life." We reviewed Lendal's loss of his family, also due to drug abuse by his parents.

Ms. H. then turned to Shaniqua and said firmly, "You hurt Lendal with that chair you threw at him. He's a person. He has feelings." At this Shaniqua began to sob, her body heaving, tears flowing. Then, her body softening, she said, "I hate Mommy. She doesn't play with me."

The group responded sympathetically, staff talking about Shaniqua's mother's drug problem, her missing out on being with her wonderful daughter, and the sadness of it all, children remaining attentive throughout. Another child began crying. His therapist, sitting with him verbalized, "It hurts so much to lose your Mommy."

In response to Ms. H.'s suggestion, Shaniqua walked over to Lendal and apologized to him. After the meeting, she shyly asked him to play with her. This time he did.

### COMMENT

Ms. H.'s individual therapy with Shaniqua helped her in the meeting to fruitfully interpret, as transference from mother, Shaniqua's having accused her of not playing with and of hurting her. The group discussion helped Shaniqua to feel validated and to organize her feelings of hurt and anger toward her mother. However, the group's being opposed to people hurting one another also stimulated in Shaniqua conflict over having hurt Lendal, thereby making underlying ideas and feelings more accessible to therapy. Finally, the group discussion seemed instrumental in inducing Lendal to stop rejecting and hurting Shaniqua.

## A Conflict in the Classroom Facilitates Work on a Conflict at Home

On a day Laura's individual therapist, Ms. H. was absent, the teaching assistant, distressed, reported that Laura had hurt Tania's feelings by suddenly refusing to play with her because Tania was black.

Laura, blond and fair-skinned, but with facial features showing her to be herself part African-American, sprang to her feet, turned her back to the group, defiantly folded her arms across her chest, and stared at the wall only inches from her face. To a therapist's request that she go to the news chair so that the matter might be discussed, she responded ángrily by stamping her foot. At this, Ms. B. took her hand, led her to the chair, sat her on her own lap, and asked her to tell her side of the story. Laura, however, would say nothing. Ms. B. gently reminded Laura that she and her family were racially mixed. Laura flatly denied this, and in slow, measured tones insisted, "I just don't like black people."

After a long moment of silence, Dr. L. submitted that while Laura did have the right to dislike whom she wished, she did not have the right to hurt the feelings of other children. Dr. L. added that he didn't think she ought to be allowed to participate with the other children until she apologized to Tania.

Laura melted into tears, blurting out, "My mommy beat me." With encouragement, she explained that her mother had spanked her on her "butt," and nodded in agreement that she might have wanted to hurt Tania as she herself had been hurt, but gave no details as to exactly what had happened. Ms. B., who worked with Laura's mother in parent guidance, indicated that she would try to get more information from her.

Believing that Laura, having cried and, to some extent, opened up verbally, had become less oppositional, Dr. L. asked her if she would now apologize to Tania. She responded by letting out a loud, defiant "Wahhh!" ("no"), triggering guffaws, restless wriggling, and nervous shouts of "dookie" from the other children, who until then had listened quietly. Order was restored by Ms. S.'s insistence on the seriousness of what was being discussed.

Laura was given a choice: Either she would apologize to Tania, or she would be obliged to stay on the mat and not participate with the other children. She reacted with rage, crying loudly, writhing, howling, and finally pummeling her own head with clenched fists. Ms. B. managed to restrain her, holding her arms in a bear hug, but Laura, squirming desperately, continued shrieking obscenities and trying her utmost to bite her. Dr. L., as the precipitator of Laura's outburst, offered to take her away from the meeting to try to sort things out with her. With the group silently looking on, he first tried to take her hand in the hope that she would walk with him. When she refused, he picked her up and tried holding her gently. When she reverted to shrieking and trying to hurt, he held her tightly and carried her to another room.

For the next twenty minutes, while the meeting proceeded without them, Dr. L. sat on a chair between Laura and the door. At first she shrieked and flailed about on the floor. Then, on her feet, she flailed at him as he fended her off by holding her at arm's length. Finally, seeming no longer driven by rage but coldly calculating, she concentrated on verbally rendering him helpless. "Asshole! Asshole!" she repeatedly intoned, her face only inches from his. Then, appearing satisfied that she had succeeded, she sat on a chair, her back to him, making it plain she wanted nothing more to do with him. Dr. L. conveyed his hope that they would again soon talk to one another.

The next day, at Ms. B.'s invitation, Laura's mother visited the nursery. In her mid-twenties, medium of build and height and, like Laura, blond and fair with Afro-American features, she was intelligent, articulate, and attractive.

After discussing matters in private with Ms. H., she spoke to the group with intense sincerity. She had indeed spanked Laura on Sunday. More worrisome, however, several times that day she had felt desperate enough to "almost not care" if she hurt Laura. Even now, her anger was making it difficult for her to talk to Laura. Her boyfriend had spent Sunday with Laura and herself at their apartment, but Laura had so pestered them they had little peace or privacy. As Laura's mother spoke, however, her anger noticeably diminished. In response to questions, she granted that Sunday had also been difficult for Laura. Their apartment is small. For reasons of safety, she does not allow Laura out alone into their crime-ridden neighborhood. Laura had no children to play with. Her room, though stocked with toys might have been painfully lonely. Ms. B. summed up: The family's circumstances were such that nightmarish days like Sunday were all but inevitable. In addition, Ms. B. proposed a plan: to provide mutual support, she and Mother would talk daily on the phone, in addition to their usual weekly face-to-face session, until feelings between Mother and Laura had been sorted out and an equilibrium restored. In the event of an emergency, Mother would be free to contact Ms. B., even outside of working hours. Laura, no longer defiant, apologized to Tania.

COMMENT

The group enabled Laura and her mother to constructively address conflict that had nearly overwhelmed them. Laura's having behaved cruelly toward another child—because it violated group standards of conduct— stood out in sharp relief, facilitating its being observed and confronted. Her stubborn refusal to apologize to the other child—uncharacteristic of her— suggested an unconscious wish on her part to communicate and get help

with the difficulties with her mother that ultimately emerged. The softening of Mother's anger as she spoke to the group, as well as her growing
empathy and sympathy for Laura, suggest the group's influence in changing
her attitude from adversarial to conciliatory. The group may also have helped
Laura and her mother by lessening their sense of aloneness and desperation. Laura's giving raw expression to her fury, opening the way for it to be
dealt with in a more organized, integrative manner, implied she felt safe
against the threats of either hurting others or being retaliated against herself. Her mother, for her part, found much needed allies in her efforts to
cope with her most difficult child.

## A Child is Removed from His Parents

After she had discussed the matter privately with Jonathan, a 4-year-
old, Ms. B., his individual therapist, holding him on her lap, announced
to the group that on the previous day he had been placed in foster
care and was no longer living with his mother and father. At this,
Jonathan—olive-complexioned, with curly brown hair, his brown eyes
already swollen from crying—burst into tears.
   "Why is Jonathan crying?" asked one child. "Why isn't he living with
his Mommy and Daddy?" asked another.
   Ms. B. explained, speaking slowly, pausing now and again to verify
she was being understood. On Friday (it was now Monday) the police
had been summoned to find Jonathan's parents lying in the street, too
drunk to stand. Jonathan's caseworker, present at the meeting, added
that Jonathan's parents had not been able to get to their feet despite
his pulling and pushing at them. The police took Jonathan with them
and reported the matter to the Department of Social Services. It was
decided that Jonathan would live in foster care until his parents were
well enough to care for him.
   At this a child blurted out that she didn't like this news, and wished
instead to present her own. She relented when Ms. H. gently insisted
that Jonathan needed the group's support. Ms. S. spoke of the sadness
of the situation. Only last week Jonathan's mother had visited the
nursery and had spoken about the Christmas tree she and Jonathan's
father had bought, and about how his father had been working steadily.
Dr. L. asked if we knew why Jonathan's parents had gotten drunk. Ms.
B. related what Jonathan's mother, through sobs, had told her on the
phone: on Friday, Jonathan and his mother had gone to meet his father after work. Then they did what Mother called a "stupid thing."
As the three of them walked home, she and father began drinking,
singing Christmas carols and laughing. Without realizing it, they be-

came too drunk to stand. "Daddy was already drinkin' on the job!" Jonathan blurted out, angrily snapping his head to look away from the group. When Ms. B. commented on how terribly hurt he was, Jonathan burst into tears and through sobs declared, "I want to go back to Mommy." His caseworker, clearly moved, tried to reassure him. His parents, she said, would be able to visit and telephone him in the nursery. "But," a girl pointed out emphatically, "they can't take him home!"

Without saying a word, Jonathan climbed down from Ms. B.'s lap, walked directly to the toy shelf and returned biting on a small wooden block. Ms. H. asked him, would he prefer a baby bottle? When Jonathan nodded yes, she fetched him one from the kitchen, half-filled with juice.

As Jonathan sucked on the bottle, Ms. B., speaking softly, summed up: children are removed when parents are unable to care for them. Jonathan's parents would have to work hard to make themselves strong enough to care for their son. A judge would now have to decide when it would be safe for Jonathan to return.

Three days after this group meeting, Jonathan's mother visited him in the nursery. Throughout the visit her distress was apparent. She left the classroom several times explaining that she was nervous and needed to smoke. While in the classroom, she appeared apathetic. She stared vacantly at a wall, and took little notice of Jonathan, who, in turn, largely ignored her. In a joint session with Jonathan and his mother, the interaction was limited to her holding him, telling him how much she missed him, and crying with him.

In the group meeting following the joint session, however, with Jonathan on her lap, his mother said she was "angry as hell" at her son's foster mother ("that bitch") for having had his hair cut from shoulder to medium length. Jonathan tentatively mumbled that he didn't like his foster mother either. Then, her voice overly loud and cheery, his mother suddenly asked Jonathan, "What's up, Buster?" Smiling shyly, Jonathan answered that his foster mother had taken him to see Santa, and, laughing, added that he had been afraid of being bitten by Santa. The group laughed as tension eased. A girl, in comforting maternal tones, assured Jonathan that Santa would not, in fact, bite him.

Jonathan asserted that he wanted a gift from Santa. Mother—anger no longer in her voice—responded softly that a good gift would be to have him home again. Looking up at her Jonathan said, "You was crying on the phone, Mommy." Mother, teary, her voice cracking, holding him to herself, replied that she and father were "sick." We "drink too much." For a time, Jonathan and his mother sobbed together while the group sat silently. At one point, Mother, apparently becoming acutely aware of herself, suddenly looked embarrassed. However, staff assured her that her crying together with her son was enabling them to feel closer to one another. Only the day before, Ms. B. continued, Jonathan had refused to talk to his mother on the telephone for fear that she would cry. Mother related how once, when she had been crying, Jonathan had stroked her head and had reassured her, "It's okay, Mommy. Don't cry."

At this point, Ms. H. interrupted. While Jonathan's mother had been crying, Coreen, age 3½, had angrily muttered under her breath, "There she goes crying' again." Coreen was reminded that her own mother also drinks heavily. Coreen, a delicately built black girl with both legs in braces, the result of a congenital spinal abnormality, confirmed, "When Mommy came to our house last night, she was shoutin' and cursin'. Nana [Coreen's maternal grandmother, with whom she had lived since infancy] yelled at her. She had no business comin' to our house and actin' that way. Nana threw her out." Had her mother been drinking? Ms. H. asked. "She wasn't drinkin," Coreen answered, "she was drunk!" For a moment there was silence, but Coreen wasn't finished. Struggling to her feet, she addressed the group. "Hey y'all. Look at my new pink jump suit!" Hearty laughter from all, including Jonathan's mother. Coreen appeared to be proclaiming, that while the pain of parental alcoholism must be faced, happy things can happen and be shared with appreciative people.

### COMMENT

The catastrophic disruption of Jonathan's life was countered—albeit *very* partially—by the continuity of the nursery setting, including the group meeting. In the latter, Jonathan was able to communicate and express himself better than he had in any other setting. He confronted his mother and engaged her in dialogue, not as a terrified, abandoned child but as one speaking from a position of strength, strength clearly drawn from membership in a supportive group. The group experience had a similar influence on the other children and on Jonathan's mother. Some of the children spoke up, most paid attention, and all behaved in a more organized manner than was typical for them. Jonathan's mother was at her most articulate, emotionally responsive and receptive during the meeting.

## A Child's Mother Commits Murder

With Aimee, age 3½, on Dr. L.'s lap, he began the meeting by announcing that the previous day (a Sunday) her mother (age 21) had been arrested for stabbing an elderly woman to death. Aimee was large framed and heavy, though not obese or unattractive. Her light brown skin and carefully braided hair reflected her being the offspring of a black father and white mother. The night before, Dr. L. explained, Aimee's maternal grandmother—her principal caretaker and custodian, whom he had been seeing in psychotherapy—had telephoned to tell him of the killing. Earlier in the day, Aimee's mother had called her, pleading for her to come fetch Aimee, as the police were on their way. She then became incoherent, but a young woman with whom she had been living took the telephone and filled in the story. Aimee's mother had been drinking heavily and using crack. When the victim, a neighbor, had complained about the loudness of the music coming from the apartment, Aimee's mother had become enraged, quarreled with her, lost control, and stabbed her. Aimee, according to the informant, had not actually seen the killing, as she had been playing in the backyard.

When Dr. L. finished the story, silence reigned. Dr. L. then asked Aimee about her thoughts. She replied without affect, "Mommy went to jail. The police locked her up." Several children responded with disbelief: "She's in jail? She's locked up?" Aimee, contradicting the story that she had been outside playing at the time of the killing, continued. "I was on the bed sleeping. The police took my mommy. I was scared." "This isn't scary," a boy interjected, wide eyed and tense. "Yes it is," Ms. H. replied firmly. The children fidgeted. "They close the door on you," another boy blurted out. "There are rats in jail," the first boy declared. Ms. H. clarified that there probably weren't rats in jail, but confirmed that Aimee's mother would likely remain in jail for a very long time—maybe until Aimee had grown up. For a time there was silence, most of the children fixing their gazes on Aimee. Two children hid their faces between their knees.

Ms. B. gently recounted that two of the children had mothers and two others had fathers currently in jail, while a fifth child's mother had been in jail. A boy, not among this group, volunteered that his father too had been in prison—though only overnight—due to a fight with the boy's mother. He added that the previous night his mother and father had again fought.

When Aimee now sadly declared, "I don't want to tell anymore news," Ms. S. gently praised her for the clear way in which she had expressed herself, and related how that morning, Aimee, on arriving, had straight away come to her and had told her what had happened.

Throughout the morning, Aimee had limited herself to drawing, and working with blocks. In her individual session, however, she had shown how pained she was as she laughed loudly and uncontrollably, and had to be restrained from shoving Play-Doh up her own nose.

During the next two weeks, Aimee spoke almost daily in meeting. She explained: "Mommy took drugs. Her couldn't think." Other children asked questions: Why had she stabbed the woman? What happens to people when they use drugs? Can drugs make you stab people? Several spoke of their own parents' abuse of drugs (all but one of the group had at least one parent who was or had been a substance abuser). One, the only middle-class child in the group, volunteered: "My mommy doesn't drink anymore, but she smokes. You can get cancer from smoking."

Two and one-half weeks after the killing, Aimee was taken by her maternal grandmother to visit her mother in prison. Prior to that, Grandmother—despite her tough street talk a bright, articulate woman of 38—indicated, her own pain had made visiting impossible for her. The day after the visit, at the group meeting, Aimee, on Grandmother's lap, seemed depressed and was less verbal than usual. "What was jail like?" Aimee was asked. "Jail," Aimee answered. Grandmother vividly yet soberly filled in details. She described the prison's many doors, the guards and inmates, the large room in which, separated by tables and overseen by guards, inmates and visitors met. Aimee had been allowed to sit on the table, touch and kiss her mother. But when Aimee asked her why she had killed the woman, her mother had cried for the remainder of the visit. Aimee had hugged and wiped her mother's tears and had even apologized to her for having hurt her feelings.

At this point, Aimee spontaneously reiterated that the police had "locked up" her mother because she had "stabbed a lady." How, Ms. H. asked, did she feel about her mother now? "I love her," Aimee answered. "She's in jail." Was she angry at her mother? "Sorry," Aimee answered.

The other children had been attentive to the point of appearing spellbound. Discussion followed. Aimee's mother had visited the nursery on several occasions—what did the children remember of her? One child recalled her sitting in the classroom, smiling and observing. Several recalled her drawing along with the children and making paper cut-outs. One child, still unable to grasp the reality of what she had done, asked if she had, in fact, struck someone with a stick.

The next day, Ms. S.—holding Aimee on her lap and displaying a small plastic knife—announced that something upsetting had just happened, and asked Aimee to tell about it. Aimee, bursting into tears, blurted out, "I stabbed Ashley in the arm." (The knife was blunt and had not drawn blood.) "I said 'sorry' to Ashley," Aimee added plaintively through sobs. "I want my mommy." "How terrible to think that your own mother killed someone," Ms. S. said softly. "I wiped Mommy's face" [i. e., in prison], Aimee said.

During the next four weeks, Aimee continued to speak regularly at meetings, though never at great length. Her ideas about the killing seemed to become more organized. "Mommy stabbed a lady. Her killed a lady. Her was not using her brains. Her [the victim] had blood on her tummy. My mommy put drugs into her mouth. Her in jail."

Then Aimee's anger broke into the open. She reported—later verified by Grandmother—that she had scolded her mother during a telephone conversation. "You shouldn't stab nobody!" she had shouted. "I hate you!" Mother had shouted back, but Aimee had retorted, "I hate you, too!" In the next meeting, Aimee expressed the worry that her mother would stab her and her grandmother, but insisted, "I stab her back." In another meeting, Aimee confirmed Grandmother's telling Ms. S. by phone that the previous evening Aimee had squeezed her pet lizard to death because she no longer wanted it. As therapists individually expressed their sense that emotional pain had driven Aimee to behave destructively, she melted into tears and buried her head in Ms. S.'s chest, on whose lap she was sitting. In the next meeting, Aimee was confronted with having slapped Mike earlier that morning, and was asked to explain her side of it. She refused, insisting she wanted to continue talking about her mother. She was given permission to, provided she would then talk about having slapped Mike. At first Aimee rambled. Mother had used drugs and had "killed the white lady. Her wanted to." She herself was afraid of growing up because "Mommy will kill me." Then, all at once, the rambling stopped, and in a remarkably adult manner, Aimee said softly, "It's sad. It's too late."

After a moment of sober silence, Mike was asked by a therapist to step forward and tell Aimee how much her having slapped him had hurt him. Aimee apologized immediately, and asked that she be given "another chance." When she was reminded by a therapist that Mike's mother, too, was currently in prison, she became teary and hugged him.

COMMENT

By providing Aimee and her grandmother a forum for organized, thoughtful discussion—enabling them to gain perspective and feel less isolated—the group helped them to cope with the tragic and traumatic experience to which they had been subjected. Similarly, it helped the other children, most of whom themselves lived in similar circumstances.

The staff also benefitted. The violence the children so often talk about is not merely a product of the children's own intrapsychic processes, but exists only too concretely in an external world in which not only they but also the staff (albeit at a greater distance) live. Because the staff is subject to the same dangers the patients are subject to, when an event such as the one discussed above occurs staff members are confronted with the need to clarify and organize their own thoughts and feelings, calm their own fears, and, most importantly, successfully struggle against the temptation to defensively alienate themselves from the patients by thinking of them in a world or even as a species apart. The group experience, in which an almost familial intimacy between staff and children is so prominent, can reduce the alienation and isolation that is a consequence of violence.

## A Nearly Nonverbal Child Communicates with Her Mother

Betty, age 3, pretty, oval-faced, and Afro-American, looked tense as she sat stiffly in the news chair. In Cornerstone for the previous eight months and in foster care since she was 3 months old, she had gone from a disorganized, barely accessible, feral-like child to one who, while at times still impulsive, intolerant of frustration, and barely verbal, had become often poignantly appealing.

Her individual therapist, Ms. B., sat next to her. On the other side of her, some ten feet away, sat Betty's mother—25 years old, slim, pretty despite her obvious tension, her face bearing a striking resemblance to Betty's. On her lap was an 8-month-old baby, her fifth child, the only one still in her custody.

Betty had not seen her mother for nearly a year and a half. A half-year prior to that, Mother had reestablished contact with her daughter for the first time since placing her in foster care, and during a six-month period had visited with her in the nursery on a once-weekly basis. Then without warning, Mother had stopped coming and her whereabouts had been unknown. A few days before this meeting, Mother had reappeared, and had requested the Department of Social Services to again be allowed to see her daughter.

Ms. H. briefly summarized this story to the group, and asked if there was anything Betty would like to say to her mother. Betty lowered her gaze and remained silent, but nodded yes when asked if she would like to ask her mother why she had stayed away from her for so long. Betty then climbed down from the chair and walked slowly and tentatively toward her mother, but before reaching her, she stopped and, seeming at a loss, turned, ran back to her therapist, started sobbing, and buried her head in her lap.

At this, Aimee rose, went to Betty and gently asked her, "You mad at your mommy? Don't be mad at her." When Betty reacted with intensified sobbing, Aimee tenderly stroked her head and returned to her place on the mat.

Ms. H. asked Betty's mother why she had come back into Betty's life at this time. She replied that she had wanted to see her daughter. "Losing a mom or a dad hurts lots," Ms. H. said softly. Near tears, several of the children and Betty's mother nodded in agreement. (Of those present only one child was living with both mother and father. Five of the children were in foster care, and another five were living with their mothers only).

### COMMENT

When, just prior to the above described interaction, Ms. B. had met with Betty and her mother alone, Betty had been mute, affectless, and physically immobile. Ms. B. had suggested using the group meeting to facilitate communication. Mother, who was familiar with this aspect of the nursery, agreed. The strategy yielded positive results, for in the meeting Betty, despite limitations, was able to convey something of her longings and pain. Clearly, the support of the group setting had facilitated Betty's access to affect. Further, Aimee, a child with similar though less severe limitations, also was able to make good use of group support. Her show of empathy for Betty was atypical of her, reflecting the capacity of the group process to deepen her emotional life.

## WORK WITH PARENTS

Initially many parents are suspicious and even rejecting of staff. However, with surprisingly few exceptions, such attitudes prove amenable to change, and with most a viable working relationship can be established. Although we strongly encourage parents' involvement, we are guided by the degree of participation each seems capable of. Actual involvement on the part of parents has ranged from daily visits, to once weekly or even less frequent attendance, to occasional telephone contact. We acknowledge parents' needing time away from their children and don't pressure them to remain in the classroom beyond what they themselves consider beneficial. This applies especially to parents who have little opportunity to leave their children in safe hands so that they might have time for themselves. However, if at the beginning of treatment a child is unable to so separate from his or her parent without undue distress, we make it a condition of accepting that child that the parent remain in the nursery for however many days or weeks it takes for the child to be able to separate. If parents find the experience of meeting individually with a therapist uncomfortable or even threatening, but are able to attend nursery sessions, we allow them to attend and gradually acclimate themselves.

Helping parents with parenting is approached primarily by way of individual discussion, and modeling. Regarding the latter, we do not imply that parents should observe how staff interacts with their children and then imitate staff behavior. The aim rather is to expose parents to the experience of adults and children interacting with one another in ways that are pleasurable, gratifying, and mutually enhancing. We do not pretend to possess formulae or answers as to how children ought to be raised, but agree with Winnicott (1958) that parents can best be helped by being understood, supported, and encouraged.

We do not hesitate to acknowledge to parents, in a straightforward manner, that their children are indeed difficult and that mistakes (ours as well as theirs) are inevitable. It can be most reassuring for parents to witness staff, in the course of work in the nursery with difficult children, react with fatigue, exasperation, and fumbling. To assume the role of "authoritative expert," in our view, can too easily undermine parents' already vulnerable self-esteem, promote distrust, and, overall, make matters worse.

A useful approach to making contact with parents has been to invite them to parties given in honor of their children's birthdays or important holidays. At these parties we try to facilitate an informal mutually supportive and respectful atmosphere. This can be problematic, as it requires of the staff that they not hide behind professional decorum but behave in a natural and, to some extent, self-exposing manner. The challenge, of course, is to do so without harmful loss of professionalism.

Four examples follow that illustrate something of the range of work with parents. These include: (1) a mother who became very much involved both in her own individual therapy and in working with the team; (2) a mother of very limited cognitive and emotional capacities who related to her children's therapist and the nursery setting as substitute parents, family, and community; (3) a mother who, while accepting therapy for her child, remained only minimally involved herself; and (4) a mother with whom we did not succeed in maintaining a working relationship.

## A Mother who Became Involved

Mrs. Connors' older children, 9 and 11, had been taken from her and placed in residential care, the result of one of them having set fire to their apartment, the other having become severely depressed, and both being out of her control. To work toward having them returned she had been court mandated to receive psychotherapy and parent guidance for herself, as well as treatment for her two younger children, a daughter, age 2, and a son, 4, both of whom were already showing signs of serious disturbance.

Initially, Mrs. Connors was so angry and suspicious that developing any form of relationship with her seemed doubtful. She avoided eye contact, gave single-word answers, and was emotionally disconnected. Because her daughter was so young, Mrs. Connors was required to stay in the nursery each day. After a few weeks of simply being welcomed, invited to join in nursery activities, and offered the opportunity, at her own pace, to talk matters over with her children's therapists, she began helping with snacks and other activities and seeking staff's opinion concerning problems of parenting.

After seven months, the following scene occurred illustrating Mrs. Connors' identification. One morning Mrs. Connors' therapist, Ms. B., found her in the waiting room with seven of the nursery children, having, as usual, come in the van with the youngsters who live in her area. Mrs. Connors had taken charge of the children, comforting one, gently reprimanding another, and holding a sheet of paper with the heading "Mat List" (a list like the one used in the nursery on which are written the names of children who have misbehaved and must remain on the mat until matters are resolved). Proudly she announced that no one's name had been placed on this list as all but one child had been "cool" and she was in the process of sorting it out with the one exception. Once in the nursery, Mrs. Connors showed Ms. B. a cassette player and two audio tapes she had played in the van for the children. She then sang bits of several of the songs to demonstrate their appropriateness.

In her twice-weekly talks with Ms. B., Mrs. Connors had been initially hyper-sensitive and defensive concerning her parenting. Nevertheless, from the outset, she showed signs of having reflected on what they had discussed; either by later making verbal reference to it or showing by her actions that she was trying to implement it. After a few months, no longer disheveled, she began dressing and grooming herself with greater care. There emerged in her therapy themes of poor self-esteem and judgment, unmastered anger, physical and emotional abuse by her parents and, as an adult, by men, and of her being rejecting of her own children as a manifestation of identification with her rejecting parents.

### COMMENT

Over time Mrs. Connors sought actively to identify with staff. She often engaged in conversation with various team members on topics ranging from grooming and cosmetics to parenting and ways of dealing with her landlord.

She also gave small gifts to the staff. Lacking an alternative support system in her life she took the opportunity offered her by the Nursery team to risk engagement.

## A Mother with Severe Limitations

Ms. Taylor, in her early thirties, mother of three sons—9, 2, and 1 year of age—presented as depressed, cognitively retarded, disheveled, dirty and smelling, and lethargic to the point of seeming barely able to speak. With the help of Ms. Taylor's Mandated Protective Services Caseworker, who accompanied her, it emerged that her oldest child had been placed with her sister—a relatively well-functioning woman—and that her 2-year-old son, Charlie, had been referred to the Center for evaluation under court mandate. The older boy, according to the worker, had defied his mother, staying out at night and refusing to go to school, while Charlie was of concern because of his blunted affect, glazed facial appearance, and inappropriate smiling. Ms. Taylor could add only that the older boy had "talked back" and that Charlie "didn't listen."

Charlie presented as a child who smiled almost continuously in a vague detached manner, although he responded easily and with obvious delight at being played with on the slide, with puppets, and by having a ball and toy cars rolled to him. More ominous was the presentation of Ms. Taylor's 1-year-old, Paul, who showed little affect or responsiveness to intense efforts to engage him. During intake Ms. Taylor tended to withdraw into combing her children's hair, to which Charlie protested and Paul was indifferent. It was decided to take both children into the nursery with the proviso—because of their age and the obvious degree of family disturbance—that, for an indefinite period, Ms. Taylor also attend daily.

For the better part of the first year, each day Ms. Taylor arrived with her children at least one hour late. When urging her to come earlier was of no avail, it was decided to accept this pattern and welcome her at whatever time she did manage to come. At first, in the nursery setting, Ms. Taylor participated minimally, keeping to herself and, other than combing their hair, hardly interacting with her children. However, as she appeared to become more comfortable, an effort was made to draw her out. She was asked to help with simple tasks such as serving food and juice at snack. Gradually her affect became more lively and warmer. At the same time, she began voicing complaints about Charlie's misbehavior at home (not eating all his food, rebelling against being put to bed), providing Dr. L. the opportunity to discuss with her practical approaches to parenting and, in joint sessions with Charlie, to give her immediate help in understanding and communicating with him. Now revealing a surprising, engaging sense of humor, she became more open with staff. For example, she asked a staff member to teach her to bake a cake and beamed with pride when applauded at snack time for her creation. She began to volunteer to help prepare snacks, chatted with staff on such topics as decorating her apartment, proper diet, and other health issues, and participated in group discussion. Despite her verbal limitations, making extensive use of the nursery's telephone she also took unexpected initiative searching for a better apartment for her family. Nearly four years later, she rarely comes late or misses a session. Both of her children are functioning at a level significantly closer to age appropriate norms.

COMMENT

Given Ms. Taylor's limitations it remains most uncertain as to how well, or even how long, she will ultimately be able to parent her children. For now, however, due, in large measure, to the extended-family-like acceptance and relief from the drabness of her life she has been able to derive from involvement in the Nursery, the quality of her parenting and of her life and her children's lives has visibly improved.

## A Mother Minimally Involved in the Treatment of Her Child

In her early twenties, no more than five feet, seven inches tall, yet weighing well over three hundred pounds, Ms. Lane had been obese throughout her life. According to records supplied by her caseworker, her school performance had been poor. Expelled from the public school system for severely disruptive behavior, she finished high school in a residential setting for disturbed adolescents, earning while there a reputation for habitually lying, verbally threatening teachers, bullying, and fighting with peers.

We believe that crucial to Ms. Lane's allowing her seriously disturbed 2-year-old son, Joey, to attend the nursery was the team's allowing for and containing her needs to "split" two of its members into "good" and "bad" and to distance herself from the situation. Relieved thereby of having to experience all as enemies, she was not forced to withdraw completely. During intake Ms. B. explained to Ms. Lane that despite having been assigned to take preliminary information, she herself would not be Joey's therapist as her quota of three patients had already been filled. Ms. Lane implored Ms. B. to reconsider, insisting that it was only to her that she could relate, other staff seeming to Ms. Lane unfriendly and unapproachable. When Ms. S. was assigned as Joey's therapist, Ms. Lane responded by ignoring Ms. B. who, she now designated as "bad"—favoring white children over black, showing prejudice toward Joey, and being "too loud"—while Ms. S. was seen as "good." To try to sort things out, Ms. S. arranged for a meeting between Ms. Lane and Ms. B. with herself acting as mediator. In the meeting, Ms. Lane denied any problem. Following the meeting, however, Ms. Lane withdrew from active participation in Joey's treatment. Despite having done so—Joey was now able to come in the van unaccompanied by his mother—Ms. Lane continued supporting her son's attendance in Cornerstone, more than once voicing her recognition of its benefit to him in furthering his development. Indeed she has requested that her younger child, 10 months old, be considered as a future patient.

## A Mother with whom a Working Relationship Could Not Be Maintained

Ms. Morgan, an overweight woman in her early thirties with stringy hair and ill-fitting clothes, had been an alcohol and drug abuser since her early teens. Her four children, 1, 3, 13 and 15 years old, had been placed in the care and legal custody of her older sister, a well-meaning woman with two children of her own, but herself quite depleted and overly burdened.

Ms. Morgan's 3-year-old daughter, April, began treatment following referral by a Department of Social Services caseworker troubled by her difficult-to-manage behavior at home and her hyperactivity. It was hoped that treatment for April and her mother might enable at least the two younger children to be returned to Ms. Morgan. Although it was more than a month after April began that Ms. Morgan first visited the nursery, thereafter for the next two months she came weekly, visiting with her daughter and having her own individual sessions with her daughter's therapist, Ms. B.

These sessions gave reason for hope. Ms. Morgan appeared to be reaching out. She spoke of a range of interpersonal and financial problems, of feeling inadequately prepared to work despite being a high school graduate, and of her long history of substance abuse and efforts to overcome it. She denied using drugs at the time. She also spoke of wanting to help herself in order to help her children and seemed to be enjoying and deriving support from interacting with children and staff in the nursery setting.

As had Ms. Lane, she asked if her youngest child, a 1-year-old son whom she feared was showing signs of emotional disturbance, could also be considered for enrollment in the nursery. When it was explained to her that because he was so young she would have to accompany him on a daily basis, she readily agreed. However, following a closing of the nursery for a one-week vacation, Ms. Morgan came back to the nursery only one time, and then abruptly, without explanation, stopped. Despite strenuous efforts by her therapist to get her to return, over the next two years up to the present, Ms. Morgan has limited her contacts with Cornerstone and her children to occasional visits, made without advance notice, interspersed with weeks and even months during which her whereabouts become unknown to the nursery and her family. When her son turned 2, he was accepted into Cornerstone, accompanied for a time by Ms. Morgan's sister.

Ms. Morgan, however, remained unavailable. We conjecture that initially Ms. Morgan had temporarily succeeded, by dint of will, in holding in abeyance her tendency to take flight from responsible human relationships into drug use, and that her ultimate withdrawal represented her having failed in that effort. Still Ms. Morgan has expressed nothing but positive feelings about her children's treatment in Cornerstone, clearly appreciating the good they have been deriving from it. All four children remain with her sister.

## LIMIT-SETTING AS THERAPY

A frequent and inevitable situation that must be handled in the CNS Nursery is the loss of control of a child. With some children this occurs when they enter the program, either secondary to anxiety related to their unfamiliarity with the environment or as a direct acting out of their problem. With others, however, the child's acting out represents an evolution in his treatment. Such children typically first present themselves as apathetic and overcompliant and need time in the Nursery to feel safe enough to express their underlying fear, frustration, and rage. For these children, their expressions of intense affect often provide the first evidence that they are reachable. When their behavioral displays are adequately handled, the children generally respond with more differentiated affects such as sadness or neediness, which can then usually be connected to ongoing anxiety—disturbing relationships or events in their lives.

Whether these episodes of loss of control occur earlier or later in treatment, their occurrence and management are not considered as extracurricular to the treatment but rather an integral part of it. Most of the children have had experiences in which their deprivation and distress have been reinforced rather than contained by their caretakers. On the one hand, their disturbing behavior has often been responded to with indifference; on the other, with aggressive attacks. In order for them to feel safe with and manage their own feelings, they must be repeatedly provided with responses to their loss of control that contain it in a manner that reduces rather than exacerbates their frustration and anxiety.

While it is easy to understand their need for patience, support, and empathy, what is often more difficult to acknowledge is their need for direct and intense expressions of disapproval of their behavior. This need exists for at least two reasons. On the one hand, they are accustomed to ineffectual responses, so that mild remonstrations are not experienced as meaningful. Second, they are accustomed to a sequence of interaction whose endpoint is usually parental attention in the form of parental rage. Such earlier experiences can be countered by staff through responses characterized by modulated anger in the service of meeting the child's affective state halfway, without which the child remains emotionally isolated. Such responses may be viewed or experienced by visitors new to the Nursery as harsh. On the other hand, they have been validated by the positive nature of the therapeutic process and material following such confrontations with the child.

Following are three examples of loss of control, each of which required from staff a different mix of support and modulated anger: (1) a 3-year-old boy with a history of running out into traffic ran away from the driver who had come to take him "home" (a residence for homeless people); (2) a 4-year-old girl in foster care, giggling maniacally, ran out of the nursery's bathroom with feces smeared over her naked body; (3) a 4-year-old boy, ignoring all verbal efforts to calm him, exploded with hostile aggression, shouting obscenities, overturning furniture, hurling anything he could at children and staff.

How were these incidents responded to? It goes without saying that they became issues to be taken up in each child's individual therapy, but that came later. First "disciplinary" steps had to be taken. The boy who ran away, when he disregarded verbal efforts to persuade him to come back, was pursued by a therapist and promptly brought back. Both immediately and the next day in group discussion he was sternly confronted with the dangerousness of his behavior. He was also prohibited for a full session from participation in nursery activities and required to apologize to the driver as a condition of their resumption. By contrast, the 4-year-old girl's agitation immediately subsided when the therapist (not her own), who happened to be close, took her gently by the hand, led her to the bathroom, and, in a sink before a mirror, bathed her, massaged her with lotion, and spoke to her about how sad it was that she had soiled her lovely body. In the third instance, the therapist took a blanket with which she first protected herself from the objects being thrown, then restrained her attacker. For the next twenty minutes, while he struggled and cursed, she and another female therapist held onto him until he finally burst into tears, after which he allowed himself to be comforted. Sensing he was now receptive, she talked to him about how pained he seemed and what his pain might be related to.

We conceptualize the behaviors described above as representing efforts to cope with states of helplessness induced in the children by the intensity of their emotional pain, especially a desperate sense of feeling alone and unloved. Such behaviors constitute efforts to deny, reverse, and thus master intense feelings of helplessness and vulnerability by engendering helplessness in the therapist.

As Winnicott (1947) argued nearly fifty years ago, suppression of their own feelings by clinicians when dealing with emotionally overwhelmed children, in effect, abandons the children to cope with their chaotic feelings unaided (see also Kohut 1977). An overwhelmed child is an emotionally isolated child in desperate need of a sustaining tie to a helping adult. Such ties cannot be created by false or self-centered affects, by outbursts of temper, or by aloof "reasonableness" on the part of therapists. Just as children's neediness, fear, and emotional pain call for tenderness and affection from therapists, so hurtful, sadistic behavior or disruptive defiance on the children's part call for *coherent* expressions of anger—even outrage—followed by firm, thoughtful limit setting. When an interaction between an emotionally overwhelmed child and therapist goes well, a developmentally positive experience for the child may result. During the time they are overwhelmed such children lose their belief or trust (Erikson 1950) in the helpfulness of adults. If, however, in the face of such a "crisis of faith," the therapist in fact is able to be helpful, a precious corrective emotional experience (Sandler et al. 1980) may be created for the child. His or her distrust is, thereby, experientially contradicted.

## EDUCATION

When psychologically healthy children enter nursery school they relate easily to adults and peers and possess a range of interests and lively curiosity. Nursery education becomes an extension of the rich learning process in which they are already engaged throughout their waking hours. To teach them, teachers need primarily to be patient and supportive and to provide them with challenging but age-appropriate stimulation.

Children making up the Cornerstone population, however, present a dramatically different picture. They tend to be inattentive, distractible, unfocused, difficult to engage, and lacking in interests and curiosity. Representational play (Greenspan 1992) is either absent or impoverished, reflecting, in addition to impoverishment of imagination and creativity, major deficits in their abilities to convey thoughts and feelings through the use of symbols (Ekstein 1966). It is difficult for them to persevere—to "stay with it"—reflecting poor frustration tolerance and lack of confidence.

Their circumstances contain at least four elements that interfere with their capacity to learn. (1) The children have been inadequately stimulated at home. Verbalization is not sufficiently used as a source of information about the world and as a basis for rational problem solving. Far more common, they are shouted at, scolded, or otherwise browbeaten. Essentially absent from their lives are having their ideas listened to and valued, having things explained to them, being read to, or being taken to zoos, parks, museums, and other venues that could enlarge their view of the world and inspire wonder. (2) In their homes and their neighborhoods they tend to be inundated with adult violence, sexuality, and drug abuse, and with threatened or actual loss of their parents. Such overwhelming threats make the world seem a place to be avoided rather than approached with lively curiosity. In addition, the sexual and aggressive impulsiveness to which they are exposed reduces their own capacity for neutralization and sublimation required for sustained thought and attention. (3) The children are lacking in adequate models to identify with. Identifications are means through which children, by becoming like loved and admired adults, take over as their own desirable aspects of these persons' feelings, thoughts, reactions, and ways of dealing with inner and outer life. Learning through identification is spontaneous and rapid, rather than step-by-step and gradual, and essential for normal development (A. Freud 1965, Rapaport 1951). Indeed, "one could say that while the gratification of instincts ensures animal survival, identification is necessary to guarantee the ontogenesis of a person in the given sociocultural context" (Thomä and Kächele 1994, p.158). The virtual absence in the lives of Cornerstone children of adults who lead coherent, socially competent lives, or who live by ideals and values whose emulation would be enriching, deprives them of models from whom to fashion a sense of themselves as people capable of doing well in the world. (4) The children, too ill-equipped and ill-protected to do otherwise, are forced into emotional withdrawal and cognitive paralysis. For many, emotional ties, other than those which are narrowly need-fulfilling, as well as complex feelings, ideas, hopes, and aspirations, all but fade away. Children simply cannot learn about a world they are not able to care about.

Enabling the children in Cornerstone to learn involves, first and foremost, drawing them out of their emotional isolation so that the world about them, indeed life itself, comes to feel safe and inviting enough for them to want to learn about it. It seems almost self-evident that such a process can take place only by way of deeply felt commitments on the part of therapists (and others) toward the children, and a sustaining milieu, which can afford the children the opportunity to form identifications with others who are invested in, and can form a bridge to, the outside world.

Each aspect of Cornerstone contributes to learning. The child's (and parent's) relationship to his or her primary therapist embedded in the nursery milieu is the central element in this bridge. The group meetings can create an experience in which words and ideas may be sources of comfort rather than attack. To the extent that parents participate in their own and the child's treatment, the children's identification with their parents' mistrust and withdrawal can be diminished. The predictable and nonthreatening imposition of rules can offer the children positive models to identify with, enhance their self-control, and contribute to their increased frustration tolerance. The constant lively interaction among staff and children that takes place in the nursery provides children with daily ongoing opportunities and challenges for learning to cope with their own and others' needs and feelings. Finally, the staff-maintained ideal that learning—learning of any kind that helps one become stronger and more competent—is good can provide the children with the necessary raw material for interrealization. While we accept that no amount of treatment can totally compensate even very young children for markedly inadequate support and stimulation during the first three or four years of life, improvements in the Cornerstone children's abilities to learn and think are often impressive (see Chapter 16). The case of Wendy, seen through the lens of individual therapy, is illustrative of such an improvement.

> Wendy was referred at age 2 by the Department of Social Services. At 3 months of age maternal neglect had resulted in her having been taken from her drug-addicted mother. At 1 year, after two temporary foster placements, she was "permanently" placed with a woman related to the family by marriage.
>
> At intake Wendy's speech was limited to single words and her interest in exploring the environment all but absent. Considered a "failure-to-thrive child," her appetite was poor and she was well below average in size.

Her foster mother, feeling rejected by not being able to get her to eat properly or to comfort her when she cried, became chronically dissatisfied. She feared Wendy was either retarded or brain-damaged due to her mother's substance abuse, and voiced reservations about keeping her. However, she was urged not to give her up by the DSS worker, as to do so might well be devastating for Wendy.

At first, in the nursery, Wendy was mostly mute, and unless stimulated would remain rooted to the spot. However, she would cry easily, especially if she had gotten "messy," for example with paints. She interacted little with other children, preferring during free play to sit on the swing which her therapist would push gently while singing to her. In individual therapy* it took Wendy at least six months of daily intensive interactions before she would look to her therapist (R.S.) as "her person."

At first, at "brainwork"—when children are asked to name letters, colors, or numbers, or answer simple questions—Wendy would stare blankly into space. If pressed, even in the gentlest way, she would dissolve into tears. At other times she would manage a correct answer only to be unable, moments later, to reproduce it.

After six months, however, noticeable changes began to take place. Wendy would "shadow" her therapist. She would stay so close to Ms. S. that at times the therapist would almost trip over her. Wendy would often "sit" on the therapist's foot as the latter walked slowly about the room carrying her. She would sink into a sad, depressed look when her therapist would work with another child, and wait for the opportunity to again "glue" herself to her "Stooy." Despite Wendy's continued relative silence and nonrepresentational play, her therapist would talk to her about the pain of the losses of her three "mothers."

As therapy progressed, Wendy increasingly verbalized what she felt and wanted, her voice growing from a barely audible whisper to nothing less than booming. She also became more playful. For example, she delighted in hiding with her therapist, then sneaking up behind another therapist and, with a loud shout, "scaring" him or her. She would also play at being powerful—first a superhero, later a teacher. As Wendy's vitality emerged, and she opened up to new experiences, so, too, did her ability to learn. She became a most enthusiastic participant in "brainwork" activities, regularly jumping up and down in triumph when she answered correctly.

Early in her third year in the nursery, each day upon going home Wendy began crying bitterly. At first, her crying was understood as a measure of her attachment to the therapist and the Nursery. However,

*Rita Stewart was the therapist.

when one day Wendy appeared with bruises on her body, investigation by Child Protective Services revealed another reason for her not wanting to go home: her foster mother admitted to hitting her, and to having her stand in a corner for hours at a time for getting her clothes dirty or answering back.

Wendy was removed from the home and placed in emergency foster care. Within four weeks, however, she was adopted by a maternal aunt. Throughout the transition, she continued attending Cornerstone, was well able to communicate about what was happening to her, and showed no sign of any appreciable loss of the gains she had made in treatment. Upon graduating from the Nursery at the end of her third year and moving on to kindergarten, she was articulate about her feelings and receptive to interpretations linking the loss of the Nursery with her prior losses. In kindergarten, and the following year in first grade, she was considered an outstanding, even gifted learner.

## SUMMING UP

Apparently to avoid re-traumatization, the children treated in the Cornerstone Nursery typically are especially guarded against accepting what for other children would be developmentally enhancing support from adults. Thus, they are markedly unable to trust, rely on, learn from, or identify with would-be caretakers. Central to their treatment is their struggle to find their way back to sustaining ties, thereby reviving what potential they still have for further development (Erikson 1950, A. Freud 1965, Kohut 1977).

Particularly for this population we think of the various aspects of Cornerstone as working together synergistically. Individual therapy within the nursery setting bears the main burden of emotionally reaching the child, of drawing him or her out of detachment, and of nurturing, sustaining, and solidifying the resulting relationship. Its main tools are (1) the intimacy of the patient–therapist relationship (A. Freud 1965), supported by the frequency and length of sessions and the therapist's focus on the patient; and (2) the therapist's ability to interpretively diminish defenses (A. Freud 1936), thereby conveying to the child that he or she is understood, appreciated, and not alone (Kohut 1977, 1984, Modell 1984). To the extent that a given child's detachment is diminished, his or her inner world of fantasy, longing, and striving is brought to life, stimulating thinking and causing the milieu aspect of the nursery (as well as the rest of the world) to become more interesting and attractive for self-expression. The milieu aspect, in turn, by promoting in the children a sense of community and of belonging

(Scheidlinger 1980) helps to diminish their sense of aloneness, making them less vulnerable and reducing their need to withdraw, thereby enhancing their ability to enter into and benefit from an individual therapeutic relationship.

Individual and milieu aspects acting together offer the children a rich range of opportunities for developmentally enhancing, "emotionally corrective" (Sandler et.al. 1980) experiences. Among them are:

- being consistently cared for—loved—by their therapists and staff
- having their ideas and feelings taken seriously
- having realistic, constructive limits set to their behavior
- being encouraged explicitly and implicitly to express themselves symbolically and play creatively
- having their states of overwhelming emotional pain responded to in a constructive manner
- being exposed to their therapists, other staff, and children as objects of positive identification
- having their therapists actively advocate in their best interests
- being exposed to the enrichment of learning to interact, cooperate, compete, share, and play with other children in a safe, supervised setting
- being consistently encouraged and helped to learn about the world around them.

Not all of the children experience the intense transference revival of emotional pain and rage associated with their parents having failed them, as experienced by Monroe and Shaniqua. In fact, most experience this kind of transference to a much lesser extent or not at all. This latter group of children seem, on the whole, even more profoundly damaged and less adequately parented than those who experience the transference more intensely. It is probable that their early object relations were more shallow, and that, among severely disadvantaged children, the degree to which painful affect is transferred and worked through may be taken as an indicator of capacity for relating in general.

In treatment the children who do not experience an intense transference revival tend to experience therapeutic efforts to explore their life conditions less as means to greater mastery than as the uncovering of a situation beyond remedy, intensifying rather than relieving their sense of being alone and unprotected. Their tending to disavow or "split off" (Kohut 1971, 1977) thoughts and feelings associated with their home situations, however, is not wholly disadvantageous to them, as they also generally turn to their therapists and the nursery setting as alternative sources of care, libidinal involvement, and protection (Sandler et al. 1980, Settlage 1994). By so doing a large proportion are able to make substantial developmental progress.

For example, when Marcus began treatment at age 3 he was hyperactive, spoke largely in incoherent "word salads," was nonrepresentational in his play (Greenspan 1992), had little attention span, and tended to flit promiscuously from person to person and from activity to activity. His treatment had two foci: (1) clarification of a home situation in which his parents' energies were greatly absorbed by their poverty, antagonism toward one another (including Mother's consistently wanting Father to move out and Father's refusing to), and chronic depression; and (2) responding to his yearnings for richer parenting, both by interpreting them to him and by creating with him gratifying compensatory experiences (playing, talking, walking, discovering, learning together, etc.). In the course of two years in Cornerstone he improved greatly in every facet of his functioning. He also became able to acknowledge, rather than defensively avoid as he had done earlier, the harsh realities of his home environment as they were verbalized to him, both by his parents in joint sessions with him and by his therapist using information gotten from the parents. Although in the latter part of his second year of treatment Marcus was able symbolically to represent in his play aspects of his loyalty conflict concerning his parents, overall he volunteered little, explicitly or implicitly, concerning his home situation. Dominant (in terms of affect) was not intense emotional pain but a subdued sadness and depression born seemingly of increasing awareness of and resignation to his difficult situation.

For Marcus and most children like him we have suggestive evidence from follow-up work that continued therapeutic help throughout most if not all of their childhoods into adolescence is clinically indicated. Even if, as a result of treatment, their symptoms are ameliorated and their development resumes, they typically remain highly vulnerable children living in extremely undermining circumstances. It seems to us, that for many, the support of a therapeutic relationship throughout their growing-up years might well be crucial to their living socially viable lives.

## REFERENCES

Balter, N., and Lopez, T. (1990). Psychological help for a disadvantaged preschool boy: the Cornerstone method. *Journal of Preventive Psychiatry and Allied Disciplines* 4:329–344.

Brenner, N. (1988). The third decade. *Bulletin of the Anna Freud Centre* 11:289–294.

Colonna, A. B., and Friedman, M. (1984). Prediction of development. In *Psychoanalytic Study of the Child* 39: 509–526. New Haven, CT: Yale University Press.

Edgcumbe, R. (1975). The border between therapy and education. In *Studies in Child Psychoanalysis*, pp. 133–148. New Haven, CT: Yale University Press.

Ekstein, R. (1966). *Children of Time and Space of Action and Impulse.* New York: Appleton-Century-Crofts.

Erikson, E. H. (1950). *Childhood and Society.* New York: Norton.

Freud, A. (1936). *The Ego and the Mechanisms of Defense.* New York: International Universities Press.

——— (1965). *Normality and Pathology in Childhood.* New York: International Universities Press.

——— (1975). The nursery school of the Hampstead Child Therapy Clinic. In *Studies in Child Psychoanalysis*, pp. 127–132. New Haven, CT: Yale University Press.

——— (1979). The nursery school from the psychoanalytic point of view. In *The Writings of Anna Freud*, vol. 8, pp. 315–330. New York: International Universities Press.

Friedman, M. (1988). The Hampstead Clinic Nursery: the first twenty years. *Bulletin of the Anna Freud Centre* 11:227–288.

Furman, R.A., and Katan, A. (1969). *The Therapeutic Nursery School.* New York: International Universities Press.

Greenspan, S. I. (1992). *Infancy and Early Childhood: The Practice of Clinical Assessment and Intervention with Emotional and Developmental Challenges.* Madison, CT: International Universities Press.

Kliman, G. W. (1975). Analyst in the nursery: experimental application of child analytic techniques—the Cornerstone method. In *Psychoanalytic Study of the Child* 30:477–510. New Haven, CT: Yale University Press.

Kohut, H. (1971). *The Analysis of the Self.* New York: International Universities Press.

——— (1977). *The Restoration of the Self.* New York: International Universities Press.

——— (1984). *How Does Analysis Cure?* Chicago: University of Chicago Press.

Lopez, T., and Kliman, G. W. (1980). The Cornerstone treatment of a preschool boy from an extremely impoverished environment. In *Psychoanalytic Study of the Child* 35: 341–375. New Haven, CT: Yale University Press.

Miller, J. (1988). A child losing and finding her objects: an unusual therapeutic intervention in the nursery school. *Bulletin of the Anna Freud Centre* 11:75–89.

Modell, A. H., (1984). *Psychoanalysis in a New Context.* New York: International Universities Press.

Rapaport, D. (1951). *Organization and Pathology of Thought.* New York: Columbia University Press.

Salo, F., and Friedman, M. (1988). The runaway bunny mother: the long-term influence of the nursery school experience. *Bulletin of the Anna Freud Centre* 11:53–74.

Sandler, J. (1987). *From Safety to Superego.* New York: Guilford.

Sandler, J., Kennedy, H., and Tyson, R. L. (1980). *The Technique of Child Psychoanalysis: Discussions with Anna Freud.* Cambridge MA: Harvard University Press.

Scheidlinger, S., ed. (1980). *Psychoanalytic Group Dynamics: Basic Readings.* New York: International Universities Press.

Settlage, C. F. (1994). On the contribution of separation–individuation theory to psychoanalysis: developmental process, pathogenesis, therapeutic process, and technique. In *Mahler and Kohut: Perspectives on Development, Psychopathology, and Technique*, ed. S. Kramer and S. Akhtar, pp. 17–52. Northvale, NJ: Jason Aronson.

Settlage, C. F., and Spielman, P. M. (1975). On the psychogenesis and psychoanalytic treatment of primary faulty structural development. *Association for Child Psychoanalysis: Summaries of Scientific Papers and Workshops* 2:32–63.

Thomä, H., and Kächele, H. (1994). *Psychoanalytic Practice: Volume 1–Principles.* Northvale, NJ: Jason Aronson.

Weise, K. (1995). The use of verbalization in the management of feelings and behaviour: a therapeutic intervention in the nursery. *Bulletin of the Anna Freud Centre* 18:35–46.

Wilson, P. (1977). The referral of nursery school children for treatment. In *Psychoanalytic Study of the Child* 32: 479–504. New Haven, CT: Yale University Press.

——— (1988). Therapeutic intervention through the nursery school. *Bulletin of the Anna Freud Centre* 11:307–316.

Winnicott, D. W. (1947). Hate in the countertransference. In *Collected Papers*, pp. 194–203. London: Tavistock, 1958.

——— (1958). *Collected Papers.* London: Tavistock.

——— (1965). *The Maturational Processes and the Facilitating Environment.* New York: International Universities Press.

Woods, M. Z. (1988). Developmental help: interventions in the nursery school. *Bulletin of the Anna Freud Centre* 11:295–306.

# 3

# Cornerstone, Steppingstone, Superstone: A Three-Phase, Long-Term Intensive Intervention for Extremely Stressed, Emotionally Disturbed Children*

*Rita Stewart*
*Laurie Mendik*

Homelessness, poverty, substance abuse, fragmented families, and a general level of hopelessness have taken a considerable toll on the lives of many young children, who are being raised in an atmosphere of anxiety, chaos, and despair. Consequently, foster care, school, welfare, legal, and mental health systems are being confronted with ever-increasing problems. Despite the catastrophic nature of the stresses placed on these children and their families, there is an accelerating trend toward cuts in essential services and emphasis on quick, short-term treatment for this population.

This chapter offers an approach that is counter to the prevailing trend of "band-aid" approaches to severe problems. The model presented here constitutes a long-term, intensive, multidisciplinary approach that has generated data that support the potential for significant remediation of child psychopathology and for strengthening of the family system upon which the child's future mental health will depend.

The children treated in this program are drawn almost exclusively from inner city areas. Virtually all of them have experienced combinations of

---

* This chapter is based on a presentation to the American Orthopsychiatric Association, San Francisco, CA, May 22, 1993.

physical abuse, sexual abuse, extreme neglect, abandonment, foster care, homelessness, moderate to extreme poverty, and/or a lengthy family illness. Most have lost one or both parents as a result of substance abuse, abandonment, imprisonment, severe mental illness, divorce, and/or death. Their homes and lives are, on the whole, chaotic and crisis-ridden, and many live in a state of chronic instability.

Behaviorally, all the children exhibit symptoms of anxiety and depression. Their cognitive functioning is significantly below their apparent potential (Zelman et al. 1985). Their object relations are often tenuous and inconsistent, and the range of their emotional life is impoverished. They all display significant arrests and aberrations in their development. Impulsive, provocative, destructive, and hyperactive behaviors are common (Balter and Lopez 1990).

On intake, these children present with severe manifestations of diagnoses, such as Oppositional–Defiant Disorder, Dysthymia, Overanxious or Generalized Anxiety Disorder, Reactive Attachment Disorder, Separation Anxiety Disorder, Attention Deficit Hyperactivity Disorder. Some of the children also exhibit psychotic features, and these are generally reactive, rather than organic, in nature. Some also exhibit features of the "borderline-child-to-be" (Pine 1985).

Preschool children are referred to the program's first phase because their level of emotional disturbance, coupled with their learning difficulties, is beyond that which may be treated effectively in a preschool special education setting or through psychotherapy alone. For some, the alternative is institutionalization. Referrals come from Child Protective Services, Preventive Services, the courts, other agencies, psychiatric hospitals, individual therapists, daycare centers, prekindergarten programs, special education programs, and self-referrals.

Twenty-seven children were involved in the long-term, intensive, three-phase program from 1987 to 1992. Demographics of the population were as follows:

- Gender:     56% Male
              44% Female
  This represents a higher number of females than is generally encountered in public child psychiatry clinics.
- Abused/Neglected: 67%
- Involvement with Child Protective Services: 74%
- History of foster placement: 52%
- Parental severe emotional problems (defined as a psychiatric diagnosis and very low to moderately low functioning): 89%

- Absent fathers: 44%
- Absent mothers: 19%
- Intact families: 11%
- Medicaid: 93%

The Cornerstone, Steppingstone, and Superstone programs of the Center for Preventive Psychiatry represent the three phases of treatment presented in this chapter. The phases are linked together in a long-term intervention for the population described above. However, it is noteworthy that each of the components can and do function as separate entities.

Cornerstone is a five-mornings-per-week program for twelve children, ages 2–5, and their families. Steppingstone is a two-times-per-week afterschool program for eight children, ages 5–7, and their families. Superstone is a one-time-per-week afterschool program for eight children, ages 8–10, and their families. All three programs use differing balances of individual, milieu, and group modalities, utilize a co-therapeutic team approach, offer family therapy and parent/foster parent guidance and therapy, and provide intensive advocacy and case management.

The Cornerstone Method is the methodological foundation for all three programs. This approach, described in detail in Chapter 2, has evolved in response to a changing population of children and families during the past twenty-five years. It is characterized by:

- Intense, affective engagement with the children on every level, from the preparation of food to the most complex and emotionally laden family issues. Of primary importance is the real relationship between child and therapist.
- All therapists participate equally to create an atmosphere of spontaneity, affection, and safety in which therapeutic interaction can take place.
- Individual, milieu, and group therapy coexist simultaneously. Therapists maintain an awareness of and can respond to all three components as they emerge and shift in the treatment process.
- The milieu and group components of the therapy promote the effectiveness of the individual therapy by countering the very prevalent emotional withdrawal and detachment among the children and by helping to sustain their investing in other group members in group activities and group processes.
- The children's personal issues and experiences are discussed freely and openly within the group and milieu setting.
- The children's intrapsychic pain is the object of focus.

- Every program session includes a group meeting and a snack, around which other activities are structured. The structure is flexible and responsive to the needs and issues of the children and varies from session to session. Therapists are alert to the difficulty of transitional periods and use them therapeutically.
- Safety and respect are emphasized for all group members. Limits are clearly defined, stated, and strictly maintained, with the goal of helping the children internalize the structure and boundaries provided. Limit setting is combined with interpretation and nurturing.
- The relationship of the members of the co-therapeutic team is respectful and open. Differences are thoughtfully discussed, sometimes within the milieu, and the team models appropriate cooperation, communication, and problem-solving skills for both the children and their parents.

## CORNERSTONE (PHASE I)

The Cornerstone Unit is an innovative early intervention therapeutic program. Twelve children, ages 2–5 (or until they attend school a full day) attend five mornings a week year round. Children typically attend Cornerstone from one to three years. Cornerstone is conceived of as a corrective therapeutic milieu with as much family participation as possible. It includes daily intensive individual psychotherapy, daily group meetings, and age-appropriate preschool activities. Parent/foster parent guidance, family therapy, and individual psychotherapy are available for family members. The Cornerstone staff also provides advocacy and intensive case management for each child and his or her family. Cornerstone is staffed by an interdisciplinary team of four psychodynamically and developmentally informed psychotherapists, two clinical social workers/psychotherapists, one clinical psychologist, and one special education teacher/psychotherapist. Interns and trainees may also work with the team.

Therapeutically, Cornerstone consists of a combination of individual, milieu, and group therapy. Each child is assigned one of the team members as his or her individual therapist, from whom the child receives, in the milieu setting, one half hour of individual psychotherapy daily. In addition, a group meeting of all the children, therapists, and family members present takes place daily. Milieu therapy and experiential learning are also provided by all the therapists in the program. The emphasis, however, is on each child's individual issues.

As in therapeutic nurseries, children learn to follow instructions, verbalize, tolerate frustration, play cooperatively, work to achieve goals, settle disputes reasonably, avoid endangering themselves or others, and to read letters, numbers, and simple words. However, in Cornerstone the children are in addition engaged in individual therapy carried out primarily within the classroom itself.

The children and the families are encouraged to share experiences in a mutual support system. In effect, Cornerstone, for many of these children and their families, becomes a supportive and nurturing familylike environment.

Cornerstone is an active and lively place. The therapist is a person who functions on many different levels at the same time—as a teacher, a parent-surrogate, an interpreter of feelings, behavior, and ideas, a mediator of disputes, and an advocate with the welfare and legal systems. Most of the children have not had the experience of a real relationship with responsive adults, so the therapists actively attempt to engage the child in a broad array of affective repertoire. For example, if a therapist is hit in the shins by an angry child, he or she will express the pain loudly and then will process the incident with the child with the goal of encouraging verbalization and insight without destructive behavior.

Parental involvement is not a prerequisite for admission to the program but is strongly encouraged. In our case sample, however, almost 100 percent of the children had caretakers who became involved in their child's and their own treatment as the child's treatment progressed.

The parents of Cornerstone children are often depressed, depleted, overwhelmed, and unsupported, with low self-esteem and painful histories. Many have experienced early abandonment, foster placements, homelessness, substance abuse, mental illness, and incarceration. Many have extreme problems with interpersonal relationships. This population often feels intimidated in individual psychotherapeutic settings and has difficulty following through in keeping individual appointments. The flexibility of this program and the nonthreatening milieu atmosphere allow each parent to become involved at his or her own pace.

## STEPPINGSTONE (PHASE II)

Before Steppingstone was created, in 1987, termination dates in Cornerstone were arbitrarily dictated by the child's entrance into a kindergarten (or first grade in some districts) at the start of the school year. Therefore, this very important transition for the children and their families would coincide with the loss of the therapist, of the intensive treatment, and of the therapeutic support system. In addition, some children were not psychologically or developmentally ready to terminate in Cornerstone and regressed significantly. These children were referred to individual therapists who would treat the child one to two times a week and work as indicated with the family members. Many families found this transition from the milieu to the individual setting too threatening and the loss of Cornerstone too painful, and they terminated therapy prematurely.

There was, therefore, a clear need for an interim treatment process in which:

- Children could continue within an intensive therapeutic environment at this time of high stress for their families and for them.
- It would be possible to maintain the relationship with the parents within the less threatening milieu setting.
- Parents and children could continue contact with their respective peer groups.
- There would be an opportunity to follow up Cornerstone treatment.

**Steppingstone Structure**

The Steppingstone program includes eight children, ages 5–7, and two therapists, at least one of whom is also a Cornerstone therapist to ensure continuity between the two programs. The program meets for two hours, two times per week, immediately after school to enable the children to come to the program without going home first. We found that this guarantees better attendance of children from disorganized households because caretakers are not responsible for getting the child to the program. The program meets during the school year and follows the school calendar. Having the children come to the program directly from school also reinforces our role as a support for the school because the teachers know where the children are going and who we are.

Parents continue involvement in the program and become increasingly able to keep appointments both during and after the program time. They continue their involvement both in the work with the children, in their own work, and in their often very important and supportive contacts with the other parents.

During the program time, spontaneous play and peer games developed by the children are used by the therapists to highlight and interpret individual issues and to develop problem solving, cooperation, and communication skills. The structure of the program time is flexible. Snack and a group meeting always occur, sometimes separately, sometimes together, but otherwise the structure and activities are responsive to the needs of the children.

When they enter Cornerstone, these children often have not developed the ability to verbalize their feelings and experiences. By the time they reach Steppingstone, however, they have the beginnings of the ability to verbalize and have some internalized ego process. Therefore, the role of the therapist changes gradually during the developmental process of Steppingstone from auxiliary ego to a facilitator and a resource. The therapists also continue to function as case managers for all the families, doing extensive collateral work with schools, and, as needed, the legal and welfare systems.

### Rationale for the Structure of Steppingstone Program

We have found, in our experience, that therapeutic issues seem to be addressed more quickly in a combination of individual and milieu therapy, as in the Cornerstone program, because this combination offers the opportunity to observe and to deal with the child's issues on several levels and from several perspectives:

- The opportunity to observe, intervene and interpret issues around peer relationships and the ways in which these are distorted by the child's individual issues and behavior styles.
- The opportunity to observe and intervene in issues related to structure and transitions, such as the need to begin and end activities, to sit at snack, to listen, and to not interrupt.
- The opportunity to deal with these problems not as reported by parents and teachers, but as they happen in front of the therapists, the group, and the child.

The philosophy of the work with the children in Steppingstone is to focus on helping children gain insight into behaviors that interfere with their ability to negotiate school, family, and peer situations and to replace these behaviors with more appropriate, effective, and satisfying behaviors. The goal is to help children successfully negotiate our society and to maximize their individual potential. The primary way that we work on this is through understanding and interpretation of the feelings behind behavior while clearly enforcing rules and providing consequences for destructive behavior.

### Steppingstone—Case Illustration (Shaniqua)

Following is a description of work done in Steppingstone with Shaniqua and her family. (Earlier work done in the Cornerstone Nursery with this child was described in Chapter 2.)

Shaniqua was enrolled in the Cornerstone Therapeutic Nursery (CNS) after the last of multiple abandonments. At age 3, her drug-addicted mother had left her and two younger brothers with a neighbor and did not return. Shaniqua and her brothers were placed in separate foster homes, the first of three for her. She entered CNS following transfer to her second foster home. She presented as a withdrawn, electively mute, oppositional, angry child who made great gains in Cornerstone through her attachment to both the milieu and her primary therapist (S. H.). Although much improved, on graduation from CNS in August, further work and support were clearly needed.

She entered the Steppingstone Program in September. In the first few months, in a new milieu, with a new therapist (R.S.), much of the clinical work focused on dealing with the loss and mourning of her previous therapist and how this resonated with her previous maternal losses. During group discussions with the seven other children in the program (most of whom had also experienced parental loss), Shaniqua would listen avidly, but remained silent.

During play periods, she dressed up as a "lady" with a lipstick (which she carried with her and applied liberally), rigidly playing the part of a mother who took care of everything in the household, and was controlling of other children in her play. During this period, Shaniqua's biological mother, Mrs. T., who was enrolled in a drug rehabilitation program, began to visit with Shaniqua and her brothers in the offices of the Department of Social Services. These visits were planned in preparation for a possible future return of the children to their mother. Shaniqua, however, had formed an intense bond to her then current foster mother, Ms. V., whom the visits with her mother exacerbated her concern about losing.

In Steppingstone, during this period, Shaniqua became more emotionally withdrawn and she avoided peer play. (Nevertheless, her kindergarten teacher reported that she was functioning adequately.) Shaniqua was able to talk about her ambivalence in individual sessions, provided in Steppingstone, but was not yet able to express those feelings in group discussions with the other children.

In November, visits with her biological mother increased. When her former therapist visited her in Steppingstone, she gave her a lipstick to use in her play. Shaniqua treated it like a precious object, and invariably held it when she seemed troubled and sad. She spent a lot of her playtime in the housekeeping area, again, being the "mother." Interpretations were made about her wishes and longings to have a permanent home with a mother who would remain with her.

In December, her ambivalent feelings in regard to her two "mothers" became more intense. Her wish to return to her mother was verbalized, along with her worry that her mother would again use drugs. She recounted early memories of her mother going into the bathroom and using drugs. She then expressed these concerns directly to her mother during the latter's visits to the program. During these visits, Shaniqua would search her mother's purse, check her pockets, and follow her to the bathroom, asking, "What she doing in there?" During the holiday period Shaniqua was more depressed and withdrawn, but in January she became more open in discussing her feelings with other children about being in foster care.

She now began a routine of telephoning her foster mother once each session. She also became more needy of food, and wanted to take home cookies and crackers. She expressed more persistently her fear of losing her foster mother and her mistrust of her biological mother. During group discussions, she now volunteered comments on issues related to losing parents.

She continued to address more of her concerns and questions directly to her mother, who was now making regular visits to Steppingstone. However, she also continued to call her foster mother even when her biological mother was present. The therapist commented on, and supported, Shaniqua's effort to do what she could to make sure she would be taken care of.

In March, Shaniqua, with the help of her Steppingstone therapist, dictated a note to her CNS therapist, stating that she still thought about her and when she received an answer, she played a game of running towards and then away from her Steppingstone therapist. When her actions were interpreted in terms of the pain of her losses and her wishes to undo them, Shaniqua covered her ears and began to sob.

Although the Steppingstone program closed for the summer, family sessions continued. The therapist met with Shaniqua, her mother, and her two younger brothers. Shaniqua began to reconnect with her mother, and openly express her fears, anxiety, and love for her. During the fall of the second year, her two brothers began regular attendance in Steppingstone and their mother frequently attended as well. Plans were discussed for a possible return of the children in December beginning with overnight visits to their mother's apartment.

Shaniqua was clearly excited about the prospect of going home, but manifested confusion about who her mother was. She referred to both her foster mother and her biological mother as "Mommy." She began to be more upset now when her biological mother left at the end of a Steppingstone visit. During this period, however, she continued to do well in school, and had received good report cards.

In December, Shaniqua was told that she would be returning home in January, although this would require a change of schools. In January, Shaniqua and her two younger brothers were indeed returned to their mother, but with poor preparation. When the children arrived, there were no beds for them, and Shaniqua and her brothers had to sleep on the floor. Shaniqua's mother was not given the extra money she needed for food for the children, and Medicaid cards were not activated for several months.

During this period Shaniqua, her mother, and brothers continued to attend Steppingstone sessions in addition to family sessions outside Steppingstone. Meanwhile the therapist increasingly functioned as an advocate with the Department of Social Services and as liaison to Shaniqua's new school. On the surface, Shaniqua managed to maintain her equilibrium during this period, although both in the roles she assigned herself in play and her interaction with her mother and siblings she suggested a parentified child.

The therapist attempted to deal with this issue, both in individual visits with the mother and family visit sessions in and out of Steppingstone, by supporting Ms. T., while pointing out the relationship between Shaniqua's need to control and her underlying insecurity. These issues were also taken up in group discussions in Steppingstone. Although the return of her children clearly generated immense stress for Ms. T., the existence of affiliative bonds between mother and children, and among the children, was evident. Nevertheless, Shaniqua still maintained contact with her former foster mother, calling her during Steppingstone sessions and having her "mothers" speak with each other on the telephone. On one such occasion, the foster mother told Shaniqua "I'll always be there for you." Shaniqua was still hedging her bets in her own interest.

In May, four months after the children had been returned, Ms. T. once again succumbed to drug abuse. The children, Shaniqua included, were abruptly removed and returned to foster care. Fortunately, Shaniqua's original foster mother, Ms. V., was available to take her back. This time one of Shaniqua's brothers accompanied her. Ms. T. entered a detoxification unit, following which she returned to a drug rehabilitation program. Shaniqua did not see her mother for two months.

Simultaneously, the therapist continued to see Ms. T. in individual sessions outside Steppingstone, in preparation for the resumption of visits between Ms. T. and her children. The first visit of Ms. T. with her children occurred in July, outside of Steppingstone, which was closed for the summer. Ms. T. had been able to express feelings of guilt, remorse, and pain in individual sessions, and felt somewhat prepared for the anger and rejection that she expected Shaniqua to direct at her. Ms. T. arrived earlier in order to speak with the therapist. She wept and berated herself for causing her children more pain. When Shaniqua (and her brothers) arrived she jumped into her mother's arms and said, "Mommy, Mommy, I love you!" Ms. T. was taken aback by the intensity of Shaniqua's expression of affections, which was so unlike her reaction to their previous reunification following a longer absence. In the interval between the two separations, Shaniqua had gained confidence in herself. The new enthusiasm with which she greeted her mother was accompanied by an ability to confront her. Shaniqua was different now. Shaniqua looked straight at her mother and asked in a steady voice, "Why did you do this?" "Where did you get the drugs?" "Did someone give them to you?" "Why did you leave us?" Ms. T. was overcome by tears, and Shaniqua comforted her.

At the time of this writing, Shaniqua is enrolled in Superstone. Individual and family visits with her mother will continue outside Superstone, as appropriate, as will contact with her foster mother. Superstone itself will be utilized to reinforce her sense of age-appropriate competence, based, as it increasingly must be, in the world of her peers.

It remains a question whether Shaniqua will again be reunited with her mother and, if so, whether her mother will be able to keep her. In any case, the long-term, intensive work done in the Therapeutic Nursery, Steppingstone, and now Superstone has served, on the one hand, to keep hope of family reunification alive, and, on the other, to sustain and strengthen Shaniqua so that she can survive, whatever the future will bring.

## SUPERSTONE (PHASE III)

Superstone is a group which meets only once a week, also immediately after school, for two hours. Eight children, ages 8–10, attend. There is one primary therapist, who is also, for continuity, a therapist in Steppingstone and one intern. Superstone is primarily a group modality, in which content and process both reinforce and reflect the children's increasing internalization of and identification with the therapeutic environment and the corrective object experiences from the previous phases. Family therapy, parent/foster parent guidance and therapy, and individual work are offered outside the group setting, and case management and close contact with schools continues.

- Individual work is rarely done within the group.
- Family members do not participate in the group process. Age-appropriate separation from families is encouraged.

- Focus is on group process, on each child's impact on group members and the group's impact on individual members. Members are encouraged to verbalize their observations of the process and their experiences of each other's behaviors.
- There is consistent use of the group to verbalize understanding and interpretation of individual problems, rather than the therapist doing it, so that the problem-solving and interpretive aspects of therapy are being internalized and used. Group members act as "co-therapists," with consistent use of peer pressure to deal with behavior problems.
- The role of the therapist is of an active group leader, facilitator of group process, and resource, who is also always available, if necessary, to deal with individual issues.
- The therapist continues intensive collateral work, as needed, with schools and other systems.

### Superstone—llustration of Group Process

Following is an excerpt of group process that is characteristic of the work done in Superstone. The Therapist is Laurie Mendik.

Everyone except Beth arrived at once and began letting off some afterschool steam and organizing some play activities among themselves. As they were beginning, Beth came in with Margaret (her mother). Beth was crying. I asked what the problem was, and Margaret said that Beth didn't want Margaret to leave. I asked Beth why, and she just hid her face in her mother's coat and cried, begging me to let her mother stay. I said that since she wasn't giving me any reason why she wanted her mother to stay I felt that it was important that we stick with the Superstone policy, agreed upon by the children, that parents do not come to the group because the group is private and for kids only. I reminded Beth that our reason for deciding this was that an important reason for her coming to group was to work on issues she had with other kids. At this point Beth said, "They don't like to play with me." I said, "Is that true?" and she said, "Yes, I play alone," and refused to say anything else. She just hid her head and cried. I said gently that I thought this was a really important problem that we needed to work out in the group with the kids.

Since Beth kept repeating that nobody liked her, I turned to Nicole, Nassime, and Alana. I didn't tell them they had to come over to us. I simply asked, "Did you three realize that Beth is upset and crying?" They had been playing in a corner and hadn't seen it, and they immediately all jumped up and ran over to talk to her. They asked her why she was crying and tried hard "to help her feel better," as they put it. This didn't have much success, however, because Beth became oppositional and walked away.

I then decided to ask Danny if he would help out because Danny and Beth had been spending a lot of positive time together recently. He said he would help only if someone like me or Dr. Ferber (the assistant therapist) would guard the gun he was making. I arranged for Dr. Ferber to do that while I went over to Beth with Danny. Danny started talking to her, stroking her hair, and saying, "Come on, Beth, I want to play with you, I love playing with you." Beth did not respond. Such behavior made it easy to see why Beth has trouble getting along with other children. Danny shrugged his shoulders and said, "Well, what can I do?" I asked Danny, "Aren't there times when you are upset and people are trying to talk to you and you don't talk?" He thought about that for a minute, as did the other group members, who had all been following this, and he agreed. I asked, "Does that really mean that you think the person trying to help you should just give up and walk away?" and there was a general chorus that that was not a good response and that they thought that Beth should be helped, and that they should stick with her, which they did in varying degrees. Although it was not clear to me that sticking with Beth was necessarily what she needed, I felt that the group members should discover for themselves what worked and what did not.

Finally, Margaret, who had been waiting in the waiting room, called down to say that she was leaving, and Beth tried to run after her. I used my body to block the door. She pushed me angrily, and I said, "I can see that you're angry at me for not allowing your mother to stay, and that's OK, but we need to help you figure out why you think kids don't like you."

Beth went off in a huff, and Nicole, Nassime, and Alana decided on their own to follow her, which they did, quite closely. I watched, wanting them to work it out themselves. I could see how helpful Nassime was trying to be, by asking what was wrong and how could they help her. Beth kept screaming, "Leave me alone, leave me alone," and they kept trying to talk to her. After a while the girls came over to me and reported that Beth was telling them to leave her alone. I said, "Well, when you are feeling really bad and you tell people to leave you alone, is that what you want?" I was prepared to accept either answer, but they unanimously said that they would not want to be left alone when they were feeling really bad like Beth seemed to be feeling. They said that they would want to be helped. So I said, "Then maybe you should stick with what your idea is about how to help Beth."

A few minutes later, Nassime came to me and told me that she was trying hard to be nice to Beth and help her but she wanted to know if she had to put up with it if Beth hit, kicked, and pushed her. I said, "No, not at all,

Nassime. I can understand if you're angry about that." She said, "I'm getting angry at her and I don't like the way she's treating me. She's yelling at me and is treating me badly." I said, "In that case, Nassime, there is really no reason why you should put up with that. If Beth is treating you badly, that is not acceptable. On the other hand, what do we know about people who are treating others badly?" Everybody said it was because they were feeling bad themselves. I told Nassime that, with that in mind, it was up to her to decide what she wanted to do.

At this point, Beth ran into the kitchen and told them all to leave her alone. Nassime shrugged her shoulders and said, "I can't do anything for her. She is really being mean, and I can't help her and don't know what to do for her." Alana looked very upset and said, "I'm trying so hard to help her, and I don't understand why I can't." I asked Alana, "Aren't there times when people can't help you?" She thought about that and said yes. I said we would have to keep working at it and see what we could do.

I went into the kitchen to see what Beth was doing. She asked me to tie her shoelace. I tied her shoelace and asked her what was going on. She said, "They're bugging me, they're being mean to me." I asked, "Is that what you think they're doing?" She said, "Yeah, they're really getting on my case." I asked if she was sure that that was what they were doing and she said yes. I called Nassime, Nicole, Alana, and Danny over and I said, "Are you all trying to bug Beth?" They all looked surprised and said no. I said, "What are you trying to do?" They said, "We're trying to help her."

That seemed to be the turning point for Beth, who decided to get into the high chair in the corner and asked me to bring her food over. I said that I wouldn't do that, that she was welcome to sit in the high chair but that she had to be part of the group. I said that we were all going to work on this together because that was what we were all here for. We were all here to help each other. She did not protest. She brought the high chair over to the end of the table.

Nassime then said, "I don't want anyone to sit next to me." When I asked why, she said, "Because I'm upset about Beth." At this point, Beth said, "I want Nassime to sit next to me." I said, "Nassime, look, she wants you to sit next to her now, maybe you did help," at which point Alana's feelings were hurt because she felt that Nassime had been able to help Beth and she had not. We talked about how sometimes different people need different other people to help them out when they are upset.

As we were passing out the food, Danny started getting upset because he said that it wasn't fair that Beth was taking out the fact that she was upset on everybody else by being mean. I said to Danny that I thought that was a very good point. Nassime said that she didn't think that was a fair point at all because, as she said to Danny, "You do that all the time." I said I thought Danny knew that he did that all the time. Danny was able to agree. I said that I wondered what everybody did when Danny did that. I asked, "Do we just dump him and say, 'Well, forget it, we're not going to deal with you'?" Everybody said in chorus, emphatically, "No, we don't." I asked what we do. Several children responded that we try to help Danny, we try to understand him but we don't put up with it if he really treats us badly. At this point, John and Nicole said that they too were angry with Beth. John had refused to pass her something and then told her he was mad at her, and Nicole was saying that she didn't like the way Beth had treated her, that she had tried to help her, and she didn't understand why Beth was so mean. I observed that Beth was looking increasingly dejected at this point, and we were almost at the end of the group time, so I said it was fine for the group members to be angry at Beth, but I wondered if they all still liked her. They all looked at me as if it were a stupid question and said yes. I said, "So you can be angry with her and still like her."

Beth then got up, and ran into the corner, shouting, "I don't care if my stepfather dies, I hate him anyway." We all looked at each other understandingly, and I said, "I think Beth is letting us know what she's hurting about. It's not OK that she hurt everyone else, but I think she's letting us know how bad and how scared she's feeling that her stepfather has been sick. Losing her first father was so hard, and now I think she's afraid that she'll lose Joe, too."

As the kids went to get their coats, I could hear them quietly talking with Beth in the coat corner. I couldn't hear what was said, but she looked immensely better when she came out. When Margaret arrived to pick her up, Margaret, Beth, and I spent a few minutes privately talking about the stress in the house since Joe had been sick and Beth's fantasies and anxieties concerning his illness.

### The Three Phase Program—Case Illustration (Nassime)

Following is a summary of the treatment in Cornerstone Nursery, Steppingstone, and Superstone of Nassime and her mother.

Nassime was referred at age 2½ by Child Protective Services (CPS) because she was acting out and unmanageable in her foster placement. Nassime's mother, Mary, had been conceived in an incestuous relationship between her own mother and her alcoholic maternal grandfather. Mary had been abandoned by her mother and then severely abused and rejected by her stepmother and her father, after which she had been placed in a series of foster homes. She developed severe psychiatric problems which resulted in frequent hospitalizations.

Nassime was an unplanned child. Her father abandoned the family after one month. Little else is known about Nassime's father other than that he had been frequently incarcerated. Mary and Nassime were homeless during Nassime's first year of life and moved four times from relative to relative. When Nassime was 2½, Mary called CPS because she had been physically abusing Nassime and was afraid the abuse would escalate. She had been beating Nassime because "nothing would get to her." It is noteworthy that Mary had also been severely abused by her mother and had been placed in foster care at 2½.

Nassime's first placement was in care with her step-grandmother, the same person who had abused Mary. The step-grandmother also called CPS because she couldn't handle Nassime's "uncontrollable screaming and tantrums for hours." It was discovered later that this woman had scrubbed Nassime's lips with Ajax and had smashed her head into a sink. CPS removed Nassime from the step-grandmother's care and placed her in nonfamily foster care.

At the time of placement, Mary and Nassime began seeing a therapist in the hope that reunification could be achieved. When Nassime was 3½, she was returned to her mother after a nine month separation. The family's functioning deteriorated, and Mary and Nassime dropped out of treatment. Mary again called the clinic for help and this time was placed on a waiting list for the Cornerstone Therapeutic Nursery.

Nassime entered Cornerstone at age 4 with diagnoses of Severe Oppositional–Defiant Disorder and Severe Attention Deficit Hyperactivity Disorder.

Nassime presented on admission to Cornerstone as angry, aggressive, and extremely provocative. She had frequent, severe tantrums that involved screaming, hitting, kicking, and biting. In addition, she was restless, hyperactive, distractible, and impulsive.

Mary viewed Nassime as "evil, malicious, and controlling." She was unable to say anything positive about her daughter and verbally abused her repeatedly. Nassime in turn provoked her mother repeatedly and ragefully attacked her at the slightest provocation. It was necessary, on many occasions, for CNS therapists to separate the two and to closely supervise them in order to prevent escalation of these destructive interchanges. Mary also seemed unable to visualize the possibility of mother and daughter experiencing mutual gratification.

After three months in Cornerstone, Nassime made a suicide attempt. She took a number of pills and required hospitalization, following which she said that she had "wanted to die."

In CNS, Nassime developed an intense attachment to her primary thera-pist. The therapist functioned as a real person who set limits, gave emotional support, and verbalized Nassime's fear and anxiety over further abandon-ment and loss. Nassime's competition with other children for the therapist's attention and fear that she would get less than the other children, which would not have been apparent in individual therapy, was highlighted, ver-balized, and interpreted. The two overriding goals of treatment were to strengthen her positive sense of self and, ultimately, to interrupt the cycle of abuse.

Mary also developed an intense attachment to Nassime's primary thera-pist and often competed with her daughter for the therapist's attention, despite being assigned her own therapist. Mary attended Cornerstone regu-larly several times per week for the entire morning and displayed an eager-ness to participate in activities, including drawing, painting, and even children's games. One objective of work with Mary was to give her permis-sion to experience childhood pleasures that she had missed herself so that she would be able to allow Nassime the same pleasures. Another objective was to facilitate empathy for Nassime's legitimate needs for positive valida-tion. The staff attempted to both model and educate Mary concerning parenting skills and functions.

Nassime graduated from CNS after two years at age 6 and entered spe-cial education first grade and the Steppingstone Program. Work in the CNS program with Mary and Nassime had diminished the abuse to a degree that enabled Nassime to remain in her mother's care. As the pair entered the Steppingstone program, however, the degree of Mary's ongoing punitive-ness was illustrated by the fact that Nassime's room was virtually bare as a result of her mother having removed all of her possessions.

Nassime was treated in Steppingstone for two years. The therapeutic in-terventions continued, initially, to address intrapsychic issues of deprivation and low self-esteem. In addition, in the peer group, direct interpretation of relational problems began to be addressed. The Steppingstone therapists began by highlighting and praising her verbal abilities with her peers and encouraging her to use these abilities to articulate her observations of peers' issues. By doing so, we began to observe an enhancement of self-esteem and the emergence of a beginning capacity for empathy.

In addition, Nassime's difficulty maintaining self-control in social situa-tions both in school—she was wandering in the classroom and provoking conflicts with peers and teachers—and in Steppingstone were addressed by such techniques as highlighting each time Nassime appeared to be losing control and asking her whether she would choose to "stay together" or to "lose it." She was able to respond to this way of handling her negative behavior by beginning to experience the extent of her own self-control and by beginning to experiment with choosing her reactions.

Finally, her provocation of teachers and peers was interpreted as related to her expectation of abandonment and abuse from others. Repeated use was made in the group of the question, "What do we know about kids who are mean to other kids?" The responses to this question, increasingly provided by other children, linked these behaviors with past experiences, negative expectations, and affects. Nassime responded well to such techniques.

During Nassime's second year in Steppingstone, as her observing ego gained strength, she showed an increased awareness of the effect of her behavior and attitudes on others. As she struggled to keep herself from maladaptive reactions and behaviors, the therapists worked with her to develop alternative ways to respond and behave and to fulfill her needs by focusing on the use of her strengths: verbal problem solving, intelligence, growing empathy, and the increasing ability to verbalize her needs.

Simultaneous with Nassime's treatment in CNS, her mother was being seen individually by Susan Howard. Mary's treatment consisted of a combination of parent guidance and self-exploratory work. The latter entailed a review of Mary's own history and its relevance to her perception of, and relationship with, Nassime. The fundamental objective of this work was to enhance Mary's empathy with, and decrease her punitiveness towards, her daughter.

Nassime spent her last year at the agency in Superstone, when she was 8 years old. This constituted her fifth year in the program.

The work now primarily focused on and utilized peer group interaction. Support for her self-esteem and reinforcement for her sensitivity to others was provided by encouragement of Nassime to intermittently assume the role of "assistant therapist" and even spokesperson for the group. She became very proud of her ability to help other children. Not infrequently she would comfort other children, verbally and with a physical embrace.

The group was used to highlight, comment on, and interpret Nassime's pressured speech, impulsive responses, hyperactivity under stress, and her intense ongoing need for the attention of the group and therapist. Thus, Nassime's peers were able to confront Nassime when these behaviors turned them off while at other times expressing appreciation for her help.

Mary and Nassime spent a number of sessions together in which they began to negotiate and work together on helping Nassime with her difficulties in school. Mary began to consistently see and respond positively to Nassime's hard work at keeping herself together and at not provoking people.

Mary began to work full-time as an executive secretary that year, and no longer needed Welfare or Medicaid. She chose to pay for Nassime's treatment so that Nassime could finish the year in Superstone with her peers. Mary was also able to find an apartment in a safer neighborhood. Nassime, who had spent the previous two years in a class for emotionally disturbed children, was now mainstreamed. At the end of that year, Nassime and her mother were deemed ready to try life on their own.

Two years after termination, and one year after a Superstone reunion party, her Superstone therapist met Nassime and Mary on the street. It was Nassime's birthday, and Mary told the therapist that running into her was the best present Nassime could get. They were both well dressed and walked arm in arm. They reported that Nassime was continuing in a regular classroom and that Mary was doing very well in her job. With great pride, Mary and Nassime together recounted how well Nassime was doing in school, and Mary took out a photo of Nassime she had in her wallet. The photo showed Nassime posing next to a prize winning painting she had made.

**Discussion**

Outcome evaluation of the triphasic program revealed the following:

- The number of intact families in the study rose from 11% to 26%
- The number of families with a working parent increased from 19% to 59%
- 80% of the children who had experienced nonfamily foster care either did not return to foster care or were adopted or returned to their biological parents
- 54% of the children were mainstreamed in school.

The cases of Shaniqua and Nassime presented here are typical of the situations in which an increasing number of children find themselves. Their endangered relationships with their primary caretakers are often embedded in generations of neglect, abandonment, and abuse. The attempt to preserve these relationships and break the generational repetition of family disruption is a complex and difficult task. The accomplishment of this task requires intensive work and continuity of care.

The triphasic long-term approach described here begins with an intensive five-day-per-week program which gradually tapers off in the subsequent two phases. The three phases, with their gradually increasing emphasis on peer relationships and processes, are in keeping with normal developmental processes, hence the shift, between Steppingstone and Superstone, away from individual and family work, and toward group process. Nevertheless, circumstances, as well as past histories of these families, require ongoing flexibility as to the kind of help needed, and individual and family work outside of Superstone are provided as needed. Follow-up treatment beyond the triphasic program may be needed as well. While the resources of time and expense are considerable, the stakes are high: keeping families together and strengthening the child so that she or he will be immune to the vertical epidemic of disaffiliation and despair that is all too threatening.

## REFERENCES

Balter, N., and Lopez, T. (1990). Psychological help for a disadvantaged preschool boy: the Cornerstone method." *Journal of Preventive Psychiatry and Allied Disciplines* 4:329–344.

Pine, F. S. (1985). On the development of the "borderline-child-to-be." *American Journal of Orthopsychiatry* 66:450–457.

Zelman, A., Samuels, S., and Abrams, D. (1985). IQ changes in young children following intensive long-term psychotherapy. *American Journal of Psychotherapy* 39(2):215–227.

# 4

# Early Intervention for ADD

*Richard Evans*
*Susan Berenzweig*

## INTRODUCTION

While Attention Deficit Disorder (ADD) can be a lifelong disorder, it is acknowledged that early intervention can reap great benefits for both children and their families. Work with children in nursery and pre-kindergarten settings often alerts us to the onset of this disorder before its more usual identification in the early grades of school. Furthermore, as we work with young children in diverse settings that span the socioeconomic spectrum, we are alerted to factors such as family history of ADD, maternal substance abuse, inadequate pre- and post-natal nutrition and exposure to lead, which can increase the risk of central nervous system-based disorders such as ADD.

The later in life a child with ADD begins to receive treatment, the more likely he is to develop serious difficulties with academic performance, behavioral control, interpersonal skills, and the development and maintenance of adequate self-esteem. Outcome studies reveal that a significant percentage of children with ADD go on to school failure and serious antisocial behavior (Weiss and Hechtman 1993). All of these negative trajectories can be mitigated by early intervention with the child, his family, and his school.

A child with the diagnosis of ADD is not meeting age-appropriate expectations in some, if not all, of the following areas: consistent focus of attention while on task (particularly in school), context-appropriate control of motor activity, tolerance for delay, organization of activities and materials, and modulation of emotional response in terms of intensity and predictability.

The child whose functioning is compromised in one or more of these areas may then be described as impulsive, hyperactive, disorganized, or emotionally overreactive. He may also be on the road to developing the demoralizing belief that effort does not bring results. With manifestations in school, at home, and with peers, the disorder may easily affect the child's entire life. The degree of impairment will depend upon the severity of the disorder as well as the timing and adequacy of treatment interventions.

Current understanding of ADD, based upon several decades of clinical observation (Barkley 1990) and recent biological research (Anastopoulos and Barkley 1988) indicates disturbed maturation within specific areas of the brain as a primary cause of the disorder. The remarkable and repeated success of treatment with psychostimulant medication, since Bradley first used Dexedrine in 1937, had early suggested that brain disorder was responsible for most of the symptoms of ADD. Research done within the past decade points towards deficit functioning of dopamine neurotransmission in the prefrontal cortex as the basis for cognitive symptoms such as inattention and distractibility (Satterfield et al. 1994). While this hypothesis has not been firmly established, and other brain areas are probably involved as well, it is an indication of increasing specificity in our understanding of the neurobiological basis of this disorder.

## DEMOGRAPHICS

A survey of fifty children served at our clinic (the Center for Preventive Psychiatry) yielded the following information:

1. *Gender:* A male: female ratio of 4:1.
2. *Age:* 80 percent of children with a diagnosis of ADD are between 6–10 years of age; 7 percent are under 5 and 13 percent over 10 years.
3. *Family composition* covers a wide range:
   a) 30 percent report two parents in the household.
   b) Of the 70 percent with no father living at home, caretakers may include single mother, mother with extended family, kinship foster, or foster care. Children have some contact with their fathers in 40 percent of these families where father is not at home.
4. *Socioeconomic Status:* 80 percent are Medicaid recipients. About half of the remainder are living at the poverty line.
5. *Parental Occupation:* 20 percent of parents are unemployed; 45 percent of parents report blue collar occupations; the remaining 25 percent are in either clerical or business occupations. A few of these are full-time students.
6. *Medication:* 80 percent of the children receive Ritalin alone; 5 percent are taking Ritalin in combination with another medication (Clonidine or an antidepressant).

7. *Co-morbidity:* 20 percent have an additional diagnosis of Oppositional Defiant Disorder; 20 percent Over-anxious Disorder. Other accompanying diagnoses such as Dysthymia and Pervasive Developmental Disorder are also seen. Over half of the children with ADD in our clinic have associated learning disabilities. Our experience suggests that the majority of children with a diagnosis of ADD who come from multi-stressed low socioeconomic backgrounds have other diagnoses associated with aggression, depression, and anxiety. Eight of nine boys from such backgrounds, treated in an ADD group described below, had such diagnoses. In fact, it is often difficult to distinguish symptoms of these conditions from symptoms resulting from ADD.

## ASSESSMENT

A clinical diagnosis of ADD is based upon a full developmental history and observation of the child's behavior in several contexts. While psychological testing can be of help in confirming the diagnosis, as well as in determining whether there are coexisting learning disorders, there is no single test which establishes the presence of ADD (Barkley1994). The symptoms and criteria listed in *DSM-IV* (1994) are a place to start when data has been assembled through developmental history, testing, and multiple observations and rating scales gathered in different settings. If the symptoms add up, a diagnosis of ADD is made (*DSM-IV* 1994). This, however, is only a beginning in terms of treatment planning for the child.

A first consideration should be the question of conditions within the child's environment that will significantly impinge upon his difficulties. At our clinic we encounter a wide range of situations, from children in supportive, secure families to those who have to cope on a regular basis with deprivation and loss. Inevitably their ADD will manifest differently in terms of the resources they and their families can bring to bear on both the primary difficulties, such as impulsivity, and the secondary symptoms, such as oppositional behavior, that develop. A number of children with ADD have accompanying anxiety and depression, as noted in a recent review of the problem of co-morbidity (Biederman et al. 1991). We have already commented on our observed association of multiple stressors with co-morbidity. These cases require a sensitive appreciation of the role each factor plays in the child's behavior so that therapeutic responses may be chosen accordingly.

Concerning academic performance, one must consider the possibility of accompanying learning problems that are sometimes obscured by ADD-related behaviors. We have found that a number of the children have con-comitant language disorders that were falsely attributed to the effects of attention problems (Riccio et al. 1994). In addition to recognizing co-morbidity and establishing a differential diagnosis, a further refinement in assessment is promised as the result of Hunt's proposal of neurobiological subtypes. This hypothesis is based upon recent experiences with the effects of medications such as Ritalin and Clonidine upon specific symptoms, and suggests that the future may hold a taxonomy based upon specific neural subsystems in the brain (Hunt 1993).

## GOALS OF TREATMENT

We acknowledge, in setting treatment goals for the child, that our objective cannot be normalization but rather the creation of a supportive, prosthetic environment in which the child is given the best opportunity to develop his potential. Interventions must reach into the home, school, and play settings. For treatment planning, we rely upon an individualized functional assess-ment that takes into account the child's unique pattern of strengths and liabilities as well as the situations which trigger problem behaviors. Just as there is no single dose of Ritalin appropriate for all children with ADD, so there is no single therapeutic approach. Some children respond to a report card sent home once a day while others need a more intensive response–cost program with consequences delivered immediately in the classroom. While research, such as the multimodal NIMH study underway at several sites around the country (Abikoff 1994), may answer questions about the relative merit of different treatments for the group as a whole, there will always be a need to tailor a child's program to his individual pattern of re-sponse. Our model for this approach is based upon the functional assess-ment described by Levine (1994), who recognizes that children who fit the same *DSM-IV* category will still comprise a heterogeneous group in terms of abilities and liabilities.

We begin forming a treatment plan with attention to observable behav-iors. These often occur in the classroom. Here, attentional dysfunction can be manifest in varying levels of alertness, inconsistent effort, distractibility, difficulty distinguishing relevant from irrelevant information, and deficit in working memory. Each aspect may then be dealt with differently. Inconsis-tent effort calls for support and immediate positive reinforcement, while working memory problems call for the teaching and repetition of "remind-ers." Impulse control problems in one child may result in skipping a step in a mathematics problem, and in another, hitting a child who accidentally

pushed him in line. A child who daydreams may miss a homework assign-
ment in class or miss a play on the soccer field, thus incurring the wrath of
his teammates.

## OVERVIEW OF TREATMENT

We have come to recognize that ADD, affecting as it does so many areas of
a child's life, must be approached with a variety of tools in what has come to
be called *multi-modal* therapy. While not all children with ADD need or benefit from every modality, the following should be considered for every child:
medication; modification of the school program; education about the disorder for child and family; guidance, support, and perhaps therapy for the
family; and finally, individual and/or group therapy for the child. Coordi-
nating all of these modalities takes some effort; in some families this may
be the responsibility of the caretaker but others may need a professional in
this role.

## MEDICATION

The positive effect of psychostimulant medication upon focus, persistence,
attention span, and impulsivity in ADD is well established. (It should be
acknowledged, however, that the efficacy of medication on learning per se
is not so well established.) The clinician will usually begin with a trial of
Ritalin but if this is not successful in terms of either efficacy or side effects
there are other options available. Recently, Clonidine has been used for
children with high emotional reactivity (Kempf et al. 1993). If accompanying depression is present, appropriate antidepressant medication may be
used, although its effectiveness in latency-aged children has not been firmly
established (Rosenberg et al. 1994). When medication has been started it is
essential to closely monitor clinical response in the setting(s) where it is being
used in order to adjust the dose to the optimal level.

The manner in which medication is introduced to child and family is
important. Frequently, parents whose personal or family history has included
drug abuse are frightened by the prospect that their child is being placed
on a "drug" which may lead to addiction. Others may expect the medication to be a magic pill that will solve all of their child's problems. Both fears
and unrealistic expectations may be countered by saying that the medication can help the child do what he wants to do better, in school and with his
friends. In this way, the child is reassured that he is not being controlled

while his parents are encouraged in the belief that their child is motivated
to do what is expected.

## INDIVIDUAL THERAPY

While it is acknowledged that non-directive play therapy alone has little
impact upon the core symptoms of ADD, individual sessions can provide a
forum for expression of the anxiety and demoralization experienced by
children struggling with this disorder. These sessions can be particularly
important when there is an established coexisting condition such as depression, and can focus upon the emotional states which disrupt a child's ability
to function. Though the children often do not agree to talk about the problem, the use of techniques such as storytelling, games, or dramatic play
often opens up expression and leads to changes in perception, feelings, and
behavior. In cases where the child can be helped to openly acknowledge
his behavioral and social difficulties, cognitive-behavioral techniques may
be used to teach anger control and social skills (Goldstein 1988, Kendall and
Braswell 1993).

## GROUP THERAPY

We have come to rely upon cognitive-behavioral techniques as modified for
use in groups (Braswell and Bloomquist 1991). Based upon the assumption
that structure and direction are prerequisite to success, our group sessions
include planned activities related to the problems being addressed at a particular time. Anger control is a major issue for many ADD children, especially those living in adverse circumstances and violence-prone environments.
In group, such children are able to identify and review the sequence of
behaviors associated with anger arousal, thus affording them the opportunity to interrupt or alter the sequence. They also have the opportunity to
explore common sources of their anger. For many of them, teasing about
mothers, issues around absent fathers, unfair accusations, and other challenges to their self-esteem are triggers in many angry sequences. In one of
our groups, we found that every child had a father who was, or had been, in
jail! The connections between the boys' anger, shame, and loss, as well as
the implications for being in trouble, were explored.

    Structure in the group is provided using a standard behavioral format,
with contracting around group rules and immediate consequences for performance. Points are accumulated, and at the end of a session, may be traded

for small toys or an activity reward such as Nintendo. The formal exercise is preceded by snack time, when the children share news about the week and review the use of lessons at home.

Group composition will determine the specific set of skills on which we focus. For children who have experienced deprivation and severe losses, anger control and managing fear are initially prominent themes. For children with more stability in their lives, we may focus upon the social and communication skills necessary for satisfying peer interactions. The groups are designed to run for a "semester" of 14 sessions. At the end we re-contract for those who wish and need to continue and who we believe would continue to benefit from participation in a second semester.

## COMBINED INDIVIDUAL AND GROUP THERAPY

While it is often not practical, because of time and financial constraints, to provide individual and group therapy for a child simultaneously, we have found that this combination can maximize the benefits of each and hasten the progress of treatment. Since the children we see typically have internal as well as interpersonal difficulties, the combination of modalities provides a complementary perspective for both assessment and treatment. On the level of assessment the group's interaction provides a microcosm of the problematic interactions reported in school. In addition, the group's interaction often triggers memories and feelings that are inaccessible in the individual session. Through modeling, role play, and feedback, new ways of dealing with stress are developed and new social skills are practiced. For the same child who benefits from the group the presence of peers may inhibit expression of crucial issues, necessitating individual work. Here, alone with a therapist, the child can feel safe to explore his feelings in a less directed manner. Finally, the focus of a one-to-one relationship may facilitate learning which cannot develop in the distracting presence of others.

If, as was true in the case reported below, the same therapist is both group co-leader and the child's individual therapist, the advantages multiply.

## FAMILY INTERVENTION

Family intervention is a central feature of our program for children with ADD. This intervention provides opportunity for education about the disorder, a clearing of misconceptions and beliefs that may interfere with effective caretaking, emotional support in a challenging and often overwhelming situation, training in parenting skills, and family therapy when dysfunctional interactions are exacerbating the child's problems. Parents who recognize that their child's disruptive behavior is neither intentional nor directed against them can begin to appreciate the energy, need to relate, and wish to cope successfully that coexist with his symptomatology.

A number of useful books, which provide an understanding of the disorder for parents and children, are now available (Ingersoll and Goldstein 1993, Quinn and Stern 1991). Another valuable source of information and support is the parent-organized group known as CHADD (Children and Adolescents with Attention-Deficit Disorders), with chapters throughout the country (CHADD, 499 Northwest 70th Avenue, Suite 308, Plantation, FL 33317; phone (305)587–3700). Parent training is well described in several publications (Barkley 1988, Garber et al. 1995, Parker1988). Our approach to family therapy uses a blend of dynamic, communication, and structural theory modified for use in families with a child who has a biologically based disorder (Evans 1988, Minuchin 1981).

The kind and amount of intervention is determined by the needs of a specific family. For isolated families living under adverse circumstances, activation of community support services is essential. Thus, family work may be carried out away from the traditional clinic location at, for example, a transitional housing site for homeless families. Areas that are covered within either an educational or therapeutic context should address not only the management of difficult child behaviors, but collaboration with caretakers (including the exchange of information and the provision of stress reducing techniques) as well. It is essential to maintain this dual focus upon children and their caretakers in order for the program to be effective.


## SCHOOL INTERVENTIONS

Each child with ADD experiences a unique pattern of difficulties in school. While ADD per se is not traditionally considered a learning disability, its presence, often along with specific learning problems, always presents an obstacle to a child's school performance. As noted in the CHADD Educator's Manual (Fowler 1992), "ADD is not just a disorder within the child. Its expression depends upon the match between child and environment" (p. 11). This is nowhere more apparent than in school, where children with ADD have trouble with control of activity, cannot follow directions, stray off task, intrude upon others, and are often overreactive emotionally. Thus, a majority of our ADD referrals come from the school, and this is the setting where significant modifications must occur to foster optimal learning.

The clinician works closely with school personnel in order to educate them about the disorder and to plan school interventions which include the following: setting up a behavioral program, maintaining contact with caretakers at home, and giving advice concerning placement decisions. Regular follow-up concerning the effects of treatment is essential.

Education about ADD for school personnel, as for families, is a crucial first step. School personnel need to have a clear understanding of a child's unique pattern of functioning and how this is affected by his/her attention disorder (Levine 1994). Often we help teachers to reframe their view of the child from one who is unmotivated and out of control to one who may have temporarily given up trying to direct his unbridled energy. A variety of behavioral interventions have been shown to ameliorate school problems (DuPaul and Stoner 1994). These begin with an analysis that identifies target behaviors, antecedents, and consequences and includes the rapid delivery of rewards when positive behavior is exhibited. Modification of the work load and a daily school–home report are other effective school-based measures that have been demonstrated to be effective. The clinician can serve as an important link between the school and the child's caretaker, fostering positive communication in both directions. Too often, caretakers of the child with ADD are blamed (sometimes covertly) and may develop a defensive mistrust and feelings of helplessness in working with the school. If this point is reached, the clinician must work to re-establish an alliance between caretaker and school or the child may become caught in the middle of a power struggle. Often the clinician's involvement brings much needed optimism and support to frustrated teachers and caretakers. Finally, there may be needed work with school special education committees to identify any specific learning disability, and to place the child in the least restrictive environment for learning. This may include "pull-out" classes for remediation of specific learning problems, an aide to sit with the child in his/her mainstream classes, or placement in a special self-contained program.

## CASE ILLUSTRATION: ANDY—INTEGRATED MULTIMODAL TREATMENT FOR ADD

The use of individual, family, and group treatment, along with caretaker support, medication, and school-based intervention, is illustrated in the case of Andy G.

Ms. G. called the clinic for the first time when her son was 8. The school had been urging her to call for several months because her second grader, Andy, was in chronic danger of suspension. Although he could draw charming action pictures of superheros with strong lines and a flair for detail, Andy was inattentive, hyperactive, and barely able to write his name or work alone in his seat. His mother feared he was headed for trouble. She felt she had done all she could do to help him by herself. In calling, she set aside the humiliation she felt in needing professional advice for what she considered to be a failure in parenting.

The initial interview (S.B.) with Andy's mother was difficult. Ms. G., a single parent, had worked at two jobs to keep her son and daughter sheltered, fed, and clothed. In the first interview, she was cordial but reticent. Background history was difficult to elicit, because she didn't want to talk about many things that she considered irrelevant or "too personal." It was not until much later that she revealed that Andy's father had been incarcerated and that his present whereabouts were unknown.

Initially, intervention was planned in three areas: consultation with the school, individual sessions with Andy, and meetings with his mother. However, during the first several months, Ms. G. remained inaccessible, while allowing the therapist to speak to the school and see Andy weekly. She was averse to the idea of medication.

## Mother's Initial Resistance

In the early phase of treatment, while Andy attended individual sessions regularly, Ms. G. avoided direct contact with the therapist. Instead, she frequently telephoned the therapist regarding school problems. She frequently agreed to appointments, saying, "You'll *definitely* see me next week!" However, she would usually cancel a few days later, citing lack of money and other demands on her time. Once she pointed out that if Andy's therapist had children, she would understand how parents need to do things for themselves. The therapist succeeded in meeting with Ms. G. only once during the several months following the intake.

## Early Individual Work with Andy

Weekly individual sessions with Andy reflected Ms. G.'s wariness in that he tended to avoid and minimize his difficulties. As with his mother, care had to be taken to stress the positive. Andy responded to this approach, showing himself eager to elicit the therapist's approval. Individual sessions required an initial focus on an appreciation of his talents before Andy could name and accept his difficulties. The therapist consistently told Andy that she knew that his intention was to be "good," while simultaneously showing admiration of Andy's excellent abilities in acrobatics, basketball, and drawing.

Andy's strong need to deny his mistakes was apparent. Small errors precipitated the trashing of beautiful drawings, wrong moves in checkers were taken back, and "do-overs" were plentiful in basketball. The therapist noted her own errors, pointing out that before she could get better, she had to make and notice her mistakes. Still, Andy continued to find it difficult to acknowledge mistakes and talk about specific negative events in school. This difficulty was consistent with the therapist's observation that Ms. G. was reacting to negative school reports with anger, blame, and punishment directed at Andy. Predictably, Andy appeared to expect similar treatment from the therapist.

## School Intervention

School questionnaires and telephone contact made at the beginning of treatment revealed that Andy's second-grade teacher had lost patience and sympathy with him. This was reflected in her giving him the highest scores ("almost all the time") for every item on the standardized behavior rating scale for ADD, as well as in the tone of her complaints about him.

On the clinician's first visit to the school, as she approached the classroom she could hear Andy's teacher loudly reprimanding him. After observing Andy in the classroom the therapist went to a meeting attended by the principal, Andy's teacher, a guidance counselor, and Andy's mother. At the meeting, the therapist's impression was confirmed that Andy's behavior had provoked in the teacher's mind an intensely negative and pessimistic view of him.

The therapist suggested a simple behavior modification program that was designed to alter the behaviors that were most disturbing to the teacher. The latter agreed to try to "catch him being good" and reward his behavior five times per day. This strategy was directed toward the goal of redirecting the teacher's attention from Andy's negative behavior to his positive potential. It was agreed that the therapist would work closely with the school and she, rather than Andy's mother, would initially be called to deal with problems. In the course of this work, the therapist received many calls from the school critical of Andy. The deflection of these calls from the mother served several purposes. It reduced her anger at Andy, strengthened her alliance with the therapist, and reduced conflict between Ms. G. and the school. In addition, the therapist's continuing efforts to help the school be more supportive of Andy also helped school personnel to be less critical of his mother. This approach succeeded in strengthening the alliance between mother and therapist.

## School Intervention: Phase II

A turning point came after ten months of treatment, when the therapist received a telephone call from Ms. G. informing her that Andy had been suspended from school for joining other boys who had assaulted a girl on the bus in an attempt to pull down her pants. His mother said she was furious with Andy because he had not told her of the incident (and prepared her for the telephone call she had received the previous evening from the assistant principal). A school conference was arranged which included the therapist, Ms. G., Andy's teacher, the guidance counselor, and the assistant principal. At this conference, the therapist again outlined several behavioral interventions based on combining limit setting with an emphasis on the search for, and reinforcement of, positive behavior. Andy's new teacher was appreciative of these suggestions and demonstrated an admirable capacity to accept his disruptive behavior and focus on his successes, however limited. In the course of a behavioral analysis, the teacher observed that Andy's behavior was most problematic in unstructured, free-play situations. She devised ways to provide extra structure and support during these periods. In addition, an assistant principal was identified for whom Andy and his mother had developed a mutual fondness. Andy was given permission to seek him out any time during the day if Andy felt he was having difficulties with control. This plan was posited on Andy's increased awareness of cues suggesting impending loss of control.

Andy's new teacher was also able to sympathize with his mother. With the therapist's help, the teacher and Ms. G. were able to persuade the school administration to pursue psychoeducational testing to investigate potential learning difficulties. Thus, mother, teacher, and therapist had formed a team working on Andy's behalf. Andy's mother was developing a very different attitude toward his troubles from the defensive and alienated picture that she had initially presented.

At first, medication had been unacceptable to Ms. G., ostensibly because of worries about chemical dependency. Now, after nearly a year of treatment, Ms. G. accepted the therapist's recommendation that Andy be evaluated by a psychiatrist for the use of stimulant medication. By now, all the information from home and school confirmed a diagnosis of ADD. A course of Ritalin was prescribed, which proved to be effective. As he became more focused, Andy's off-task behavior diminished, and he became more productive in school. However, he was still having social difficulties, mostly related to his impulsivity. These would be addressed specifically in family sessions and in group, as described below.

## Joint Family Sessions

After one year of weekly individual visits with Andy, and after the crisis of Andy's suspension from school had resulted in a strengthening of the alliance with the therapist, Ms. G. began to accept invitations to join her son in family sessions. A primary ostensible goal of these joint sessions was the enlistment of Andy's mother to help him work on interaction with peers. At first, she blamed the therapist as well as Andy for his lack of dramatic change in this area. The therapist sympathized with Ms. G.'s wish for faster progress and used it to encourage her more active collaboration. This began with school-related incidents, which were relatively easy for her to discuss. Ms. G. alternately blamed Andy and the school for these incidents. The therapist, with Andy's assistance, attempted to reframe these incidents in terms of problem situations for which there were constructive solutions. Ms. G. at this point showed herself capable of responding to this nonjudgmental approach with greater empathy for Andy. Soon he was able to help engage his mother in problem-solving discussions of alternate behaviors, some of which he could use at home with his sister. Predictably, as Andy observed his mother's growing capacity to acknowledge his difficulties without anger and disappointment, Andy himself became less resistant to discussing incidents as they happened. Mother and child were now increasingly hopeful.

This work with Andy and his mother was affected by two incidents which dramatically highlighted the chronic environmental stress to which Andy and his mother were exposed. One day, after three months of joint sessions, Andy found a bullet on the street as he walked to school. He picked it up, brought it to school, and showed it to a child on the playground. Word spread quickly, and shortly Andy found himself sitting in the principal's office, suspended again. This time his mother was told at once. She responded to Andy less punitively than earlier and was able to explore the incident with empathy. As a result, Andy tearfully acknowledged the fear and isolation he had been experiencing on a daily basis. Further discussion focused on ways in which, with his mother's help, Andy could protect himself.

The second event occurred exactly one month later. Shortly after Christmas, the family's apartment building burned down and they were left homeless. Ms. G. was able to mobilize herself and quickly relocate the family.

For several weeks following these events, a recurring theme in Andy's individual sessions was "scary surprises." His mother reported similar behavior at home, in that he frequently jumped out of a hiding place to scare her. The parallel effects of these events on his social behavior were observed in group. He used individual sessions to further explore his fears and identify ways to calm himself and ask for help from supportive adults.

By the end of the second year of individual treatment and after much work with the school and his mother, Andy could gradually acknowledge feelings of worry about the unpredictable nature of his life and sadness about his failures and losses. His confusion about his mother's conflicting reactions to him, from loving and accepting to angry and punitive, were eventually acknowledged in individual sessions.

**Group Treatment**

Andy participated in three consecutive series of fourteen-week group sessions for ADD boys, beginning six months after his admission to the clinic. The focus of the group was to teach cognitive-behavioral techniques to the children that would help (1) reduce impulsiveness, (2) understand nonverbal communications of others, and (3) problem-solve in social situations.

Although Andy was withdrawn at first and was slow to feel comfortable, he gradually felt safe enough to display many of the behaviors seen in the school setting. Andy had considerable difficulty sitting in his seat. In nearly every session he fell out of his chair and frequently played the clown. He giggled uncontrollably at times and provoked others to laughter. In the group, as these behaviors were problems for everyone, we spent time role playing "how to ignore someone trying to get you to laugh." This exercise led to lessons that focused on coping with teasing and aggressive provocation (described further below).

Andy's participation in the group enriched the work of individual sessions. The therapist could make use of her observations in the group of interactional sequences and the triggers of negative behavior. These sequences could then be pointed out to Andy and alternative behaviors could be explored and role played with a greater likelihood of success. When role playing, the therapist generally first took Andy's role as provocateur. In this way, Andy was able to distance sufficiently to reduce his tendency to feel criticized.

The group offered Andy support for his anger and frustration at being "singled out" as a troublemaker in school. Other group members discussed similar perceptions of being "the first to be blamed for everything." These perceptions of unfairness, even if distorted, provided therapeutic leverage insofar as they reinforced group cohesiveness.

Individual and group work done following the destruction of his home by fire illustrates the synergy of these two modalities. Andy did not speak of the fire in the group. However, the therapist noted that Andy's anxiety-driven laughter increased significantly. In addition, she observed that his silliness was often preceded by someone telling a sad story to the group. The therapist, in individual sessions, made this connection for Andy, noting how hard it was for him to stay in control and follow the rules when he was sad or disappointed. During a group session a few weeks later, the boys in the group "mutinied" and refused to play a game that had a heavy emotional content. In the course of a discussion of the boys' resistance in his subsequent individual session, Andy spoke for the first time of his embarrassment about so often being in trouble. At the last group session, Andy told everyone about his absent father and speculated that if his father was around, he imagined his mother wouldn't frustrate and disappoint him so much. Thus, the combination of group and individual treatment enhanced the work of each and afforded an opportunity for observation, confrontation and support that neither modality could accomplish alone.

**The End of Treatment**

The completion of Andy's third cycle of group treatment coincided with the end of his second year of treatment. Many of the initial goals had been accomplished and reliable therapeutic alliances had been established with Andy and his mother. Medication and remediation were becoming effective in improving Andy's school behavior and ability to focus on academic work. What followed was two years of gradually tapered individual sessions that used a combination of psychodynamic expressive therapy and cognitive-behavioral techniques to accomplish much reparative work in self-esteem. Andy's feelings of insecurity and vulnerability (to which both Andy's unreliable impulse control and his risk-filled environment contributed) were explored, while sources of security and comfort were reinforced.

During the third year of treatment, Andy came to individual sessions an average of twice a month. During this period, he was increasingly able to engage in direct discussion of his problems and to acknowledge mistakes without inordinate loss of self-esteem. Most striking, however, was the deepening of the transference in spite of the decreased frequency of visits. Anger at the therapist now alternated with frank expressions of yearnings for her. The anger could be connected both to abandonment by his father and the previously excessive expectations and criticism that had been directed at him by his mother. As the therapist's summer vacation and termination of therapy approached, Andy became angry. In an ensuing discussion of previous losses, Andy confessed that he believed his father was dead. A connection was made to his preoccupation with ghosts, which had been a frequent theme in his play and a source of his nighttime fears.

For six months following the summer vacation, he was seen monthly during which time his fear was the main theme. One day he drew a huge, scary ghost and named it "BaBa." The therapist wondered if he meant DaDa. The next month he drew the same figure. It was still called "BaBa," but it had been reduced to a mere two inches and was now a protective "angel." Soon after, Andy announced that he was ready to end treatment. Three more months went by with no further requests for sessions. During a pre-planned termination session, four years after treatment had begun, Ms. G. recalled how scared she had been at the outset, expressed her appreciation, and embraced the therapist as she left. Andy walked out proudly, promising to keep in touch.

**Discussion**

Andy lived in an environment, familial and community, of significant psychosocial stress. Like many children with ADD, living in such circumstances he initially had a second diagnosis, in this case Oppositional Disorder. There was little direct evidence of biological vulnerability, although the improvement obtained in Andy's behavior and attention following administration of Ritalin can be viewed as evidence for CNS dysfunction.

Regardless of whether primary CNS dysfunction underlies some or most cases of ADD, the suspicion of such a dysfunction is useful insofar as it encourages a multidimensional concept of the disorder. This concept, in turn, opens up many possibilities for intervention.

In any given case, including the one presented here, multiple modalities may be needed. In other cases, careful assessment may reveal a single point of intervention that, when adequately addressed, may be sufficient to eliminate or reduce to an acceptable degree the ADD symptomatology. When ADD is diagnosed in a child coming from an intact and/or stable single parent family, the chances are decreased of a coexisting diagnosis, especially Oppositional Disorder. Such children can often be treated with medication and a small amount of parental guidance.

The symptoms and diagnosis of ADD can be confused with problems, both internal and external to the child, that may be more threatening to the child's development and well-being than ADD itself. The greater the degree of family and community disintegration and/or dysfunction, the more likely it is that intervention will have to be complex and intensive.

Conversely, the more one sees, on assessment, such manifestations as fear, anger, or severe anxiety, the more closely one should scrutinize the child's family and community milieu. With the majority of ADD children seen in public clinics, special attention has to be given to psychosocial factors, using a variety of individual, family, and group modalities, as well as close collaboration with the school.

The successful use of Ritalin by itself should not be assumed to constitute adequate treatment. As illustrated in the case of Andy, much work had to be done, utilizing individual, family, group, and school consultation modalities, both before and after Ritalin had been prescribed. Hence the diagnosis of ADD and prescription of an effective medication, such as Ritalin, are no guarantee that treatment can be short and simple.

## REFERENCES

Abikoff, H. (1994). *Multi-modal treatment of ADD: one year treatment outcome data.* Presentation at the Sixth Annual International Conference on ADD. New York: CHADD.

Anastopoulos, A. D., and Barkley, R. A. (1988). Biological factors in ADHD. *Behavior Therapist* 11:47–53.

Barkley, R. (1988). *The Defiant Child.* New York: Guilford.

——— (1990). *Attention Deficit Hyperactivity Disorders: a Handbook for Diagnosing and Treatment.* New York: Guilford.

——— (1994). *The ADHD Report.* New York: Guilford.

Biederman, J., Newcorn, J., and Sprich, S. (1991). Comorbidity of ADHD with conduct, depressive, anxiety, and other disorders. *American Journal of Psychiatry* 148(5):564–577.

Braswell, L., and Bloomquist, M. D. (1991). *Cognitive-Behavioral Therapy with ADHD Children.* New York: Guilford.

*Diagnostic and Statistical Manual of Mental Disorders,* 4th ed. (1994). Washington, DC: American Psychiatric Association.

DuPaul, G. J., and Stoner, G. (1994). *ADHD in the Schools.* New York: Guilford.

Evans, R. (1988). Child centered family therapy. In *Handbook of Clinical Assessment of Children and Adolescents,* ed. C. Kestenbaum and D. Williams, pp. 1066–1083. New York: New York University Press.

Fowler, M. (1992). *C.H.A.D.D. Educator's Manual.* Plantation, FL: CHADD.

Garber, S., Garber, M., and Spizman, R. (1995). *Is Your Child Hyperactive? Inattentive? Impulsive? Distractible? Helping the ADD/Hyperactive Child.* New York: Villard.

Goldstein, A. (1988). *The Prepare Curriculum: Teaching Prosocial Competencies*. Champaign, IL: Research Press.

Hunt, R. D. (1993). *Neurobiological Sub-types of ADD*. Nashville, TN: Center for Attention and Hyperactivity Disorders.

Ingersoll, B., and Goldstein, S. (1993). *Attention Deficit Disorder and Learning Disabilities: Realities, Myths, and Controversial Treatments*. New York: Doubleday.

Kempf, J. P., Lindsay, D., Levin, G., et al. (1993). Treatment of aggressive children with clonidine: results of an open pilot study. *Journal of the American Academy of Child and Adolescent Psychiatry* 32:577–581.

Kendall, P. C., and Braswell, L. (1993). *Cognitive Behavioral Therapy for Impulsive Children*, 2nd ed. New York: Guilford.

Levine, M. (1994). *Educational Care*. Cambridge, MA: Educator's Publishing Service.

Minuchin, S., and Fishman, H. C. (1981). *Family Therapy Techniques*. Cambridge, MA: Harvard University Press.

Parker, H. C. (1988). *The Attention Deficit Disorder Workbook for Parents, Teachers and Kids*. Plantation, FL: Impact Publications.

Quinn, P. Q., and Stern, J. (1991). *Putting on the Brakes: Young People's Guide to Understanding Attention Deficit Hyperactivity Disorder (ADHD)*. New York: Brunner/Mazel.

Riccio, C. A., Hynd, G. W., Cohen, M. H., et al. (1994). Comorbidity of central auditory processing disorders and ADHD. *Journal of the American Academy of Child and Adolescent Psychiatry* 33(6):849–857.

Rosenberg, D., Holttum, J., and Gershon, S. (1994). *Textbook of Pharmacotherapy for Child and Adolescent Psychiatric Disorders*. New York: Brunner/Mazel.

Satterfield, J. H., Schell, A. M., and Thomas, N. (1994). Preferential neural processing of attended stimuli in ADHD and normal boys. *Psychophysiology* 31:1–10.

Weiss, G., and Hechtman, L. (1993). *Hyperactive Children Grown Up*, 2nd ed.: *ADHD in Children, Adolescents and Adults*. New York: Guilford.

# II

# FOSTER CHILDREN

# 5

# Use of a Personal Life History Book in the Treatment of Foster Children—An Attempt to Enhance Stability of Foster Care Placements

*Gilbert W. Kliman*
*Arthur B. Zelman*

The fact of a child's placement in foster care more often than not constitutes a marker for a set of events and processes, many of which are highly threatening to the child's ongoing development. The extent to which his development has already been compromised depends on such factors as the child's innate resilience to stress, the frequency and intensity of stressors to which he has been exposed, the degree to which earlier needs have or haven't been met, the extent of the losses he has endured, and the availability of continuing supports in his environment. Far too often the dice are loaded against him in most of these areas.

The very fact of placement in foster care implies a profound discontinuity in caretaking, usually not the first loss of caretakers. Let us take an "ideal" situation necessitating foster care: the placement together of two latency age siblings, children of a well-functioning single mother who is hospitalized for an acute illness that is quickly resolved. The reason for the placement is simple and easily understood by the children, and the placement itself is predictably brief. Unfortunately this kind of scenario is the exception, not the rule.

Typically the foster child comes from a background that includes poverty, severe family disruption and pathology, deprivation, abuse, and previous rejections and abandonment. It is difficult to believe that children in such circumstances, as well as their caretakers, are not in need of supportive mental health services of some kind. For a variety of reasons, a primary one being that they have become "carriers" of deprivation, these children generally do not receive such services.

Kline and Overstreet (1972), despite their earlier recognition of the threat to the emotional well-being of the child of having to enter foster care, recommended that psychotherapy should be used in the early phase of foster care only when environmental approaches are blocked and ineffectual. They differentiated psychotherapy from preventive and therapeutic casework help that is an integral, routine part of foster care service. This conservative approach to clinical intervention turned a blind eye to a sequence that frequently occurs in foster care. Initially there is a "honeymoon" period during which all goes well and the hopes of foster parents are unrealistically raised for a trouble-free adjustment. This is followed by unanticipated difficulties that may lead to abrupt removal of the child from the home or to a longer period in which the foster parents experience increasing ambivalence and resentment such that seeking help is resisted or rejected as just one more burden the child has placed on their shoulders. Again, the end point is "bouncing" of the child from one foster home to another.

That a scenario of this kind can be anticipated, in many cases, is borne out by the data. A Stanford University study (Wald et al. 1985) concluded that the major criticism of the foster care system pinpoints its instability. Most children, especially those who remain in foster care for longer than six months, are subjected to multiple placements (Knitzer and Allen 1978, National Commission on Children in Need of Parents 1979). It is common procedure for a child to be in three or more placements in a period of one to two years.

In addition to the stress generated by foster care placement, the child's behavior is frequently problematic because of pre-existing disturbances. There is much evidence to suggest that foster children have a relatively high incidence of behavioral and emotional problems (Dinnage and Pringle 1967, Fanshell and Shinn 1978). In view of the frequency of family problems prior to foster placement (Wolkind and Rutter 1973, Lambert et al. 1977) it is likely that many of the children's problems antedate their placement. This is confirmed in a study done by Kliman and colleagues (1982), one of the few in the literature in which children were evaluated on entering their first foster placement. Twenty-eight percent of the children were found to have a diagnosis other than adjustment disorder. (The authors thought this number to be minimal, in view of the young age of the subjects and the tendency of adjustment disorders, from which they virtually all suffered, to obscure other diagnoses.) At seventeen-month follow-up, Kliman found a significantly higher rate of "bouncing" in the group with diagnoses other than adjustment disorder.

These findings provide a rationale for clinical assessment and treatment of children at or before placement in foster care, insofar as diagnosis may predict likelihood of bouncing. In fact Kliman and colleagues (1981) did attempt to study the effect of clinical interventions on bouncing. They initially reported on a series of 30 foster children, 8 of whom had been referred for emotional problems, and 22 of whom had been routinely and consecutively referred by the Department of Social Services for preventive reasons. These children received a variety of psychodynamically oriented treatments, varying, as needed, from brief crisis intervention to intensive psychodynamic psychotherapy. Their foster parents also received help in varying degrees. The results of these interventions were encouraging in that no bouncing occurred during a one-year period in comparison to a calculated expected rate of 25 percent.

These results led Kliman and his group to launch a more systematic study. Much of the treatment employed in the pilot study had been intensive and was provided by senior therapists. Kliman was interested in studying a preventive approach that would be less costly and might therefore be more likely to be utilized, if proven effective. He decided on a relatively unstructured model utilizing inexperienced therapists under the supervision of an experienced child psychiatrist. The focus was on helping the child to mourn his lost relationships and lost environments.

Two versions of this model were tested, a 15 session version and a 40 session version. There was no specific focus on the prevention of transfers from one foster home to another but it was hypothesized that facilitation of the mourning process would reduce the child's need to act out and therefore reduce the transfer rate. The results obtained were somewhat disappointing. Neither the 15 nor 40 session modality reduced transfers, although the 40 session modality was effective in reducing indicators of behavioral pathology (Kliman et al. 1982). It was Kliman's impression that a more structured and concrete approach to intervention might be more effective.

There are compelling theoretical reasons to be concerned about the foster care transfer rate. Foster children generally come from homes with high rates of parental psychopathology and family dysfunction. Thus, a combination of poverty, social isolation, and inadequate parental and family functioning has led to a situation in which the vast majority of children placed in foster care have experienced neglect, abuse, and abandonment by their primary caretakers.

Both brief and intensive work with these children, examples of which will be described in this and the next chapter, confirm the prevailing view in the literature that such negative experiences with primary caretakers result in varying degrees of trauma. In the classical psychodynamic sense, trauma leads to the evocation of the repetition compulsion to repeat the original anxiety-provoking experience. In the case of foster care, the trauma to be repeated is the neglect, abuse, or abandonment of the child by his primary caretakers. If the child "succeeds" in his unconscious attempt to test or provoke rejection, the original trauma and the child's need to repeat it will be reinforced. The result is a child who is even less able to allow himself to be cared for. Thus, "bouncing" may be viewed as a negative indicator of the foster child's capacity to sustain a positive human relationship.

As predicted from the theoretical considerations enumerated above, follow-up studies do show greater functional impairment of those foster children who have lacked stable placement. Zimmerman (1982) found that youngsters who transferred among homes had a high rate of dysfunction. In his long-term follow-up of 61 former foster children, nearly half of the frequently moved youngsters had inadequate functioning as opposed to only 14 percent of the stably placed long-term youngsters. An orderly association was found between the number of homes in which a child had lived and his functioning in adulthood. Over one-half of the inadequately functioning group had lived in five or more homes. In contrast, only one-sixth of those in the adequately functioning group had lived in that many homes.

## RATIONALE FOR THE PERSONAL LIFE HISTORY BOOK

Wheeler (1978) reported on caseworkers' use of an unstructured life history book with children in foster care. Aust (1981) described the use of life story books in weekly psychotherapy with children in foster care. She reports that this tool can help a child to understand the reality of his past and identify and counter "irrational negative beliefs the child holds about himself and his parents in order to allow him to see himself, his life, and the future in a more positive and realistic way" (p. 558). Several theoretical considerations suggest the usefulness of a personal life history book for this population.

First, as in other traumatized populations, these children tend to excessively employ a group of defenses that makes access to their disturbing experiences particularly difficult. Such defenses include avoidance, denial, forgetting, splitting, idealization, psychic meandering, depersonalization, derealization, and projection. These defenses may preclude spontaneous communication, in words and even in play, of material that can be used to recover traumatic experiences and associated affects. The opportunity to see printed statements and pictures of situations that have potential relevance to their lives makes communication easier for at least two reasons. First, these media in and of themselves are structured and so may provide protection from the chaos threatened by the underlying anxiety and affects connected to the children's disturbing experiences. Second, the concreteness of the written word or the drawn picture or photograph can enhance the child's sense of control over the communication process. At the same time, the authority and permanence of the printed word and picture affirms the importance of the child's experience and, by extension, the importance of the child himself. Such validation is an essential antidote to the rejection and devaluation these children have experienced. Terr (1991) quotes a 7-year-old-boy who had been repeatedly physically abused by his stepfather.

> I used to pretend I was at a picnic with my head on mommy's lap. The first time my stepdaddy hit me, it hurt a lot. But then I found out that I could make myself go on Daddy's lap [in imagination] and Winston couldn't hurt me that way. I kept goin' on Mommy's lap—I didn't have to cry or scream or anything. I could be someplace else and not get hurt. I don't know how many times Winston punched me out. I wasn't always payin' attention. Like I told you, first I'd be at a picnic on Mom's lap. Now if somethin' makes me bleed, I don't think of no lap at all. I just don't feel no pain. [p. 17]

Many foster children have been given cause to deny their capacity to think, feel, and remember. This dilemma suggests a variation of Descartes' proposition, "I think, therefore I am," to "I don't think, therefore I don't exist." The personal life history book, and the efforts of the therapist and caretakers to collaborate with the child in writing it, insofar as it facilitates the child's recovery of his experience, can help him to recover a sense of himself.

## DESCRIPTION OF THE PLHB

The personal life history book, as most recently formatted by Kliman (1993), consists of a page for identification and twenty-one "chapters," covering all aspects of a child's life, past, present, and future. It includes spaces for photographs and drawings, as well as some already drawn pictures of common scenes of childhood. Most of the book, however, consists of statements (rather than questions) followed by blanks for the responses. This form of eliciting information is designed to reduce the child's fear of giving a wrong answer at the same time that it conveys a message that the child does have a response. The statements range from references to neutral facts to preferences and positive experiences, to dislikes and negative experiences.

Items are arranged from neutral and concrete at the beginning to more charged later. Topics include: birth, biological family members, special things about the child, friends, previous homes, games, TV shows, reasons and circumstances of placement in foster care, foster care plans, information regarding foster parents, school information (including teachers and peers), people I miss, hopes and wishes, memories (best, worst, earliest, happy, unhappy, past significant figures), and visitation (past and anticipated) from biological family or others. The book also provides space for medical information (for foster parents to complete), birthdays, report cards, and a personal directory with space for addresses and telephone numbers.

The four cases which follow are illustrations of a psychodynamically informed, supportive-expressive time-limited treatment with a focus on experiences of object loss. They were carried out by experienced psychotherapists who used the PLHB as a structured organizer of the supportive-expressive treatment. As part of a study to determine the efficacy of this method each child received 30 treatment visits of 45 minutes each. Although these were supposed to have occurred on 30 separate days, one day a week, in many instances for logistic reasons double sessions were provided. By its strict emphasis on time limits, the method enabled the children to anticipatorily mourn for the loss of the therapist.

## CASE ILLUSTRATIONS

Following are four examples of the application of this treatment approach.

### Case 1

A developmentally moderately delayed and speech-slurring Hispanic-Jamaican 5-year-old girl, Lakisha, had witnessed the unpremeditated murder of her mother by her uncle. Not only was the child having to assimilate this extraordinarily painful history, her capacity to do so was being undermined by the same uncle. In visits with him, the uncle maintained to Lakisha that her mother was still alive.

In a series of visits with the therapist, Lakisha's uncle, the sole surviving caregiver, was actively delusional. The child's caseworker accepted a recommendation that the uncle should be psychiatrically examined and treated

before the child and he had further visits. The uncle did not accept this recommendation but enhanced its credibility by informing the child's caseworker that his sister was following him around with video cameras.

The PLHB treatment method was like an anchor in heavy storms for
Lakisha. She could ignore it much of the time, but it kept her safe and oriented. After fifteen sessions she was clearly reactive to a vacation break. She
then pretended not to remember the therapist, but immediately recalled
her book. She had by now started kindergarten and was doing increasingly
well in language and cognition, and teased the therapist in an acerbic, lanc-
ing fashion rather than being vague and unrelated as at first. By the end of
the post-vacation session she verbalized: "I missed you. Where were you? I'm
mad."

Soon after this confession of yearning, Lakisha was able to discuss her
uncle and mother with keen articulation of hatred and mourning. "Uncle
Simon is a lazy old junkie. He does a lot of cocaine. He don't get no work,
don't want to do no work, just drugs."

Drawing Simon's pipe, she added, "I miss my mother," and looked very
sad. Previously, for fifteen sessions, she had looked retarded and dull whenever her mother was mentioned. Warned now that only ten minutes were
left in this session, Lakisha responded forthrightly, "I don't want to go. I
want to see you. I want to come tomorrow."

In the final fifteen sessions of her treatment Lakisha demonstrated
marked developmental, cognitive, and speech progress. She seemed stimulated by the challenge of dealing with a termination known for weeks in
advance and discussed openly with the departing person. In the sixteenth
and seventeenth sessions, the therapist found Lakisha expressing memory
of the murder scene with unexpected lucidity. At first Lakisha used an intro-
ductory story of "dumplings they make in Jamaica." Then she switched to
castigating her uncle. "Simon was once so mean he ate all the dumplings."
Then Lakisha had a dumpling become an immense ball, a rock on a hill
that could kill a person by "crushing, shushing, blood all over, pieces sticking out." The therapist interpreted this fantasy as related to a real memory
of mother's smashed body. To this, Lakisha responded, "I don't ever want
to see Simon again. . . . He's so mean . . . he hurt Mom so bad . . . he hit
her, so hard, she was bleeding all over . . . blood came out of her. . . . He hit
her. . . . I'm so scared. He's crazy in the head. He made my Mommy go away.
I miss her." Crying, limp like a ragdoll, Lakisha was held by the therapist at
this point.

In the combined eighteenth and nineteenth hours of treatment, Lakisha
reached a hair-raising intensity of emotion, as her therapist perceived the child.

Looking through her PLHB, Lakisha seemed to be in a reverie, and reported an episode from two years earlier. "[It was when] we used to live in Jamaica, me and Mom and Kitty and Simon. They all started arguing because I peed on myself. Simon said 'She can't sleep in my bed anymore because she wets the bed.' I was ashamed. Simon yelled at Mom and she hung her head and went to the barn. Then Simon slept in my bed and I wet it anyway."

After being given some perspective on this poignant bit of her life history ("Children aren't really responsible for their family arguing"), Lakisha briefly became hyperactive. She wiggled, crammed her head under the therapist's chair, and put her head on the therapist's lap. Pretending to be asleep, Lakisha's hyperactivity ceased and she became flaccid. She wouldn't "wake up," occasionally opening an eye to look up, staying in the therapist's lap for about half an hour in what seemed a nurturance-seeking, psychologically and physically relaxed state until the session ended.

This seemed to be a regression in the service of the ego, and it was accepted and interpreted as a form of mourning. "You would like to be mother-cuddled, if only your mother could do that for you."

Lakisha spent a large portion of the final sessions drawing details of the treatment room, using a level of artistic ability (including geometric perspective) never evident earlier. She seemed to be memorializing the setting.

When only four sessions remained, the therapist made a chart with calendar boxes on which the patient and therapist checked off the impending sessions—a countdown.

Lakisha colored in the boxes and gave some unsolicited details of her self-concept, apparently spurred on to ask for help in the setting of an impending and carefully anticipated loss. "I talk funny . . . a boy in my class talks like this and everyone laughs at him."

As the countdown proceeded session by session, Lakisha grew more silent, and copied details of the room with increasing care, scanning back and forth from the actual room to her drawing. Her silence and visual taking in of the room were clearly a preparation for her loss.

With increasingly frequent moments of highly intelligible speech, she spoke of her uncle, and his murder of her mother. "You know, Simon smokes drugs. . . . He's gonna be a robber. . . . He had a gun under the other end of my bed. Soon as the cops come, he hide it under the bed. He shoot her and then he hides the gun. He tells me not to say, not to tell." (The above and earlier material about the uncle's alleged homicidal activity was reported to the appropriate district attorney. Although it was used during treatment, the page was not put into the child's PLHB lest the uncle ever have custody of the child and be punitive to her.)

As material about her mother's murder emerged, there was a positive change in Lakisha's quality of speech and a parallel change in the quality of her drawings. When treatment began, Lakisha's pictures were unrecognizable squiggles without apparent sequence or meaning. Lakisha now drew competently and admired her own expressed artistic products.

She reproduced the room around her in further detail, showing the wall switches, a desk and chair, a ventilation shaft and intake duct. The therapist found herself silently reacting to this product as "a phenomenal piece of work . . . indicative of a higher level of visual-motor functioning than one would expect of her." In a healthy countertransference resonation, the therapist silently remembered a major bereavement of her own.

The therapist commented to the child about what "a clever way this is to remember the room and the good times we had together in it after we stop working together." This insistence on the termination relevance of her work led to new recall of memories of her dead mother. The child completed the previously incomplete section on her mother in the PLHB, volunteering new descriptions of domestic events: "Mommy used to iron my clothes . . . always woke up happy, singing in the morning."

Lakisha and the therapist sang a song together which the child and mother had also sung:

Lucy had a baby,
She named him Tiny Tim
She put him in the bathtub
To see if he could swim

She drew a picture of both her mother and uncle for the PLHB, and after a long silence asked the therapist for help in spelling, "I love you, Mommy."

The therapist linked the child's sadness and missing Mommy with the feelings of sadness "that we feel because we won't see each other any more." The therapy ended with mutual sadness and a sense that both the therapist and Lakisha had grown.

Lakisha was referred for further assistance with her speech pathology and surveillance of her developmental progress. Her foster parents' ratings of Lakisha's progress are shown in Table 5–1.

## Case 2:

Five-year-old David was seen with his 8-year-old brother, Terry, during most of his thirty -session individual treatment and occasionally with another older brother, Ulrich.

**Table 5–1.** Child's Problems and Symptoms as Stated and Rated by Foster Parent on a Scale From 1–7

|  | At Intake | At Termination |
|---|---|---|
| Touching other people's things | 4 | 2 |
| Crying about mother | 3 | 1 |
| Talking about everything | 6 | 1 |
| Wanting food immediately | 3 | 2 |
| Total | 16 | 6 |

Transportation problems dictated that sessions were doubled up to ninety minutes rather than the traditional forty-five minute child therapy session. Fifteen such double sessions were held instead of thirty single sessions.

At the beginning of treatment, David sat rigidly and silently in whatever position he first assumed. He refused eye contact and met all overtures with stony indifference. He appeared electively mute. On the rare occasions he did speak in the first sessions, David was generally monosyllabic and unspontaneous. He became much more assertive, loquacious, and spontaneous when his siblings were present. Usually his spontaneity took the form of corrections of their history giving.

During the combined twenty-first and twenty-second sessions, both of David's brothers were present. Because David was calm, the therapist (Mary Courtney) felt she could suggest working on an emotionally difficult chapter. That was the still unworked-on chapter concerning his mother. Resistance to this suggestion was strong. David's brother Ulrich was evidently furious at the mother and said he would not talk about her. Ulrich also consistently refuted statements his siblings tried to make about his mother, and even tried to silence them for being disloyal.

The therapist only slightly changed the subject to where the children used to live. In response, David became quite intensely engaged in drawing a house, showing round windows and bars. His brother Terry insisted the windows were square. An argument ensued over colors and other details.

This irritable, angry squabble was interpreted from a loss-related view. "You boys are getting upset because you know we have only a few sessions left to work together."

Noteworthy responses occurred to this interpretation. The first was that David became busy in contributing to his PLHB with increasing detail. He began making a drawing which he described as bunkbeds that broke when Ulrich was on top. Mom bought a new bed, he reported. The two older siblings discussed this contribution in depth. Ulrich had the opinion that Mother had fixed the bed that time. It was another time that she had bought a new one, not the time Ulrich broke it. The discussion was amiable.

The next and more important and sudden breakthrough of communication in apparent response to the interpretation above was in the form of a lengthy account of events leading to placement. David recalled being in the bed with Ulrich on top when a knock came at the door. Robert answered the door, which made David blame Robert. "If Robert hadn't answered the door (and Mom told us not to answer the door) the police wouldn't have come in. They said 'Where is your mother?' and David and Terry told them, 'At work'." Ulrich, however, maintained that mother always was at school. All the boys agreed there was an uncle who took care of them months earlier but stopped coming because he stole Mother's money and was afraid to come back.

In their final session, more personal history poured out, despite continued resistance by the oldest child. The boys all agreed the police were nice. David now stated he liked being in foster care "better than home," and this led Ulrich to become furious. He tried to stop the younger boys from talking to the therapist. His interference was irritating and not accepted by either the therapist or the other boys. Nevertheless, Ulrich's attitude was respected by the therapist as resulting from an understandable loyalty conflict, one which she firmly said should not be allowed to spoil this goodbye moment. This resulted in the children all continuing to complete David's PLHB energetically.

The foster mother's rating of David's problems and progress is summarized in Table 5–2.

**Case 3**

Eleven-year-old Michael had an unfortunate but not rare systems adaptation problem. Multiple foster home transfers had already occurred prior to the start of treatment. Michael was initially anxious, overactive, and enuretic. Disruptive at school as well as in foster homes, he had been shifted to four different foster homes in one week.

Michael was very attached to the PLHB. He made a written product in each session, usually involving an affect-laden memory (i. e., "It made me sad"). At first he idealized his mother, who had neglected and abused him for years prior to his placement in foster care, but in the fifth session he wrote a story in which his mother seemed negligent and unable to help him. "I'm at the beach, and my mother lets me go way out. I start to drown. She

**Table 5–2.** Child's Problems and Symptoms as Stated and Rated by Foster Parent on a Scale from 1–7

|                        | Initial | Final |
| ---------------------- | ------- | ----- |
| Bedwetting             | 6       | 2     |
| Uncommunicative        | 5       | 1     |
| Fighting with brother  | 2       | 2     |
| Wary of adults         | 4       | 1     |
| Nightmares             | 2       | 1     |
| Total                  | 19      | 7     |

can't swim." The therapist made an interpretive comment concerning the above fantasy. "Mother wasn't able when you really needed help." Michael reacted to this interpretation by giving a realistic account of his mother having bruised him, spontaneously giving up his previous account that the substantial bruises with which he had entered foster care were self-inflected.

In the next session, he recounted a dream. "Mom committing suicide . . . shooting herself in the head . . . she was so sad the kids aren't with her." The dream was not interpreted, and the patient simply gave his associations that he felt both "sad and glad about the dream . . . glad because mother wouldn't have to suffer anymore because it hurts her to have me be away."

This confiding of a dream seemed a remarkable result of Michael's growing trust in the therapist, who had been putting persistent emphasis on the child's inner life and helping him to deal continuously with the theme of object loss. But it showed a marked reversal of roles, in that the child felt sorry for the mother, rather than angry or lonely or feeling sorry for his neglected and abandoned self.

Michael soon made a startling correction of his perspective on his mother. It occurred when stimulated by an anticipation of absence from the therapist due to her imminent vacation. He expressed curiosity about the therapist's activities outside of the clinic, and whether she had other patients. The therapist interpreted this curiosity as part of the child's hope that he would not have to share the therapist with anyone, and that "maybe this is how you would like your mother to feel about you." The patient confirmed the interpretation with a surprisingly forthright yes, and stated, "You know, I don't think my mother likes me."

Michael expressed increasing sadness as he made a genogram, which showed his concept of his history was that he had "five fathers," none of whom he could name except for one who is an alcoholic athlete. As his sadness became somewhat ameliorated through persistent work on the genogram, he brought up two people of whom we knew nothing before— a 3-year-old little sister living with a maternal aunt, and a 2-year-old little brother living with his maternal grandmother. By the seventh session, Michael was straightforwardly discussing his recent historical situation and realistically explaining reasons for his placement. "The trouble is my mother's boyfriend. I'm not going to be able to go home until he stops spending money on cigarettes, movies, and drinking. Mom's not going to have enough money to take me home."

By the fifteenth session Michael was filling his PLHB with very charged material. He was bitter because his mother had not yet visited him in three months of placement, although his grandmother had told him on the phone that his mother missed him. "Yeah, sure. She never wanted me to be born. She wanted an abortion. My grandmother talked her out of it. . . . I am afraid I will be in foster care all my life."

Reacting to his growing interest in her person, Michael noticed the therapist was pregnant, and expressed concern that she would give up her baby. This question was interpreted. "It's a way you have of showing me how worried that your mother didn't want you and doesn't want you." Michael confirmed that his grandmother has made him very worried about this, and that whenever grandmother and mother fight—which is often—they bring this up. "Even though I want my mother to take care of me, I don't think she can ever do it anymore."

He also revealed a contrary concern, by telling a fantasy of great relevance. "I sometimes think that if I am bad, my mother will come and take me back." Using the principle of focus on object loss, the therapist worked vigorously with this loss-related fantasy. She interpreted his actual misbehavior as understandable in light of this fantasy but likely to produce an undesired result. "Instead of getting what you really want, what you get is trouble. You might get yourself moved again, but I don't think you can really get your mother to take you back this way."

By the end of his thirty-session treatment, Michael continued to show straightforwardness rather than defensive distortions and denial regarding his mother's abuse and neglect of him. His aggressive behavior in school had diminished, as had his enuresis.

By the last session the court had taken custody of Michael and this was discussed in his PLHB. His mother had called Michael to tell him she had found a four-room apartment, without even mentioning the possibility of him coming to live with her. He was able to see that his mother's lack of active involvement with him reflected her problem and was not his fault or responsibility. He recalled having been threatened by his mother with foster placement if he disobeyed household rules about going outside or spending money.

As part of the last two sessions, Michael spoke of good mothers and bad mothers, hoping the therapist would be a good one and not abandon her baby. He thought about having children himself, and that he would like to keep them out of foster care. He made a connection to saying goodbye to the therapist with having to say goodbye to his grandmother when he left for foster care. Then Michael was able to be angry in a modulated, expressive rather than action-prone way. "I'm angry at you. I don't like saying goodbye. I always have to say goodbye. Foster care is rough. You never know when things are going to end."

Michael then reviewed the four brief placements prior to his current one. He created a story in which the protagonist asks for freedom, a tale of Oscar the Grouch, Big Bird, and Cookie Monster in which Big Bird asks, "Let me go!" In this fashion he turned passive abandonment into an active quest for freedom.

In the final session, Michael was appropriately quiet and sad, but also withdrawn. He said, "This is the final page to my life story book," and pretended to be dying, saying, "This is the final page of my life." The direness of the situation could not have been made more clear. He then expressed frank wishes to be a baby again so his mother would take him. He expressed continuing but realistic uncertainty about what life in foster care would bring, and the difficulty of predicting events.

In the final moments Michael remarked on the novelty of actually deliberately saying goodbye instead of just leaving without saying anything. "I'm not used to that."

The PLHB method appeared to be a corrective and fortifying experience to Michael. He accepted the therapist's model of courageously facing inner life. Calmly and without regression he told of his disappointments, bitterness, and burdens. At the end, he used no façade or camouflage, and suspended his extravagant prior defenses of denial and avoidance. He ceased trying to provoke a rejection as a compulsive way of taking charge of loss. He accepted his losses, accepted the associated affects, bound them up, and continued his sublimative activity of making a book with the therapist up to the final moment.

David experienced no further transfers among foster homes during the 30-week time frame of the study. Table 5–3 shows his foster parent's ratings of David's progress.

## Case 4

Victor, age 11, entered foster care when his mother voluntarily placed him because of inability to provide a home. She lived with a violent man. Victor

**Table 5–3.** Child's Problems and Symptoms as Stated and Rated by Foster Parent on a Scale From 1–7

|  | Initially | At Termination |
|---|---|---|
| Nervous | 7 | 3 |
| Bad manners | 7 | 5 |
| Hyperactive | 7 | 6 |
| Bad temper | 7 | 6 |
| Easily distracted | 5 | 4 |
| Poor discipline | 7 | 5 |
| No structure | 7 | 6 |
| Depressed | 7 | 3 |
| Poor behavior | 7 | 6 |
| Selfish | 4 | 3 |
| Total | 65 | 47 |

had a recently married, 17-year-old brother, who he claimed had married Victor's former "girlfriend."

Victor's functioning in the year prior to treatment was rated highly impaired. He had little interest in school and he was failing most subjects. In addition, he was highly disruptive and spent much time in detention.

The child elicited a disconcerted reaction from the therapist, who found Victor to be a prematurely adult person who appeared strikingly self-possessed. While he seemed friendly at first and amenable to treatment, he was resistant to discussing any emotionally charged topic. In contrast to his appearance of maturity, he unexpectedly talked of "soft fuzzies" and other babyish things in a high sing-song voice.

The PLHB was seized on avidly by Victor, who populated it at first with magazine photos of wrestling heroes. His mother and he, it soon became clear, had shared an interest in this sport. The emphasis on wrestling was interpreted as a way of feeling close to his absent mother, as well as representing an identification with powerful persons. It was quickly apparent that Victor had been unable to acknowledge the disturbing realities concerning his family or the reasons for his placement. Accordingly, he denied certain threatening facts known to the caseworker, for example, that Victor had been beaten and choked by his grandmother, who disliked and did not want him.

Victor stated that when it came to "sad things, I just throw them away. I don't pay no attention to them. I just try to stay happy all the time." The therapist acknowledged this might work a lot of the time, but is hard to keep doing when "the sad builds up inside." Victor responded to this interpretation of his defensive dilemma with an acknowledgment that he needed physical care (for sunburn, for example) and that his mother just tells him to be tough.

By the combined tenth and eleventh hours of his treatment, Victor was articulating many details of his daily life. He managed to obtain numerous photos, including some of his previous birthday party, which was at his foster home. This led to many domestic details being shared, including some of an embarrassing nature such as his blushing in one picture. He dictated an extensive, unrealistically positive story about the party. The therapist (Mary Courtney) at times found herself irritated by the child's incessantly Polyanna view of life, and pointed out to Victor how much else there was to his emotional life besides these happy thoughts. Victor responded to this explorative remark with articulation of his other pleasant interests—drawing and writing about his jogging route, his go-cart hobby, his interest in the Yankees.

While avoiding, in early sessions, negative feelings concerning his situation, Victor continued his avid use of the PLHB. He filled in almost every available chapter and line. However, there were notable defensive avoidant operations, such as filling in his grandmother's telephone number but not his mother's. Victor focused on siblings and tended to avoid adults when responding to family items on the PLHB. His most intense conscious conflicts were over his brother's marriage, including a question as to whether or not he had been invited to the wedding, which he had not attended. He inserted many extra pages into his PLHB, filled with photos and anecdotes of the wedding.

His biological father was a particular source of confusion for Victor and he lamented, "I don't know what his address is. I don't know where he's at. I don't care." The simple task of trying to list his family members' whereabouts led to an immense constructive turmoil and revelation not only for Victor, but also for his biological mother. Victor expressed the conviction that his father was living in a veteran's facility for mentally disabled veterans. The therapist, trying to enlist the biological mother's participation in the PLHB method, was finally able to get her to have a long telephone session. It was then learned there was indeed a male friend of hers who fit the description of the disabled veteran. However, this man was not Victor's father. She expressed surprise at Victor's confusion regarding his father's identity, and after much urging from the therapist, took particular trouble to discuss and correct the misunderstanding first by telephone, then in a visit with her son.

The PLHB method thus brought to light a fundamental misconception and enabled Victor's mother to actively be of help to him. During the course of her efforts, she learned more about Victor's misunderstandings, which included confusion as to which children were his biological siblings. Two children who were not biologically related to him, Victor regarded as bio-logical siblings and his mother tried to help him comprehend the true relationships.

Victor's response to these endeavors and the discovery of his father was an important one. He began taking his PLHB book home, with the therapist's permission, so he could call his older brothers for information on some points. A few weeks after his mother's interventions Victor began to exhibit an increased curiosity about academic matters. It appeared that the help he had received to "get the facts straight" about his own origins and family had the effect of giving him generalized permission to correct other intellectual confusions and inhibitions. His grades began to improve markedly. Such an intellectual recovery phenomenon has been noted by both authors among severely stressed children who have received intensive treatment. This effect of treatment has been documented via post-therapy IQ gains (Zelman et al. 1985).

In the twelfth and thirteenth sessions, Victor discussed his biological father and several half siblings. He now expressed scorn, and sarcastically described his father's stinginess and tendency to waste money on gambling. From his disappointing father Victor went on to discuss his relationship to the school principal, in whose office he was spending a good deal of time for disciplinary reasons. Victor projected his need for the principal onto other children, per-ceiving that they enjoyed seeing Victor get in trouble. Victor thus lacked in-sight into his role in seeking the discipline of the head of the school, and no effort was yet made to clarify the matter. The session ended with Victor taking Polaroid pictures of a male security guard he had met outside the treatment room while waiting with the therapist for transportation.

Sessions fourteen and fifteen included a revelation by Victor that he had a tender relationship with a girlfriend now, and that he was gaining a favor-able perspective on his biological family in comparison with his foster fam-ily. "One trouble with my [biological] family is that we don't do nothing together. We don't even go anywhere together."

In the next sessions he brought up sadness as well as mild reproach toward his mother, who was regularly missing visits with him. He expressed worry about his school average having been dragged down by earlier poor work, and was clearly becoming academically ambitious.

Victor's PLHB was now a catalytic agent for well-articulated memories of his extended family. He reported amusing tricks previously shown him by a disabled "favorite uncle." He filled in details of the genogram, including the divorce of his mother from his biological father and her marriage to a man who had seemed to be his father even though his mother hadn't yet met him when Victor was born. Memories of this man emerged with sadness, and were associated with profound sadness concerning another deceased relative to whom Victor attributed both anger and generosity.

As the sixteenth session was ending, Victor spun a poignant fantasy, indicating his hope for a permanent attachment to the PLHB. "Let's practice like when I was older." He pantomimed blowing dust off the PLHB, opening it, and flipping through the pages as an adult. The therapist understood this fantasy of a future visit as implying a self-concept sufficiently strong and positive to provide continuity through time. She responded with a "heart-wrenching" mixture of hope and concern that Victor could sufficiently internalize the PLHB and the associated therapeutic process so as to be able to sustain and fortify his beginning experience of himself as a person.

In his final sessions, Victor reported on his accelerated attachments to his foster parents. He was able to enjoy a summer vacation in a small cabin with them, and developed the ability to enjoy mountain scenes silently for an hour at time. This was an unprecedented aesthetic sensitivity for Victor, paralleled by increasingly constructive involvement with school work. His grades soared from D's and F's to A's and B's, and his frequent detentions and disciplinary comments on report cards ended. He no longer seemed learning disabled, in sharp contrast to an intake psychiatric evaluation which had concluded he had a reading disability as well as an adjustment reaction disorder. Table 5–4 summarizes his foster parents' ratings of Victor's progress.

## DISCUSSION

A matched pairs study of eight treated children, including the four cases presented here, showed a statistically significant treatment effect on the sta-

**Table 5–4.** Child's Problems and Symptoms as Stated and Rated by Foster Parent on a Scale From 1–7

|                                | Initally | At Termination |
|--------------------------------|----------|----------------|
| Whines and cries a lot         | 6        | 1              |
| Clinging to adults             | 6        | 6              |
| Refuses to defend self/victim  | 5        | 1              |
| Poor academic performance      | 7        | 2              |
| Few friends/too smothering     | 6        | 2              |
| Holds everything inside        | 3        | 6              |
| Total                          | 33       | 18             |

bility of foster care placement. During the period studied only one of the eight treatment cases was transferred from his foster home, while five of eight control children were transferred, one control child being transferred twice. This study is encouraging but requires replication using a much larger sample.

Both the clinical process and the foster parents' pre- and post-treatment ratings presented here are typical of a group of twenty-four foster children treated with the PLHB method. Only one of these cases showed possible worsening in treatment. That case was of a child who at first improved markedly but deteriorated when transferred to another foster home against the therapist's recommendations and the foster parents' wishes.

As illustrated in these cases, associated with a decreased transfer rate from the foster home is a more positive view of the child by the foster parent. Although we have focused on the transfer rate as a convenient, concrete marker of the effects of interventions, the crucial underlying issue is the potential of this technique to enhance the capacity of stressed foster children to sustain positive relationships.

An early objective toward the accomplishment of this goal is the enlistment and enhancement of the biological (as in the case of Victor) and foster parents' acceptance of, and empathy with, the child. Active involvement of the child's primary caretakers in helping the child to obtain information for the PLHB as well as reviewing the book with the child on a regular basis (even a few minutes each night) can help to achieve this objective.

In view of the past histories, as well as the clinical presentation of the children described, one may wonder about the brevity and time-limited nature of the PLHB technique. As mentioned earlier, this treatment approach was formulated in the context of a research project, in an attempt to investigate, and hopefully provide evidence for its efficacy. The clinical process as well as the foster parents' pre- and post-treatment ratings of the treated children do suggest the method's effectiveness for short-term work, as does the small matched control study. We believe, however, that for most of these children a more extended course of treatment would be needed to sustain and extend the gains made.

Perhaps the most salient aspect of the PLHB is its ability to facilitate the child's communication of his experience. Such communication both strengthens the child's sense of self and enhances his capacity to trust others, without which a satisfactory life is highly improbable. For this reason, use of the PLHB should be considered for hard to reach children in situations other then foster care.

## REFERENCES

Aust, P. (1981). Using the Life Story Book in treatment of children in placement. *Child Welfare* 60:535–560.

Dinnage, R., and Pringle, M. (1967). *Foster Home Care: Facts and Fallacies.* London: Longmans.

Fanshell, D., and Shinn, E. (1978). *Children in Foster Care.* New York: Columbia University Press.

Festinger, T. (1983). *No One Ever Asked Us . . . A Postscript to Foster Care.* New York, Columbia University Press.

Kliman, G. (1993). *My Personal Life History Book.* San Francisco, CA: Children's Psychological Trauma Center.

Kliman, G., Schaeffer, M., and Friedman, M. (1982). *Preventive Mental Health Services for Children Entering Foster Family Care: An Assessment.* Monograph of The Center for Preventive Psychiatry, White Plains, NY.

Kliman, G., Schaeffer, M., Friedman, M., and Pasquariella, B. (1981). Children in foster care: a preventive service and research program for a high-risk population. *Journal of Preventive Psychiatry* 1(1): 47–56.

Kline, D., and Overstreet, H. (1972). *Foster Care of Children: Nurture and Treatment.* New York: Columbia University Press.

Knitzer, J., and Allen, M. D. (1978). *Children without Homes.* Washington, DC: Children's Defense Fund.

Lambert, L., Essen, J., and Head, J. (1977). Variations in behavior ratings of children who have been in care. *Journal of Child Psychology and Psychiatry* 18:335–346.

National Commission on Children in Need of Parents (1979). *Who Knows? Who Cares? Forgotten Children in Foster Care.* New York: National Commission on Children in Need of Parents.

Terr, L. (1991). *Childhood Traumas: An Outline and Overview.* American Journal of Psychiatry 148(1):10–20.

Wald, M., Carlsmith, J., Leiderman, P., et al. (1985). *Protecting Abused/Neglected Children: A Comparison of Home and Foster Placement.* Stanford, CA: Stanford Center for the Study of Youth Development.

Wheeler, C. E. (1978). *Where Am I Going? Making a Child's Life Story Book.* Juneau, AK: Winking Owl Press.

Wolkind, S., and Rutter, M. (1973). Children who have been 'in care': an epidemiological study. *Journal of Child Psychology and Psychiatry* 14:97–105.

Zelman, A., Samuels, S., and Abrams, D. (1985). IQ changes in young children following intensive long-term psychotherapy. *American Journal of Psychotherapy* 39(2):215–227.

Zimmerman, R. (1982). Foster care in retrospect. *Tulane Studies in Social Welfare,* vol. 14. New Orleans, LA: Tulane University School of Social Work.

# 6

# Treatment of Foster Children: Working through Loss to Facilitate Attachment

*Shirley C. Samuels*

## INTRODUCTION

All bereaved children, who do not mourn previous losses, are at risk for developing serious emotional problems later in life (Bowlby 1980, Furman 1974, Hoopes 1982, Kliman et al. 1982, Lindholm and Touliatos 1980, Schaeffer et al. 1981, Simon and Senturra 1966). Foster children are especially vulnerable to developing emotional problems because of stress in their parents' lives before being separated from them. Disturbed early object relationships can result from abuse, neglect, drug and alcohol use, illness, and/or the effects of poverty. In a recent study of 4 to 16-year-old children, Stein and colleagues (1994) found that the children who had been exposed to substance abuse, criminal behavior, and psychiatric problems had significant pathology for one or more disorders.

Festinger (1986) reported that 23.6 percent of foster children had been abandoned by their biological parents. In a federal study looking at the characteristics of children entering foster care, it was found over ten years ago that three-quarters of children entering foster care at that time were there because of abuse and neglect (National Committee for Adoption 1985). The crack epidemic, AIDS, and homelessness are problems leading to current increases in the numbers of foster children whose families cannot rear them or who have abandoned them (Barden 1990). It was reported that in 1988 in the USA there were 323,000 children in foster care (Committee on Finance 1990). The number had increased to 360,000 by January, 1990 (Barden 1990).

Additionally, after children leave their biological parents, other factors that often exacerbate their ability to attach to new caretakers are loyalty conflicts and multiple placements (Burland et al. 1981, Kliman et al. 1982, Samuels 1990, 1995). It is not uncommon for a foster child to have multiple placements, so they have to mourn not only their first loss but also subsequent ones.

The negative effects that all of these events have on the children's self-esteem is tremendous. Children separated from their biological families below the age of 6 are likely to blame themselves for losing significant others, due to the fact that it is developmentally normal for preschool children to be egocentric (Piaget and Inhelder 1969). They are less likely to regard themselves as worthy or competent or to have a sense of belonging, all indicators of high self-esteem (Samuels 1977). The impairment of ego functions in children separated from significant others is also common (Bowlby 1980, Furman 1974, Kliman et al. 1982, Milrod 1988, Sorosky et al. 1975, Warfield 1972, Wolfenstein 1966, 1969, 1973).

Young children suffering from the loss of a parent are predisposed to later pathology in dealing with object loss (Bowlby 1980, Burland et al. 1981, Furman 1974, Kliman et al. 1982). Even separation from primary caretakers during the first year of life is significant. Recent infant research has shown that the newborn can discriminate between self and other within the first few weeks of life (Flashman 1992, Mayes and Cohen 1992, Pine 1985, Stern 1985) and can detect visual, tactile, auditory, olfactory, gustatory, and vestibular stimuli (Haith 1986). Evidence from these studies supports the fact that children from earliest life form early representations of their experiences with others (Mayes and Cohen 1992). The impact of these early life experiences affect the ways the child copes with separation.

Bowlby (1969, 1973) emphasizes the factors of attachment and separation. This viewpoint stresses that the grief response of the infant is caused by the breaking of a bond between the baby and the mother. This bond develops as a result of the child's recognition that, in order to survive, the mothering figure is essential. Bowlby states that this attachment behavior continues throughout life. As a result, whenever an attachment figure is lost, the earlier life feelings of loss and fear of survival are reexperienced by the individual.

The more intense the attachment with previous caretakers, the greater the pain of loss. If an earlier attachment had occurred, it has been estimated that for older adopted children it takes one year to eighteen months for mutual attachment between the child and the new caretaker to become reality (Cohen 1981). If no previous attachment existed, there would be severe pathology with a guarded prognosis for future emotional health.

Whatever the age of separation, children with unresolved bereavement live in the past and do not detach internally from the earlier object. Successful mourning enables an individual to work beyond denial, anger and depression to acceptance of the loss of significant others (Kubler-Ross 1970). According to Freud (1917), after the loss of an individual to whom the child had an attachment, the primary work of grieving is to work through the memories and feelings towards the lost individual. At the end of that process, the bereaved person is able to accept the ending of a physical connection to that person and can move on to form new attachments. Mourning is completed when there is identification with the person lost, that is, the biological parent becomes part of the child's ego.

If earlier life experiences are negative, a child's ability to move on and to invest in new relationships becomes problematic. The memory and its attendant emotions related to the early-life caretaking person are powerful in that the child recreates versions of his reactions to primary caretakers in subsequent relationships with new caretakers. Maladaptive defenses such as rage, chronic depression, and chronic dependency are frequently utilized to try to ward off sadness. If the child's early experiences are developmentally inappropriate, before moving on developmentally he must first work through possible unresolved earlier life trauma, as well as deal with the expected sadness of the normal mourning process described above.

If this is not done, social and cognitive failure is probable. These failures would likely further lower self-esteem, leading to an increase in maladaptive behavior which often results in rejection and the giving up of the children by the foster parents (Samuels 1990).

For children who have had minimal disruption and a relatively stable earlier life, caseworkers and foster parents may be able to provide adequate help with their ambivalent feelings and memories, and help them to reinvest in new relationships. Even for these children, the availability of a clinician to assist the foster parent in understanding and facilitating the processes in the child of mourning and reattachment should be routine.

There are increasing numbers of severely disturbed young children in foster care, however, who need therapeutic intervention to prevent later-life negative consequences for them and for society. There have been few studies in the literature showing the effectiveness of intensive psychotherapy for children traumatized as a result of being separated from their parents. There are case studies in the literature reporting the effectiveness of intensive therapeutic intervention with children following the death of a parent (Furman 1974, Harmon et al. 1982, Lopez and Kliman 1979, Wolfenstein 1973). In other studies, several of the children were treated for a short period of time and some of the children were later adopted by their foster parents (Ament 1972, Auestad 1992, Brandell 1992, Clifton and Ransom 1975, Defries et al. 1964, Demb 1993, Fraiberg 1962, Frankel 1991, High 1982, Kaplan 1982, Kaplan and Turitz 1957, Kegerreis 1993, Kliman et al. 1982, Lush et al. 1991, Reeves 1971, Samuels 1995, Schaeffer et al. 1981, Warfield 1972).

The Center for Preventive Psychiatry has been a pioneer since its inception in 1965 in utilizing intensive psychotherapy for severely disturbed foster and adopted children (Kliman et al. 1982). Samuels (1995) has reported on the process of psychoanalytic psychotherapy with two children treated in the Clinic. This chapter reports on two other children treated with psychodynamic psychotherapy by this author.

The aim of the paper is to show that long-term psychotherapy can be effective in helping foster children who had unhealthy attachments with their biological parents to work through their memories and the attendant feelings related to their primary caretakers and to move on to form new healthy attachments. Both children were subsequently adopted, although they had been in more than one foster home after leaving their biological parents. The case material reveals the maladaptive reactions of these children and the therapeutic interventions used to help them. The interactions between the therapist, social services, and foster parents are discussed.

## CASE OF BENNY

Benny, an African-American 6-year-old, was placed in the home of his foster mother five weeks before being brought to our agency. He had never lived with his biological mother, but had lived with his maternal grandmother for the first four years of his life and in a series of foster homes for the next two years. In some of the foster homes, his older sister, six years his senior, was not with him. She left the biological home with him and was with him in the first and last foster homes before being separated from him again for the last time. The goal was originally to keep them together because they were so bonded to one another. However, his sister was a profoundly behavior-disordered girl and the last foster home that they were in together could not keep both children, as she encouraged her brother to misbehave and to be oppositional and regressed. She was placed in a residential school and remained there, and Benny was placed separately in a foster home.

There was relatively little history about the children's extended family. The records state that their biological mother had a history of multiple psychiatric hospitalizations and drug addiction. The maternal grandmother took the children in and their mother appeared at her mother's house infrequently to see them. The grandmother had multiple emotional and physical problems and it was reported that she could not adequately mother Benny. The two children had different fathers unknown to them and to their grandmother. There was some extended family but they were unavailable and the grandmother gave the children up with relative ease. Since neither she nor the children's mother visited them in the various foster homes, they were released for adoption.

Benny's latest foster mother was a single African-American woman. She was in her middle forties and had a daughter away at college. She wanted an older foster child she could ultimately adopt. When Benny first entered the home, there was a short honeymoon period. Soon, however, the foster mother was overwhelmed by his regressive and oppositional symptoms. Within a month, he wet his bed every night, masturbated excessively, sucked his fingers almost constantly, and his oppositional symptoms became manifest. He began to destroy things, refused to comply with any demands, and denied or blamed other people or circumstances for his misbehavior. Benny's foster mother was overwhelmed by Benny's regressive and oppositional symptoms. He was unmanageable in school, where he provoked the teacher and other children. He had serious deficits in his fund of information and functioned cognitively at the preschool level. On the WISC-R, he was found to have a full scale IQ score of 91.

Benny was most unmanageable when he saw his sister. It was clear, when the therapist saw the two children together during early sessions and in the material that emerged as therapy progressed, that his sister had been the major caretaker throughout Benny's early life. His older sister came to one of the sessions and admitted to liking to boss Benny around and to getting upset when he did not listen to her in opposition to adult demands. His sister remembered more about their biological mother. She provided her version of interactions and information about them to Benny. She also revealed that, in their previous common foster homes, there had been other children. When she was brought for visits to Benny's home, which was considered important for Benny, he was encouraged by his sister to disobey this new foster mother. The foster mother also observed that his sister would baby and tease him unmercifully to the point where he would withdraw and masturbate, therefore the home visits were stopped. Subsequently, the children saw each other with a social worker present in the residential center.

During the first session with the therapist, it was noted that Benny's affect was generally constricted. He became hyperactive and regressed (sucked his thumb) as he talked about anxiety-ridden material, such as missing his sister, when he and his sister ran away from the last foster home to find their biological family, and when he got scared by "bad people" who carry knives. Benny's speech was pressured and his language was concrete and limited. He told the therapist that he had to leave his last foster home because his sister had taken him away to their old neighborhood to find their grand-mother and mother. He said his sister "be telling me things that's not right." When asked what he would like the therapist to help him with, he said he wanted to stay in his new foster home. Later in the session, he said he missed his sister and his last foster mother but he liked being the only child. He went from activity to activity and seemed to enjoy throwing a ball back and forth with the therapist. He teased the therapist by throwing the ball away and laughing when she could not retrieve it. When it was time to end, he started painting and refused to leave the session.

It was clear in meeting the foster mother for the first time that she liked Benny. However, she was overwhelmed by his pathology and regression. She said she knew it was important for him to see his sister, but that she needed help in coping with him, especially after he visited or talked on the phone with his sister.

The child was diagnosed as having Oppositional Defiant Disorder. The treatment plan was to see the child twice a week and the foster mother once a week. This report will focus on the three years during which this treatment plan was carried out.

During the first six months of therapy, Benny's play consisted mostly of playing with a ball and hero figures. The play was repetitive and Benny had difficulty elaborating on it. At times, he became disorganized and provoca-tive, requiring active limit setting. This occurred especially at the end of sessions. When the therapist had to bring his foster mother in at such times to help to control him, he would claim it had been an accident or the thera-pist had made him do it. The therapist interpreted his behavior as a reac-tion to the pain of being thwarted and/or separated from someone he wanted to be with.

Increasingly during this time, as he realized the therapist was not mak-ing value judgments about his verbalizations, and as she accepted his long-ing for his sister after visits with her, he did talk about their interactions. He said she told him he didn't have to listen to his foster mother if he didn't want to. In one session he admitted he didn't want to listen to his sister, but during others, when he was angry at his foster mother, he said he wanted to live where his sister was.

The foster mother needed a great deal of support during this time. She began to doubt whether she could keep the child because his symptoms had not sufficiently subsided. Her extended family began to question her motivation to adopt the child. With the therapist's help, however, she became more supportive of the child. It was discovered in talking to her that she had not been knowledgeable enough about the need to be consistent and firm as well as having the empathy she already exhibited with the child. With parent guidance by the therapist and parenting classes required by the Social Service agency, she realized that this traumatized child was not like her own. She became more able to discipline him appropriately. This was observed in some joint sessions the foster parent attended with Benny.

In therapy during the next three months, Benny regressed much of the time in his sessions. He sucked his thumb more, crawled around the room, pushed toys back and forth repetitively, and destroyed materials and pictures he occasionally drew. This behavior commonly was stimulated by drawings in which Benny represented a considerable amount of violence, including police, jail, and frightening creatures. He would structure himself during some sessions by writing pages of words he was learning in school and he proudly read them to the therapist. In one session, he revealed that his sister liked to see his work. He would give the therapist some of his work as gifts. He also made things for his sister.

At home, he began to show signs of wanting approval, although he still destroyed toys and wet his bed when stressed, particularly after having contact with his sister. However, his foster mother now felt sufficiently encouraged to reaffirm her wish to adopt him. After she told him, he asked her if she could adopt his sister too. When she told him she couldn't, Benny became angry and broke an expensive lamp. The foster parent was very distressed and required a lot of support. Benny accused his foster mother of not caring about him if his sister could not live with them. This issue came up repeatedly in therapy. At times, especially late in therapy, he said he could understand why it was impossible for his sister to be adopted with him, but when he was upset, he often expressed a wish to join his sister where she was.

At the end of the academic year, his school behavior improved and he was catching up cognitively. On the other hand, he was still not up to grade level, he had trouble following rules, and he teased children who would not befriend him.

During the weeks prior to the therapist's month-long vacation, Benny was uncontrollable and regressed in all settings. He denied being concerned and stated he hated the therapist and therapy and said he wasn't coming back. He said his sister told him he didn't have to. Interpretation focused on his reaction to the pain of feeling rejected by the therapist. This was linked to past rejections as well as his need to be loyal to his sister.

That summer was a very difficult one for the child. He had a bad camp experience and his foster mother finally removed him from the camp before it ended. Benny was oppositional with the young counselors and unmercifully teased the other children, who in turn rejected him. It was felt by everyone involved that the environment was too unstructured for him and the young, inexperienced counselors were incapable of helping him. He did have a good experience with his 19-year-old foster sister, who was home for the summer from college. She was a good model for him, he generally listened to her, and she genuinely liked him. The family also went for a short vacation to another part of the country to visit his foster mother's large extended family and that was reported to have been a generally positive experience for him.

Immediately after the summer vacation, the child tested the therapist for a few sessions by telling the therapist she was ugly. He tried to provoke her by tearing up paper and writing on tables after drawing pictures of bad guys who shot and hurt each other. The therapist related this behavior to his feeling rejected and angry at the therapist's absence during her vacation. He neither denied nor affirmed this, but within a few weeks his play became richer and more expansive. For about six months he enacted a theme in which puppets of animals that did bad and violent things were defeated and put into jail. There were still periods when the aggression in his play became overwhelming for him and he expressed his disorganization by throwing something or creating disarray. He generally was able to stop himself and would sit down and suck his thumb. Ending sessions continued to be difficult for him. During this time, he often took things from the room and would run out to his foster mother with the toy. The mother would return the toy with him in tow. The therapist interpreted his wish to keep the therapist with him.

As he realized that the therapist was not going to punish him for his behavior by rejecting him, greater trust developed. Before this time, he resisted saying much about his sister. A major change during therapy came about during the second half of the second year. More verbalized sadness appeared relating to his separation from his sister. He talked about memories of their family that she had provided for him. Many of the memories revolved around not having enough food, and men with guns and violent activities, with some idealized statements about the biological mother whom Benny could not remember. During these times, the therapist empathized with Benny's love for his sister and his biological mother. He still controlled the therapist in play but the activities that he controlled were more organized and less aggressive. For example, he would play games and would arbitrarily determine the rules to which the therapist had to adhere. The therapist verbalized the need for him to be in charge of the rules of his life and to know what they were. She reflected on the confusion of the previous rules and circumstances of his life.

At the end of the second school year after starting therapy, he had almost caught up academically. He still had peer problems but he had a few friends that the therapist encouraged the foster mother to invite home after school. This was done and the foster mother said she noticed he tried to control the play of these children. Generally, these children were passive and he teased them as his sister had teased him.

The second vacation was much more productive for the child. He had a better camp experience. The bedwetting, stealing, and excessive masturbation were no longer present before this vacation from the therapist. At times, he still was oppositional and destroyed things and sucked his thumb when stressed, which continued to occur mostly after visiting his sister. He used verbal arguments more when he didn't want to do things requested of him.

After the vacation and for the rest of the last year in therapy, Benny spent more time with higher level games, toys, and creative materials. He enjoyed playing cards with the therapist, although he still changed the rules to suit his need to control the therapist. He drew pictures of valorous men and animals and either gave them to the therapist or brought them home to give to his foster mother. When he had gotten into trouble at home or at school, he would draw a picture for his foster mother as a gift indicating contrition and a wish for forgiveness. This was interpreted as a wish to be good and to be loved. At such times his upcoming adoption, about which Benny expressed mostly positive anticipation, was frequently discussed.

However, once an actual court date for the adoption was set during the third year of his therapy, he again began to test limits everywhere. He again told the therapist with anger that it was unfair that his sister was not being adopted with him. As his misbehavior and the guilt and anger related to it were worked on in therapy, Benny's foster mother again expressed ambivalence about adopting him. The first sign of this ambivalence was her inactivity in calling her attorney to push for a date for final court approval of the adoption. The therapist brought this to the fore and she admitted she was discouraged by his regression. She acknowledged her worry that he would never be normal if his sister's presence in his life persisted. Having expressed this concern, she was able to recapture her understanding of the importance of his sister to Benny. At the same time, the therapist reaffirmed the foster mother's greater importance for Benny's ultimate well-being. After a few sessions, she moved to call her attorney to set a court date.

The adoption was finalized at the end of the third year of therapy. In therapy, he continued to express his feelings of sadness and guilt related to his adoption and not being with his sister. He sometimes used a game about feelings to make it easier for him to talk about them. He played games more according to the rules and was better able to tolerate losing. His intensity and need to control showed evidence of increasing sublimation, for example, his persistence at games and his ability to correct (albeit somewhat obsessive) and complete pictures and schoolwork he sometimes brought. He teased the therapist if she made a mistake, such as when a letter of the alphabet she wrote was not up to his standard. The therapist verbalized the positive aspect of his persistence, his wish to be smart, and his wish to do things the right way.

Before the therapist's vacation at the end of the third year, the intensive therapeutic work ended, as the therapist was moving to another geographic location. Benny was now functioning at grade level for his school. His foster mother decided to transfer him to a private school for the following academic year because she was not happy with his peer relationships and she wanted him to have more academic stimulation. It was decided that she would be in contact with the therapist at the new site if the child regressed again, but she wanted to see how things progressed without therapy.

During the last month before the vacation the child revealed ambivalent feelings about ending. He had difficulty actually saying he would miss the therapist. He listed all the positive things he could do with the time. He was told by his mother that he could see the therapist in the future if he had to and he repeated this to the therapist during his last session. He drew a happy picture of himself in this session and gave it to the therapist. The therapist verbalized his wish for the therapist to remember him and told him that he could remember the things and feelings in therapy to help to do the grownup things he now showed he wanted to do.

## CASE OF SANDRA

Sandra was brought to Westchester County Children's Services when she was 5 years old. Her mother had come to New York from South Carolina. She said she had lived in a home for unwed mothers, after which she had lived with friends. Other than saying that the child had lived with her extended family, the mother was vague about the child's background. The mother did say that the child was conceived when the mother was 13 years old, that the father was unknown, and that she could not take care of the child in New

York. After the information was given, she refused to answer any more questions. She did, however, repeat a conviction that Sandra would be better off in a good adoptive home than she would be living with her extended family. She denied that this might upset the child, saying, "She is stronger than I am."

In the foster home into which she was placed, Sandra was superficially independent and conforming. At school, she was friendly, helpful and creative and was functioning academically as a normal kindergartner. She was referred to our agency two months after she had been given up by Social Services because she had shown little apparent visible reaction to her separation from her mother. When her mother came to visit, she assumed an adult, reassuring role while her mother behaved like a child. Her mother told her not to cry after she left.

Sandra was an attractive African-American child with an alert appearance. During the intake evaluation, she acted in a pseudo-adult manner, and there was much apologizing, conformance, and meticulousness in her play. She had a sad, forlorn look on her face when the therapist asked her if she knew why she had come to see her. Sandra then picked up two cups and a coffee pot which was already filled with water and said there was coffee in them. When the therapist asked her who the coffee was for, Sandra picked up a large baby bottle, poured water into it and said sadly, "She's hungry." However, Sandra did not feed the doll. The therapist said, "The baby is hungry but it looks like the mommy isn't feeding her." The child partially acknowledged this with a half nod and again filled the two cups with water and asked the therapist to drink the coffee with her. Later in this initial session, she played out being taken care of by a grandma doll while the mommy doll (a Barbie doll) was in bed with the Ken doll. The therapist clarified for Sandra that she was telling a story of her worries. The session ended with Sandra pouring torrents of water into the baby, suggesting both the intensity of her oral needs and her anxiety.

The school psychologist's report on a WISC-R, given to Sandra at school entrance, showed a total IQ score of 94. It was felt by the tester that the result did not reflect Sandra's potential. It was reported that she had been apathetic while being tested, although friendly and cooperative on the surface. She was given a diagnosis of an Adjustment Disorder with Depressed Mood, which later in therapy was changed to Dysthymia. The recommendation was made that she be given twice-weekly dynamic psychotherapy and her foster parents were to be seen biweekly. The goal was to help her to work through the loss of her biological family so that she could move on to form new healthy attachments and relationships. It was clear to all who observed her that she had learned to comply and to please people in order to avoid rejection and loss.

Her foster parents were a young, childless African-American couple who had tried to conceive a child of their own for five years without results. They said they had preferred to take a younger, healthy male baby but one had not been available, so they had agreed to take Sandra. Sandra's mother continued to be clear and unambivalent about wanting the child to be adopted by a good family and this couple expressed a wish to adopt her from the start.

Her early therapeutic sessions focused on her past relationships with her mother and her extended family. Her play clearly indicated that she had mothered her mother. She called herself a dummy and said that she did not do a good job making her mother's coffee in the morning. The social worker, who had observed her with her mother the few times they saw one another after Sandra was in the foster home, said her mother criticized her even when she tried to respond to her mother's inappropriate expectations of her. The therapist made a few appointments to meet with her mother but she never appeared.

A predominant defense Sandra used early in therapy was reversal of affect. It was common for her to sing and to become manic when sadness would have been the more appropriate emotion. She rarely completed anything. During one session early in therapy, when the therapist verbalized the fact that Sandra seemed to be running away from something and that maybe she was trying to forget something, the child abruptly stopped running and drew a partial face on the blackboard and intensely scribbled over it. The therapist said, "It looks like you want to blot out that face." She than gave the therapist a dog puppet that she said was lonely. The therapist responded that she wondered if Sandra was lonely for the person with that face. Sadly, the child nodded her head. For quite a few sessions following this one, she called her mother, her grandfather, and other relatives on the play phone. She asked her mother if she was at work. Frequently, she would say in a pleading voice, "Where are you?" Also, during this time, her mother was not showing up when she was supposed to be seeing her.

For many sessions after this one, the child was annoyed with the therapist if she did not mirror Sandra's every action. The therapist had to draw a picture like hers alongside her. This narcissistic defense was present throughout therapy whenever Sandra felt lonely, depressed, and unloved. It appeared the therapist had to mirror her every action to bolster Sandra's self-esteem.

After being in therapy for about six months, Sandra began to suck on a bottle and talk like a baby during her sessions. As her demand to be babied was interpreted, she began to show anger about being abandoned. In one session, she sang Rock-A-Bye-Baby to a doll, then threw the doll at the therapist. The following session, she told the therapist to be the little girl and she was going to be the mommy. She started to spank the therapist and when asked why the spanking, she said because the baby did not listen to Mommy. The therapist wondered if Sandra felt that her mother would not have left her if she had listened to her. Sandra exclaimed, "I cooked and took care of my mother, even when she was sick, even when she didn't want me to. I want to take care of my mother."

For many sessions after this one, Sandra talked about her life with her mother. There was a fantasy of another baby (a boy) taking her place with her mother. She somehow knew that her foster parents had wanted a baby boy. She talked to the therapist about wanting her foster parents to get a baby boy and that she would help them care for him.

Just about this time, six months after the child had last seen her mother, Sandra was informed that her mother had disappeared. Sandra expressed a fantasy that her mother was very sick and that was the reason why she hadn't come to see her. Sandra began to show despair and depression in her foster home. Her foster parents expressed increasing impatience with her nightmares, babyish whining, psychosomatic cough, and sleeplessness. They alternately tried to ignore and stop the behavior.

In therapy during this period, the child continued to order the therapist to do exactly what she did. Session after session they painted and drew pictures together. She shouted at the therapist if she didn't do exactly what Sandra did. Depression was evident in both her psychomotor sluggishness and her symbolic material, for example, tear drops, represented in her pictures. This was mixed with anger during one session, when she drowned the Barbie doll in a tub of water after she sadly dressed and undressed the doll. Interpretation focused on her painful feelings related to her earlier life memories and the loss of her biological mother. Simultaneously there were times when she played age-appropriate games with the therapist. She was able to be competitive at these times and acknowledge her wish to win. Some of the material revealed during sessions seemed to indicate she had earlier received a measure of good care and had had positive emotional interactions with her extended biological family. For example, she knew a Dr. Seuss book by heart. When asked how she had learned it, she said her grandmother had read to her.

As treatment proceeded, and the honeymoon period passed, Sandra began to manifest her underlying feelings and needs through regressive "babyish" behavior or frank depression. Her foster parents began talking again of wanting a baby boy, a reflection of their increasing ambivalence toward Sandra. Rather than discussing this ambivalence they began cancelling visits with the therapist. Finally they told the foster care case worker that "if she is unhappy with us she should be placed with someone else who can make her happy." Shortly after, Sandra was removed from the foster home.

Before this was done, there was a meeting of the child and the social worker. Although the foster parents had clearly lost empathy with Sandra, they were helped by the case worker to try to reassure her that her removal from their home was not her fault. They accompanied her and talked to the new foster parents in the new home she entered. After several of these visits, Sandra was transferred to her new foster home.

In treatment, Sandra was overtly depressed. She resumed the themes expressed early in therapy, alternating between the wish to be babied and the attempt to please by taking care of the dolls and the therapist. She now had another loss to mourn and found it difficult to believe that it was not her fault her first foster parents were not able to meet her needs. When the depression became too painful in therapy, she again asked the therapist to function for her as a mirror in order to bolster her depleted sense of self. Upon entering her new foster home she reverted to the overcompliant behavior she had first manifested in her earlier home.

Sometime after this the therapist took a month's vacation. Sandra told her foster parents, and later the therapist, that she did not think the therapist would return. In a subsequent session, Sandra brought in three Barbie dolls and took care of them all. The therapist reflected on how she had had three mommies, how much she wanted to be good enough for all of them, and how she might feel she would not have been given up if she had taken better care of them.

Four months after entering her new foster home, Sandra was told that her foster parents wanted to adopt her. She responded by testing them. She sometimes didn't come home directly after school, dawdled over food, and resisted cleaning up her room.

In therapy, she told the therapist she had wandered into another neighborhood when she should have been walking home from school. She said she imagined she saw her biological mother there. She spent many sessions idealizing her mother. She spoke of her mother's pretty face, how her mother took her places, and her belief that her mother was sick and might die. She said her mother's sickness was the reason she hadn't come to claim her. Alongside these themes, there was an expression of confusion about her mother's abandonment of her. She said, "I think my mother is back with my grandfather. When I grow up , I'm going back to see her and my grandfather and my cousins." With the therapist's encouragement, her future adoptive parents allowed her to talk about her biological family. They told Sandra that she had a right to try to find her roots when she was grown. Still, she expressed ambivalence in therapy towards her future adoptive family. She made pictures for them with great effort and left the pictures at the clinic.

Sandra told the therapist she was better behaved than her brother (the 11-year-old biological son of her foster parents). She followed this by drawing a picture of herself with her future adoptive parents and with her adoptive brother. She showed the three of them looking alike while she was isolated and looked different. At the end of the second year of therapy when the adoption was about to become final, Sandra's adoptive father was to be transferred to another part of the country. They had three more months in their present location. The termination phase of therapy was devoted to helping Sandra separate from the therapist and to use the feelings stimulated by this separation to work through further her earlier trauma related to loss.

When she first heard that her family was moving away, she told the therapist she did not know whether she was going with them. When the therapist asked her what she meant, she said, "It's all the same." The therapist suggested that she might need to protect herself against the fear and pain of being left. She responded, "My mommy left me after I came here."

Providing food for others from whom she had separated previously was repeated with the therapist as her separation from the therapist approached. Sandra routinely met with the therapist before lunch. She would ordinarily eat her lunch in the car on the way back to school. During the last month of therapy, she decided to eat her lunch in the therapy room, saying she was hungry. She wanted to share her food with the therapist and seemed to experience pleasure in feeding her. She talked about a party before leaving her previous foster home. She was appropriately sad during the last session and acknowledged the significance of eating with the therapist. The therapist helped the child relate the feelings of not seeing the therapist anymore to earlier separations and clarified her attendant feelings and their meanings.

Gradually, during the last weeks, Sandra dealt with her feelings related to being a member of her new family. She began to talk excitedly about her new house and her new room. She seemed genuinely pleased that her adoptive parents would allow her to choose the room she wanted. At the same time, she remembered and with appropriate sadness talked about her past experiences and the people she missed. One day, she wrote after her name the last names of all the people who had ever been important to her, starting with her biological father who she had never met and ending with the name of her new adoptive family . Each one revived a memory. In one session she directly expressed anger about her abandonment by the therapist, by her first foster family, and by her biological mother in favor of someone else. This anger emerged while comparing a picture she had done with one done by a previous child (a boy). The therapist reflected that maybe she thought the boy was preferred to her.

In the last session, she was able to share memories and wishes, both positive and negative, related to her earlier life with her biological family. She said her mother had come to New York to get married and the man hadn't wanted Sandra around. This was the first time she had told this to anyone.

At the time she ended therapy, Sandra was one of the best students in her first-grade class, was accepted socially by other children, and was a well-functioning member of her new family. Although the therapist encouraged her to write if she wished to do so, no further communication was received from her or her family.

## DISCUSSION

The therapeutic goal for the two children described here was to help them work through their previous (and concurrent) losses. Both the losses and the quality of the relationships that preceded them placed in jeopardy the children's ongoing development and their capacity to attach to their new caretakers. As a result of the gradual working through of their feelings and conflicts linked to these earlier life experiences, they were able, in varying degrees, to reverse their developmental delays and invest in their new caretakers.

Both children had been abandoned by their biological families. Sandra's memories included positive interactions with her grandparents. Benny appeared to have been mothered primarily by his sister and his memories revolved around her and the stories she told him about their earlier life with family members. These earlier significant extended family members were central to the formation and maintenance of the emotional lives of these children. For Sandra, her grandparents appear to have been a more stabilizing force. Her earlier attachments enabled her to trust and attach more easily in new relationships, in spite of the rejection by her first foster parents.

The fact that the major caretaking role in Benny's earlier life was played by his 6-year-old sister, herself severely deprived, placed Benny at predictably higher risk. His loyalty to, and identification with, his sister represented his struggle to keep himself emotionally alive. At the same time this identi-fication not only impeded him from attaching to his foster mother, but threatened her ability to attach to him. Treatment involved intense and persistent work on both sides.

The literature supports the importance of siblings to each other after they leave their biological parents (Samuels 1990). It is not uncommon in the face of inadequate parenting for an older sibling to assume the role of par-ent who makes sacrifices for the younger child (Bank and Kahn 1982). During World War II, children in England whose parents had died and who took care of each other in a concentration camp became upset and suspi-cious of adult intervention when separated (Freud and Dann 1951).

Similarly Benny was stubbornly attached to his sister. In spite of his iden-tification with her rebelliousness, this attachment provided him with a foun-dation based on which he was better able to benefit from a good foster home and therapy. It is probable that adult(s) earlier in life had also provided some islands of care and nurturance, but a complete history was not available.

Abandonment has a profound negative effect on children's self accep-tance and self esteem (Samuels 1995). This was true of these two children. Their sense of worthiness and being loved, appreciated, and good was shaken (Bibring 1953). There was intolerable injury to their fantasied omnipotence (Wolfenstein 1969). The children expressed fears of further abandonment and revealed feelings of not being good enough. Sandra indicated in play and verbalization that she had not done a good enough job of taking care of her mother and called herself a dummy, and Benny destroyed his pictures.

Lags in ego functions, regressive symptoms, anxiety, anger, depression, guilt, and narcissistic rage were symptoms seen in these children. These symptoms are reactions to the children's pain and confirm reports in other studies (Brinich 1980, Burland et al. 1981, Frankel 1991, Kliman et al. 1982, Nickman 1985, Samuels 1995, Smith 1979). As can be seen in the present study, these reactions are reenacted in later situations that resemble the children's earlier life traumatic experiences.

Their reactions to separation support the literature on the negative ef-fects of loss on ego functioning (Bowlby 1980, Furman 1974, Kliman et al. 1982, Milrod 1988, Sorosky et al. 1975, Warfield 1972, Wolfenstein 1966, 1969, 1973, Zelman et al. 1985). As their conflicts were dealt with in therapy and they mourned and appropriately reworked their feelings related to their previous caretakers, they reached higher levels of ego integration and func-tioning (Loewald 1971). At the end of therapy, both children were func-tioning better cognitively, and many of their regressive behaviors and mal-adaptive symptoms were reduced or were no longer present. Both children expressed their narcisstic rage, especially when faced with the risk of another abandonment. The narcissistic rage at being abandoned and made to feel helpless leads to an attempt to get away from the helpless and passive feelings of rejection and low self-esteem. Mastery is commonly attempted through turning passive into active. Benny teased and tested his foster mother and the therapist when he felt helpless. Before and during the therapist's first vacation he regressed and his oppositional symptoms increased. Sandra was sure the therapist was not coming back from vacation. This belief was her way of trying to master the loss in advance. The child may also actively search for the lost parent, a common reaction of adopted children (Sorosky et al. 1975). Sandra went for a walk in her neighborhood and imagined she would find her mother.

Each child reacted differently to anger about being separated from significant others. Sandra blamed herself more for not doing a good enough job of taking care of her mother. When her mother totally abandoned her, she was afraid her mother had died. Her regression to magical thinking led her to fear that her angry wishes would come true (Fraiberg 1957). Later in therapy, she was able to be more irate about her mother's not being there for her. She also felt freer to test her limits in her second foster home where she felt more secure about expressing her feelings. Benny's anger was uncontrollable at times and more problematic, probably reflecting the degree of his earlier deprivation and helplessness. Similarly, the difficulty he had taking responsibility for his hostile behavior reflected the degree of his unneutralized aggression and primitiveness of his self and object representations.

Especially early in his placement and in therapy, it was observed that Benny had widespread development arrest and unmanageable, impulsive behavior. His reactions to his separation from his sister caused an upheaval and he became disorganized and overwhelmed. He needed more structure and control from without. He was regressed and lacked higher level ego functioning. His symptoms were, at times, uncontrollable in all settings. Sandra had a higher level of ego development and did not regress as much as Benny did. She was a likable child and was able to relate positively to others, suggesting that there was a positive primary attachment in her early life. She was less impulsive and unmanageable. She was constricted and "too good," especially immediately after being separated from her mother. She was also intellectually blocked, as revealed by early testing of her intellectual ability.

Anxiety about being abandoned again was easily stimulated by any possibility of rejection. Benny acted out whenever he became anxious. He teased other children in school when he couldn't perform academically, threw things, teased the therapist and refused to leave her office when it was time to end sessions. Sandra was "too good" after her mother abandoned her. She acted like a pseudo-adult, took care of the therapist, was conforming and meticulous at home, and complied with her mother's injunction not to cry. This behavior appeared to be a way for her to ward off the anxiety of not being a good enough girl, as well as her fear of her mother's retribution. It was maladaptive, however, because it prevented her from protesting her abandonment. Later in therapy, when she was anxious about being abandoned again when the foster family was planning to move, she shrugged her shoulders and said, "It's all the same."

The affective response of depression can occur when an individual feels helpless and resigned in the face of pain (Sandler and Joffee 1965). In therapy, the children were more and more able to tolerate their depression and to mourn their previously lost relationships. Subsequently, their regressive and maladaptive behavior decreased as well. Sandra was able to tolerate more depression than Benny although he was able to express his sadness without acting out later in therapy. Sandra drew teardrops on water and, as she did so, she sadly and pleadingly called her mother on the play phone asking her where she was. She was depressed when she was removed from her first foster home and when she had vacation separations from the therapist. When feeling depressed, she commonly made the therapist do exactly what she did, such as their drawing side by side. It appeared to be an attempt to control and manipulate the therapist as a perceived powerful person to assure herself that she was not weak, inadequate, and helpless (Kohut 1971). Early in therapy, she defended against depression and sadness of her loss by using the defense of reversal of affect. She would become manic and sing when sadness would have been the more appropriate emotion. Benny tended to express his helplessness and feelings of emptiness related to separation from his sister and his therapist through his provocative and oppositional behavior.

Three special aspects of psychotherapeutic work with disturbed foster children, illustrated in the cases of Benny and Sandra, should be mentioned. First, the frequent absence of information concerning their earlier history and relationships requires that the therapist pay especially close attention to their communications, especially nonverbal, and their modes of relating to the therapist. This is essential if the therapist is to reconstruct with the children an emotionally relevant account of their experience. An understanding of developmentally determined defenses and reactions to trauma and loss is needed for this work.

Second, the therapist must be prepared for a variety of intense transference reactions: with Sandra, the need to please the therapist and deny anger or disappointment with her; with Benny, his compulsive provocativeness. Awareness of such transferences will allow the therapist to master and make productive use of the corresponding countertransference reactions: complacence with Sandra and anger with Benny.

Third, because of the predictably low self-esteem of children who have been abandoned, it is especially important to identify, support, and acknowledge children's strengths and adaptive capacities. Accordingly, the therapist frequently encouraged and commended Benny for his persistence in doing things until they were right and supported his wish to win in games. Such positive "real person" interventions play a role in opening up obstacles to more normative development (Cohen and Solnit 1993).

The foster care workers assigned to the two children discussed in this paper realized these children needed therapeutic intervention. They were helpful in recognizing the importance of introducing Sandra to her new family slowly and in making the transfer to the new home a cooperative one between the first and second families by explaining the reason for her leaving her first foster home, and in taking care not to blame the child for the failure (Jewett 1978, Samuels 1990). In Benny's case, they made it possible for him to continue seeing his sister, who was a primary caretaker and significant link to the child's earlier life.

Contact with biological parents has been recommended by others, whether the children are in foster homes or are adopted (Burland et al. 1981, Colon 1978, Fanshel and Shinn 1978, Kliman et al. 1982). The need to find connections with one's biological heritage is strong in many adopted children (Samuels 1990). One study found that foster children who maintained contact with their biological parents showed significantly greater emotional and intellectual gains than did those who did not (Fanshel and Shinn 1978). Sandra's adoptive mother said she was in favor of the child's looking for her mother when she grew up. This was judged to be a sincere belief on her part and it is expected that she will help her to do so when she is of age. Benny's adoptive mother had a difficult time after he came back from visits to his sister. Nevertheless, she verbalized the recognition that it was important that they be in touch with each other and allowed his sister to visit overnight during holidays, despite her misgivings. Throughout therapy, Benny wanted his sister to be adopted with him and had a hard time accepting his happiness in his new home. It is suggested that he felt guilty about his adoption, especially since he was the only child in his adoptive family, perhaps accentuating the exclusion of his sister.

Meeting with the foster parents is considered to be essential to prevent them from reacting inappropriately to the children's behavior. Without supportive parent guidance, such children often repeat negative behaviors that lead to rejection by foster parents. Accordingly, Sandra was rejected when, after a honeymoon period common following placement, she began to manifest maladaptive symptoms (Samuels 1990). Fortunately, her second family was well chosen.

Benny's foster mother needed a great deal of support and met with the therapist weekly throughout therapy. Sandra's foster parents met with the therapist bimonthly. The foster parents were reassured that they were important partners with the professionals in helping the children. The therapist empathized with their problems and reactions to the children's behavior. They were helped to not react "personally" to the children's negative reactions and to learn appropriate management techniques to cope with the children's behavior. For example, with the therapist's help and in sessions with the child, Benny's foster mother was able to become more empathetic. This reduced his symptomatology significantly. With the therapist's support, she, as well as Sandra's parents, was helped to answer the child's questions and to encourage and accept the oftentimes idealized memories of the biological family. The parents were encouraged to verbalize to the children that they were wanted and would remain in the family regardless of their misbehavior.

Both children's symptoms increased when they were told they were going to be adopted, a common reaction in such children, since the hope of acceptance intensifies fear of rejection. After being told they were going to be adopted, the children tried to master this fear by acting out in their future adoptive homes. Both children were rejected from previous foster homes after expressing symptoms not acceptable to their foster parents, as unfortunately happens all too frequently. Without therapy and parental help by the therapist, the acting out could have led to another abandonment.

It is unlikely (and perhaps impossible) that these children have mourned totally the loss of their biological parents. Without getting involved in the debate as to whether children are capable of mourning fully or not before the end of adolescence (Wolfenstein 1966), it can be assumed that children such as Benny and Sandra, who have suffered early losses coupled with chronic stress, will be vulnerable to stress later in life. Adolescence in particular, when identity problems are predominant issues for adopted children, may restimulate old conflicts.

However, both children were developmentally on track when therapy ended. Sandra said she would write to the therapist but neither she nor her parents did so. Benny was seen intermittently by the therapist for many years. The last time he was seen, he was 15 years old. He was having some adolescent conflicts with his foster mother, which she needed help to deal with. He had a B average in the private school he was attending and he was planning on going to college. He had friends and he coped without regressing. He was able to talk with appropriate sadness about his sister's involvement with drugs and its negative effect on her. It is felt that therapeutic intervention at a critical time had helped these children to develop sufficient inner stability to enable them to cope adequately with future losses and stress.

## REFERENCES

Ament, A. (1972). The boy who did not cry. *Child Welfare* 51:104–109.

Auestad, A. M. (1992). I am father's baby—you can have the turtle: psychotherapy in a family context. *Journal of Child Psychotherapy* 18:57–74.

Bank, S., and Kahn, M. (1982). *The Sibling Bond*. New York: Basic Books.

Barden, J. C. (1990). Foster care system reeling, despite law meant to help. *The New York Times*, Sept. 21, Al, pp. 18–19.

Bibring, E. (1953). The mechanism of depression. In *Affective Disorders*, ed. P. Greenacre, pp. 13–48. New York: International Universities Press.

Bowlby, J. (1969). *Attachment. Attachment and Loss (Vol. I)*. New York: Basic Books.

——— (1973). *Separation. Anxiety and Anger (Vol. II)*. New York: Basic Books.

——— (1980). *Loss. Attachment and Loss. Sadness and Depression (Vol. III)*. New York: Basic Books.

Brandell, J. R. (1992). Psychotherapy of a traumatized 10-year-old boy: theoretical issues and clinical considerations. *Smith College Studies in Social Work* 62:123–138.

Brinich, P. M. (1980). Some potential effects of adoption on self and object representations. In *Psychoanalytic Study of the Child* 35:107–133. New Haven, CT: Yale University Press.

Burland, J. A., Kliman, G. W., and Meers, D. (1981). Psychoanalytic observations of foster care. *Journal of Preventive Psychiatry* 1:37–45.

Clifton, P. M., and Ransom, J. W. (1975). An approach to working with the "placed child." *Child Psychiatry and Human Development* 6:107–117.

Cohen, J. (1981). *Adoption Breakdown with Older Children*. Toronto: Faculty of Social Work, University of Toronto.

Cohen, P. M., and Solnit, A. J. (1993). Play and therapeutic action. In *Psychoanalytic Study of the Child* 48:49–63. New Haven, CT: Yale University Press.

Colon, F. (1978). Family ties and child placement. *Family Process* 17:289–313.

Committee on Finance, United States Senate (1990). Foster care adoption assistance and child welfare services. Washington, DC: U.S. Government Printing Office.

Defries, Z., Jenkins, S., and Williams, E. C. (1964). Treatment of disturbed children in foster care. *American Journal of Orthopsychiatry* 34:615–624.

Demb, J. M. (1993). The written word in psychotherapy with a latency age girl. *Journal of the American Academy of Child and Adolescent Psychiatry* 32:26–31.

Fanshel, D., and Shinn, E. (1978). *Children in Foster Care: A Longitudinal Investigation.* New York: Columbia University Press.

Festinger, T. (1986). *Necessary Risks: A Study of Adoptions and Disrupted Adoption Placements.* Washington, DC: Child Welfare League of America.

Flashman, A. J. (1992). The moment of recognition. In *Psychoanalytic Study of the Child* 47:351–369. New Haven, CT: Yale University Press.

Fraiberg, S. (1957). *The Magic Years: Understanding and Handling the Problems of Early Childhood.* New York: Scribner.

Frankel, S. A. (1991). Pathogenic factors in the experience of early and late adopted children. In *Psychoanalytic Study of the Child* 46:91–108. New Haven, CT: Yale University Press.

Freud, A., and Dann, S. (1951). An experiment in group upbringing. In *Psychoanalytic Study of the Child* 6:127–168. New York: International Universities Press.

Freud, S. (1917). Mourning and melancholia. *Standard Edition* 18:3–64.

Furman, E. (1974). *A Child's Parent Dies: Studies in Childhood Bereavement.* New Haven, CT: Yale University Press.

Haith, M. M. (1986). Sensory and perceptual processes in early childhood. *Journal of Pediatrics* 109:158–171.

Harmon, R. J., Wagonfeld, M. D., and Ende, R. N. (1982). Anaclitic depression. A follow-up from infancy to puberty. In *Psychoanalytic Study of the Child* 37:67–94. New Haven, CT: Yale University Press.

High, H. (1982). The consequences of severe deprivation as they emerged in the psychotherapy of a girl in foster care. *Journal of Child Psychotherapy* 8:37–55.

Hoopes, J. L. (1982). *Prediction in Child Development. A Longitudinal Study of Adoptive and Non-Adoptive Families.* New York: Child Welfare League.

Jewett, C. L. (1978). *Adopting the Older Child.* Harvard, MA: Harvard Common Press.

Kaplan, A. (1982). Growing up in foster care: one boy's struggles. *Journal of Child Psychotherapy* 8:57–66.

Kaplan, L. K., and Turitz, L. L. (1957). Treatment of severely traumatized young children in a foster home setting. *American Journal of Orthopsychiatry* 27:271–285.

Kegerreis, S. (1993). From a gang of two back to a family. *Psychoanalytic Psychotherapy* 7:69–83.

Kliman, G. W., Schaeffer, M. H., and Friedman, M. J. (1982). *Preventive Mental Health Services for Children Entering Foster Home Care. An Assessment.* White Plains, NY: Center for Preventive Psychiatry.

Kohut, H. (1971). *The Analysis of the Self.* New York: International Universities Press.

Kubler-Ross, E. (1970). *On Death and Dying.* New York: Macmillan.

Lindholm, B., and Touliatos, J. (1980). Psychological adjustment of adopted and non-adopted children. *Psychological Reports* 6:307–310.

Loewald, H. W. (1971). The transference neurosis. In *Papers on Psychoanalysis*, pp. 221–256. New Haven, CT: Yale University Press, 1980.

Lopez, T., and Kliman, G. W. (1979). Memory, reconstruction and mourning in the analysis of a four year old child. In *Psychoanalytic Study of the Child* 34:235–271. New Haven, CT: Yale University Press.

Lush, D., Boston, M., and Grainger, E. (1991). Evaluation of psychoanalytic psychotherapy with children: therapists' assessments and predictions. *Psychoanalytic Psychotherapy* 5:191–234.

Mayes, L. C., and Cohen, D. J. (1992). The development of a capacity for imagination in early childhood. In *Psychoanalytic Study of the Child* 47:23–47. New Haven, CT: Yale University Press.

Milrod, D. (1988). A current view of the psychoanalytic theory of depression. In *Psychoanalytic Study of the Child* 43:83–99. New Haven, CT: Yale University Press.

National Committee for Adoption (1985). *Adoption Factbook: U.S. Data, Issues, Regulations, and Resources.* Washington, DC: U.S. Government Printing Office.

Nickman, S. L. (1985). Losses in adoption. The need for dialogue. In *Psychoanalytic Study of the Child* 40:365–398. New Haven, CT: Yale University Press.

Piaget, J., and Inhelder, B. (1969). *The Psychology of the Child.* New York: Basic Books.

Pine, F. (1985). *Developmental Theory and Clinical Process.* New Haven, CT: Yale University Press.

Reeves, A.C. (1971). Children with surrogate parents: cases seen in analytic therapy and an aetiological hypothesis. *British Journal of Medical Psychology* 44: 155–171.

Samuels, S. C. (1977). *Enhancing Self-Concept in Early Childhood. Theory and Practice.* New York: Human Science Press.

——— (1990). *Ideal Adoption. A Comprehensive Guide to Forming An Adoptive Family.* New York: Plenum.

——— (1995).Treatment of Two Foster Children to Help Them Mourn Past Relationships. In *Psychoanalytic Study of the Child* 50:308–326. New Haven, CT: Yale University Press.

Sandler, J., and Joffee, W. G. (1965). Notes on childhood depression. *International Journal of Psycho-Analysis* 46:88–96.

Schaeffer, M. H., Kliman, G. W., Friedman, M. J., and Pasquariella, B. G. (1981). Children in foster care: a preventive service and research program for a high risk population. *Journal of Preventive Psychiatry* 1:47–56.

Simon, N. M., and Senturra, A. G. (1966). Adoption and psychiatric illness. *American Journal of Psychiatry* 122:858–868.

Smith, W. R., Jr. (1979). The foster child. In *Basic Handbook of Child Psychiatry. Development (Vol. I)*, ed. J. D. Noshpitz, pp. 348–356. New York: Basic Books.

Sorosky, A. D., Baran, A., and Pannor, R. (1975). Identity conflicts in adoptees. *American Journal of Orthopsychiatry* 45:18–27.

Stein, E., Rae-Grant, N., Ackland, S., and Avision, W. (1994). Psychiatric disorders of children in care. Methodology and demographic correlates. *Canadian Journal of Psychiatry* 39:341–347.

Stern, D. M. (1985). *The Interpersonal World of the Infant.* New York: Basic Books.

Warfield, M. J. (1972). Treatment of a two-year-old in preparation for adoption. *Social Casework* 53:341–347.

Wolfenstein, M. (1966). How is mourning possible? In *Psychoanalytic Study of the Child* 21:93–123. New York: International Universities Press.

——— (1969). Loss, rage and repetition. In *Psychoanalytic Study of the Child* 24:432–460. New York: International Universities Press.

——— (1973). The image of the lost parent. In *Psychoanalytic Study of the Child* 28: 433–456. New Haven, CT: Yale University Press.

Zelman, A., Samuels, S., and Abrams, D. (1985). IQ changes of young children following intensive long-term psychotherapy. *Journal of Psychology* 34:215–217.

# III

# HOMELESS CHILDREN

# 7

# The Treatment of Homeless Children and Families: Integrating Mental Health Services into a Head Start Model*

*Paul J. Donahue*

Providers of educational and other service programs designed for homeless children and families have been forced to confront the mental health needs of this population (Buckner et al. 1993, Goodman et al. 1991, Hausmen and Hammer 1993). Increasingly, they have come to recognize that service plans are often derailed by inadequate assessment and treatment of mental health problems. There is also an emerging consensus among researchers and clinicians that to be effective, mental health interventions with homeless children and adults must be coordinated with other community-based services (Goodman et al. 1991, Toro et al. 1991).

This paper will describe an attempt, over the course of six years, to integrate mental health services into a Head Start program for homeless children. The two collaborating agencies are The Center for Preventive Psychiatry (CPP), an outpatient child psychiatry clinic specializing in the treatment of young children and families, and St. Bernard's Center for Learning, which serves over 100 homeless, primarily African-American children and their families each year. Both programs are located in White Plains, NY.

Recent reports suggest that the majority of Head Start programs serve many children in need of mental health services and that such services must focus on prevention and family interventions (Piotrkowski et al. 1994). Like many homeless pre-schoolers (Molnar et al. 1990), the children at St.

---

*This chapter is based on a presentation to the American Orthopsychiatric Association, Washington, DC, April 29, 1994.

Bernard's present additional challenges. Many are underimmunized and see health providers for acute care only. Chronic respiratory illnesses, fatigue, and poor nutrition are common. Most of the children exhibit speech and language delays, poorly developed social skills, and a limited repertoire of play behaviors. Fighting, cursing, and other impulsive, oppositional, and aggressive behaviors are frequently seen in the classrooms. Many of the children have short attention spans and little tolerance for frustration. Some attach to adults indiscriminately; others remain isolated and withdrawn. Teacher observations at St. Bernard's have corroborated research findings indicating that homeless children suffer from depression, anxiety, and other forms of emotional disturbances in disproportionate numbers (Bassuk and Rosenburg 1988, Bassuk and Rubin 1987, Molnar 1988).

From the beginning, the administrative staff of St. Bernard's recognized that they had to make adjustments in the Head Start model to effectively serve these children. Classrooms had fewer children and more teachers, transitions were kept to a minimum, extra food was served, and a curriculum was designed that more accurately reflected the children's developmental abilities. These modifications were helpful, but the teachers were still hard pressed to cope with the children's anger and sadness and the tales of violence and deprivation they brought to school every day.

Typical play, for example, included establishing a "jail," and making "arrests" for violent crimes or drug offenses. One group of children repeatedly set the "breakfast table" with "beer." It was not unusual for mealtime talk to include descriptions of physical fights involving parents. Many children were extremely frightened by fire alarms during routine drills, painful reminders of the frequent, forced excursions out of shelters in the middle of the night. Some wondered aloud if the police or child protective workers were coming to take them away. Teachers were unsure how to respond or make use of these communications.

The severity of the problems presented by the families of the children also presented challenges to the staff of St. Bernard's. Many of the mothers had limited self-care skills and were ill-prepared to cope with the responsibility of living on their own and rearing children. While they were eager to enroll their children in the program, they were often impatient or noncompliant with Head Start regulations regarding attendance, intake procedures, and parent participation. Still in their late teens and early twenties, many were the sole caretakers of three or more preschool children. Few of these women were in stable relationships. Many were veterans of many shelters and had been homeless for years.

Other factors complicated the work with parents. It became apparent that many had substance abuse problems. The most recent report by the social workers at St. Bernard's indicated that 63 percent of the families had a parent struggling with alcohol or drug abuse, more than double the number reported in other surveys of homeless adults (Buckner et al. 1993). Teachers usually chose to steer clear of references in the children's play to drugs and alcohol use, as they were not comfortable addressing these issues with them or their parents.

Less easy to avoid was the mothers' obvious emotional distress. Many were clearly depressed and some spoke openly of being victims, past or present, of sexual or physical abuse. The social workers' reports on the frequency of abuse would place this population towards the high end of research estimates (ranging from 27–64 percent) of the number of homeless women who have been victims of violence (Browne 1993). One mother casually reported a history of 15 suicide attempts. Many verbalized wishes to be rid of their children.

## THE INITIAL COLLABORATION

The Center had always welcomed referrals from St. Bernard's, but transportation problems, lack of child care, and other logistical difficulties often prevented even the more motivated families from receiving services from The Center's nearby clinic. Three years after the establishment of St. Bernard's, its director invited The Center to join forces to serve these multi-problem families. In the first year of the collaboration, two social workers from The Center began work as mental health consultants at St. Bernard's, meeting regularly with teaching staff from each classroom, with the executive director, and with other administrative and support staff. They adopted a model that had been successfully applied to a number of other area daycare and Head Start programs, who utilized The Center's consultants to assist staff in developing classroom structure, behavioral management techniques, and nurturing and flexible environments. The consultants observed and screened individual children, assisted teachers in working with them, and facilitated referrals when needed.

For a variety of reasons, this model proved to be insufficient for the needs of the staff and children at St. Bernard's. Severely strained by the constant demands of the children, the teachers had little energy left over to focus on the advice of other professionals. Although some of them were reassured by the presence of the consultants and welcomed their input, the majority seemed not to benefit greatly from their interventions. Some of the difficulties encountered were typical, as mental health clinicians and daycare personnel have been shown to differ in their ideas about such child development issues as the use of rewards and punishment, the importance of dependency needs, and the value of the expression of negative feelings (Zelman et al. 1986) (see Chapter 13).

While some teachers did learn, with the consultants' help, to tolerate and even facilitate their students' expression of sadness and anger, it was difficult for them (and at times, the consultants) not to take a judgmental stance towards the children and their caretakers. For example, children who hoarded toys might be seen as "greedy" rather than deprived, while children who inconveniently locked doors and were ever alert for intruders were seen as disruptive rather than fearful. Attempts by the consultants to reframe these behaviors often left the teachers feeling criticized or invalidated.

The consultants' observations about the children's emotional distress were often seen by the teachers as labeling or stigmatizing the disenfranchised families they served. Like other providers who serve homeless children, many of the staff members at St. Bernard's initially believed that the children's problems could be traced primarily to their living situation, and could be overcome by providing them adequate housing and a nurturing school environment.

However, the greatest obstacle to the success of the consultation model was posed by the magnitude and intensity of the needs of the children themselves. With some coaching, one teacher tried to reach an abused, withdrawn boy through puppet play, but as he began to communicate his fears, she became frustrated by not knowing where to go next. The teachers were puzzled by another boy who sometimes washed his face with milk and once became petrified by a religious icon, thinking it was dripping real blood. They grew disconcerted and frightened by a third boy, who had witnessed violent fights with knives at home. He bit his hand until he bled, drank from a toilet, and threatened to jump off a balcony, announcing "I want to kill myself." The teachers were confused and discouraged by what they heard and witnessed, and they tread lightly when confronted with troubling material, fearing that they might open a Pandora's box of feelings that they could not contain or alleviate.

The consultants from The Center were also feeling a sense of helplessness, due in part to the limitations imposed by their roles. They were not sure, for example, how much family information to divulge or how many prescriptions to offer to the teachers, for fear of overwhelming them with the children's distress and of burdening them with additional work. A situation resulted in which both parties felt disappointed and unappreciated.

At the same time, the children showed a need and an ability to communicate their experiences, and they often attempted to draw the consultants into their play. One 3-year-old boy, whose father had recently left his family, went immediately to the doll house each time the consultant entered his classroom. He would enact for her a scene of abandonment with adult and child figures, sensing perhaps that she was someone who could understand and help him.

These frustrations were compounded by the failure of the referrals made to The Center's main clinic. In one year's time, only 2 of the 24 families referred to The Center became engaged in treatment in any meaningful way. Typically parents would request help for their child, agree to an initial treatment plan, but not return.

The commitment of the staff of St. Bernard's and particularly the work of the social workers, who helped parents with concrete services such as housing searches, school registrations, medical appointments, and food deliveries, had laid the foundation of trust necessary for the formation of therapeutic alliances. As this Head Start program gradually transformed itself into a full service community agency, it became increasingly clear that mental health services would likely be better utilized if provided on-site and under the auspices of St. Bernard's.

## ON-SITE TREATMENT: THE "BOYS GROUP"

By the third year of the collaboration, the clinicians from The Center had joined forces with the staff of St. Bernard's to evaluate most of the older children at St. Bernard's, with the aim of developing individual educational and treatment plans prior to their entering kindergarten. These assessments revealed that many of the children were in need of intensive therapeutic and educational interventions. As a result, a twice-weekly play therapy group for boys aged 4 and 5 was established, with a psychologist and social worker from The Center as the leaders. Seven boys who exhibited severe behavioral problems in their classrooms were referred to the group. Parents met with the therapists at monthly intervals to discuss their child's progress and any other issues that emerged at school.

Once given a safe opportunity to express themselves, the intensity of the boys' distress became apparent. Though engaging, they were extremely active and impulsive, and they displayed much hostility and sadism towards the therapists and each other. For example, the boys often pretended they were dogs, with one as master who brutalized the others. In playing the role of teachers, they were aggressive and vicious. One boy repeatedly slammed down his instruction book to frighten his "students." Another screamed at his "assistant," "I hired you and I can fire you!" The boys' bravado seemed to represent an attempt to ward off fears of being punished or devoured by merciless forces. They often wanted to be turned into monsters, lest they be eaten by one. In addition, the boys often expressed fear that the therapists would hit or scream at them, or tell the teacher of their "bad" behavior.

As the group evolved, themes of rejection and abandonment were increasingly expressed. One boy told the group that he wanted to "divorce" his parents because they did not pay attention to him. Another boy, whose father had left him as an infant and whose mother was a heavy substance abuser, sadly stated, "My parents died." The boys surprisingly demonstrated a capacity for tolerating such expressions of vulnerability and could offer words of comfort to each other.

Gradually hostility gave way to group cohesiveness. For example, the boys staged a weekly dance contest, and allowed an awkward boy, previously an outsider, to participate as the emcee. At the same time their play became less rigid, more coherent, and more positive. "Good dogs" could be differentiated from "bad dogs" by their behavior, and the police could intervene in helpful ways to protect the former. Similarly a "good drink" could turn the monsters back into normal boys, and the male therapist into a "superhero" who could protect everyone.

The boys grew more open in their requests, albeit ambivalent, for nurturance, especially from the female therapist. For example, they asked her to be the "kissing shark" who would protect them from monsters. The boys also more readily acknowledged their fears and worries to each other, as well as their wish to be safe and cared for. During the final weeks of this six-month group, the boys "built" a home for themselves, a "safe house" with smoke alarms and locks on the doors, that would keep all frightening things away.

The group thus proved to be an effective method for reaching these boys, and it showed that the careful use of dramatic play techniques could be a powerful intervention with traumatized homeless children. In providing a safe arena for the boys to express their anger and aggression, the group facilitated their socialization and fostered the development of empathy. The group provided the boys a secure place to reveal their fears, while at least temporarily setting aside their counterphobic bravado. Over time, they were able to request comfort and support from the group leaders, and showed evidence of identifying with them as strong yet benevolent adults.

Despite these gains, sustaining the group another year seemed a difficult proposition. The therapists often felt overwhelmed by the boys' intense hostility on the one hand and their profound neediness on the other. Compounding this stress was the lack of integration of the boys' group in the overall structure of St. Bernard's. The therapists were not full-fledged members of the classroom teams, and were painfully aware that the insights and gains provided by the small group process were not integrated into the daily classroom routine. For children who clearly benefited from these dual services, this seemed a wasted opportunity. The therapists also had little time for meetings with the social service staff, who often had greater access to, and information about, the families.

Both the successes and limitations of the group forced a reevaluation of The Center's role at St. Bernard's. It was clear that many children could benefit from an intensive group treatment model. On the other hand, it was also evident that a greater investment of clinical staff time would be needed both to ensure the continuation of the program and to maximize its effectiveness. It was also apparent that on-site mental health services would have to be more integrated into the overall Head Start experience. In order to develop adequate working relationships with parents, for example, the therapists would have to play a more active role at St. Bernard's, and become part of the nonthreatening community that made families feel welcome there.

## TOWARD AN INTEGRATED MODEL:
## THE THERAPEUTIC NURSERY

In the fourth year, the two agencies agreed to join forces to form a therapeutic nursery located at St. Bernard's. The nursery was modeled after the Cornerstone nursery (Kliman 1975, Lopez and Kliman 1980) originated at The Center in the late 1960s utilizing principles of child development, education and psychodynamically informed therapy. The model has evolved into an intensive milieu for disadvantaged children who have been abused, abandoned or otherwise traumatized, and cannot be maintained in other preschool environments (see Chapter 2).

The therapeutic nursery was designed as a half-day treatment program for the Head Start children who manifested the most severe behavioral and emotional problems. It operates five days a week, three hours per day. It is staffed by a psychologist and social worker from The Center, and by a masters-level teacher and two assistant teachers from St. Bernard's. Enrollment is limited to 12 children. Parents are encouraged to attend at least two nursery sessions a month and to join in monthly family group activities at the school. However, the parents are made aware that the nursery is always open to them. There is great variability in parents' utilization of this opportunity. One parent, for example, attended the nursery almost every day for a month in order to get support to avoid a relapse of drug use. Other parents are only able to tolerate infrequent attendance.

During the first year, the nursery staff members were quickly put to task. Like the boys in the group the year before, the children who were referred to the nursery were angry and aggressive, highly anxious, and sexually precocious. One boy frequently banged his head on the floor. Another seemed lost in fantasy. An attractive, diminutive girl cursed compulsively.

The children in the nursery all came from chaotic family situations, and had experienced more traumas than any group seen previously by the clinicians at St. Bernard's. A large proportion of the children had been physically abused, and many of their families were already involved with child protective services. Nearly all of the children had been witness to violent acts. Most had a family member struggling with a long-term substance abuse problem.

The combination of the children's profound sadness and longings for connection, and their intense rage, forced the staff to be both active, nurturant caretakers, and strong, physical presences capable of limiting their destructive behavior. The latter responsibility, in particular, pushed the therapists into fierce and intimate contact with the children, as the teachers expected them to intervene when the children lost control. They found that physically restraining and struggling with the children was the most draining and emotionally wrenching aspect of the work. Despite recent evidence of the validity and importance of physical encounters with children (Bath 1994), the therapists were often hard pressed not to question their professional self-concept when they heard a child protest, "Stop, you're hurting me!" or "I'll tell my mother you beat me." Often unsure of how the teachers would react to these encounters, the therapists at times felt alone and unsupported by them.

Four years into the nursery, all the team members now recognize the importance of confronting violence in the nursery, and they take turns responding to the children's angry outbursts. The teachers readily accept the idea that feelings of helplessness and insecurity often lie beneath the children's bravado, and they understand that physical restraint is not only inevitable but necessary in order to reduce the need for such defenses. The staff's interventions with 4-year-old Billy, who often threw chairs or punched other children, illustrates this work. When confronted, his behavior would escalate, and he would kick and scratch his therapist. After a prolonged struggle, he would break down and cry, often saying, "I want my Mommy," and admit that he was sad and lonely and wished to be close to people. Another 4-year-old boy, Gerard, often entered the nursery in an enraged state of mind, and would attack other children. While being held by a staff member, he would sadly acknowledge, "I was put in the corner [at home] again this morning."

The nursery is intended to function as a therapeutic milieu—a safe, predictable setting designed to protect and validate the children, and to help them connect with positive aspects of the larger world. For many, it is the one stable environment in which they can enjoy the rituals and rites of childhood free from fear of intrusions or disruptions. These are children who sometimes fear that Santa Claus might be coming to kill them rather than deliver presents. Holiday celebrations, birthday parties, group outings, and graduation festivities solidify and intensify the bonds the children form with each other, the teachers, and the therapists. The children are also active participants in the two daily meals in the nursery, delivering and serving the food, and sharing stories of home and tales of the day while eating together with members of the team.

The children's involvement in the group is not intended as a substitute for their family ties. Parents are encouraged to attend and participate in birthday parties and other special events, as well as biweekly meetings. Such events often serve the dual functions of meeting the parents' needs and validating and reenforcing their parental role. Some parents seem to enjoy them more than their children, and want to participate in all the group activities. Many celebrations are aimed specifically at enhancing the children's connections to their parents. The teachers and the children work together on cards for parents on Valentine's Day, and on making gifts and learning songs for Mother's Day. On one such occasion, 3-year-old Marcus presented his mother with a six-pack of soda at a Mother's Day party, a tribute to her thirty days of sobriety.

Parents are often helped to speak about difficult issues in the daily group therapy sessions in the nursery. A major objective of these sessions is the discussion of events in the children's lives. One child or parent is generally the main speaker, but all the children are invited to share their experiences. In one session, a mother told the children of her arrest, which had been made in her 4-year-old daughter's presence. "I was drinking too much beer, and I pulled the fire alarm. . . . It was a mistake, I shouldn't have done it."

Such revelations are not unusual but reflect the everyday realities of these children and their families. A goal of the milieu is to provide a facilitating environment in which such experiences can be acknowledged. No issue is *a priori* considered too disturbing for the group, and stories of jail, drug use, violent fights, and sexual relations are common. The children are helped to listen and respect each other and the adults present, and to identify with the concern shown by the staff for their families' difficulties.

A full description of this group discussion component of the nursery is beyond the scope of this paper (see Lopez 1994 for a more complete description of these techniques), but the essential elements include (1) recognizing the reality of the children's experience, (2) normalizing and validating their responses to the threatening situations to which they are exposed, and (3) helping them to develop strategies to cope with their environment. In one recent group 4-year-old Shanda cried openly and told the others of missing her baby sister, who was living with her violent and abusive father. The other children responded with tales of their own losses: a father down South, a brother in foster care, a mother lost to depression. Shanda was not comforted. "My mother just doesn't understand." Her friend Dina suggested, "Give her a hug, try to be friends with her."

An essential function of these group discussions is the public assessment of risk and the reassurance provided to the children that they can be protected. Four-year-old Anthony reported to a therapist that he had been hit in the head by his father. The therapist informed the group that he would call Child Protective Services because "his father shouldn't do that, parents shouldn't hurt their kids; we'll have to help Anthony's father with that."

These reassurances can facilitate further revelations concerning the risks to which the children are exposed, even in the face of parental discouragement of such disclosures. Juanita, age 5, complained to the group of her mother's drug use. "There's crack vials in the bathroom. She's smoking . . . she leaves me alone. . . . My mother told me to hide under the table at school and to curse at you. . . . I'm not going to!"

Ultimately, a main objective of the nursery is to forge a shared assumption between parents and staff that the safety of the children is of primary concern. This goal is, not surprisingly, more easily achieved with parents who are active participants in the group. In these cases, if necessary, Child Protective Services can be contacted by staff and parents together. When successfully utilized, such interventions can reduce the risk to the child and enhance parents' caretaking skills without severely straining their alliance with the nursery staff.

## THE CURRENT MODEL

During the past two years, the collaboration between the two agencies has expanded, and The Center is now providing additional treatment, consultation, and evaluation services at St. Bernard's. The therapeutic nursery remains the cornerstone of the on-site clinical services, and is now the most intensive among a range of treatment modalities, including crisis intervention, brief assessment and treatment, and individual and group psychotherapy. St. Bernard's has also recently been designated by the state as an official satellite clinic of The Center.

Crisis intervention services are available for children or adults suffering from acute trauma, including recent physical or sexual abuse, domestic violence, or parental imprisonment. A psychologist and social worker from The Center are available to do immediate assessments, both in the classroom and in an office remodeled as a play therapy room. They assist the identified child's attempt to understand and master these stressors by validating the child's emotional responses to the trauma, including fear, anxiety, and rage, as expectable and universal. They also encourage them to turn to trusted adults for help, including teachers, therapists, and other caretakers. A third task of the crisis team is to determine if additional individual or family treatment is warranted, and in the case of abuse, to act as liaisons to the appropriate child welfare agencies and criminal justice officials.

Often an initial display of behavior in the classroom that raises suspicion of trauma becomes a more detailed narrative in the treatment room. One 4-year-old girl, Amy, who had previously been compliant with her teachers, became extremely defiant and provocative soon after her father entered a drug rehabilitation program. In her first individual session with The Center's social worker, Amy revealed that she and her siblings had been repeatedly sodomized by their father, and she reenacted the abuse in dramatic fashion. Her revelations were later confirmed by her younger sister, also a student at St. Bernard's. The social worker helped Amy work through her fears and her anxiety regarding her parents' reaction to her revelations. She also offered reassurances regarding the investigative process, and accompanied Amy when interviewed by the police and Child Protective Services.

The effectiveness of crisis intervention in this setting depends to a large extent on the clinicians' ongoing participation in it. The social worker had been a regular visitor to this girl's classroom, and was well known to Amy and the other children. She had an understanding of Amy's typical affect and play, and agreed with the teacher's assessment that her behavior had shifted markedly. These joint appraisals are critical in sorting through the myriad classroom behaviors which could potentially be linked to traumatic events in the children's lives.

Brief assessment and treatment services are available to those children who are identified by classroom teams as in need of psychological intervention but are not necessarily suffering from either acute trauma or severe emotional disturbance. The most frequent referrals are for children with behavior problems or those with symptoms of depression or anxiety. Intervention is based on the assessment of (1) the level of distress in the children, (2) the extent of their family's stressors and conflicts, (3) the strengths of the family, (4) the family's capacity to utilize support and (5) the kind of supports (e. g., clinical or concrete services) needed.

Many of the children's symptoms stem, in large part, from their living under chronically stressful and unpredictable conditions. A goal of treatment is to provide them with a greater sense of internal control and security, so that they might feel more capable of influencing and coping with their environment. A second goal, and one that is often more difficult to achieve, is to help parents understand and relate to their children's concerns and to reinforce their own attempts to cope with their environment so that they may be better equipped to respond to their children's needs. A third goal of the assessment and brief treatment process is to provide feedback to the educational staff regarding the children's concerns and conflicts and the ways in which these can continue to be addressed in the classroom.

Four-year-old Tawan was referred for brief treatment after his teachers became more aware of his isolation and self-deprecating remarks and behaviors. Tawan's mother was depressed and overburdened, and she was unable to offer much support to him. She frequently referred to him as "bad," compared him negatively to his younger brother, and expressed a wish to be rid of him. In the early phase of treatment, Tawan would repeatedly depict a mother rejecting and killing her son and then running off with her younger child.

Tawan's therapist openly discussed his mother's difficulties, but also emphasized and attempted to engage his strengths and skills, particularly his keen intelligence. She supported and facilitated Tawan's creative use of materials and his dramatic and symbolic play. She also helped his teachers to likewise identify and support his strengths and need for nurturance. They readily accepted these suggestions and began to apply them to other children in the class as well, focusing on how each was a "special person."

Work with Tawan's mother was often frustrating, as she was out of touch with his feelings as well as her own. She did however, support his treatment and the classroom interventions, and gradually began to identify with the positive view of Tawan communicated to her by his therapist and teachers. After leaving St. Bernard's, Tawan was granted a scholarship to a local Catholic school. Proud of his achievement, Tawan's mother was an enthusiastic participant at his graduation, and became more actively involved with his schooling the following year.

Leah, a conspicuously bright child, was referred for treatment in order to address her lack of affect and her confusion over her mother's mental illness. Leah's mother had suffered a series of psychotic breaks in recent years, but was not under psychiatric care while Leah was enrolled at St. Bernard's. In treatment, Leah began to express feelings of sadness and concern over her mother, as well as her worries about who would be able to care for her. At one point she asked her therapist to write a letter to her mother explaining her concerns, especially her fear that her mother would be unable to care for either Leah or herself.

After a short time, Leah began to display a greater range of emotions in the classroom and relate to other children in a more differentiated manner. These gains, sadly, were not sustained, as Leah was abruptly removed from St. Bernard's during the middle of the school year, and returned only intermittently afterwards. Although her mother expressed interest in receiving help for herself, the family's constant moves and her disordered thinking prevented her from forming any lasting treatment alliance or following through on scheduled meetings with The Center's psychiatrist.

As was the case with Leah, brief treatment often leads to a recommendation for additional mental health treatment or other interventions with the children and their families. Sarah, an extremely anxious girl, was referred for treatment when her teachers became disconcerted by her constant hair-pulling. In the classroom she often pulled out large clumps of her hair. This behavior occurred at home as well and was also of concern to her parents. Assessment sessions revealed that Sarah was mourning the loss of her father, who had recently left her mother for another woman. Her mother had become depressed following this loss, and Sarah had adopted the role of caretaker for her mother and her two younger siblings.

Sarah was referred to twice-weekly psychotherapy, where she articulated her ambivalent feelings towards her father, and expressed her anxiety over her new caretaking role, which had also impacted on her relations with her classmates. Over the course of the academic year, Sarah gradually grew less tense and slowly relinquished her adultlike attitudes and behavior. She also devised a new strategy for allaying her anxiety, stroking tissues at home and in school to soothe herself instead of pulling her hair.

Kevin was among the most difficult children in his class, a large, angry boy with few friends who could become assaultive when denied his wishes. Kevin was often dejected and critical of himself after these episodes, and expected to receive harsh punishment from his father and grandmother, who shared in caring for him. As there were no openings in the therapeutic nursery, Kevin was first referred to the newly reconstituted boys' group to address his socialization issues. Like the original boys' group, the new version, led by the psychologist and social worker from The Center, sought to enhance the boys sense of security and competence and to strengthen their bonds with their peers.

The early group sessions focused on Kevin's neediness and his wish to control the play. He felt isolated and rejected by the other boys, who in turn were repelled by his anger and stubbornness. Yet during one group Tyrone offered to share his dinosaurs with Kevin, and then, one by one, each of the boys in the group followed suit. Kevin felt welcome for the first time, and began to join the boys in an animated yet contained dinosaur battle.

However, this group cohesion could not be sustained, as Kevin grew more insistent in his demands and more aggressive towards the other boys and the group leaders. After much consultation with his teachers, with whom they shared their travails, the therapists reluctantly concluded that Kevin was not ready for the group. Instead, he was referred to individual treatment. In this modality Kevin was able to speak of the harsh treatment he received from both his father and grandmother, and how he expected to be punished severely for all his "bad" school behavior. Work in the child guidance sessions focused on the ways Kevin's father and grandmother chose to discipline him, and its impact on his self-esteem. They gradually became more responsive to Kevin and less punitive, and also agreed to psychological testing for him and to a referral for special services in kindergarten.

These evaluation services are another important component of The Center's work at St. Bernard's. The psychologist administers developmental screenings to all the children and performs psychological evaluations on the children most at risk for developing more serious cognitive deficits or emotional delays. Evaluations by the psychologist and psychology trainees are used for educational planning, referrals for relevant services, and for Committee on Special Education hearings for determining appropriate school placements for children as they leave St. Bernard's. A psychiatrist from The Center is also available to evaluate children displaying symptoms of severe emotional disturbance and for medication consultations.

The expanded collaboration has also facilitated work with parents. The Center's psychologist and the teachers often together review screening test results with parents, and collaborate in the formation of classroom strategies to confront learning or speech and language problems. Information is now more readily shared between the St. Bernard's social work staff, who are often the main contacts with parents, and the teachers and clinicians. Although parent involvement is still far from ideal, steady progress has been made in transforming the classrooms from isolated educational environments into family-oriented centers. As in the therapeutic nursery, holiday celebrations, field trips, and other group rituals that include parents continue to be mainstays of the other Head Start classes. The mental health and educational staff have also joined forces to work as advocates for the children and families, and to serve as community liaisons on their behalf, preparing them for kindergarten and other situations that they will encounter when they leave St. Bernard's.

In addition to providing timely clinical interventions on an as-needed basis, the main objective of The Center's clinicians working at St. Bernard's is to foster the development of a supportive milieu in the classroom that can address most of the children's educational and emotional needs. Under the supervision of the program coordinator, the psychologist and social worker from the Center provide consultation and support to the five teams of teachers. In weekly team meetings and ad hoc conferences, they provide a developmental perspective to the teachers and help them interpret and understand their student's responses to the traumas they have experienced. Psychological test data are also reviewed at these meetings. Staff members from The Center also meet weekly with the executive director, educational coordinator, and social workers from St. Bernard's to review specific clinical issues and referrals, to monitor ongoing evaluations, to discuss staff development and educational planning, and to coordinate services between The Center, St. Bernard's, and other child welfare agencies.

The constant demands and neediness of the children at St. Bernard's continue to test the ability of the teachers and the therapists to provide the much-needed combination of firmness and support. Progress has been made however, particularly when the team members have worked together to address difficult issues. The children's experiences in the shelters, including the constant moving, the lack of privacy, the loss of friends, and the threat of danger, are now more openly discussed in the classrooms, especially during meal and circle times.

When the staff learned that the mother of 4-year-old Charles had been stabbed by another mother, the clinician from The Center met with him, and then reviewed with his class what had happened, eliciting supportive comments from his teacher and other children. The teacher, who had formerly shied away from such sensitive issues, this time welcomed the support, and continued to follow up on the child's progress in team meetings.

In another class a discussion of hitting among the children enabled several children to speak of their experiences as the recipients of their parents' violence. The teacher and the clinician helped to focus the discussion, highlighting the empathic comments from the children regarding their shared dilemma: that they cared for their parents yet feared their anger. Plans were then made to follow up with individual parents. Though not routine, these exchanges have become more a part of the daily experiences of nearly all the children and staff at St. Bernard's.

## CONTINUING CHALLENGES

The greatest challenge facing the staff of The Center and St. Bernard's lies in the difficulty of the task undertaken. The children and families at St. Bernard's are under such stress, both internal and external, have such few resources, and require such intensive services that the staff of both agencies are themselves under constant stress. Staff members frequently experience feelings of helplessness, hopelessness, and despair. Many of the families have been homeless for years and appear to have made little progress towards living independently. There is a dehumanizing quality to their existence that is frightening and can feel engulfing.

Other families move out of St. Bernard's catchment area without warning, often in the middle of the academic year, threatening the continuity of services for the children. As was the case with Leah, many children do not remain long enough to consolidate their educational and therapeutic gains. The stress of the work is compounded by these sudden changes, for despite the best efforts of both agencies to provide follow-up, treatment plans, educational strategies, and social service agreements often have to be abandoned midstream.

In recognition of the profound impact that these issues have on staff morale, two social workers from The Center have recently developed a weekly support group for teachers. The goal of this group is to foster communication and support among team members, so that they might more readily share the burden of the work. It also serves as an advocacy and liaison group for the teachers, and gives them an opportunity to raise their issues and concerns with the executive director and administrative staff of St. Bernard's rather than to passively endure what they at times feel are unrealistic and unfair work expectations.

The intense stress communicated by these families can also lead to tension between the mental health professionals and educational staff and exaggerate differences in philosophy, ethnicity, training, and compensation. To combat the potential for staff splitting into fractured alliances, a portion of team meeting time is now spent discussing systemic and interpersonal issues. Staff members from both The Center and St. Bernard's have developed more open communication and mutual respect, and increasingly rely on interdisciplinary team planning rather than hierarchical decision-making.

## ACHIEVEMENTS

The collaboration between an early childhood educational program and a child mental health center has had a positive impact on homeless children with intense emotional, educational and material needs. This joint effort has allowed staff from both agencies to work together to provide a comprehensive and flexible treatment plan for each child and family in need. Together the two agencies have entered the lives of these families in a deeper and more meaningful way than either could do on its own. Through its affiliation with St. Bernard's, with its many educational and support services and outreach efforts, The Center has been able to forge solid and lasting treatment alliances with many homeless families, something that had been attempted but not achieved in its more traditional outpatient clinic modalities. Support from The Center's clinicians has allowed the educational staff of St. Bernard's to maintain relationships with some of the most provocative and difficult children and with highly resistant and stressed parents. Joining together under one umbrella has also reduced, if not completely eliminated, the stigma associated with mental health services in this population.

The collaboration has also allowed parents to view the staff of St. Bernard's and The Center as members of one team, each with different roles in meeting the children's needs. This is essential for this population of homeless families, who, in our experience, are often inundated with service providers who do not coordinate their efforts. These shared service arrangements often tend to overwhelm and confuse the families. Though the agendas of The Center and St. Bernard's do clash on occasion, the staff members of both agencies must coordinate their efforts every day and deliver a unified message to the families they serve if they are to maintain their connections with them.

The collaboration has also helped team members from both agencies develop more realistic expectations for themselves and the families. They have worked together to maintain a strong investment in the children and families without becoming overwhelmed or consumed by their distress. The clinicians from The Center and the staff of St. Bernard's have learned to share both the emotional burden and concrete tasks, as well as the pleasures and successes of the work. They have also learned that relying on each other is the best way to enhance their resilience in working with these families.

## FUTURE DIRECTIONS

The staff of St. Bernard's and The Center have made plans to expand their partnership and enhance the services available to the children and families. Among the programs currently underway are a craft workshop for parents and a mothers' group, both led by social workers from St. Bernard's. Staff from both agencies are currently working with outside consultants to institute more formal curricula on dealing with substance abuse and children's exposure to violence. They have also increased outreach efforts to local school districts who will be receiving these children, and to shelters and transitional housing providers.

The director of St. Bernard's and program coordinator for The Center have also begun to focus on the issue of continuity of services for these families. They are scheduled to meet with representatives from the Department of Social Services, which oversees housing decisions, transportation, and daycare for homeless families, and from the State Office of Mental Health, which coordinates treatment planning and program oversight for this population. The aim of these discussions is to highlight the need for ongoing Head Start and mental health services for the children and families of St. Bernard's that could remain in place when they change shelters or enter transitional or permanent housing. The notion that young children develop their cognitive competencies and a sense of security when they have stable relationships with adults is widely accepted by most officials and other advocates for the homeless. In our experience, however, these relationships rarely take precedence when logistical difficulties and additional costs are weighed.

Similar work needs to occur with parents, most of whom need ongoing guidance and support regarding their children's educational and psychological needs. Although many are connected to St. Bernard's, few parents make decisions regarding housing and work options based on their ability to continue their child's (and often their own) schooling and treatment. This is not surprising given the multiple stressors with which these homeless families must contend. The solution to this problem lies in enhancing the awareness of both parents and the community.

As this joint work progresses, The Center hopes to institute a formal evaluation design that will allow its staff to document gains in the children's cognitive and social development and their family functioning. Preliminary results from a pre/post administration of a developmental screening measure have been promising, with nearly all children showing marked gains in their scores after four to six months at St. Bernard's. The creation of a solid clinical and research data base would allow the achievements of the program to be presented in a more formal and forceful manner. It is to be hoped that this research will encourage other Head Start and early childhood programs to advocate for similar intensive collaborations with mental health providers.

The conditions that have led to feelings of helplessness and despair in many of the homeless children and families of St. Bernard's are, unfortunately, far from unique in America today. If, as our ongoing experience suggests, the model described here can be clearly demonstrated to effectively counteract these forces, it will be worthy of wider application.

## REFERENCES

Bassuk, E. L., and Rosenburg, L. (1988). Why does family homelessness occur?: a case-control study. *American Journal of Public Health* 78:783–788.

Bassuk, E. L., and Rubin, L. (1987). Homeless children in America: a neglected population. *American Journal of Orthopsychiatry* 57:279–286.

Bath, H. (1994). The physical restraint of children: Is it therapeutic? *American Journal of Orthopsychiatry* 64:40–49.

Browne, A. (1993). Family violence and homelessness: the relevance of trauma histories in the lives of homeless women. *American Journal of Orthopsychiatry* 63:370–384.

Buckner, J. G., Bassuk, E. L., and Zima, B. T. (1993). Mental health issues affecting homeless women: implications for intervention. *American Journal of Orthopsychiatry* 63:385– 399.

Goodman, L., Saxe, L., and Harvey, M. (1991). Homelessness as psychological trauma: broadening perspectives. *American Psychologist* 46:1219–1225.

Hausmen, B., and Hammer, C. (1993). Parenting in homeless families: the double crisis. *American Journal of Orthopsychiatry* 63:358–369.

Kliman, G. W. (1975). Analyst in the nursery. In *Psychoanalytic Study of the Child* 30:477–510. New Haven, CT: Yale University Press.

Lopez, T. (1994). *Cornerstone children speak out from within: group discussions in the Cornerstone nursery.* Unpublished manuscript.

Lopez, T., and Kliman, G. W. (1980). The cornerstone treatment of a pre-school boy from an extremely impoverished environment. In *Psychoanalytic Study of the Child* 35:341–375. New Haven, CT: Yale University.

Molnar, J. M. (1988). *Home is Where the Heart Is: The Crisis of Homeless Children and Families in New York City.* New York: Bank Street College of Education.

Molnar, J. M., Rath, W. R., and Klein, T. P. (1990). Constantly compromised: the impact of homelessness on children. *Journal of Social Issues* 46(4):109–124.

Piotrkowski, C. S., Collins, R. C., Knitzer, J., and Robinson, R. (1994). Strengthening mental health services in Head Start. *American Psychologist* 49:133–139.

Toro, P. A., Trickett, E. J., Wall, D. D., and Salem, D. A. (1991). Homelessness in the United States: an ecological perspective. *American Psychologist* 46:1208–1218.

Zelman, A. B., Friedman, M., and Pasquariella, B. (1986). Use of a questionnaire to compare day care staff and mental health staff attitudes: an aid to mental health consultation to daycare. *Journal of Preventive Psychiatry* 3(1):87–101.

# IV

# CHILDREN BEREAVED OF A PARENT

# 8

# The Use of Parentally Bereaved Adolescents as Therapeutic Assistants in Groups for Parentally Bereaved Children*

*Aviva Levy*
*Arthur B. Zelman*

## INTRODUCTION

Bereavement work is sufficiently difficult for children and adolescents that the very ability to mourn prior to the completion of adolescence has been called into question (Wolfenstein 1966, 1969). More recent work has stressed the complexity of childhood mourning and its open-ended character (Baker et al. 1992, Silverman et al. 1992). One can assume, for example, that the bereavement will have to be reworked at each succeeding development period.

Efforts to treat parentally bereaved children and adolescents, whether individually, in family therapy, or in groups generally encounter defenses against narcissistic injury, further complicated by developmentally determined difficulties such as the relative weakness of the developing ego, an incomplete process of individuation, and idiosyncratic needs and defenses characteristic of each individual child. In light of these difficulties, the authors have over a period of years developed a relatively open ended and unstructured group modality whose most distinguishing characteristic is the inclusion of both bereaved children and adolescents.

---

*This chapter is based on a presentation to the American Orthopsychiatric Association, San Francisco, CA, May 21, 1993.

The model presented here thus utilizes a "naturalistic" setting in which parental bereavement, common to all group members, is an expected and normative topic of concern and communication. Everyday events as well as anniversaries can serve as stimulants of verbal and nonverbal expression of bereavement-related material, interspersed with other developmentally determined activities and discussions.

Several considerations led us to expect that the use of adolescents as "therapeutic assistants" (TAs) would reduce the resistance of both groups to dealing with their bereavements.

One of the predictable consequences of bereavement in childhood and adolescence is the loss of self-esteem associated with the self-perception of being different or defective. For the adolescent who is functioning as a therapeutic assistant, this difference is turned to advantage insofar as his own bereavement gives him an advantage in understanding and helping the children in the group.

The adolescent, meanwhile, is an admired object to the child who therefore strives for his approval as a source of self-esteem. This approval is obtained and self-esteem enforced in part by acknowledging and reflecting on his bereavement. For both child and adolescent, then, we postulated that the group context could transform the issue of bereavement from one that diminishes self-esteem and therefore generates resistance into a source of self-esteem and diminished resistance.

The dual purpose of this chapter is to describe in some detail clinical process engendered by our group model and in so doing to provide evidence for its efficacy in reducing resistance by documenting the richness of bereavement related material and attempts at active mastery that the model can facilitate.

## REVIEW OF LITERATURE

Group therapy has been a frequently employed form of intervention with the bereaved. The majority of groups described, however, whether self-help or professionally led (Yalom and Vinogradov 1988), are for adults.

The literature includes fewer descriptions of groups for bereaved children. These groups tend to be either for latency-aged children (Davis 1989, Kalter et al. 1984, Madonna and Chandler 1986, Sugar 1975, Vastola et al. 1986, Zambelli and DeRosa 1992) or for adolescents (Jones 1985). They are generally time-limited (6 to 12 sessions), and highly structured (Madonna and Chandler 1986). In these groups, play is used mostly for the release of tension rather than as a means of creative mastery.

We found two groups that included both children and adolescents (Masterman and Reams 1988). One was formed secondarily for the children of widows who were already enrolled in a group, and was also structured and time-limited. The second was organized by Helen Fitzgerald (1995, 1996). Fitzgerald describes in detail techniques she has developed and employs in various bereavement groups for children. Her preferred model is the openended group, and there appears to be much overlap, regarding her goals and techniques, between her approach and ours. (She mentions that adolescents are often placed in such groups, and may even function as "temporary assistants" to the therapists as we do.) Fitzgerald's description, however, does not focus on clinical process of such groups, nor does she include clinical material illustrating the role or experience of the adolescents.

## DEMOGRAPHICS OF THE GROUP

The material presented here is taken from four groups, conducted over a period of four years serving a total of 45 children, from 31 families. Group members ranged from 6 to 18 years. Sixteen of the participants were above the age of 14 years. Mean age was 11.8 while the median age was 11. Twenty-two of the children were male, 23 were female. Twenty-four had siblings in the group. Twenty of the children and adolescents remained in the group for one academic year and 14 others remained longer.

Some bereavement-related characteristics of the cohort were as follows:

1. Sex of deceased parent: 33 group members (16 boys, 17 girls) had been bereaved of their fathers and 14 (6 girls and 8 boys) had been bereaved of their mothers. Two boys had been bereaved of both parents, one due to an automobile accident, the second over a period of 7 years.

2. Nature of the death: 28 parents had died suddenly (the parents of 9 children had been killed in a violent manner) and 19 had died following an illness.

3. Time between bereavement and entry to group: 9 children joined the group within 3 months of their parent's death, 19 children had been bereaved between 3 months and a year, and 17 had been bereaved between 1 and 12 years at the time they joined the group.

4. Age at bereavement: 15 children (8 boys and 7 girls) had been bereaved before the age of 6 years, 20 (11 boys and 9 girls) during latency (6–11 years), 4 between ages 11 and 15, and 6 after age 15.

Fifteen children had been in individual treatment at some point prior to joining the group. None of the children had been in a group before. Those who were not in individual therapy were usually seen individually by the group therapist once every 4 to 6 weeks.

The groups were heterogeneous with regard to academic performance, psychopathology, educational level of parents, and ethnic and racial characteristics.

During the 4 years reported on, only 6 children from 3 families withdrew against the therapist's advice, while 5 children from 4 families were referred elsewhere because of inability to make use of the group. Hence, the modality appeared usable for a broad cross section of bereaved children and adolescents.

## METHODS OF TREATMENT

Children and adolescents are recruited for the group both from the clinic and the community. Adolescents are recruited with the understanding that they will be therapeutic assistants (TAs) to the therapist. A single therapist (A.L.) led the group the first three years, and the fourth year a co-therapist/ trainee was added.

Prior to entering the group, children and TAs are screened by the therapist. Criteria for entrance are liberal and depend on the clinician's judgment that the child and/or adolescent can tolerate a group experience.

Caretakers of the children and the TAs themselves are told that, should they choose to join the group, they are committed to 6 sessions, after which they can choose to leave or remain for the duration of the school year. Children and TAs are sometimes admitted during the course of the school year. Following the end of the school year, group members may choose to participate in the following year's group.

Between 6 and 16 bereaved children and adolescents meet weekly for 75–90 minutes, in accordance with the school calendar. A snack is provided toward the end of these meetings.

The group process is characterized by a semi-planned rotation among discussion, structured activities, and spontaneous play. Activities and discussions initiated by children or TAs are generally given priority over those initiated by the therapist.

Materials and activities are chosen that are thought likely to elicit bereavement-related themes. Activities include arts and crafts, creative writing, group readings, dramatic play, special group projects, and games.

Games are chosen to facilitate group process or elicit specific themes, for example, "Simon Says" to maintain control, and balloon or bubble games to elicit separation and loss, although content is deliberately not limited to bereavement-related themes. The calendar is used to bring to awareness bereavement-related anniversaries.

Parents may be invited into the group for specific purposes. For example, a parent and child may discuss their family tree or bring in artifacts, and discuss memories and feelings about the deceased and the bereavement.

## The TA Meetings

The TA group usually consists of 3 to 6 adolescents. Prior to each large group meeting, the TAs meet with the therapist for 45 minutes. Following the large group meeting, the TA group reconvenes for 15 minutes.

The content of the TA meetings fluctuates between a focus on helping the younger children on the one hand (including planning activities) and discussing themselves on the other.

As in the larger group, much of the focus is on bereavement, but not exclusively so. Don, age 17, tells the other TAs that he joined the group "to get to understand myself better at the time of my father's death when I was 6." He is especially interested in 6-year-old Harry and notices that Harry becomes agitated when the subject of death is discussed. He recalls that he himself was hyperactive as a child. His comments about Harry lead to a discussion in the TA meeting of the adolescents' current anxieties and nightmares about death. At a group meeting with the children, Don is patient with Harry's acting out behavior, lets Harry play at beating him in a fight, and declares "I'm dead." At the meeting's end, he carries Harry on his back and brings him to his mother.

For several weeks during the TA meetings, Don champions Harry and explains Harry's disruptive behavior to the other TAs. One week, however, he admits, "I hope Harry doesn't come. It's so hard to stand him." He wonders whether his family and teachers may have sometimes felt that way about him. He decides to make a contract with Harry who, he knows, wants his approval. Harry signs a statement to the effect that he will try to behave better.

The TAs are interested in the causes of negative or disruptive behavior and strive to be tolerant and supportive. They volunteer to pay more attention to particular children. Tracy, age 16, tells the other TAs she intends to help two brothers, Thomas, age 12, and Paul, age 8, to be more tolerant of their 4-year-old sister. She then recalls how angry she had been when, at age 4, her mother left her to visit her dying father in the hospital.

The TAs express pride in their ability to help the younger children. They even suggest meeting with the children without the therapist so that the therapist can meet with the parents, and often see themselves as intermediaries between the parents and their children.

The task-oriented aspects of the TA group—to help the younger children and to plan for the large group—achieve the purpose of generating (TA) group cohesiveness and reducing anxiety. The TAs discuss current peer relationships, including fears of intimacy and loss. They are also able to verbalize their ambivalence towards both deceased and surviving parents. On occasion, even suicidal preoccupations are acknowledged.

Having been able to tolerate the expression of such feelings, the TAs are able to help the children with the latter's ambivalence toward the group. Hence, Don responds to some children's complaints about the group, "No one is making me come. I love the group, even when it hurts."

The impact of the younger children is apparent in the TA group. The age and bereavement-appropriate fantasies and fears of the younger children resonate with suppressed or partially repressed fantasies of the TAs and help bring them to consciousness. For example, during one TA meeting while planning for a large group meeting that was to take place before Halloween, the TAs discuss their own fears of ghosts.

## THE LARGE GROUP

### Beginnings

Upon introducing themselves, both children and adolescents tend to avoid the issue of bereavement, whether at the initial meeting of a group or when a new child enters the group. By the end of the first meeting, however, there is acknowledgment and discussion of bereavement.

Jennifer begins the first meeting of the year. "My name is Jennifer. I am 9. I go to Public School 5. I am in the fourth grade." "I play field hockey," says Larry, age 12. "I dance and play the flute," says Debbie, age 10, as if these bits of information are sufficient to account for their presence in the group. Later in the meeting, however, Naomi, age 13, says, "I'm a Cancer [i.e., born in July] and my mother died of cancer when I was 6," and other children begin to speak briefly about their bereavement. The younger group members sometimes speak of a pet who died before speaking of their deceased parent.

In general, both children and TAs start with facts, including age at bereavement, without much affect or elaboration. Karen's first reference to her bereavement comes after 2 weeks in the group. "My father died 3 years ago. I was 8. My dad just went to work and died. No one could believe it. It was so sudden."

As the children grow more comfortable further details emerge. Karen, for example, elaborates on her original account. "I came back from school and saw all these people . . . and my grandma . . . and I knew something bad had happened. My mom came out and told me my father died and . . . I really didn't hear what else she said, just that he died."

"My father died when he was on a business trip," says Debbie, age 10, in her first account. In a meeting a few months later she struggles to articulate the name of the disease that caused her father's death and adds, "He was fine, he was not sick at all when he went, just a cold, but then he couldn't breathe and they called the ambulance to the hotel, but he died." Karen, on hearing this, gives further details about the cause of her father's sudden death.

The TAs often lead the way and give more details early on. Lenore, age 15, toward the end of her first meeting in the group says, "My father was sick for a long time; he had lung cancer. He was in the hospital and back home and then in the hospital again, on and off for about 2 years. We were sure he was going to get better just like before, but he didn't . . . not this time. It was such a shock; we were totally shocked." Lenore's 12-year-old brother Robert describes his father's last day, the visit of the priest, the gathering round of the family, the medical explanation that was given to them, and he begins to weep. Lenore and Robert's 8 year old sister whose deceased father had been a plumber, draws a picture of a man repairing a leaky faucet. Three or four meetings later she is able to talk about her father's death.

**Remembering**

The group generates a culture in which memories related to the bereavement process as well as to the deceased parent are highly valued. Anniversaries of the deaths and birthdays of parents and children, as well as holidays, facilitate remembering.

Terry, age 9, tells the group that following the first Thanksgiving dinner after his father's death, "I choked on my food, and couldn't eat more than two bites. I sat on the armchair just opposite my father's empty armchair. Last year at Thanksgiving my dad played the organ and we all danced, even my grandpa. It was a lot of fun . . . then . . . I ate a lot." Wendy, age 14, writes to her mother on Mother's Day, which is also the anniversary of her death, "Mom, I want you to know I will always love you even though you are not living anymore . . . you are very special to me, you were the best mommy anyone can have. You're #1! Happy Mother's Day."

The content of the children's memories (including distortions) is determined by their age at bereavement, in keeping with Buchsbaum's (1987) observations. Nine-year-old Jennifer, for example, recalls her father's death when she was 3 in terms of action. "Daddy was in bed when it all happened— I held Mommy's hand and threw flowers on the grave." Six-year-old Sally, whose mother has just died, relates how her mother had braided her hair. Fourteen-year-old Wendy, whose mother had died the previous year, shows her awareness of the interests and the personality of the deceased. She draws her mother's "favorite tree . . . Mom planted 5 of them in our yard and took good care of them." She also recalls cooking with her mother on holidays.

The adolescents can verbalize guilt about not wanting to remember. Wendy says, "I tried to forget but I felt guilty." Christine, age 17, says she used to be afraid that she was going to forget her mother, who had died when she was 10. She reports telling a friend about her mother "so she would help me remember." Now that her older sister has left for college and her father is remarrying, Christine says she is trying harder to remember. She cuts her hair short and brings her mother's photograph to demonstrate her resemblance to her mother.

Children and TAs alike describe other concrete attempts to remember. A 6-year-old girl says she keeps her father's pillow and shirts unwashed in order to retain his smell. Two girls, ages 12 and 16, wear their fathers' shirts. Several children bring pictures of the deceased parent. One 12-year-old girl uses audio tapes to remember her father's voice. Younger children bring to the group gifts that they had received from the deceased parent. Adolescents bring artifacts that symbolize the deceased parents' values, such as a key chain and a shirt with a peace logo.

The group can also facilitate the verbalization of grisly aspects of the bereavement. Barry, age 12, tells the group about the car accident in which both his parents were killed. Several weeks later he adds that he had asked to see his parents' bodies but had not been permitted. One child says the body of his deceased parent "was made up to look like everything was fine." Another asks, "Do you go and buy a dress to rot there?" Twelve-year-old Barry describes cremation to the group. Another 12-year-old asks, "Can you imagine what it must have felt like for my mom to stay alone with the corpse for ten hours?" Terry, age 9, describes his father, bloated due to kidney failure. "He looked awful, many times larger than even his big, big brother, and you should have seen his fingers." Far from overwhelming the children, such descriptions seem to enhance mastery. Terry's father had been murdered. When he tells the group that the murderer has not been caught, the group attempts to solve the crime. Terry later brings a newspaper article to the group about a murderer who is brought to justice.

Children describe their experiences of the funerals and burials of their parents, using varying degrees of intellectualization in accordance with their ages. The younger children are more concrete; for example, they describe the food at the funeral or the number of cars parked in the street. The older children are more likely to verbalize their feelings. Each age group both stimulates and is stimulated by children of other ages to contribute their developmentally determined piece of the tapestry. Sometimes, children who had been very young when bereaved complain of their lack of memories. They may turn to their older siblings for material.

### Feelings About the Deceased and the Surviving Parent

A broad range of affects and attitudes toward the deceased parent is expressed in the group. Both children and TAs express love and longing in writing, dreams, and to a lesser extent direct verbalization. "Mom, there's so many things I wish I could tell, say, and do with you. . . . I am confused about everything—make it go away" writes Christine, age 17, 2 months before her high school graduation. "Just call my name—I'll come running." A 9-year-old writes to her father, "Where are you? . . . I love you." In signing the letter she uses the name that "only Daddy used to call me." Tara, age 6, writes, "Please Daddy come back! I really miss you Dad. I think you are the best dad . . . love."

Similarly, the group members express through dreams their longing for and fantasies of the deceased parents' survival. Jennifer, age 9, tells of a dream in which her father "was alive and then he died and came back to life and died again and came back and then he died but I could see him, only I . . . but he died." Barry says he dreamed that "my father was around . . . he woke up and came back to life also. I could see him."

Longing for the deceased is combined with ambivalence toward the surviving parent. Fifteen-year-old Lydia rhetorically asks the group, "Did you ever have a dream like one parent died and not the other—like the opposite one died? I had a dream once that my mom died and not my dad." Nine-year-old Jennifer, whose father had died 6 years before, says she dreamed that "I came home from school and my mother had died and I said, 'Oh, good, my dad is back alive!'" Debbie, age 10, reassures the group and herself that while she used to like her deceased father a lot more than her mother, now there is "only a very tiny difference between how much I love Mommy and Daddy."

Along with expressions of longing and attempts to reverse the loss in dream and fantasy come attempts at mastery through identification and idealization. A 6-year-old boy states, "I am my dad's twin," and draws a picture of two boys. Lenore, age 16, often wears shirts her deceased father had bought for her. She tells the group how kind and sensitive her father had been and later asserts that she both looks like him and possesses his character. The therapist and group are thus given an opportunity to reinforce or counter such mechanisms, depending on their age-appropriateness and adaptive value.

The children also discuss their fear of grief. Younger children articulate the fear that crying may cause more sickness and death. As an antidote, one child says, he "tries to make Mommy smile" by forcibly moving her lips.

On the other hand, the TAs in particular may be critical of the surviving parent for not showing sufficient evidence of grief. Wendy, age 15, is angry with her father for not expressing more grief. Eric, age 14, is disturbed by his father's apparent lack of affect. "I know my dad inside out, after all, I have been with him for 14½ years. I can see by the way he combs his hair if he wants to cry. . . . Except at the funeral I have never seen him cry." The view of the surviving parent as not sufficiently caring or sensitive seems to be more characteristic of children with more disturbed family relations prior to the bereavement.

As expressions of longing intensify, feelings of unreality surface. Jennifer, age 9, begins a conversation, "I was really close to my dad. I was probably the closest to him." Debbie, age 10, says, "It is all like a dream." Sabrina, age 16, adds, "It is absolutely bizarre." Karen, age 11, says, half smiling, "You can think he just went on a long business trip." Debbie responds, "Sometimes it's really—why did he die? Yesterday, I wished so much that my father was there. I hit a home run—all the fathers were there . . . weird."

Associated with such descriptions of fluctuating levels of reality testing are verbalizations of fears of the dark, strange sounds and lights, ghosts, kidnappers, and separation anxieties. Several children speak of nightmares and inability to fall asleep because of fears of the return of the deceased parent in the form of monsters and ghosts who might take revenge. Terry, age 9, says he sometimes sees his bedroom door or dresser drawer open and is convinced his deceased father has done this. His 6-year-old sister, on the other hand, tells the group that she sometimes feels her father's beard touching her cheek as he kisses her goodnight.

Obvious attempts at mastery of these fears also occur. The children frequently draw "scary" pictures of such things as ghosts or buried bones. Halloween is an occasion of particular importance in this regard, the TAs taking the opportunity (as mentioned above) to play out with the children such fears.

Expressions of fear often appear in connection with verbalization of guilt. Terry says that his dreams always come true, which terrifies him. He mentions several events, including his father's death and an injury to his mother's finger, that he claims had previously occurred in his dreams. He adds that he feels "terrible" because he did not tell anybody about his dream of the murder of his father. "If I had warned them, I could have saved my father's life. Last night I again dreamt about death; this time I told my mom, 'We have 24 hours to wait, to see if someone will die'." Barry, age 12, who had lost both parents in a car accident and who had frequently spoken disparagingly of his father, says, "I had a feeling that night that something bad was going to happen, but I didn't want to tell them, because when I used to say it they always thought that I was just saying that because I didn't want them to leave." He repeats this story several times, each time verbalizing guilt and regret at not having prevented them from leaving. Molly, age 9, thinks she should not have gone to summer camp so that she could have prevented her father from smoking. Lenore, age 16, confesses that she had wished her father would die so that his pain would stop. She says she hasn't said this before to anyone because she had felt guilty.

The discussion of negative feelings toward the deceased, usually first expressed by the TAs or older children, often follows the expression of loss and longing. Glen, age 12, refers to his deceased father's smoking and drinking and calls him "a bum." Lydia, age 15, says, "My dad really did annoy many people . . . he did bad things. I'm not sure of where he is now that he is dead." The younger children can then follow suit. Derek, age 6, tells the group his father died "because he was drinking too much but my mom said I can't tell more about it, 'cause it is bad for you."

Such negative statements may be quickly counterbalanced. Thus Lydia qualifies her statement, "I just get pissed—I think my dad is alive (somewhere) and well." Gradually the awareness, acceptance, and expression of ambivalence emerges. Wendy, age 14, says her mother had favored her younger brother, and claims that on their last visit to the hospital her mother had squeezed her brother's hand and not hers. Wendy adds that while her mother had been alive she had wanted her aunt to be a mother to her. Now she finds herself saying to her aunt, "You are not my mother . . . it's none of your business."

The surviving parent is often depicted as vulnerable and in need of the child's support, help, and protection. The children worry about their parents' financial security and health. They are sensitive to signs, real or imagined, of parental illness or upset. Todd, age 8, is worried that "our dad's back pain is the beginning of something, because this is what happened to our mom." Lenore, age 16, expresses concern about her mother's physical and emotional vulnerability while she is grieving. Both children and adolescents describe their efforts to comfort and make life better for their surviving parent.

## Loyalty Conflicts

Both children and adolescents use the group to work through the loyalty conflict generated by the wish for a substitute parent. The group tends to polarize on this issue according to age. The children generally express the wish for a substitute, while the adolescents speak of betrayal of the deceased parent. Sally, age 6, tells the group that her father promised to find her a new mother with whom he will make her a little brother. Jennifer, age 9, talks about the fatherly function of her father's brother, who therefore deserves a gift on Father's Day.

Most girls above age 12 are disturbed by the idea of their mothers' dating (the TAs often talk about this in their group). Christine's (age 17) father is engaged and Jena's (age 14) mother is dating shortly after her father's sudden death. Christine says she wants her "father's happiness" but she acknowledges a wish "to annoy him and make him worry" when she dates. Jena states flatly, "It's my turn to date, not my mother's." On the other hand, 16-year-old Tracy, unlike her peers, says she wants her mother to socialize more, after 12 years of widowhood.

The loyalty conflict is literally acted out in a play entitled Sleezy Vinnee, developed by the group over a period of 3 weeks. In the play, a widow wishes to meet a man but her children object. The oldest daughter tries to persuade her mother not to make this "mistake." The mother explains to her children how lonely it is to be a single parent. The mother's boyfriend is given the name "Sleezy Vinnee" and is arrested by the police for criminal activity. Two scenes are enacted involving a widower. In one he finds a nanny whom the children dislike. In the other he dates a woman and the children get into a very serious accident. The father expresses his concern about his children as well as his loneliness and depression, while the woman is depicted as unfeeling and selfish.

## The Group Versus The World

Group members frequently state that no one understands their situation. They express anger at and alienation from others, both peers and adults, in connection with their bereavement. Again, it is the adolescents who are more able to articulate such feelings.

Wendy, age 14, cries as she recalls that some of her school friends had been laughing during her mother's funeral. In an essay she had written on euthanasia, that she reads to the group, she criticizes the doctors for not understanding her family's pain. "Just merciful death it is not, because that family undergoes a loss that causes more pain than cancer. I know this is a fact because I have felt this pain." Other group members also speak of teachers who don't understand them. Lenore, age 16, describes walking out of the classroom during a discussion of a Shakespearean tragedy in which her teacher says, "One can get over death; it's not such a big deal." Sabrina, age 16, whose mother had died the previous year after a long illness, is enraged at her teacher's threats to call her mother to discipline her.

The younger children resonate with these feelings. Terry, age 9, thinks that "people in school are staying away from me since my father's murder," and Sally, age 6, feels that her peers and teachers pick on her.

Such stories strike a chord with all group members and facilitate the expression of feelings of alienation, rage, shame, and isolation. As with all other aspects of bereavement discussed in the group, however, along with, and even as a result of, the expression of negative feelings, a more positive, balanced view of things usually emerges. Often it is the younger children who initiate these positive expressions. Molly, age 9, says, "I want them to be my friends but not because they feel sorry for me." Lenore, age 16, then expresses gratitude to the people who came to her father's funeral and provided food and other forms of support, but adds, "I don't want them to treat me so nicely. I don't want to be pitied."

## Endings

When children leave the group, direct opportunities present themselves to deal with separation and loss. Whenever a group member leaves without warning (as occasionally happens), however, the children tend to feel devalued and disparage themselves and the group. The therapist may take this as an opportunity to connect self-denigration caused by the loss of a group member to the loss of self-esteem caused by the loss of a parent.

When a child leaves the group in a planned manner, reactions are quite different. Lydia, age 15, leaves for a month to go to Europe, promises to keep in touch, and tells the group when she will return. Group members enthusiastically prepare cards and posters for her return. Don, age 17, says he has to leave the group before the end of the school year to prepare for graduation. Glen, age 12, perhaps the most hostile member of the group, says to Don, "You will be missed. Thanks for being here and for coming to say goodbye." The warmth the children display when they speak of Lydia and Don contrasts markedly with their refusal to make contact with members who come only a few times and disappear.

The imminent termination of each group as summer approaches is always acknowledged. One year, it led to the creation of a book. Initiated by the therapist, it expanded into a series of drawings and writings to which virtually every group member contributed—a striking example of the group's capacity to support each member's efforts to master the bereavement.

## DISCUSSION

The model described here has certain developmentally derived advantages for overcoming resistance and for bringing to awareness underlying feelings, fantasies, and attitudes concerning bereavement.

The adolescents serve as powerful models whom the young children wish to emulate. The latter learn from the adolescents that reactions to bereavement are not only acceptable but that exploration in the group of such reactions meets with approval and support. Similarly, their positive identification with the bereaved adolescents reduces the stigmatization and sense of inadequacy engendered by their own loss. For the adolescents, the opportunity to serve as models for, and supporters of, the children provides a context in which efforts to come to terms with their own bereavement can resonate with their developmental need for enhanced control and autonomy rather than constituting a threat to it.

The presence in the group of individuals of different ages also provides the group members with opportunities to deal with the bereavement at different developmental levels. Thus, the young children, in addition to being supported in their age appropriate attempts to cope with the bereavement, also have the opportunity to anticipate and/or practice future developmentally determined phases of the bereavement work.

Conversely, the presence in the group of the children, who had experienced their bereavement at varying ages, also provides special therapeutic opportunities for the adolescents. For example, older children and adolescents who had been bereaved in early or mid-childhood are given a direct opportunity to recapitulate, through regression and identification with younger children, the earlier stages of their own bereavement.

The fact that the bereavement has occurred at varying periods of time prior to admission to the group gives children and adolescents who had experienced the bereavement a long time before an opportunity to reexperience acute bereavement at a safe distance. On the other hand, acutely bereaved children acquire a base for a long-term perspective provided by those group members whose bereavement had occurred years before.

The question arises, "Which children need such a group?" Rather than answer a question via a sickness versus health model, we prefer Silverman and colleagues' notion (1992) that "bereavement should not be viewed as a psychological state that ends or from which one recovers. . . . The emphasis should be on negotiating and renegotiating the meaning of the loss over time" (p. 502).

The richness of bereavement-related content elicited by the group with such a heterogeneous cohort of children and adolescents provides support for this viewpoint, as well as for the intervention described here. It further suggests that a broad range of children at varying stages of development and in various phases of their bereavement process could benefit. Finally, our experience with this technique leads us to speculate about the usefulness of this multi-age model for other populations, for example, children and adolescents of divorce, or children in foster care.

## REFERENCES

Baker, J. E., Sedney, M. A., and Gross, E. (1992). Psychological tasks for bereaved children. *American Journal of Orthopsychiatry* 62(1):105–116.

Buchsbaum, B. (1987). Remembering a parent who has died: a developmental perspective. *Annual of Psychoanalysis* 15:99–112.

Davis, C. B. (1989). The use of art and group process with grieving children. *Issues in Comprehensive Pediatric Nursing* 12:269–280.

Fitzgerald, H. (1995). Developing and maintaining of children's bereavement groups: Part 1. *Thanatos*, Fall 1995, 20(3):20–23.

—— (1996). Developing and maintaining of children's bereavement groups: Part 2. *Thanatos*, Winter 1996, 20(4):20–23.

Jones, K. W. (1985). Support for grieving kids. *Home Healthcare Nurse* 3(4):269–280.

Kalter, N., Pickar, J., and Lesowitz, M. (1984). School-based developmental facilitation groups for children of divorce: a preventive intervention. *American Journal of Orthopsychiatry* 54(4):613–623.

Madonna J. M., Jr., and Chandler, R. (1986). Aggressive play and bereavement in group therapy with latency-age boys. *Journal of Child and Adolescent Psychotherapy* 3(2): 109–114.

Masterman, S. H., and Reams, R. (1988). Support groups for bereaved preschool and school-age children. *American Journal of Orthopsychiatry* 58(4):562–570.

Silverman, P. R., Nickman, S., and Worden, J. W. (1992). Detachment revisited: the child's reconstruction of a dead parent. *American Journal of Orthopsychiatry* 62(4): 494–503.

Sugar, M., ed. (1975). Group therapy for pubescent boys with absent fathers. In *The Adolescent in Group and Family Therapy* pp. 49–67. New York: Brunner/Mazel.

Vastola, J., Nierenberg, A., and Graham, E. H. (1986). The lost and found group: group work with bereaved children. In *Mutual Aid Groups for Vulnerable Populations and The Life Cycle*, ed. A. Gitterman and L. Shulman, pp. 75–90. Itasca, IL: Peacock Publications.

Wolfenstein, M. (1966). How is mourning possible? In *Psychoanalytic Study of the Child* 21:93–123. New York: International Universities Press.

——— (1969). Loss, rage, and repetition. In *Psychoanalytic Study of the Child* 24:432–460. New York: International Universities Press.

Yalom, I. D., and Vinogradov, S. (1988). Bereavement groups: techniques and themes. *International Journal of Group Psychotherapy* 38(4):419–457.

Zambelli, G. C., and DeRosa, A. P. (1992). Bereavement support groups for school-age children: theory, intervention, and case example. *American Journal of Orthopsychiatry* 62(4):484–494.

# 9

# Strengthening Attachment in Anticipation of Loss: Treatment of a Paternally Bereaved (due to AIDS) 5-Year-Old Girl*

*Elissa Burian*
*Arthur B. Zelman*

The AIDS epidemic has created a situation in which each year thousands of children at developmentally vulnerable ages can anticipate the loss of a parent. Furthermore, since many AIDS victims contract the disease through sexual contact with spouses and common-law partners, as well as through shared intravenous drug use, the child of one parent with AIDS is at high risk for having two parents with AIDS. These children are, therefore, often in the position of having to anticipate the loss of both parents. This chapter describes a psychotherapeutic intervention with a child, Jennifer, whose father had died of AIDS-related illness and whose mother was HIV-positive.

## PARENTAL BEREAVEMENT AND ITS RISKS

Abraham (1911) and Freud (1917) drew attention to similarities (as well as differences) between reactions to loss and bereavement on the one hand, and melancholia on the other. Early work on childhood bereavement, therefore,

---

*This chapter is based on a presentation to the American Orthopsychiatric Association, New York, NY, May 1992.

189

focused on depression as a possible consequence. Spitz (1946), for example, coined the term *anaclitic depression* for the early childhood syndrome resulting from the absence of a reliable caretaker. Similarly, Van Eerdewegh and colleagues (1982) found depressive symptomatology including sadness, crying, and emotional withdrawal to be present in a parentally bereaved group of children compared with a nonbereaved group. Rafael's group (1980) found a 25 percent incidence of depression in a group of 20 bereaved children she was studying prospectively. In addition, she found that virtually all of the surviving parents of the depressed children were themselves depressed.

Caplan and Douglas (1969), on the other hand, found that a group of children with a primary diagnosis of depression had a higher incidence of previous separations and losses, including bereavement, than did a "mixed neurotic" group of children.

There is also evidence that childhood bereavement may result in depression in later life as well as in childhood. Brown's group (1982), for example, found a higher incidence of childhood bereavement before the age of 11 in a group of depressed women compared with a nondepressed control group. He also showed, however, that this difference only occurred when there was a provoking factor active during the previous year, suggesting that childhood bereavement acted as a factor increasing vulnerability to depression. Bowlby's (1980) work also suggests that childhood bereavement may result in decreased resiliency to loss later in life. Finally, Adam (1982) reported a higher rate of suicidal ideation and attempts in a group that had suffered parental loss before the age of 16.

Nevertheless, while it seems clear that children react to parental bereavement with depressive symptomatology in the short run, the long term effects of childhood bereavement remain controversial. Tennant and colleagues (1980), for example, after reviewing studies attempting to link bereavement in childhood with adult depression, conclude that any apparent correlation would be negated if methodological inadequacies of the studies were eliminated.

Our own view, in accord with Bowlby, is that bereavement, like many other stressful life events in childhood, does constitute a potentially significant threat to the child that may or may not lead to detrimental consequences, depending on other factors.

## PREVENTIVE IMPORTANCE AND ENHANCEMENT OF THE SURVIVING PARENT–CHILD RELATIONSHIP

It is also our contention, in agreement with Furman (1974) and Bowlby (1980), that a major (perhaps *the* major) factor in determining long-term outcome, is the quality of the child's relationships with his caretakers both pre- and post-bereavement. The nature and quality of the pre-bereavement relationship will influence the child's interpretation of the bereavement. For example, a highly ambivalent relationship between the child and his deceased parent often leads the child to respond with excessive fear and guilt based on projections of, and identification with, hostile feelings.

With regard to post-bereavement relationships, the one between the child and the surviving parent is usually most important. At least three key aspects of this relationship can be identified. First is the manner in which the surviving parent interprets and communicates with the child about the death of the other parent. Second is the degree to which the surviving parent's own grief and mourning process affects his or her availability to the child. Third is the degree to which the surviving parent is able, in the absence of the other parent, to maintain a supportive and developmentally appropriate relationship with the growing child. All three of these processes closely relate to the surviving parent's ability to mourn the death of his or her partner. If the surviving parent is herself afflicted with a life threatening illness such as AIDS, the adequate performance of these parental tasks will be severely threatened.

The surviving parent's own condition and anticipatory mourning may lead to self-absorption and withdrawal from the child on the one hand or clinging to, and dependence on, the child on the other. In the instance of AIDS, the likelihood that the deceased parent transmitted the disease to the surviving parent may complicate the latter's capacity to mourn and ability to help the child to mourn the loss of the first parent. Treatment must address these interferences with mourning so that the parental functions elucidated above may be supported.

AIDS-afflicted families are faced with an additional problem insofar as society's attitude towards this disease includes moral disapproval and ambivalence towards its victims. This stigmatization can result in social isolation of the parent, even from extended family members. These processes of isolation and alienation can manifest themselves at varying levels of consciousness. Hence a family may be consciously supportive and even be perceived by the ill person to be such. Closer scrutiny, however, often reveals evidence of denial and distancing on the part of family members.

Often it is the lack of an adequate support system that brings people in such circumstances to the clinic in the first place. In some cases, support systems can be mobilized. Often however, familial and community support systems are absent or inadequate thus exaggerating the surviving parent—child mutual dependency and isolation that has already been engendered by the loss of the first parent. On the one hand, this relationship is crucial to the child's survival; on the other, its very exclusivity may burden it with excessive mutual ambivalence.

## THE CHOICE OF A TRIPARTITE APPROACH TO INTERVENTION

We believe that the major treatable threat to the short- and long-term well-being of the child in this high-risk situation is the threat to the child's remaining primary attachment. The maintenance for as long as possible and enhancement of the quality of this relationship, paradoxically, will enable the child to cope in a nontraumatic manner with the inevitable loss when it comes and, equally important, enhance the child's capacity to sustain object relationships such that the child will be able to attach to new caretakers. (This approach runs counter to the well-intentioned separation of parent and child, in the service of "protecting" both.) For these reasons, a psychotherapeutic modality is indicated whose focus is on the attachment between parent and child.

We therefore decided to treat Jennifer and her mother with a modification and expanded application to older children of Margaret Mahler's "tripartite" method (Mahler 1968), which the present authors have described in Chapter 10. We will attempt to describe the application of this approach and provide evidence for its effectiveness through a case report. During the two years of treatment described here the therapist saw the mother twice weekly, once alone and once with her daughter. This approach we hoped would best achieve our treatment objectives in four ways. First, the technique would counter the mother's tendency to withdraw from her child by making the here-and-now relationship a major focus of attention. Second, the therapist could hold, and then make acceptable, the enhanced ambivalence in the relationship. Third, as the mother could be helped to mourn her husband and her illness in individual work with the therapist, her enhanced emotional availability to the child could be directly reenforced in the joint sessions. Finally, joint mother–child sessions could be used to help the mother to avoid overidentifying with her child as she was helped to mourn.

In broad outline the treatment consisted of two phases. During the first phase, work centered on helping the child and her mother to mourn the death of the child's father. In the second phase, work with mother and child focused on the mother's illness. In the course of the latter work, mutual ambivalence between mother and daughter, heightened by both past and anticipated losses, was exposed and worked through to a considerable extent.

## CASE REPORT

### Background

Five-year-old Jennifer and her 34-year-old mother, Gail M., came to the clinic two weeks after the death of Gail's husband, the father of Jennifer, of AIDS-related complications. The couple had no other children.

Mrs. M. had grown up as a parentified child in a family with alcohol-related problems. She had married her husband knowing he was drug-abused, believing that she could help him. Jennifer's father had, in fact, managed to conquer his addiction to heroin when Jennifer was about 1 year old. When Jennifer was 4 years old, however, her father was diagnosed as having AIDS Related Complex. Further testing revealed that Mrs. M. was found to be HIV-positive, while Jennifer was HIV-negative. Mr. M. remained well enough to work until three months prior to his death. He held a nighttime job while his wife worked during the day. Prior to his death, Mr. M. had been intensely involved in raising his much-adored daughter and may have been the more nurturing parent.

At the time of admission, Jennifer and her mother had been living with Jennifer's maternal grandmother. Mrs. M. had a support system consisting mainly of her mother, her brother, and her sister-in-law, all of whom while consciously supportive denied the seriousness of Mrs. M.'s condition, and avoided all discussion of it. All three declined the therapist's (E.B.) invitation to participate in the intervention.

### Treatment

#### PHASE 1—MOURNING THE LOSS OF FATHER/HUSBAND

Although Mrs. M. had been referred to the clinic three weeks prior to her husband's death, she didn't come until two weeks after his funeral. Her main preoccupation at this time involved feelings of guilt. She told the therapist that her husband had wanted to speak with her about his impending death but she had been unable to do this.

Mrs. M. also expressed regret that she had prevented Jennifer from seeing her father the last few weeks of his life, her reason at the time being that she had wanted Jennifer to keep intact the image of her father as a healthy man. She recalled that she had been unable to tell Jennifer when Mrs. M.'s own father had died, when Jennifer was 2½ years old and that Jennifer had only inadvertently learned of the death of her grandfather six months after the fact. Mrs. M. also recounted an incident that had occurred about one year earlier, after the diagnosis of AIDS had been made. Jennifer had been standing on line with her father in a toy store, clutching a large stuffed rabbit that she named Peter (probably a multi-determined choice, since in addition to the traditional Peter Rabbit character, she had a favorite uncle by that name).

At the checkout counter, the salesgirl pointed out that the stuffed animal that Jennifer had selected had only one eye and she offered a substitute. Jennifer insisted on keeping the rabbit in spite (or because) of his defect and said she would take good care of Peter.

During her first session, Jennifer drew a picture of a family. All the people in the family were smiling but they lacked arms and legs. As she drew the picture Jennifer matter-of-factly informed the therapist (E.B.) that she used to have a daddy and a grandpa but they had both died. As she discussed these losses further her smile disappeared and her affect became palpably sadder. She then drew a picture of herself, this time with arms and hands.

During Jennifer's second visit, while playing Richard Gardner's Talking, Feeling and Doing Game, she was asked to state three wishes. She responded, "I wish I had my daddy and grandpa back," and began to cry, attributing her tears to an eye irritation. Her mother then had to answer the question, "What is the worst thing you ever did?" Jennifer indignantly interjected, "I know what it was! You lied to me about Daddy staying in the hospital."

Jennifer's final card asked, "If you could turn into any animal, which would you choose?" Without hesitation she replied that she wanted to be a kangaroo. Among the reasons she gave for this wish was the pouch used for carrying babies. The therapist pointed out that the loss of her father might make Jennifer want to stay very close to people she cared about.

The first Christmas after her father's death arrived about six weeks into therapy. Jennifer had gone to see Santa Claus with her uncle Peter. She had intended, but had forgotten, to bring a photograph of herself with her father and Santa taken the previous Christmas. Jennifer, her mother, and the therapist then discussed the importance, as well as the difficulty, of remembering. In a subsequent session Jennifer brought in pictures of her father to put in an album she and her mother were making in therapy. During this session she referred to her father in the present tense.

For a while Jennifer drew pictures of her extended family, giving each member her last name so as to accentuate their common bond. She brought Peter Rabbit into sessions as well. She gave him turns at playing games until she said he was tired and had to rest. She spoke of Peter as "lazy, like Daddy" because he worked nights and slept during the day. However, she then reported that "Peter got sick in the moonlight" and speculated that her father might not have gotten ill had he worked days.

During one session, Jennifer denied a problem her mother had brought to the therapist's attention, namely that Jennifer had been crying at school and had refused to make a Valentine's Day card for her mother. She appeared to assent to the therapist's interpretation that it was easier not to make a card for her mother since she could not make one for her father. She was able to volunteer the fact that a classmate had also suffered a bereavement, the death of a grandfather.

The therapist noticed that Jennifer consistently pushed herself to continue an activity, even though she had obviously tired of it. She appeared to need an opportunity to regress. She gradually allowed herself to do so, via the use of primitive materials such as water and dough. Her mother had to be helped to tolerate this change in the quality of her play. Mrs. M. was soon rewarded with the emergence, in Jennifer, of more genuine and animated affect, to which she responded with corresponding enthusiasm.

Jennifer now began to articulate longings for her father. At home, during this period, Jennifer told her mother that she wished to be a threesome again and verbalized her wish that they both die so they could be with her father, yet simultaneously she showed increasing pleasure during the sessions. Sometimes she played with her mother, sometimes with the therapist, sometimes with both, enjoying herself whatever the combination. One day, the therapist suggested that Jennifer was working on ways to enjoy her life with her mother, despite her feelings of missing her father. This comment seemed to intensify Jennifer's engagement and she expressed a wish to prolong the session.

Meanwhile Mrs. M., first in her individual sessions and later in the joint sessions, was able to review, with a mixture of pleasure, longing, sadness, and regret, the experience of having been a happy threesome with her husband and child. She nostalgically recalled, for example, days in which her husband had taken the family to the country. She expressed guilt and regret that, without her husband, she did not feel capable of initiating such activities. Having ventilated these feelings, she expressed her determination to continue traditions begun by her husband, for example, buying Jennifer chocolates on special occasions.

One day, about six months into therapy, Jennifer arrived, happily clutching her rabbit with one hand while holding her mother's hand with the other. The therapist commented that she, her mother, and Peter seemed to be able to be happy together even though Peter had only one eye and

Jennifer only one parent. Mother and child responded with confirming affect. Following this sequence, however, the therapist found herself contemplating, with feelings of intense sadness, Mrs. M's prognosis and its implications for the mother–child relationship. These feelings brought into relief the paradoxical nature of the therapeutic task, namely the achievement of a more secure attachment so that Mrs. M. would be able to accept, and Jennifer to survive, the loss of the other.

### PHASE 2—COMING TO TERMS WITH MOTHER'S ILLNESS

Gradually, the focus of treatment shifted from the mourning of Mr. M. to issues related to the mother's illness. This shift was facilitated by the therapist's impression that the pair were ready to deal with Jennifer's ambivalence toward her mother.

In sessions at this time Jennifer often manipulated games so that her mother would win. This behavior became exacerbated when her mother showed signs of mild illness. On one such occasion Jennifer spoke of her father's absence at a school play along with the recollection of his having attended another play when he was alive. The therapist took the plunge and asked Jennifer if she feared her mother would also disappear. She nodded in reply.

Shortly after this exchange, Jennifer began to express anger at her mother. During one joint session Mrs. M. was having difficulty assembling a toy. Jennifer called her mother "stupid." Jennifer began to draw while the therapist sorted the markers into "usable" ones that would be kept and "non-usable" ones that would be thrown out. "Thank God that's not me," said Jennifer, referring to the non-usable markers. The therapist asked who Jennifer thought might throw her out if she wasn't good. "Mommy," Jennifer replied, "and I'll throw her out if she doesn't shut her mouth."

Jennifer looked frightened and the therapist encouraged her to make up a story about her angry feelings. She dictated the following story: "There once was a mother who never shut up, so her daughter, named Patricia, who was 8 years old, threw her sleeping mom into a garbage pail. The garbage men picked the mother up and she found herself in the garbage dump. She ran all the way home to her little girl and told her never to do that again." Following this open expression of fear and anger in relation to her mother Jennifer allowed herself to regress, using baby talk and requesting that her mother push her in a baby carriage.

As Mrs. M. gave further indications of acceptance of her husband's death (for example, the disposition of some of his possessions), she began to talk more, in individual sessions, of her fear of her own illness.

By the end of the first year of treatment, Mrs. M. had reached a new level of frankness with the therapist concerning her illness. She talked of her wish to eliminate the word AIDS, as if that would eradicate the disease itself, reflecting both her fear and hope. She began to acknowledge her illness as a fact she had to face in planning and living her life. This enabled her to take a more active approach to her condition (including getting information about and requesting medication), which, in turn, led to increased feelings of mastery and self-esteem.

Simultaneous with Jennifer's articulation of anger towards her mother, her play became more varied and creative. This increasing freedom of expression was paralleled by her mother. One day Mrs. M. came to her treatment session more informally dressed than usual and exclaimed that she wanted to "let it all hang out!"

As Mrs. M. evidenced coming to terms with her illness, she began to show greater confidence and firmness in her handling of Jennifer. One day, over and against Jennifer's remonstrations, she insisted on reporting to the therapist an incident in which Jennifer had been unpleasant. Jennifer was then able to tell her mother that she had been angry because her mother had laughed at her when she had lost a tooth. Mrs. M. was able to reassure Jennifer that she had laughed out of pleasure at the fact that the loss of a tooth meant that she was growing up.

A further expression of Jennifer's fear and anger regarding her mother was reported to Mrs. M. by another mother who had been at a school picnic that her mother had been unable to attend due to illness. At the picnic, Jennifer had called her mother "stupid" and had explained her mother's absence as due either to her mother having gotten lost or having had an accident.

The more open expression (and resolution) of conflict between mother and child both triggered, and was a manifestation of, a move by Jennifer toward greater psychological separation from her mother. For example, in one session Jennifer expressed a wish to play a game alone with the therapist but acknowledged a fear that she would hurt her mother's feelings if she did. For a while, in the treatment sessions, she alternated between clinging to and attacking her mother. The clinging gradually gave way to more autonomous behavior including a preference for foods her mother did not like. She began to show a marked increase in appetite, which seemed especially significant in that she had always been described by her mother as an indifferent eater. Jennifer's poor eating may also have represented a fear-engendered identification with her mother, who had lost weight due to her illness. Jennifer now felt safe enough to show anger at the therapist for being in control of ending the sessions, even as she decreased her efforts to prolong the conjoint sessions.

At home, as well, Jennifer began to share more feelings with her mother. For example, Mrs. M. reported in a joint session that Jennifer had told her mother of nightmares in which someone took her mother away.

At about this time, Jennifer was home with her grandmother when an electrical fire started. It was Jennifer rather than her grandmother who had the presence of mind to call the fire department. The therapist suggested that although her mother hadn't been there to help her, the part of her mommy inside of her knew what to do. Jennifer emphatically corrected the therapist, saying, "My *daddy* taught me to dial 911!"

The therapist responded that she was glad that her father, too, was inside her and could help her to take care of herself when she needed to. Jennifer now began to complain to her mother that she didn't want to come to therapy because it made her feel sad and bad. Meanwhile, at home she continued to share her fears with her mother. One day Mrs. M. brought the therapist a note Jennifer had written the previous day and had left in her bookbag for her mother to see. The note read, "I know you are very sick, will you be okay? I love you, you are the best mommy."

Toward the end of the second year of treatment, the therapist made a home visit necessitated by Mrs. M.'s weakened physical condition. During the visit, Jennifer said that a friend had called twice to inquire about her mother. The therapist suggested that this friend was probably worried about her mother and asked Jennifer if she was worried too. She nodded yes. The therapist further inquired about what she thought happened to people when the medicine that the doctor prescribed didn't do a good enough job. Jennifer responded that they go to the hospital. When asked what happens then, she said that they die. The therapist responded that while that was sometimes true, often the hospital can help people to get better. Mrs. M. thanked the therapist for having facilitated the preparation of her child for her hospitalization, adding, "I couldn't have spit that out myself."

Although Mrs. M. said she had been unable to prepare Jennifer for the next phase of her illness, and in spite of Jennifer's previously stated wish to stop therapy, both now proved themselves able to utilize the therapist's help to put into words what each was ready to hear. In part, Jennifer's understandable resistance was tempered by her apparent identification with her mother's gratitude toward the therapist. One day the therapist offered to bake Jennifer a cake for her birthday. Jennifer declined, saying she would bake her own cake. When the therapist asked why Jennifer wouldn't allow her to do something special for her on her birthday, she answered, "You already have. You have taken away my bad feelings."

Precipitated in part by her more frequent medical crises and hospitalizations, Mrs. M. was able to be increasingly communicative about her illness in individual sessions. In parallel, the therapist gradually found herself disturbed by, yet able to tolerate, an awareness on a daily basis of the gravity of Mrs. M's illness. The suffering entailed by this awareness resulted in an ability of the therapist to both face with the patient the possibility of the worst and, following this, to encourage the patient to explore positive opportunities that remained to her.

During one session, for example, Mrs. M. acknowledged feelings of resentment and abandonment after being informed that a member of her extended family with whom she had been very close was moving across the country. The therapist said to Mrs. M., "You have actually lost someone you loved [i.e., her husband]; you know the difference between someone being in this world and out of this world. What makes you think your friend won't be able to be with you when you need her the most? In the meantime, you are feeling well; why can't you go there for a vacation?" Mrs. M.'s response to this encouragement was more dramatic than the therapist had anticipated. "Mrs. B., you have given me back my future." Indeed, she did go to visit.

Paradoxically, but not surprisingly, the falling away of Mrs. M.'s denial of her illness was accompanied by decreased feelings of anxiety and depression and an enhanced optimism and ability to enjoy and participate in life.

At the end of the second year of treatment, four weeks elapsed between sessions due to the therapist's vacation. During this time Mrs. M. had lost sixteen pounds, yet upon the resumption of therapy she expressed enthusiasm about a part-time job that had been offered to her by a friend who had been unaware of Mrs. M.'s diagnosis. This position was especially suitable because of its proximity to Jennifer's school.

Mrs. M. reported a conversation that had ensued when Jennifer noticed a book on AIDS that the therapist had offered her mother. Jennifer asked her mother what the book was about. Mrs. M. replied that the book consisted of a memorial of quilts for people who had died of AIDS. Jennifer wanted to know what AIDS was. Mrs. M., who one month before had said that she could not "spit out" to her daughter the possibility of her hospitalization, now was able to answer her child candidly. She told Jennifer that AIDS was an illness that affected the body's protective system, making it difficult to fight infections. Jennifer then asked how a person gets AIDS. Her mother replied directly, "Through sex and through infected needles used by drug addicts." Mrs. M. later commented to the therapist, "I decided that if she had to hear the word AIDS, I wanted her to hear it first coming from my mouth."

When Jennifer arrived for her next joint session with her mother, the therapist remarked, "Mommy tells me that you were very interested in this book." Jennifer nodded as she proceeded to walk to a table to set up a game that she had brought out to play. She looked up at the therapist earnestly as the therapist commented, "I know that there are stories in the book about a lot of daddies who died of AIDS and who had little girls." Jennifer nodded and went on to teach the therapist the new game.

During the game, the therapist mentioned to Jennifer that she knew her mother had not always been feeling well lately. Jennifer indicated that she did not feel like thinking about anything sad on this day. The therapist suggested she might want to take a vacation from the subject. She vehemently nodded. "Okay," the therapist responded, "we'll take a vacation, but let's make a deal. Mommy regularly goes to the doctor, who usually tells her about his plans for helping her. From now on, I'd like Mommy to share with you some of what the doctor tells her so that you'll better know what to expect." Both mother and daughter nodded their assent.

The next time Mrs. M. returned from the doctor, Jennifer asked her mother, "What did the doctor say?" Her mother replied, "I gained a pound, I will get some new medicine for the muscle aches, and I'll see the doctor again soon." "You mean you won't have to go to the hospital?" Jennifer asked. "Not this week," Mrs. M. replied.

During her next individual session, Mrs. M. expanded on her visit to the doctor. He had been encouraged by her slight weight gain but was concerned about her worsening anemia. She appeared able to tolerate the ambiguity of her medical situation.

Later in the session, Mrs. M. reported that a close friend had told her that Jennifer looked depressed. The friend had asked Jennifer what was bothering her. Jennifer made reference to her mother's illness and asked if her mother was going to die. The friend replied, "I hope not." Jennifer then inquired about who would take care of her if something happened to her mother. The friend reassured her that there were many people who loved her and who could take care of her. The friend included herself on this list. The therapist asked Mrs. M. if she had considered this person as a viable caretaker. Mrs. M. said she hadn't, but liked the idea now that she thought of it. She now indicated a desire to include Jennifer in the planning of Jennifer's care by others should that become necessary.

In Jennifer's next joint session, the therapist brought up the fact that her mother had said that Jennifer was worried about who would take care of her if her mother was not able to do so. Jennifer was asked who she thought would be best able to do this. Jennifer started a playful interchange about who she and her mother most certainly would not choose, eventuating in the choice of three candidates of whom they did approve.

Jennifer then expressed a wish to play a board game. She chose the Talking, Feeling, Doing Game that she had not played for over a year. With mischievous glee, she now played by the rules and said, "Don't ask me. I answered my question; now you answer yours." The therapist's card read, "If you were to write a book, what would you write about?" The therapist replied, "I think I would like to write about a child." "Yes," Jennifer exclaimed enthusiastically, "write about a child with five parents." "Who would that be?" asked the therapist. Jennifer first mumbled two names so that they could not be understood (very likely her indistinctness reflected her anxiety/acknowledgement of her losses), presumably her parents, or her mother and the therapist. She then clearly articulated the three names of the potential caretakers she and her mother had just settled on.

Mrs. M's next card requested that she sing a song. She chose a song of hope from the musical about Little Orphan Annie, repeatedly singing the word "tomorrow" from the refrain "The sun will come out tomorrow."

## DISCUSSION

Among Mahler's many observations of the separation–individuation process, the temporary loss of the object during the second year of life after the establishment of object permanence but before the establishment of object constancy would seem to have special relevance with regard to bereavement. She observed clinically (Mahler 1968), as did Ainsworth in the laboratory (Ainsworth and Wittig 1960), the effect of the absence of the parent on the capacity of the toddler to function autonomously. These observations have been used again and again to inform our understanding of impasses at later stages of development. Masterson, for example, draws extensively on this aspect of separation–individuation theory in his treatment of the borderline adolescent (Masterson 1972). According to Rochlin (1961) real object loss is likely to result in narcissistic injury, resulting in a loss of self esteem, once the object qua object has become important to the child. This is consistent with the depression observed in children following parental bereavement (discussed above). Kohut (1971), in turn, stressed the importance of a real selfobject for the development of an adequate sense of self on which the capacity for object relations depends.

Mahler understood that, like other developmental processes, both the separation-individuation process and the later development of the sense of self can never be fully completed and will after the first three years of life remain a dynamic process open to fluctuations and regression. The younger the child when parentally bereaved, the greater the threat to both his self-esteem and the stability of the self and object representations underlying the child's capacity for object relations. The most effective reinforcement of this threatened stability is the presence of a compensatory real object. This developmental importance of the compensatory object probably continues well into adolescence. Underlying our attempt to help Jennifer (and her mother) deal with her bereavement and losses, past and future, was the ultimate goal of preserving and strengthening her capacity for object relations. To accomplish this goal, joint sessions with mother and child were successfully employed.

We have already spoken of the specific goals addressed in the conjoint treatment. Essential to the conjoint work, however, was the work in individual sessions with Jennifer's mother. Mrs. M.'s initial concern had been guilt she felt concerning her prior inability, first with her husband and second with Jennifer, to face the tragic circumstances of their lives. In her individual work the facts and feelings concerning her affliction with AIDS were gradually acknowledge and detoxified, and denial subsided. As the mother's need to deny fell away a bi-directional improvement in communication between mother and child could be both observed and reinforced in the joint sessions. This communication included an enhanced ability of Mrs. M. to be firm with Jennifer, which facilitated Jennifer's age-appropriate individuation from her mother. This individuation manifested itself first in expressions of anger toward her, followed by open curiosity about her illness. Simultaneously, we were able to trace movement from a constricted affect toward greater spontaneity, creativity, and self-confidence.

The death of one parent from AIDS and the confirmation of HIV antibodies in the other obviously constitute a threat of enormous proportions to both parent and child. In this situation the child's need for support is intensified at the very time the parent is feeling most vulnerable. This result is an intensification of mutual ambivalence. This heightened ambivalence is experienced as a threat to the relationship and must be acknowledged and worked through. Meanwhile the threatened relationship itself must be "held" (Winnicott 1958) in order to prevent the polar pathological solutions of mutual withdrawal on the one hand or symbiosis on the other. These dynamics are characteristic of parental bereavement in childhood in general, but are likely to be amplified in situations in which the surviving parent is additionally stressed. We believe that the treatment approach described here should be considered in all cases of childhood parental bereavement, but especially where there is a high level of stress and a low level of support for the surviving parent.

## REFERENCES

Abraham, K. (1911). *Notes on the psycho-analytical investigation and treatment of manic-depressive insanity and allied conditions.* In *Selected Papers on Psycho-Analysis,* pp. 137–156. London: Hogarth.

Adam, K., Lohrenz, J., Harper, D., and Streiner, D. (1982). Early parental loss and suicidal ideation in university students. *Canadian Journal of Psychiatry* 27:275–281.

Ainsworth, M. D. S., and Wittig, B. A. (1960). Attachment and the exploratory behaviour of one-year-olds in a strange situation. In *Determinants of Infant Behaviour,* vol. 4, ed. B. M. Foss, pp. 113–136. London: Methuen.

Bowlby, J. (1980). *Loss: Sadness and Separation.* New York: Basic Books.

Brown, G. (1982). Early loss and depression. In *The Place of Attachment in Human Behavior,* ed. C. M. Parkes and J. Stevenson-Hinde. New York: Basic Books.

Caplan, M., and Douglas, V. (1969). Incidence of parental loss in children with depressed mood. *Journal of Child Psychology and Psychiatry* 10:225–232.

Freud, S. (1917). Mourning and melancholia. *Standard Edition* 14:239–258.

Furman, E. (1974). *A Child's Parent Dies.* New Haven, CT: Yale University Press.

Kohut, H. (1971). *The Analysis of the Self.* New York: International Universities Press.

Mahler, M. (1968). *On Human Symbiosis and the Vicissitudes of Individuation.* New York: International Universities Press.

Masterson, J. F. (1972). *Treatment of the Borderline Adolescent: A Developmental Approach.* New York: Wiley.

Raphael, B., Field, J., and Kvelde, H. (1980). Childhood bereavement: a prospective study as a possible prelude to future preventive interventions. In *Preventive Psychiatry in an Age of Transition. Yearbook of the International Associations for Child and Adolescent Psychiatry and Allied Professions,* vol. 6, ed. E. J. Anthony and C. Chiland. New York: Wiley.

Rochlin, G. (1961). The Dread of Abandonment. In *Psychoanalytic Study of the Child* 15:451–470. New York: International Universities Press.

Spitz, R. A. (1946). Anaclitic depression. *Psychoanalytic Study of the Child* 2:313–342. New York: International Universities Press.

Tennant, C., Bebbington, P., and Hurry, J. (1980). Parental death in childhood and risk of adult depressive disorders: a review. *Psychosomatic Medicine* 10:289–299.

Van Eerdewegh, M., Bieri, M., Parilla, R., and Clayton, P. (1982). The bereaved child. *British Journal of Psychiatry* 140:23–29.

Winnicott, D. W. (1958). *Through Paediatrics to Psycho-Analysis. Collected Papers.* London: Tavistock.

# V

# CHILDREN OF SYMBIOTIC AND PSYCHOTIC PARENTS

# 10

# Successful Treatment of an 8-Year-Old School-Phobic Girl Using Tripartite Psychotherapy

*Arthur B. Zelman*
*Elissa Burian*

Melitta Sperling, in an influential paper published in 1967, reviewed the psychodynamics and treatment of school phobias. She, as well as many writers preceding and following her, regarded separation anxiety as a central issue. Sperling also noted similarities in behavior, parent–child dynamics, and course in puberty and adolescence between chronic induced school phobias and childhood "symbiotic schizophrenia."

Meanwhile, Margaret Mahler and her colleagues, working in the late 1950s and early 1960s at the Master's Center in New York, elaborated on and elucidated in detail the components and phases of the separation–individuation process in early childhood. Mahler both based her theory on, and attempted to apply the theory in, the treatment of a condition that she referred to as "symbiotic childhood psychosis." She concluded that the key to the child's pathology could be found in the attachment phases of the separation process, in particular the *symbiotic* phase, occurring from about the second through the sixth month of life. Sperling (1967) spoke of phobias as being characterized by "pregenital impulses . . . and fixations" and found the "anal-sadistic" period of development to be of particular importance. This latter period would roughly correspond to what Mahler referred to as the *rapprochement* phase. Mahler also described the establishment of object constancy, which included the rapprochement phase, during the second eighteen months of life.

Sperling concluded that at least one type of school phobia was "induced" by the needs of the parent figure(s) and that in such cases a pathological parent–child relationship lay at the heart of the matter. Mahler and her colleagues similarly concluded that a disturbed parent–child relationship was a necessary component of the child's symbiotic psychosis.

Since, from a psychological point of view, the psychotic child was not yet a separate entity, Mahler's group conceived a treatment in which the "patient" could be viewed as the parent–child unit.

This treatment technique was called *tripartite* (in contrast to dyadic) in that it included the presence of three people, the therapist, the child, and the parent. From a theoretical point of view, the label *tripartite* was confusing, since the technique's raison d'être was that psychologically the child did not yet exist apart from the primary caretaker. In any case, the major goal of the tripartite treatment of Mahler's psychotic children was the provision of a "corrective symbiotic experience."

Sperling viewed the treatment of induced school phobias as being directed primarily toward the pathological needs of the parent. Although she identified separation as a central issue in school phobias, she prescribed individual treatment of the parent with or without individual treatment of the child, depending on the child's age, chronicity of the condition, and so on.

Mahler's use of the simultaneous treatment of parent and child to address a disorder of the separation-individuation process stimulated us to consider the use of the technique in the treatment of another disorder, school phobia, whose core issue was also believed to involve the separation—individuation process. However, since the symptomatology of school phobia suggested that the rapprochement phase had gone awry, the overriding goal of treatment would be the re-working of this phase. Accordingly, the attempt would be made to provide a "corrective rapprochement experience." The technique as we applied it involved regular joint visits with mother and child and individual visits with the mother. Following is a description of the tripartite treatment of an 8-year-old school-phobic child.

## CLINICAL NARRATIVE

Jan T., age 8, was brought to the clinic by her mother, age 32, because Jan refused or was unable to attend school regularly. Mrs. T. had been referred by another clinic, which had provided intermittent brief therapy for the same problem since Jan had attended kindergarten. The referring clinic had taken a behavioral approach to Jan's symptom. They had encouraged Mrs. T. to ignore the frequent vomiting that had occurred when Jan was about to go to school.

Jan was seen for a few sessions individually as was her mother, with apparent improvement of school attendance. The problem recurred during the first grade but seemed to have been contained with some further brief work. As second grade commenced, Jan again began resisting attending school. She began to complain of stomachaches. When her mother insisted that she attend school anyway, Jan would fly into a rage, punching and biting and accusing her mother of not loving her. At the end of one such episode she asked her mother to kill her. Upon reevaluation, she was diagnosed as having a serious school phobia requiring more intensive treatment than the referring clinic felt capable of providing. One week before contacting our clinic, Jan had gotten so out of control that her mother had called the police. The police brought Jan to an emergency room where she received an intramuscular injection of a phenothiazine.

Mrs. T.'s usual response to Jan's rage was to relent and allow Jan to stay out of school. Jan would then become solicitous of her mother and promise to go to school the following day but not before extracting a promise that her mother would take her out of school early. When Jan did go to school she worried that her mother would have an accident or fall ill and be unable to come for her.

During the first month of second grade Jan missed school entirely one-third of the time. On days she did attend, her mother routinely took her home after two or three hours. On days Jan did not attend school at all, Mrs. T. left her at her own mother's house while she attended secretarial school. We were aware that one effect, therefore, of Jan's school refusal resulted in an increased dependency of Mrs. T. on her own mother.

## FAMILY HISTORY

Mrs. T. initially gave an impoverished account of her own childhood. Over the span of treatment she added details often recalled during the conjoint work with Jan. She first said she had had a happy childhood, but could not elaborate. She was an only child. Prior to her birth her parents had had a daughter who had died in infancy. The latter's death was presumed to have been due to sudden infant death syndrome. She remembered little of her preadolescent years, except that they were "pleasant," both in school and socially. She was a compliant child and was overprotected by her parents, especially by her mother. She spent much time fantasizing about venturing out more. She recalled that at about age 14 she became aware that she felt resentful at not being able to stay out as late as other teenagers.

Upon completion of high school, Mrs. T. obtained a job requiring that she return home later than the family dinner hour. Her mother, according to Mrs. T., felt rejected and stopped talking to her. After two months of silence, Mrs. T. moved to her own apartment and communication was not resumed until one year later, when she returned to her parents' home following a fire in her building.

Mrs. T. remained at the same job for four years, at the end of which time she felt ready to marry the previously married man she had been seeing since high school. Her parents disapproved and she moved to a distant city where her future husband's brother and sister-in-law lived. There she married, but soon felt lonely and after four months returned with her husband to her hometown. Jan was born a few months after their return. Mr. T. had difficulty obtaining work and he began to use and sell drugs. He also accused Mrs. T. of loving Jan more than him. Indeed, Mrs. T. reported that since the day she was born Jan was the most important person in her life.

The T.'s divorced when Jan was 18 months of age. At the time Mrs. T. contacted us she occasionally called upon her former husband to help with Jan's rages. She also maintained contact with her ex-husband's girlfriend with whom he had had a child. Mrs. T. and Jan readily accepted this child as Jan's brother.

Since her divorce, Mrs. T. had been on public assistance. She had also been receiving assistance from her parents, whom she saw weekly. Her parents lived a reclusive life. Her father was a retired factory worker, and her mother was a housewife who had not worked since Mrs. T.'s birth.

At the time of admission, Mrs. T. had a boyfriend, Richard, to whom she had been introduced by her ex-husband's sister. He had a secure, menial job, lived at home, and had an invalid brother whose care he shared with his mother. He had been married before and had two children who lived at some distance. Neither Mrs. T. nor Richard wished to get married for fear of having to take on each other's burdens. They saw each other several times a week, although Richard never remained overnight because Mrs. T. did not consider this proper for Jan. The couple had sex when Jan was asleep, at school, or at Richard's house.

A year into treatment, Mrs. T. described her boyfriend as "childlike." She said he was impatient with Jan, often "got down to Jan's level," and withdrew when Jan misbehaved. As she had with her husband, Mrs. T. felt "caught in the middle" between Jan and Richard in that she perceived them as vying for her attention.

## JAN'S HISTORY

Mrs. T.'s pregnancy with Jan was unplanned. Mrs. T.'s husband did not want the baby and encouraged her to abort it, but Mrs. T. refused. Jan was born via natural childbirth. Mrs. T. was elated at the birth. She found it easy to raise Jan as a baby. (About a year into therapy, she recalled that she had never allowed Jan to cry and wanted to meet all her needs so that she would be happy at all times.) Jan always enjoyed food and gradually began to overeat. Her mother found it difficult to suggest that she substitute fruit for cupcakes, even though Jan responded if her mother persisted.

As an infant, Jan was easy to put to sleep. According to Mrs. T. it was only after the divorce, when Jan was 18 months old, that she insisted on sleeping with her mother. At the time of admission they were still in the same bed. Mrs. T. said she found it difficult to sleep with Jan but it hadn't occurred to her to insist that Jan sleep in her own bed.

Jan drank milk from a bottle until age 3, at which time a dentist advised her mother against this. Mrs. T. substituted water for milk, after which Jan refused the bottle and never asked for it again.

According to Mrs. T., Jan walked at age 8 months and was viewed by her mother as an active child. Her language developed rapidly and her mother enjoyed talking to her. Mrs. T. reported that Jan had been toilet trained without difficulty at age 2.

Mrs. T. denied having concerns about Jan prior to Jan's entry into kindergarten, at which time she did not want to separate from her mother. Mrs. T. had wanted to stay in the classroom until Jan felt more comfortable, but this had not been permitted in spite of Jan's vomiting each school morning.

## INITIAL CONTACT WITH MOTHER–CHILD DYAD

Jan was large for her age and moderately overweight. She had a sometimes pleasant, sometimes vacant, facial expression. She wore a doll-like dress (during the first six months of treatment, she often wore light pastels in contrast to plaids or the darker schoolgirl clothes she wore later). She smiled tenuously, denied she had a problem, and declined an offer of apple juice. She was intrigued by a game called Rings on Your Finger and asked shyly if her therapist (E.B.) would teach her how to play. She angrily pushed the game away when she didn't win. She then began manipulating dolls and doll furniture, having turned her back on her mother and therapist.

During the second session, Jan immediately asked for juice and the Rings on Your Finger game. She announced that she must be the winner and proceeded to manipulate the spinner to ensure the result. Jan played with a doll whose hair had been cut and tried to comb it. She acknowledged irritation that the doll wasn't the way she wanted it to be and made it pass gas. She then played with the dollhouse and furniture and insisted that the house had no toilet. She took two baby dolls and had one take a bottle from the other. A third doll angrily announced that she would kill the thief.

Later, in an effort to assess her reality testing during a moment of stress, the therapist asked Jan if she knew what day of the week it was. She answered that she did not, but a few minutes later, she added defiantly, "If yesterday was Monday, this must be Tuesday." She softened when asked if she thought the therapist was nosy. Jan answered "yes," and the therapist explained that she had to ask her things to understand better how she thought and felt. Jan then volunteered that she killed a lot of dolls at home and took a bottle away from a doll. She assumed that the therapist would know they were buried in a cave, and that "they were dead." She added, "They were pretend, not real." Jan then acted out with dolls a morning ritual of a mother frantically rushing to work, leaving her baby with a sitter.

After these two visits with Jan and her mother, the therapist met with the mother alone. Mrs. T. was asked about her reactions to the first two sessions. She commented on two of Jan's play sequences. First, she viewed Jan's removal of a bottle from a doll as a justifiable response to what she had done to Jan. Second, she remarked that the threat of one doll to kill the other reflected feelings toward her that Jan expressed and acted out at home. It seemed that Jan's anger at her mother loomed large and was viewed as justified in Mrs. T.'s mind.

The therapist initially recommended twice weekly joint sessions for Jan and Mrs. T. in addition to a weekly session with Mrs. T. alone. She explained to the mother her rationale for this approach as being based on the concept of the mother as Jan's co-therapist. She framed the problem as relational in nature and viewed it from a positive perspective. Jan, according to the therapist, needed help from her mother before she could comfortably separate from her, but did not know how to ask for it.

The therapist further elaborated on a formulation focusing on the issue of ambivalence. She explained in nontechnical language that the relationship tended to oscillate between the two opposite poles of idealized love on the one hand and disappointment and rage on the other. In the first situation, mother and child shared the illusion of perfection (i. e., merging), in which conflict was denied, thereby precluding help. In the second, the com-

bination of the child's rage and the mother's fear also seemed to both
mother and child to preclude the possibility of help. The therapist chose to
delay bringing up the issue of the mother's rage and the child's resulting
fear.

The history Mrs. T. had given concerning her own past was also utilized
by the therapist in her initial attempt to make comprehensible to Mrs. T.,
in terms she could accept, the relational dilemma. Hence, while the therapist supported Mrs. T.'s positive view of her upbringing by acknowledging
the care and nurturance she had received, her ongoing struggle for autonomy and its implications for her difficulties with her own daughter was
emphasized. In the ensuing individual sessions with Mrs. T., these dynamics were repeatedly revisited in connection with the clinical process observed
in the mother–child sessions.

## THE MOTHER–CHILD THERAPY

The third and fourth tripartite sessions provided early examples of what
could be accomplished by seeing mother and child together. During the
third session, Jan engaged in frenetic doll play: a mother waking, rushing
to work, dropping off her child at Grandma's where she had been making
"gusha" [defecation], and returning to take Jan home. The therapist verbalized the baby's need for mothering and suggested that she might feel
lonely and be afraid to ask her mother for help when she needed it. At the
end of the session, Jan said to her mother, "I don't feel like carrying all these
things." Her mother responded by handing her some items and taking the
rest. The therapist commented that this was a way of asking for and accepting some help rather than "all or nothing," and that this constituted appropriate behavior for a child who was neither a baby nor an adult.

In the fourth mother–child session, the central issue as we later came to
see it was introduced into the therapy. Jan had not gone to school, claiming
a painful hip, and she had even refused to go to her grandmother's house,
which she ordinarily would have done. Mrs. T. remained home with Jan and
missed her own school.

Since this was supposed to have been Mrs. T.'s individual session, she
asked that Jan stay in the waiting room with the secretary. Jan was unable to
do this. She became angry and began to twist her mother's arm. Her mother
only mildly protested. When the therapist asserted that she could not allow
Jan to hurt her mother, Jan picked up an ashtray and threatened the therapist. This threat to the therapist mobilized her mother to take the ashtray

from Jan. Jan's rage abated and gave rise to a complaint about the contents of the therapy room. She demanded a doll from another room, stating that there was nothing good in the therapist's room, and ultimately told the therapist to "shut up." The therapist replied that Jan could tell her how she felt, and ask her not to talk about some things for a while, but that she could not stop the therapist from doing the job of helping her and helping her mother do the job of mothering her.

During the same session, Jan drew a picture of herself and her mother. In Jan's picture was a single figure labeled "Jan and Mom in my bed." The therapist pointed out that only one person appeared in the picture. Jan explained that her mother was behind her. She drew a second picture which again contained a single figure. This time she identified the figure as her mother and explained that she too was in the picture, but invisible. The content of this session thus brought into juxtaposition struggles over power on the one hand and separation on the other.

The first three months of treatment were intense and extremely difficult for the therapist, yet they led to a turning point in the mother–child relationship as well as in Jan's development, only after which her school refusal receded. During this period, the focus in both mother–child and individual sessions with mother was on mother's ability to take control of Jan, as well as on Jan's ability to allow her mother to help her. At home Jan's rage and physical attacks on her mother continued. Whenever Mrs. T. yielded to these rages by allowing her to stay home from school the episodes escalated, resulting in fights during which mother and child hurled abuse at one another. On days that Jan refused to go to school, her mother called, and as the therapist's time allowed, extra mother–child sessions took place. Gradually, Jan herself began to avail herself of the therapist's suggestion that she call her on the telephone so as to accept help to control herself.

One day, Jan was losing in a board game she was playing with her mother and therapist. She changed the rules many times. Her mother became upset and literally turned her back on Jan. The therapist pointed out to Jan that games were not worth playing unless all the players enjoyed them. Jan responded by throwing pieces of the game, following which her mother stalked out of the room. Jan, enraged, hurled a pocketbook, which hit the therapist in the face. She then bolted from the room. In doing so she injured her finger and blamed the therapist for her injury. This was the first time that she had accused the therapist, as opposed to her mother, of hurting her. Jan then tried to crawl into her mother's lap. Her mother refused. The therapist suggested that mother and child simply sit close to one another. Jan began to sob as the therapist pointed out that her mother's anger did not mean that Jan would be thrown away. Following this clarification and implied suggestion to the mother, Mrs. T. held her daughter.

In many mother–child sessions during the first three months of treatment, it became necessary for Mrs. T. to hold Jan for a different reason—in order to restrain her. One day on which Jan had refused to go to school, her mother called the therapist and asked if she should accede to Jan's desire to be taken to religious instruction. The therapist suggested that it would be more appropriate for Mrs. T. to bring Jan for an extra therapy session. Upon her arrival, Jan hid behind her mother. She denied everything her mother described concerning their confrontation at home. Meanwhile, Jan picked up some playdough and warned, "I need to throw something." The therapist asked whether she was worried that if she lost control her mother would not be able to help her. She screamed at the therapist to "shut up." Her mother in turn raised her voice, "How dare you scream at the one person who wants to help you?" Jan retorted, "I hate you." The therapist suggested that Jan had mixed feelings about seeing her mother being helped to do for Jan what she was not yet able to do for herself.

Jan continued to throw objects and taunted her mother, saying that she couldn't stop her. Her mother grabbed Jan, forced her to the floor, and, with the therapist's support, straddled her. Jan pleaded with the therapist to make her mother get off. Each time her mother began to relinquish her hold, Jan lost control. Mrs. T. insisted that Jan calm down before she would release her. Jan alternately wailed and blew mucus from her nose in a helpless, infantile rage. Mrs. T. remained firm and Jan eventually calmed down. She then begged to go to the bathroom, where she regained her composure. At the end of the session, she asked for a note for school explaining her absence. She couldn't think of what she wanted the note to say. She asked her mother, who deferred to the therapist. Mother and child accepted the suggestion that the note read, "Jan missed school because she was worried and had to see Mrs. B." Jan attended school the next day, fortified with the note.

Often, however, Mrs. T. was so worn out from similar confrontations both at home and in treatment that she could not muster the energy to help Jan return to school the following day. During another session during these difficult but crucial weeks, Jan again threw clay at the therapist. Her mother started to restrain her but acknowledged that she was not sure that she could do so. She asked as an alternative that a clinic psychiatrist recommend hospitalization for Jan.

This request led to a turning point in the treatment. Mrs. T.'s uncertainty and despair resonated with the feelings of the therapist. In her discussion with the psychiatrist (A.Z.) who had also been supervising the case, the therapist also wondered whether it was time to hospitalize Jan. The supervisor, having the luxury of viewing the case from a distance, pointed out how much had been accomplished in only two months of treatment. It was concluded that both the speed of the process and the intensity of the countertransference was due in large part to the therapist's degree of direct exposure to the problem due to the tripartite sessions.

A small amount of medication (Mellaril, 10mg) was prescribed for Jan, which the mother could give on an as-needed basis. More importantly, in our opinion, the therapist insisted on increasing visits for Jan and her mother from two to three times per week (in addition to the weekly visit with Mrs. T. alone). Mrs. T. accepted both the medication and the extra weekly visit and never again spoke of giving Jan over to the care of others. Having been offered additional help with Jan, she in turn took the initiative of asking her boyfriend for more help in controlling her. Soon after, she decided to take a temporary leave from secretarial school in order to be more available to Jan.

Following this incident we became aware that Jan's outbursts seemed to be associated with attempts to function at a level above her capacity. For example, Jan had the therapist's permission to establish special rules if she needed to when she played games in therapy. Jan rejected this option and insisted on playing by established rules. However, she usually ended the game when her opponent was about to win. If the therapist did win she was ignored, while Jane engaged her mother in a private conversation. Mrs. T., for her part, engaged in these "pleasant" conversations as if nothing was wrong, thus collaborating with Jan to isolate the therapist. The therapist had to struggle with the feelings of impotence engendered by this situation and stood her ground as she commented that Jan sometimes asked too much of herself and that it was the therapist's job to help her mother so that she didn't have to attempt things that were too hard for her.

Joint sessions with mother and child provided frequent opportunities for the therapist to observe and focus on mother's anxiety-driven communications to her daughter. One day Jan complained that her eye hurt. Her mother suggested that her problem was an allergic itch caused by the medication. Jan denied that her eye itched. She said that it was a pain similar to the pain she felt when her ears had been pierced. The therapist praised her effort to put into words how she felt physically and then asked her whether she could try to do the same with her feelings. For instance, how did she feel when her mother was not in school with her when she wanted her to be there? Jan answered, "Scared." The therapist suggested that "scared" might also feel like a kind of pain. Her mother listened with interest and expressed surprise at Jan's response.

Jan's growing ability to ask for help could be seen in two joint sessions which occurred soon after. In the first, Jan assumed the role of a harsh teacher and stated that teachers don't help children. The therapist made the interpretation that when a child is afraid a mother is unable to help, she is afraid to ask for her help. The next day, Jan went to school not feeling well but afraid that her mother might not believe her. She felt unable to remain in school and told this to the teacher. The teacher called Mrs. T. to inform her that Jan had a stomachache. The therapist supported Jan's effort to go to school and to allow teachers to help her when it was too difficult to handle matters alone. During the next session, Jan at first again assumed the role of a mean teacher but switched to the role of a helpful one.

Jan still tested to the hilt, however, and her mother's (and perhaps the therapist's) tenuous confidence in her ability to support her child again wavered, resulting in an attempt to externalize the problem. One day she read an article on Tourette's syndrome. She brought the article to a joint session with Jan. Jan tried to rip it out of her mother's hand. Jan responded angrily when the therapist asked what was bothering her. She tried to stop the therapist from talking and complained that there weren't enough doll beds to play with. She picked up a clock and threatened to throw it at the therapist. Her mother restrained her, and the therapist sent Jan home early with the statement that work on better controls would continue when she returned for her session the next day. In retrospect, we understood the exacerbation of Jan's anger as probably related to the mother's recurring doubts that she and the therapist could provide Jan with what she needed. Also in retrospect, the therapist's uncharacteristic action of cutting short a session may have represented a countertransference to the mother's despair and implied devaluation of the therapy.

Early in treatment the mother had expressed doubt that she would be able to attend regular individual sessions with the therapist. Her reason for this was that if Jan was absent from school she would not be able to tolerate separation from her mother while her mother was seeing the therapist. As Jan's attendance improved (after about 2 1/2 months of treatment), her mother came more regularly. However, she still couldn't tell Jan of these visits for fear of her reaction. As the individual visits became more frequent, the work turned to Mrs. T.'s own history. She began to recall her own early feelings of inadequacy and pain. She now revealed to the therapist that she, like Jan, had been overweight and had suffered from asthma. Meanwhile,

Jan demonstrated increasing tolerance of her own dependency needs. Four months into treatment, Jan wrote on the blackboard, "Jan was here." She erased this message and changed it to "Jan wuz here." The therapist suggested that Jan might be feeling like or wish to be a smaller child who didn't yet know how to spell. Jan responded by asking for juice, albeit in an imperial tone. Hence, Jan's acknowledgement of her own neediness seemed to emerge in tandem with her mother's.

Jan's enhanced ability to tolerate her neediness also seemed to correlate with an increased self-tolerance. During one session she made a mistake while drawing intricate letters and was able to remedy it by saving the "good" letters. Later in the same session, she fell and wailed like a toddler. She was able to seek her mother's comfort, however, by moving towards her. Previously, in similar circumstances, she had become increasingly enraged and immobilized. Thus, the therapist could witness directly the transformation of Jan's representation of her mother into an increasingly "good object." As her mother's ability to assert control of Jan increased, Jan's play and verbal communications became more expressive, reflecting a growing ability to use the joint sessions for regression in the service of the ego.

During one session, in response perhaps to the fact that her mother was not feeling well, Jan could not find a comfortable emotional niche until she gave a doll a shampoo while talking baby talk and crawling into her mother's lap. This led to a discussion about which pretend age made her feel the best. Jan answered with conviction, "Two, before I had to go to school." For the first time, Jan brought up anal material. She referred to a piece of blue dough that had fallen onto the floor as "doodie." The therapist picked it up, inquiring whose "doodie" it was. She laughed and told her mother that the therapist was nasty. She and the therapist made a series of "doodies" and filled a toy toilet into which she placed a figure. She then announced, "Everyone makes peepee." She dribbled water from a doll's bottle, pretending she was urinating, then held the bottle filled with soapy water to her mouth. Finally, she asked for permission to have a bottle in therapy and requested that the bottle be blue.

This emergence of anal play occurred together with a diminished need to treat the therapist as an anal object. Also, Jan's ability to play with, rather than act out, anal issues coincided with her mother's enhanced ability to set limits on Jan's behavior. Predictably, Jan responded to these demands with more vigorous testing but also quicker capitulations, similar to that of a healthy 2-year-old.

Jan now openly acknowledged the value of the therapist to her. She now wrote a less ambivalent message on the blackboard, "Jan was here last year and will be here next year." She also took measures to protect a container in which were kept artifacts she had made. She put the therapist's name on the door, and posted a note instructing other patients to sign their names in a column headed "Who Comes to This Room." She placed her name at the top of the page. Due in large part, we believe, to Mrs. T.'s active participation in Jan's treatment, Mrs. T. showed little ambivalence towards Jan's expressions of trust in the therapist.

One day, when Mrs. T. was sick, the therapist spoke to Jan on the telephone. She was introduced to Jan's imaginary friends, who ranged in age from 3 to 9 years. Before hanging up, Jan asked the therapist to remain on the telephone and meet one more, a baby Melissa (a play on the therapist's name), who babbled. Ms. B. commented that Melissa sounded like a nice baby. Jan came to the next day's session accompanied by her imaginary baby.

From the fifth through ninth month of treatment, Jan attended school every day for a full morning. Her mother picked her up and remained with her in the afternoons. During this period, Jan's school refusal was brought more directly into the treatment as she tested her mother's (and the therapist's) resolve to leave Jan with her maternal grandmother in order to attend regular weekly sessions with the therapist. Her mother proved able to meet this challenge.

One day Mrs. T. brought Jan to therapy in spite of Jan's complaint that she wasn't feeling well. During the session Jan began to "shampoo" her doll's hair, reluctantly accepting the therapist's request that she not cut the hair. Jan then took the role of a punitive mother to her 5-year-old child. The therapist observed to Jan that she as the mother was responsible for the kind of child she had. In response Jan's play mother became kinder. Jan announced that when she grew up she would be a teacher. Her mother interjected that teachers had to remain at school all day. Jan laughed and said that by then she would.

It was eight months before Jan simultaneously included both her mother and the therapist in her play. This event seemed to signify an increased capacity to tolerate ambivalence and a decreasing need to split the therapist and her mother into good and bad objects. In all but dramatic and symbolic play, the therapist, in mother's presence, became firmer in her expectation that Jan not treat her like a part object who must immediately gratify her. For example, Jan was now expected to make requests in a civil tone. The therapist pointed out that she responded to Jan's tone of voice and her facial expressions as well as to her words and that she would comply with her requests only if she felt well treated by Jan. The therapist also told Jan that it was possible for all three people in the room to enjoy being together, but this required an acceptance of the fact that some, but not all of her wishes could be gratified. Mrs. T. gave much evidence of an increasing understanding of the importance of making similar demands on her daughter.

Compliance with the therapist's expectations that she request rather than demand temporarily increased Jan's vulnerability to feelings of disappointment and rejection. One day she verbally insulted the therapist and looked anxiously at her mother. Mrs. T. responded by expressing anger at Jan for mistreating the therapist. Jan's counterattack focused on feelings of deprivation. She complained that her mother did not buy her enough food when on an outing. Mrs. T. answered that Jan was insatiable. A discussion ensued concerning how a finite amount of money could best be appropriated. The therapist pointed out that father, mother, and child could feel deprived when resources were limited. Jan herself then suggested that they could make sandwiches rather than buy them, to allow for more visits to the swimming pool.

Two significant new behaviors now appeared. First, Jan frequently started sessions by talking about "problems." Secondly, when Jan hurt herself, she now expressed pain without blaming it on others. A recurring sequence of dramatic play emerged in which Jan portrayed an unpleasant, demanding baby who the therapist, in the role of landlord, did not like. However, Jan also allowed the therapist to be a nice neighbor who protected the baby and met the baby's needs.

Summer approached and school personnel recommended that Jan be enrolled in a program to enable her to experience increasing separation from her mother. The therapist strongly recommended the opposite, namely a summer together with her mother, during which time Jan could, with her mother's approval and support, venture forth at her own pace. Underlying our recommendation was the assumption that the school phobia would resolve itself when the parent–child ambivalence was sufficiently reduced that the child would voluntarily leave her mother, as occurred in the normal rapprochement phase. The therapist now felt that, given a little more unpressured time together, this would occur. The school reluctantly agreed to this plan on condition that Jan's mother help Jan with math.

Indeed, upon her return to school in September, she quickly took a liking to her teacher, and now commenced regular full time attendance. The therapist told Jan she wanted to talk to her teacher to tell her that Jan was in treatment so that she could be sensitive to Jan's anxieties. Jan protested. In her mother's presence the therapist persisted and called the teacher during a tripartite session. Far from continuing to protest, Jan told other clinic staff members with pride what the therapist had done on her behalf.

As Jan's school attendance and functioning at home with her mother improved, her transference to the therapist deepened (together with thickening resistance) and was more clearly expressed in the joint sessions, much as one might have expected in individual treatment. Her partial ability to acknowledge dependence on the therapist now alternated with overt hostile rejection. In conjoint sessions, Jan became contemptuous of "baby" play and she refused to speak about school or home. However, she let slip the name of a new kitten. Such sharing with the therapist threw her into conflict. She seemed to need to deny her and her mother's dependence on the therapist, especially when she perceived the therapist as getting closer to her mother. At such times she deprecated the therapist, for example, calling her ugly.

At Jan's request the tripartite sessions were reduced from three to two visits per week so that she could take part in afterschool activities. About one month later, Jan questioned the need to come to therapy altogether. She was given the choice of either discontinuing her therapy or continuing "just for fun" as long as her mother was satisfied that they were getting along adequately. However, it was made clear to Jan that the therapist would continue to meet with her mother in order to enable her mother to continue to help Jan and that tripartite sessions would resume should her mother determine that it was necessary.

Jan chose to continue on a twice-weekly basis, perhaps out of fear that a symbiotic alliance would develop between mother and therapist that would exclude her much as her alliance with her mother had excluded the outside world.

Jan continued to make use of the treatment despite her denial of the need for it. In dramatic play, her mother no longer had to assume the role of an ideal person, and the therapist was no longer asked to take only rigid, negative, and devalued roles. For example, the therapist was assigned the role of a student who could get a C instead of an F. Her mother, meanwhile, generally received Bs.

Another significant change, in addition to regular all-day school attendance, was Jan's newfound ability to express to her mother, as opposed to the therapist, specific worries or difficulties. One of her concerns involved a reading lab teacher who accused Jan of knowing more than she admitted to. Her mother offered to speak with the teacher, but Jan declined the offer. Mrs. T. at first respected Jan's wish. She soon discovered, however, that Jan's anxiety over the matter was causing Jan to bite the inside of her cheek. During a joint session, Jan decided that she herself would ask another teacher, whom she trusted, for help. In the event that this was not effective, Jan agreed to allow her mother permission to speak to the lab teacher.

During this same session, Jan played telephone operator. Mrs. T. picked up the telephone and asked to speak to Jan. Jan insisted she had no mother or father, only a lawyer whom the therapist was asked to portray. The therapist answered the telephone as her lawyer, who suggested that Jan was in need of someone to defend her. Jan laughed.

As her trust in her mother increased, Jan could now make direct use of and take pleasure in the triangular treatment situation. She now often assigned her mother and the therapist equal status in role playing. In one scenario, Jan was a Sears order clerk, her mother was a customer named Jan Long who lived on Green Street, and the therapist was Jan Short who lived on Blue Street. The therapist was also a customer named Wendy Plump who lived on Ice Cream Street, thus allowing the sensitive issue of her weight problem to surface. This material was directly followed by Jan's statement that she was smart in reading lab.

As Jan began to allow herself to feel more vulnerable, she was able to work through some of her ambivalence and fear of abandonment. In play, she assigned the therapist the role of an orphan in an orphanage. Jan played the role of the therapist's mean teacher who, however, also gave her student dolls to sleep with. The therapist noted that the mean teacher could also be kind. Jan also resumed playing baby. Often the baby was a child prodigy who filled the best museums with her artwork. For this purpose she made many pictures which she hung for display and she invited other clinic staff to view her exhibition. Work in this vein continued for several more months, during which time regular school attendance and even participation in after school activities continued.

Despite the need for further work on relational issues for both mother and child, enough of the mother–child problem had resolved to generate confidence in both Jan's mother and the therapist that the school phobia had been genuinely resolved. More importantly, and not coincidentally, Jan's development, if not unimpaired, could still proceed in an adequate fashion.

## DISCUSSION

Jan's case illustrates the early emergence in the treatment of a power struggle between parent and child. In the face of this challenge, Jan's mother wavered, falling prey to such mechanisms as denial, externalization of the problem, and splitting, in which therapist and child alternated roles of good and bad object, including devaluation of the therapist and the therapy.

The parental mechanism of experiencing the therapist as bad object and the devaluation of therapy are of particular importance in their potential to generate a negative countertransference in the therapist, resulting in pessimism regarding the progress of treatment. This countertransference reaction reflects the parent's increased resistance when forced in the conjoint treatment to frustrate her child, thus laying the groundwork for the child's individuation. This resistance, if not dealt with, will usually be acted out by the child.

Viewed from this perspective, the countertransference reaction of despair may signify that the core conflict has entered into the therapy. As with all countertransference not due to the therapist's own conflicts, it is the task of the therapist to contain and utilize it.

As we implied at the outset, the concrete focus in tripartite treatment on the as-yet undifferentiated parent–child unit may be appropriate and even necessary in the treatment of disorders originating in the separation–individuation process of the first two or three years of life. If this be the case it is also true that the attempt to address this fundamental impasse directly is likely to intensify the parental transference and countertransference reactions discussed above, as compared with more traditional individual approaches to parent and child.

For this reason, an essential ingredient of the total therapeutic interventions are regular, frequently individual meetings with the parent, the first goal of which is to build and maintain a therapeutic alliance that will withstand the inevitable onslaughts of negative transference and countertransference phenomena. For this reason also, it is strongly advisable, if not absolutely necessary, that the therapist have access to another clinician either as supervisor or clinical collaborator (e. g., to evaluate the need for medication, respite care, etc.). In fact, both authors doubt that the treatment described here could have been sustained without their collaboration.

The major crises that both threatened to interrupt Jan's treatment on the one hand, and the resolution of which constituted a major therapeutic breakthrough on the other, occurred within the first three to six months of treatment. The tripartite psychotherapeutic technique applied in this case of school phobia proved to be relatively rapid as well as effective.

In reviewing the literature describing this technique as applied to childhood psychosis, we noted a similar rapidity of response. Elkisch (1971), for example, had intended to treat a mother and her 2½ year old child individually but "found it necessary" to treat them together for a period of four months. Improvement was such that after this period of time she was able to return to her original plan. She reports that although the child and mother each had many more years of treatment (the mother with many therapists), twenty years later the mother attributed her son's positive subsequent healthy development to the four months of simultaneous treatment he and she had received.

Bergman (1971) described the tripartite treatment of a 4-year-old symbiotic child as follows: "Rachel's mother responded well to the demands of the intensive treatment program. She was willing to give all. Rachel too responded very rapidly to the creation of the symbiotic milieu. Her angry shrieking stopped within the first four weeks and was quickly replaced by pleasure in physical closeness. She loved to be held, fondled, rocked, carried about and covered up, which she would call 'making cozy'" (p. 332).

In both of these cases we have the impression that it was the child who changed first in spite of, or because of, the fact that it is the parent who is the senior partner in the pathological relationship. It is as if the safety of the tripartite situation removes a barrier to development against which the child is already pushing. Nevertheless, it is important to recognize that the parent must be helped to give permission before the child can change (i. e., separate). We choose to believe that the parent, too, has a developmental need to psychologically separate from the child, even if there is greater resistance to this change.

The relatively rapid improvement of the child obtained in the case described here, correlated with the mother's newfound, albeit incomplete, confidence in her ability to say no to her child. It is as if the successful negotiation by the child of the separation–individuation process, especially the rapprochement phase, is predicated on the parent's ability to say no to her toddler before he or she can say yes. This is consistent with Spitz's (1965) observation that the child learns the concept of negation before that of affirmation.

Following the establishment of adult control in the tripartite situation, regression in the service of the ego, that is, symbolic play, soon followed. Simultaneously, from an object relations perspective, we could observe the shift of the child's self and object representations in the direction of decreased polarization, followed by increased integration.

As noted earlier, Sperling (1967) had observed similarities between chronic (parentally) induced school phobias and "symbiotic schizophrenia."

The intensity of Jan's rage, her use of premature defenses, and her tenuous hold on reality initially suggested a psychotic or near-psychotic condition. We postulate a continuum of disorders of the separation–individuation process that depend for their manifestations of the specific phase of the separation–indivduation process that was problematic. In Jan's case, adequate attachment during the first year of life had apparently been achieved. Thus, the clinical process revealed Jan's relative potential to trust, because of which rapid progress followed rather than disintegration. It also confused the main issue, which appeared to be separation rather than attachment. In this case at least, a "corrective rapprochement experience" as facilitated by a tripartite approach did both seem to occur and to result in the resolution of a school phobia.

There has developed an increasing awareness over the past three or four decades of the earlier origins of much childhood pathology (oppositional disorders, for example) that had previously been regarded as oedipal. This being the case, one or another of the phases of the separation–individuation process is likely to be involved in their etiology. We believe, therefore, that the tripartite method should prove itself of broad value through its facilitation of a corrective experience of one or another phase of the separation–individuation process.

## REFERENCES

Bergman, A. (1971). I and you: the separation-individuation process in the treatment of a symbiotic child in separation-individuation. In *Essays in Honor of Margaret Mahler*, ed. J. McDevitt and C. Settlage, pp. 325–355. New York: International Universities Press.

Elkisch, P. (1971). Initiating separation-individuation in the simultaneous treatment of a child and his mother in separation-individuation. In *Essays in Honor of Margaret Mahler*, ed. J. McDevitt and C. Settlage, pp. 356–376. New York: International Universities Press.

Mahler, M. S. (1968). *On Human Symbiosis and the Vicissitudes of Individuation*. New York: International Universities Press.

Sperling, M. (1967). School phobias: classification, dynamics and treatment. In *Psychoanalytic Study of the Child* 22:375–401. New York: International Universities Press.

Spitz, R. A., (1965). *The First Year of Life*. New York: International Universities Press.

# 11

## The P.A.C.T. Therapeutic Unit: Treating Mentally Ill Parents and Their Children Together in a Therapeutic Nursery*

*Bernard G. Pasquariella*
*Nancy Berlin*
*Janet Brown Lobel*

### INTRODUCTION

Much information has emerged over the last two decades concerning the factors which contribute to placing a child at high risk for psychiatric disorder. One of the most powerful predictor variables is the existence of a high level of parental psychopathology (Goodman and Isaacs 1984, Jensen et al. 1990, Landau et al. 1972, Sameroff and Seifer 1981). Despite this long-standing awareness, there was little systematic evidence for the existence of primary or secondary prevention programs directed toward this high-risk population of children of mentally ill adults. Goodman and Isaacs (1984) noted that:

> Viewing individuals in the context of their families has led to more frequent involvement of parents in the mental health treatment of a child. However, it is still a rare occurrence when a woman enters a psychiatric facility for the mental health professional to assess or intervene into the needs of her chil-

*This chapter is based on a presentation to the American Orthopsychiatric Association, Chicago, IL, April 28, 1995.

dren. Even more unusual is the provision of preventive intervention for this population. [p. 388]

In the mid 1980s, the lack of preventive programs for children parented* by mentally ill adults was regarded as a problem not only in The Center's mental health catchment area of Westchester County but throughout the entire New York State mental health system. The lack of necessary resources, exacerbated by multiple and separate funding streams for adult and child treatment services, made it extremely difficult to implement programs of integrated psychiatric intervention for these families. As a consequence, many of the children from these families did not come to the attention of mental health agencies until the risk of disturbance had escalated to the point of manifest psychiatric symptomatology. In 1986, the New York State Office of Mental Health issued a request for proposals from state and voluntary agencies for a pilot program to establish therapeutic nurseries for children whose parents had been diagnosed as severely or chronically mentally ill.

In response to this announcement, The Center for Preventive Psychiatry (CPP), through the Westchester County Department of Community Mental Health, submitted, and subsequently received funding for, a proposal to provide a comprehensive and intensive program of assessment, treatment, and case management services to parents with high levels of psychopathology, their preschool children, and their families. The funded project, originally designated as the C.M.I.P. (Children of the Mentally Ill Parents) Project has evolved into the P.A.C.T. (Parent and Child Together) Therapeutic Unit to more accurately reflect our mandate to meet the mental health needs of children and their psychiatrically ill parents in a single setting. In order to provide an empirical context for the objectives and multimodal structure of our intervention model (i. e., treating parents and children together in a therapeutic nursery), it is necessary to sample the mental health literature that addresses why this population of children is at high risk (i. e., what are the factors which mediate the pathogenic impact of their parents' illnesses upon, and the psychiatric and developmental disorders common among, these children), and past and present efforts to intervene in their mental health needs.

---

*Since the work to be described here reflects a focus on the primary caretaker of the child and since most mentally ill parents who take care of their young children are mothers, parents and mothers are used interchangeably unless otherwise indicated.

## OVERVIEW OF THE LITERATURE

### Correlates of Risk

Considerable research and clinical evidence suggests that children with a mentally ill parent have a greater risk for delayed or deviant development than children from more stable, mentally healthy families. Studies convincingly demonstrate the increased risk to these children of emotional and behavioral problems.

Perhaps the most frequently cited association of parental mental illness with mental illness of the child is the rate of schizophrenia in the offspring of schizophrenic parents. While the rate of schizophrenia in the general population is 1 percent, it is about 10 percent for children with one schizophrenic parent (Sameroff and Seifer 1981), and 50 percent with two. There is also a well-established empirical relationship between schizophrenia in a parent and the likelihood that the child of this parent will have other problems. About 50 percent of children with a schizophrenic parent will be psychiatrically maladjusted (Heston 1966, Neale and Weintraub 1975). While twin and adoption studies suggest a significant genetic contribution to the transmission of mental disturbance from parent to child, at least one-half of the variance appears to be due to environmental factors.

Children born to psychotic parents evidence language delays, eating and sleeping problems, impaired reality testing, disorganized thought, depression, difficulty expressing themselves, and higher rates of delinquency (Landau et al. 1972). In this particular study, the mental health or illness of parents was more predictive of juvenile delinquency than size of family or socioeconomic status, as previously thought. Children of mentally ill parents evidence lowered social initiation and responsiveness (Kochanska 1991) that may indicate aberrant ego functioning, are angrier, more withdrawn and anxious, are less able to focus and sustain attention, and often have unresolved attachment and separation issues (Musick et al. 1987, Stott et al. 1983). Delayed language development, enuresis, eating and sleeping problems, physical aggression against peers, difficulties in sexual identification (Landau et al. 1972), anxiety disorders (or any of 42 diagnosable childhood disorders), and conduct disorders (Fendrich et al. 1990) have also been identified in these children. Furthermore, school-age children with severely mentally ill (SMI) mothers have been found to exhibit major behavioral disturbances in school. In the Stony Brook High-Risk Project (Neale and Weintraub 1975), teachers rated these children as impatient, disrespectful, defiant, inattentive, and withdrawn. They manifest acting out and impulsive behavior and seem unable to perform within the demands of the classroom.

Other studies have indicated that more than 70 percent of the offspring of depressed mothers have experienced diagnosable disorders (Hammen et al. 1987, cited in Hammen et al. 1990), such as affective psychopathology (Zahn-Waxler et al. 1984). Field's (1992) work points out the effect of maternal depression on infants. Infants with a depressed mother show less positive affect and lower activity levels. This persists into toddlerhood in the form of sadness, minimal verbalization, and less exploratory behavior. Studies of children with affectively ill parents suggest that characteristics of these caregiving environments place children at high risk for developing insecure attachments (DeMulder and Radke-Yarrow 1991).

Interaction with a disturbed parent is likely to combine with a child's genetic vulnerability to further predispose a child to psychiatric disorder or developmental anomalies (Gochman 1986, Goodman and Brumley 1990, Goodman and Isaacs 1984, Landau et al. 1972, Musick et al. 1987, Stott et al. 1984). Thus, the mother's illness may be expressed emotionally and behaviorally and exert its effect via the quality of parenting. Not surprisingly, studies document maternal dysfunction for most women who are SMI, especially concerning social contacts and responsiveness to the child (Mowbray et al. 1995).

Attachment theorists have long maintained that the infant's first attachment relationship is of paramount importance in the genesis of healthy socioemotional development or psychopathology (Bowlby 1973). Research has shown that the emotional availability of the infant's mother or caregiver, such as sensitivity and responsivity to the child's needs, is associated with the quality of the attachment (Ainsworth 1969). Mahler and colleagues' (1975) observations of mother–child interactions set the ground for, and confirmed the significance of, the mother's emotional availability for the child's normal growth toward separateness and independent functioning. Maternal care, therefore, includes not only physical but also psychological care. Psychological needs of the child include the need for parental attunement, empathy, love, and stimulation. The manner in which the parent responds to these needs will, to a large degree, shape the child's developing sense of self and his capacity to relate to others.

Given what we now know about the significance of early mother–infant relationships, we recognize that aberrant mother–infant or child interactive patterns may preclude the normal negotiation of the attachment and separation behaviors vital to healthy growth in the child (Stern 1977). The specific nature of the vulnerabilities that arise in an infant depends in part on the kind of "relational partner" that mothers and infants are able to become for each other, especially how flexible and adaptive the mother is in relationship to her child (Elkind 1992).

Analyzing mother–child interactions, DeMulder and Radke-Yarrow (1991) found that maternal psychopathology was related to attachment classification. Sixty-seven percent of 112 1- to 5-year-olds with a bipolar mother were classified as insecure; further, these children evidenced more anxiety compared to insecure children with a well or unipolar mother. Lewis and colleagues (1984) have studied longitudinally the link between a mother and child's early social relations and later child psychopathology. Psychiatric diagnosis aside, mothers who exhibited maternal dysfunction in the form of insecure mother–child attachments had more children who developed psychopathology at age 6. Thus, the quality of parent–child attachment appears to constitute a significant mediating variable between maternal and child psychopathology. The fact that dysfunctional parenting and parental psychiatric disorder have been linked to psychiatric and behavioral problems in children, and that this relationship seems to be mediated via the quality of mother–child attachment, suggests that a major focus of intervention should be on the early parent–child relationship.

While other studies (e.g., Jensen et al. 1990) have confirmed that the severity of parental pathology was the most salient variable (even when considering life stress and divorce) associated with child psychopathology, this transmission of pathology to the child may also be exacerbated by other mediating factors, such as the absence of a well spouse, few resources for economic, social, and psychological support, frequent disruptions in child care, or age of the child at the time the mother's disorder began (Goodman and Isaacs 1984). Sachnow (1987) found that children are affected not only by their parent's mental illness, but by the psychiatric hospitalization as well.

**Interventions For The SMI Mother and Her Child Together**

Since the early SMI mother–child relationship appears to be a major, potentially alterable, mediating variable in the transmission of mental disturbance from parent to child, the fundamental objective of preventive intervention is the enhancement of the early mother–child relationship. Furthermore, the younger the child, the more salient for the relationship and the more amenable to influence are issues of attachment and separation–individuation. We believe that the most effective and economical way to exert this influence is through a "naturalistic" milieu in which both parent and child participate and in which focus on the mother–child dyad plays a primary role.

Gochman (1986) advocated dyadic intervention for extremely disturbed mothers with their children. Her approach included supportive measures, interpretation of the dynamics of the interactions, and interpretations of the mother's transference to her child. Modeling, behavioral directives, and suggestions are directed at the in vivo mother–child interaction.

The UCLA Family Stress Project (Hammen et al. 1990) study compared high-risk children of unipolar depressed, bipolar, diabetic, or arthritic medically ill mothers, and children of normal mothers. Children were followed longitudinally and the functioning of mothers and children were assessed with multiple measures and through direct observations of interactions. Findings confirm that impairment of maternal functioning associated with psychiatric illness, rather than diagnosis per se, is one mechanism accounting for negative developmental and psychological outcomes for the children. At the same time, child characteristics may influence maternal variables. For example, children who were older, who had more negative self-concepts, and who were negative and critical in their interactions with their mothers appeared to have mothers who were more dysfunctional apart from parenting. In keeping with these findings, the UCLA group conceptualized a transactional model in which the child's dysfunction, arising partly in reaction to the mother, in turn increases the mother's stress and overwhelms her coping mechanisms, thereby further contributing to impaired maternal role functioning. The authors use this model to advocate for the treatment of mother and child together.

Goodman and Isaacs (1984) included mother–infant groups and home maternal coaching sessions in their primary prevention programs for the children of SMI mothers. Their program also included community outreach support, educational groups for mothers, and specialized day care for the children.

A growing body of clinical research provides support for beneficial short- and long-term outcomes of intervention aimed at the SMI mother–child dyad (Tableman 1981, cited in Lucas et al. 1984). Lieberman et al. (1991), for example, reported a preventive intervention study of anxiously attached dyads. One and one-half hours per week infant–parent psychotherapy targeting the dysfunctional mother–child pair enhanced maternal empathy and interaction with the child, decreased toddler avoidance, resistance and anger, and enhanced a goal-directed partnership.

Three separate groups reported on multimodal and milieu interventions with SMI mothers and their children. The first project, Thresholds, a psychiatric rehabilitation center in Chicago, targeted SMI mothers who had undergone hospitalization during their children's early years (Musick et al.

1987, Stott et al. 1983, 1984). To participate, a woman had to be at least 18 years old, have a child younger than 5, have a diagnosis of psychosis, and have no diagnosis of drug addiction, alcoholism, or mental retardation. Women and their young children attended a center-based program four days a week. The impact of variations in parenting as well as preventive intervention upon the developing child was studied in this group of 101 children of schizophrenic, affectively ill, or borderline and other character-disordered parents.

Intervention for the mothers included supervision of medication compliance, crisis intervention, and parent groups. For the children, a therapeutic nursery was provided which the mother attended once a week. Two components of the program involved the mother–child dyad. First, mothers and children ate lunch together under staff supervision three times per week. Second, mothers and children participated in a video exercise in which dyadic problems were identified and role played.

Oyserman and colleagues (1994) reviewed Detroit's Loving Attachment of Mothers and Babies (LAMB) program, which targeted severely disturbed schizophrenic and depressed mothers of very young children. It was modeled on the Thresholds program, and provided similar intervention services. The DENVER Mothers' and Children's Project (Waldo et al. 1987) also addressed the mother–child dyad, albeit in limited form. This program taught mothering skills to schizophrenic mothers. The children lived at home or in temporary foster homes, and the mothers received ongoing care from a clinic or private therapist. The intervention was comprised of a two-and-a-half-hour meeting held once a week in a community church with the mothers and their children. For half the session the mothers played with their children under the guidance of child development experts. The children then played separately while mothers met in separate groups. The session ended with lunch. Again, this program did not involve the dyad together for an extended period of time in the therapeutic nursery.

## The PACT Program

We can summarize the literature with the observation that over the last two decades there has been increasing recognition, gradually put into practice, of the value of a multimodal and milieu approach in which the SMI mother and her child are treated together. The PACT program, both in concept and structure, represents a further commitment to this approach.

We believe that the treatment of the SMI mother with her child is not only effective in prevention of the transmission of mental illness to the child, it may also be the treatment of choice for SMI mothers themselves. Gross (1984) described the treatment of a schizophrenic mother, using the parent–child dyad. The primary need of the mother (as is the case with most SMI mothers with whom we have worked) was for more nurturing, which she could more readily accept in the context of the dyad. There is evidence that the high attrition rate of psychotic mothers in individual treatment is reduced when mother and child are treated together.

Our experience has confirmed this finding. SMI mothers frequently enter our program with mistrust and apprehension on the one hand and low expectations on the other. These feelings are reflected in a high absentee rate at the beginning. At the same time they may be more able both to trust and entertain hope on behalf of their children than themselves. Yet the early developmental issues, around which work with the mother–child pairs revolves, invariably resonate with the parents' problems and histories. Through the work with the children their case difficulties become more accessible and amenable to influence. As a result it is not common for SMI mothers, when referred by adult treatment programs, to terminate with these agencies and accept the status of patients in their own right within the PACT program.

## PROGRAM DESCRIPTION

The target population served by the PACT Unit is made up of severely and chronically mentally ill adults, their children, from birth through age 5, and their families. Specific criteria include the presence of at least one child under six years of age, at least one mentally ill parent with a major (*DSM-IV*) psychiatric disorder (excluding a primary diagnosis of Adjustment Disorder or Substance Abuse), and ongoing contact between the mentally ill parents and their children.

In order to ensure maximum utilization of the program, we established and currently maintain a county-wide referral network comprising adult inpatient and outpatient private, state, and voluntary psychiatric hospitals and agencies, and children and family services and child care agencies. At the outset, our networking efforts, particularly among adult mental health providers, involved not only finding cases for the program, but also underscoring the importance of considering the needs of all family members, especially the youngest children, in treatment and discharge planning.

The modal family treated is white, low income (public assistance and/or SSI subsidized), and parented by a single mother, who is on psychotropic medication and has had one or more psychiatric hospitalizations. Psychotic (Schizoaffective, Paranoid Schizophrenia, Delusional) and mood (Bipolar, Major Depressive) disorders are the major diagnoses among the parents. For the children, Reactive Attachment Disorder and Parent–Child Relational Problem are the predominant diagnoses. The mean age of the children is 33 months. The demographic profile of the children treated in our nursery corresponds to the profile that studies have documented to be the most vulnerable sub-sample of this high-risk population, namely the youngest children with the most severely and chronically mentally ill parents living in low-income families without adequate socioeconomic and psychological support systems (Goodman and Isaacs 1984).

The major objectives of our program are: (1) To provide primary and secondary preventive intervention to the children in order to decrease the likelihood of their developing psychiatric disorders, and to reduce the intensity and duration of existing symptomatology; (2) To provide support, guidance, community outreach, and therapeutic services to the parents in order to enhance their mental health and level of functioning and, in turn, to strengthen and stabilize the family system.

## Intervention Components

### 1. Assessment

At time of intake, a Unit psychotherapist conducts a comprehensive evaluation, which includes a family history, a developmental history and a mental status examination for each child, an assessment of the childrearing environment in the home, an assessment of the parent–child attachment relationship, and a psychiatric and treatment history on each of the mentally ill parents obtained from the parents' previous or ongoing mental health provider.

### 2. Treatment

Treatment takes place in a three-mornings-per-week therapeutic nursery staffed by three clinicians with extensive experience in child and adult psychotherapy. (The Unit staff also includes a psychiatrist and a clinical supervisor.) Unlike the traditional therapeutic nursery in which the child is the exclusive focus of intervention, with the parents being seen, as needed, on behalf of the child, parents participate in each session so that the parent(s) and child(ren) can be provided with an integrated course of treatment in a single setting. The average nursery census is six families. The treatment program utilizes a combination of psychodynamic and cognitive-behavioral interventions within a multimodal framework including: individual therapy for the children and for those parents not in treatment outside of our program; parent–child dyadic (tripartite) therapy; and parent group therapy. Following is a brief description of the intervention modalities.

*Individual therapy* for the parent and for the 3- to 5-year-old child focuses upon those identified issues and problems which can best be explored and worked through in the more traditional one-to-one treatment approach. For the parents, the goal of individual treatment is the amelioration of their symptomatology through a psychodynamic approach that facilitates both the development of healthy object relations and insight into the origins and nature of their mental illness. Individual treatment for the children centers on helping them accomplish age-appropriate developmental tasks (for example, acquiring a sense of trust or autonomy) within the context of parenting by a mentally ill adult.

*Tripartite or dyadic (parent–child) therapy* is directed toward enhancing parenting motivation, competence, and confidence and, in turn, on facilitating the development of a secure attachment relationship between parent and child. One of the ways in which this is achieved is by enhancing the mother's ability to attune sensitively to the communications of her child (Stern 1977, 1985). The establishing or reconstituting of an emotionally secure parent–child attachment is relevant particularly to the needs of these families (in which parent–child bonds are often insecure or often disrupted, as when a parent is hospitalized).

Through a combination of parenting discussions and training, demonstrations (i. e., modeling), and both structured and spontaneous dyadic interactions, the sessions focus upon the acquisition of knowledge and skills in areas such as: (1) developmental needs and expectations as a function of the age of the child; (2) how children communicate needs, feelings and thoughts, both verbally and behaviorally at various ages; (3) how to communicate effectively with a child; (4) how to comfort and nurture a child; (5) how to discipline and set limits; and (6) how to facilitate a child's emotional, social, and intellectual development through play, structured educational activities, and everyday interactions.

In session, the three therapists work simultaneously with several parent–child dyads, modeling and then encouraging the parents to interact with the children in ways that both strengthen the bond and stimulate the children's development. For example, we might demonstrate and then have the parent engage the child in reciprocal play, reciprocal vocalization, or in mutual displays of affection. (In the latter interaction, our goal would be not only to encourage affection between parent and child but also to promote mutual feelings of gratification and comfort from having received such displays of affection.) The strengthening of the child's reality testing and coping skills also serves to reduce the negative impact of the parent's symptomatology and reinforces attachment. Children are helped in work with the parent–child dyad, as well as individually, to develop an age-appropriate understanding of the parent's mental illness.

In the process of providing the mentally ill adult with the knowledge and skills necessary for effective parenting, we also work to develop in the parent: an appreciation of, and a sensitivity and responsiveness to, the child as an individual; an emotional commitment to the child's health and well-being through infancy, the preschool years and beyond; and an increased sense of gratification in being a more effective caretaker. Enhancing the ability and motivation to be an effective parent can have a profound impact that extends beyond the parent–child dyad. Perceiving oneself as a meaningful and competent parent can contribute to an adult's psychiatric recovery (State Communities Aid Association 1991). Also, increased experiences of success in the parenting role can enhance the parent's sense of competence and self-efficacy, which can lead in turn to better functioning in other areas.

*The Parent Group Modality* provides emotional, social, and practical support in helping the parents function in their adult and parental roles. The parents' needs, feelings, problems, and concerns are acknowledged and discussed and they receive help (both from the therapists and from each other) in learning to cope with the difficulties of day-to-day living. One of the most important goals of the group process is the creation of an ongoing social support system that is available to each family both within and outside of the nursery.

Some of the recurring themes which are explored in a group session include: feelings related to being a mentally ill parent and an adult; differentiating the parents' needs from those of their children and the problems which arise when their needs come into conflict; issues related to being a single parent; and problems and concerns common to parents in general and those common to the mentally ill.

### 3. CASE MANAGEMENT

The Unit maintains linkages with outside agencies (e.g., Department of Social Services, Social Security Administration, the courts, adult mental health centers, daycare centers, and schools) in order to ensure that our families receive necessary support services beyond those provided through the program. We are also instrumental in the placement of support personnel (e.g., homemaking and parenting aides) in the home in an effort to enhance the childrearing environment and to help the families better manage their households and cope with the problems of daily living. We are in regular contact with agency and support personnel to exchange information and to consult on treatment planning. The overall goal of the case management component is to help increase family stability and reduce the psychological vulnerability of the child in the home by providing needed social, economic, and domestic support, by reducing conflict and disruptions within the family unit, and by minimizing the adverse impact on the child of the day-to-day exposure to the parent's mental illness through increased interaction with healthy alternate caretakers.

### 4. Services to Siblings

While the primary focus of the program is on the preschool child and parent, the Unit also provides a comprehensive assessment and, when indicated, treatment for the school-aged child. Some of the participating families have one or more children who are of school age and are, therefore, not appropriate for the nursery treatment model. The provision of age-appropriate intervention services to this older population is, however, quite essential if our program is to achieve its major objectives.

### 5. Post-Program Services and Aftercare

Discharge planning is based upon our experience that most, if not all, of the families will require aftercare and support services following successful program completion (with success defined as the achievement of the major treatment objectives that had been established jointly by the family and Unit clinicians during the program intake phase). When indicated, a child's and/or parent's treatment continues, in a less intensive form, with the same therapist in the Unit's post-nursery service. After leaving the nursery, the child's educational and social needs are met through referral to a special education or daycare program or through placement in a mainstream classroom. The appropriate outside agencies are engaged prior to discharge in order that the necessary support services are in place by the time a family leaves the program. Comprehensive planning and implementation of aftercare and service delivery to meet any continuing social, economic, and psychological support needs among these families serves to ensure that program gains are maintained.

The structure and application of the multimodal intervention model and the specific treatment objectives our program is designed to achieve will be illustrated through a description of the activities comprising a typical nursery session, followed by two case summaries, the first of which will include examples of treatment process.

## DESCRIPTION OF PACT THERAPEUTIC NURSERY

The PACT Nursery is set up like a typical preschool classroom, with toys and activities appropriate for children from infancy through age 5. Surrounding the child-size table and chairs are a circle of adult chairs for parents and therapists. The Nursery is in session for two hours, three times per week, with each session structured so as to allow shifting emphases on the treatment needs of the parent, the child, and the parent and child together.

During the first half-hour of the session, parents meet in a group with their therapists, while the children play freely with the various toys and materials. Parents and therapists are grouped informally around the room, with each of the three therapists available to make contact with each of the adult patients, who often arrive feeling overwhelmed and in need of the therapist's attention in order to subsequently be able to attend to the needs of their children. Both case management and individual therapeutic issues of the parents are addressed at this time. Although each therapist is formally responsible for two of the six nursery families, therapists can and do work with each other's patients, both in the instance of a given patient's therapist being unavailable (as when that therapist is engaged intensively with another patient), and in order to support the intervention of the primary therapist, using the "Greek chorus" approach of CPP's Cornerstone nursery (see Chapter 2). In addition, the therapists often support, elaborate upon, and even occasionally disagree with each other's ideas in the presence of the patients.

The structure during this first half-hour is fluid and unpredictable, in that sometimes the mothers and therapists come together as a group to respond to the needs of one parent or discuss a common issue, while at other times patients work individually with their primary therapist within the group setting. Often, a therapist will use the group modality to facilitate the participation of a silent mother by inviting her to respond to the issues and feelings being brought up by another mother. Although this is the time officially set aside for the needs of the mothers, attention may also shift to the needs of the children and to those of the parent–child dyad, as the children often arrive in varying states of need. No attempt is made to shield the children from the adult conversation, as it is our position that the children are already experientially familiar with their parents' problems. Further, an opportunity is thus afforded to enhance the child's understanding of parental stress to which the child is exposed.

Another advantage of having a team of therapists familiar with all of the patients is highlighted during this first half-hour by the frequency with which a given mother and her child each require the attention of a therapist. This is particularly important with paranoid mothers, who often become acutely anxious when observing a therapist intervening with their child and may require simultaneous support from a second therapist.

The second half-hour is devoted to what is called Parent–Child Time. Parents are encouraged to play with their children in an age-appropriate activity chosen by both. This time is used for the purpose of: (1) communicating to parents the educational and psychological importance of playful interactions with their children as opposed to purely caretaking interactions; (2) educating parents, who often were never played with appropriately themselves as children, as to what are developmentally appropriate activities for children of different ages; (3) enhancing parents' ability to take pleasure in their children and to perceive themselves as competent parents; (4) fostering the cognitive and emotional development of the child within the context of a pleasurable interaction with the parent; and, most importantly, (5) allowing the therapist to observe the parent's ability to attune to the child's needs and assess the need for remediation of parental attunement.

After Parent–Child Time, parents, children, and therapists sit together for Snack Time. As in Parent–Child Time, parents are encouraged to remain with their children. Since feeding is a crucial parent–child interaction that often highlights the sorts of attunement problems many parents have with their children, Snack Time provides a valuable opportunity for intervention on the part of the therapist. Parents frequently misread their child's signals around food. One mother, for example, typically force-fed her 2½-year-old son to the point where he would cry and gag after clearly telling her, "I don't want anymore!" Another mother would absentmindedly feed her 3½-year-old boy, although he was quite capable of feeding himself, and ignored his signals of both hunger and satiation.

After Snack Time, parents and children separate; the parents and one of the three therapists (who rotate this function on a weekly basis) go to an adjacent room for the Parent Therapy Group, while the children stay in the nursery with the two remaining therapists.

During this time, the therapists may work individually with the children or provide them with the cognitive and socioemotional benefits of a pre-school experience in an individualized, small group setting. Therapists provide: (1) infant developmental stimulation; (2) facilitation of age-appropriate language and social skills; (3) encouragement of symbolic play; (4) help with academic readiness skills; and (5) older children with under-standing of nature of the parent's mental illness and behavior. The ongoing access to the parents enables therapists to become aware of and counter-vail the transmission of psychotic ideas and behavior to the children. One mother, for example, insisted that her 3- and 4-year-old daughters run from the car into their home as quickly as possible because she expected an immi-nent attack. She also instructed her daughters to flush public toilets with their feet for fear that they would be contaminated and become ill should they ever touch a public toilet with their hands. Of special interest is the observation that parents seem more able to allow, and perhaps take in, chal-lenges to their delusional thinking when it is done in the interest of help-ing their child.

The parent group is led by a different therapist each week. Parents under-stand that group process will be shared with the two therapists not present, and we find that this often gives patients the opportunity to send indirect messages, via the therapist running the group, to an absent therapist whom they are afraid to confront on a given issue. In addition, this system of rotat-ing the therapists facilitates the therapists' ability to work with the patients for whom they are not the primary therapist. Parents are free to set the agenda for these meetings, and the modality ranges from one of traditional psychodynamic group therapy, in which transference issues between group members and between members and therapists are addressed and psycho-dynamic interpretations of current behavior are offered, to parent guidance, in which child development issues are discussed and problem solving tech-niques are explored, to a support group, in which mothers not only receive help and support for their own problems but also derive a sense of mastery from their ability to help their peers.

Following the parent group, parents and children reunite for a goodbye song, and the nursery session ends for the day.

## CASE STUDY 1

### Presenting Problem

Carol was referred to the PACT program from a drug rehabilitation program because staff had noticed that her social and caretaking interactions with her 2-year-old, Martin, were "mechanical" and she appeared to lack emotional investment in her maternal role. Carol, at 27 years of age, had a history of alcohol and drug abuse dating back to her early school years. The abuse ended the day she gave birth to Martin. Following the birth, she entered a drug/alcohol rehabilitation program which she successfully completed two years later. In spite of the remission of her drug abuse, however, Carol was observed to be withdrawn and extremely emotionally constricted. During her evaluation for the PACT program, she described herself as a "person who doesn't feel." Carol reported that during her first year in the drug program, while she had attended all group therapy sessions, she hadn't spoken to the session leaders or her peers. She expressed guilt over her drug use when she was pregnant, and stated that the only "amends" she could make to Martin was "to do the right thing for him now."

Carol's pregnancy with Martin had been unplanned and Martin was an unwanted child. She acknowledged, however, that she had never considered an abortion because "at the time of my pregnancy, I was so heavily addicted to drugs and alcohol that my being pregnant was not important to me; I was too busy getting high and staying high." Martin was born three weeks premature and tested positive for cocaine. In his first year he suffered lead poisoning requiring medical intervention. He also had an early history of multiple ear infections and bronchial asthma. Martin had consistently scored below age-appropriate norms on assessments of growth and development. For example, when tested by his pediatrician at 22 months of age, his level of cognitive development was that of a 16-month-old. He was also described as emotionally needy, hyperactive, and oppositional (resistant to limits in the home and prone to physical assaults toward older children and to temper tantrums), with an attention span and expressive language functioning significantly below age expectations. His behavioral and emotional symptoms, and his developmental delays, were thought to be due to the interaction of physical factors (i.e. prenatal addiction, premature birth, and lead poisoning) and a pattern of inconsistent, ineffectual, and emotionally detached parenting on the part of his mother.

**Family History**

Carol and a 6-year-old brother and 7-year-old sister were raised on public assistance by their mother and a stepfather. The latter entered the family when Carol was 5 years of age. Her biological father had left home when Carol was 2. She had intermittent contact with her biological father over the years but "I was not close to him" and "did not feel really sad when he died [in Carol's adulthood]." She was and continues to feel close to her step-father who, while an alcoholic like her father and highly ineffectual as a father surrogate, did give her time and attention while she was growing up.

In Carol's early years, her mother developed chronic multiple sclerosis. Due to repeated and often long-term hospitalizations as well as the debilitating nature of her illness, Carol's mother was often unavailable to her. During her mother's hospitalizations, Carol's siblings repeatedly taunted her, insisting that "it was my fault that my mother was sick" and told her that she was not allowed to visit her mother in the hospital because her mother blamed Carol for her sickness. Because of her mother's repeated absences from the home, together with the ongoing teasing by her siblings, Carol experienced, and acted out, intense feelings of rejection, loss, guilt, and anger. During elementary school, Carol was placed in a special education program for emotionally disturbed children. (In the latter stage of her therapy, Carol's insight would come to include an understanding of how her guilt, anger, and especially her fear that she would again make her mother sick caused her to distance herself from her mother and "take to the streets," and how her concern that her intense emotions might get out of control, putting herself and others around her at risk, caused her to isolate herself socially and immerse herself in drugs and alcohol.)

Carol reports that she also had her first experience with alcohol when she was 5 years of age. "I began sipping the drinks I made for my stepfather." She recalled, "I liked the warm feeling it gave me." Her access to "hard liquor" continued until at age 9, with the encouragement of peers, she switched to drinking beer and smoking marijuana. Between ages 9 and 16, at which time she became addicted to crack (which, along with marijuana, she continued to use up to the day she went into labor with Martin), she had abused numerous drugs.

At 16, she dropped out of school and left home ("too many restrictions") and lived until age 18 with a boyfriend who, like her, was drug-addicted; during that time, her life centered on "getting high." She returned home at age 18, remaining long enough to finish high school. Again leaving home, she lived for three years with another addict, from whom she separated. Following her second reconciliation with her previous boyfriend, Andrew (also a drug addict), she became pregnant with Martin. Throughout her pregnancy she continued to abuse drugs. She did not avail herself of prenatal care, readily acknowledging, "I didn't want the baby." During her pregnancy, she lived part of the time with her maternal grandmother and part of the time with her mother and stepfather. Following the birth of Martin, and while she attended the rehabilitation program, she lived with her maternal grandmother. She separated from Martin's father following the revelation that he was seeing other women. At age 27, Carol, Martin, and a new boyfriend, Fred, moved into her first apartment. Fred was 28 years of age and had been "clean and sober" for four years.

## Diagnostic Formulations and Treatment Goals

### CAROL

On presenting at the clinic, Carol spoke in a monotone and maintained a fixed, blank facial expression. The constricted affect and the interpersonal detachment, evidenced both in individual sessions and in the nursery with the other therapists and mothers, were consistent with the description of Carol originally provided by the staff of the drug program.

During the first individual sessions, Carol herself claimed that "I am out of touch with my feelings" and said that her being unable to feel grief or sadness (over, for example, the then-recent death of her biological father) is "strange," while adding, "But I don't get distressed about it [her lack of feeling] because I can't feel distress about anything." In the first nursery session, while exploring with her the dynamics underlying her readily apparent isolation both from the other mothers and therapists (she often sat by herself, mute, still, and attending passively), she offered, "I feel detached from people, even those I've known for some time." And, in a characteristic matter-of-fact tone, she admitted that "I don't feel part of the group [the parent group] and have no desire to be part of the group."

Both clinical observations and Carol's self-description supported a pervasive pattern of social detachment and a restricted range of affective expression within a social context that was consistent with a diagnosis of Schizoid Personality Disorder.

Despite a lack of desire for greater social relatedness, she recognized, on an intellectual level, that if she is ever to "do something about having a future" for herself and her son (e.g., getting off welfare and realizing her long-held wish for a professional career in working with retarded children), she would have to learn to function more effectively in the social world.

The mutually agreed-upon treatment plan centered on Carol's gaining insight into and working through the dynamic issues and conflicts which impeded her social and emotional functioning, the primary goals being: (1) enhanced capacity to express a greater range of affect and to feel comfortable with and in control of her emotions; and (2) enhanced social competence and confidence and heightened personal gratification in social relations.

MARTIN

Upon his introduction to the therapeutic nursery, Martin, age 26 months, was a physically attractive youngster whose overall level of social, emotional, and cognitive development was below age-appropriate norms. During the first month's sessions, the most clinically striking finding was the inordinate degree to which Martin was distracted by the auditory and visual stimulation in the Nursery. He moved from toy to toy in rapid succession, his hands manipulating one toy while his head twisted and turned, his eyes searching for the next toy to be apprehended and exchanged. He appeared driven and stimulus bound, unable to focus his attention on one toy long enough to employ it in gratifying play. Sedentary activities (e. g., looking through a picture book, sitting for story time, completing a puzzle) were difficult if not impossible for him, even with external encouragement to help keep him engaged in the task.

His expressive language was also below expectation for age, his ability to communicate thought, need, or feeling generally limited to two- or three-word phrases. Receptive language functioning was also delayed and he usually needed repeated verbal prompting before he would respond to a request. Her mother complained, "He doesn't listen," feeling that he deliberately ignored her.

He also evidenced extremely low frustration tolerance and manifested severe temper tantrums. Many of the tantrums occurred in his interaction with his mother, especially when her needs came into conflict with his, as will be demonstrated below when discussing the mother–child dyad. This was a major problem for Martin, despite his mother's conscious and stated intention to devote her life to him in compensation for the damage that her drug and alcohol abuse had caused him.

Treatment goals for Martin included: (1) age appropriate acceptance of limits; (2) enhanced capacity for sustained attention; (3) greater social responsiveness; (4) a greater ability to modulate behavior and affect and to express needs and feelings in socially adaptive (i.e., nondisruptive) ways; and (5) more age-adequate expressive language functioning.

**Treatment**

During the early months of treatment, it became readily apparent that there existed a wide disparity between Carol's repeated assertions of her devotion to Martin's health and well-being, with its implication of an emotional investment in the mother–son relationship, and the quality of Carol's actual behavior. Her insight was limited concerning this discrepancy. This disparity was demonstrated repeatedly in the Nursery. On the one hand, Carol was able to make accurate observations of the insecure attachment relationships of the other mothers and their children. In contrast, she saw herself tuned into Martin and as "giving him all the love and affection I am capable of giving him so he won't experience the emotional deprivation I went through in my early life with my family."

However, the nursery therapists were in agreement with the primary therapist's characterization of Carol as behaving like an automaton in her interactions with her son. Her social and caretaking behavior could best be described as continuous episodes of "noncontingent interactions" (Gochman 1986), in contrast to "contingent interactions," in which mother and child react to each other in a harmonious display of mutual attunement. Carol's interactions with Martin lacked synchrony and reciprocity; she was unable to behave in relation to him in concert with his emotions, signals, and behaviors. She cared for Martin but was, in effect, insensitive to his emotional and developmental needs. This problem was much in evidence during Snack Time. Carol repeatedly over-enforced the Nursery rule that children sit at least five minutes at the table during Snack Time. Eight months into therapy, she still hovered over Martin and admonished him to "sit still and eat," often placing food in his mouth despite his repeated attempts to resist and despite repeated attempts (to be described below) on the part of the therapists to intervene.

It was apparent that Martin for his part was avoidant, and insecurely attached to Carol. During his first six months in the Nursery, he demonstrated an indiscriminate sociability. When in need of physical or emotional comforting, or when seeking out an adult for social stimulation or play, he was likely to turn to an adult other than his mother. During the third month, for example, Martin was observed selecting a book about "fire trucks" (his favorite toy) and, with his mother present and accessible, walked past her to another mother and requested she read it to him. When the therapist asked about her reaction to Martin's behavior, she shrugged her shoulders and said "It's O.K. with me . . . he goes to anybody he wants to."

Therapeutic efforts were increasingly aimed at facilitating and reinforcing Carol's attunement and responsiveness to Martin's emotional, social, and developmental needs with the goal of a more secure emotional attachment relationship between the two.

During the first weeks in the Nursery, the primary therapist (with the assistance of the other therapists and even of some of the mothers) modeled strategies for Carol to assist Martin in achieving his treatment goals, for example: (1) verbalizing the Nursery rules and their rationale, employing positive reinforcement and time out (to facilitate an age-appropriate level of compliance with rules and limit setting); (2) gradually increasing the amount of time he would be expected to remain seated while being read to, doing puzzles, or drawing (to increase his attentional activities); and (3) object and color naming, shape discrimination, identifying parts of dolls, reinforcing the use of words rather than gestures or sounds to express needs, feelings and thoughts (to facilitate expressive language functioning).

Initially, Carol was actively resistant to engaging Martin in the interactions being modeled for her. In turn, Martin, seeming to take his cue from Carol, displayed an attitude of indifference to his mother (especially noticeable during Parent–Child Time) as shown by his disinclination to share with her his excitement or pleasure in an activity or newly acquired skill.

It wasn't until well into the third month that Carol spontaneously took an active part in Parent–Child Time. One day, she spontaneously set up a drawing activity for Martin and worked on several pictures with him. This was the first time we had observed the two displaying mutual enjoyment of a shared activity. She was commended by staff for her efforts to work with Martin and his obvious enjoyment of the interaction was pointed out to her. (Operant, or instrumental, conditioning strategies employing social reinforcers are a principal component in the facilitation of behavioral learning and change among both parents and the children in the Nursery.) This kind of involvement with Martin gradually increased. When exploring with her the reason for her increasing involvement with Martin, she said that what "finally got through to me" was the staff's repeated belief in her motivation "to do the right thing" for him, coupled with the repeated assertions of the unique importance of Carol's role in supporting her son's development.

In her individual therapy, Carol gained additional insight into the dynamic factors that, prior to her work in the Nursery, had interfered with the kinds of interactions that lead to consolidation of a strong attachment relationship. For example, she eventually recalled (now with sad affect) that her mother "never played with me when I was a little girl." Further, she was receptive to the suggestion that her own deprivation as a child could make it difficult for her to play with and otherwise take pleasure in Martin.

Much of the dyadic work in the Nursery involved the issue of limit setting, regarding which Carol alternated between passivity and intrusiveness. Early on, despite efforts of Nursery staff to model for and educate her, Carol's attempts to set limits vacillated between extremes. She was frequently hypervigilent, monitored Martin's every move, and would intervene before Martin began to lose control. At other times she seemed oblivious to his disorganized or aggressive behavior. Carol was first helped to notice these behaviors, following which she was helped to identify her responses to them. "Sometimes he wants to play and won't listen. . . . It takes too much effort to calm him down . . . so I let him go."

The treatment of a parent and child together within the context of multiple mother–child dyads and multiple therapists makes it possible to simultaneously meet the treatment needs of both. While attempting to strengthen Carol's relationship to Martin in her son's interest on the one hand, she required much support for herself on the other. It was understood that underlying Carol's social withdrawal as well as her emotional distance from her son was a fear of her own feelings.

Carol's regular contact with other mothers and therapists within the safe, supportive milieu provided ongoing opportunities to become more comfortable with her feelings in a social context. Given the severity of Carol's fears, however, these opportunities were predictably slow to generate insight and change.

Evidence of the therapeutic value of the milieu crystallized around a single incident. One day about eight months into treatment, Carol was severely criticized by four mothers for letting Martin run wild and not stepping in when Martin deliberately hurt a peer. Carol withdrew, sitting motionless, head down, eyes closed for the remainder of the session.

The next day, all of the mothers, Carol included, requested an extended Parent Group session. Surprisingly, Carol, for the first time since entering the Nursery program, shared "a part of myself" with the other mothers. She told the group that she sometimes did experience strong emotions, especially anger, which frightened her. She said she feared the damage she might do to herself or to others were her anger to get out of control.

She went on to provide the group with an unexpectedly forthright and sophisticated account of her earlier history. She said her drug and alcohol abuse had served to suppress her anger and aggressiveness. When she gave up drugs and alcohol "for Martin," she also lost a secondary defense against experiencing and acting on the anger that had its origin in the abandonment rage generated when her mother was hospitalized and Carol was separated from her for a year. (The explanation for her rage and its relation to her substance abuse had recently emerged in her individual therapy sessions.)

The mothers were moved by Carol's revelation. They now expressed long-withheld feelings of caring about her and Martin, thus rewarding her for her acknowledgment of affect, albeit negative. The mothers reaffirmed that the Nursery was a place in which feelings could be safely expressed.

With further exploration in individual sessions Carol gained considerable insight into the dynamics of her interpersonal problems, formulated by the therapist as her "schizoid dilemma" (Guntrip 1961). Fearing loss of control and destructiveness should she experience the intense anger she harbored, she closed herself off from those feelings (emotional blunting) and sought to avoid or withdraw from people or situations that might evoke negative affect. In the Nursery, she used fatigue ("I'm too tired to talk today") and subterfuge (e. g., focus on the facts of her history of alcohol/substance or her recovery, unaccompanied by affect) to distance herself from others.

The support of the group following her revelation and the further dynamic insight gained in individual sessions created the impetus for major changes in Carol. A common occurrence in subsequent Nursery sessions were the mothers and therapists sharing with her their observation of how much more related and involved she was with the others in the Nursery and how much more attuned and responsive she was to her son's needs. During the last three months in the Nursery Carol took an active role both in relation to her son and to the other mothers. Our observations of Carol and Martin in a variety of situations now revealed what could best be described as a healthy, secure attachment relationship. Carol verbalized intense feelings of affection for Martin and was overjoyed when the results of a psychological evaluation, conducted during Martin's last month in the Nursery, revealed that he was at or near age-appropriate levels in the cognitive, sensorimotor, social, and emotional areas sampled by the testing. She also provided evidence of an enhanced understanding of her own role in the promotion of her son's achievement of individuation and autonomy. "When I set limits, we both get what we need—I feel in control and Martin feels protected and secure." The forced feeding of her son had become a thing of the past.

Toward the end of her participation in the Nursery, she became more emotionally attached to several of the mothers, as evidenced by her increased interaction with them. She became something of an auxiliary therapist to some, listening sympathetically and giving them appropriate advice. She appeared to take a genuine interest in the lives of the mothers and children and became surprisingly open in her displays of emotion. She also demonstrated a sense of humor.

Carol and Martin left the Nursery after seventeen months, at which time there was mutual agreement that the major treatment goals had been substantially achieved. As of this writing (eight months following termination of nursery treatment), Carol has completed a college preparatory program and has entered a community college. She intends to pursue her goal of working with the mentally retarded. Martin is currently enrolled in a mainstream daycare program on the campus where Carol attends college. Mother and child continue to be seen in weekly therapy to consolidate and extend their gains.

## CASE STUDY 2

A second, dramatic case example of program effectiveness is provided by a family who attended the nursery for twenty-one months. The mother, Alice, was 26 years of age and five months pregnant (with her future daughter, Margaret) when she and her 15-month-old son, John, entered the PACT Nursery. Jason, the 28-year-old father, was highly resistant to program involvement and provided little support to our treatment efforts. Alice's history of severe mental illness (beginning in early adolescence) included twenty-three hospitalizations and continued maintenance on multiple psychotropic medications, which began at age 18 when she was first hospitalized. She had been variously diagnosed with Paranoid Schizophrenia, Bipolar Disorder, and Schizoaffective Disorder, the latter being her diagnosis at the time of program referral.

During the intake assessment, it became readily apparent that Alice was extremely ambivalent about her pregnancy and that she displayed or expressed little motivation to form a secure attachment relationship with her son, John. In turn, John, with a diagnosis of Reactive Attachment Disorder of Early Childhood, was markedly delayed in social, emotional, and cognitive, especially expressive language, development.

Within the Nursery, individual, dyadic, and group interventions focused upon reducing the pervasiveness and intensity of Alice's symptomatology, enhancing John's personal, social, emotional, and intellectual development and facilitating a healthy and secure mother–son bond.

Despite two brief hospitalizations during Alice's first six months in the Nursery, the treatment had a most powerful impact in all areas of intervention. Of special note is the high degree to which Alice was able to transfer the gains she made in her parenting and bonding capacity during treatment with her son to her work with her daughter, Margaret, who essentially had been "born" into our Nursery. At time of program termination, Alice's major symptoms were either in remission or greatly improved, her Global Assessment of Functioning (GAF) classification (see p. 356) was 85, from an intake level of less than 50, and she was functioning without need of psychotropic medication for the first time in almost ten years. In addition, she was enrolled in a community college and was making plans to secure (her first ever) full-time employment.

Clinical assessment at time of termination indicated that she was relatively securely attached to both of her children and that the children displayed no evidence of developmental delays or deficits or of emotional or behavioral symptomology.

A follow-up at one year revealed that all gains for mother and children had been maintained. Alice had not been hospitalized and was still functioning well without medication. She had received an AA degree, and had been employed full time for six months in a lower management position with an insurance company.

Her son John was enrolled in a mainstream pre-K program and daughter, Margaret, was in a full-time daycare program. Teachers for both reported that socially, emotionally, and intellectually they were functioning well within age-appropriate expectations.

## EVALUATION OF THE PROGRAM

### Treatment Compliance

In view of the nature and severity of the mothers' pathology, as well as their erratic treatment histories, we were interested in the degree to which they were able to persevere in this relatively intensive and interpersonally demanding program. Following are some statistics concerning this issue.

To date, thirty-four families (39 parents and 45 children) have participated in the program (8 families are currently in treatment). Of the thirty-four, 20 families (23 parents and 25 children) have successfully completed a course of treatment (with success as previously defined as achieving the mutually agreed-upon major goals and objectives for each family).

Nine families were transferred to non-PACT programs as the parents and/ or children in these families were in need of more specialized treatment than that provided in our program. For example, two mothers with dual diagnoses were referred to drug/alcohol treatment programs, two children from difficult families were transferred to The Center's more intensive Cornerstone Program (see Chapter 2) for children with severe developmental and psychological disorders, and one family had to leave the nursery after six months as the mother became physically unable to continue attending sessions. This family was able to continue in individual and tripartite treatment through home visits with a PACT therapist. Follow-up of these nine families three to six months after referral revealed that all were participating in the programs to which they had been referred.

Five families withdrew from the nursery, refusing further treatment, following an average participation time of five months. Our efforts to reengage them in the program were unsuccessful. The referral agencies were notified of the families' withdrawals and treatment case management recommendations were provided.

Thus, approximately 60 percent of the families remained in the program to completion, 25 percent were successfully referred to more suitable programs, and 15 percent withdrew against medical advice. Given the severity of the pathology, dysfunction, and disorganization within the families referred to our program, an attrition rate of 15 percent markedly exceeded our expectations. That we were able to retain a majority of the families strongly suggests the effectiveness of our efforts to establish long-term therapeutic alliances and to maintain a high level of parental commitment to the treatment. Mean time spent in the program by the twenty families who completed it was 21.6 months (range was between 9.7 and 48 months).

In considering the question of which parent characteristics precluded utilization of the program, the number of families that withdrew is too small to permit a definitive answer. Our experience suggested, however, that parents with diagnoses of Paranoid and Antisocial Personality Disorders, and parents with dual diagnoses still using drugs/alcohol at time of admission, are less likely to be able to develop or sustain an adequate alliance. Yet the presence of this kind of parental psychopathology implies a greater disturbance of the parent–child relationship and therefore greater risk for the child. In some of these cases, therefore, referral to Child Protective Services needs to be considered, if referrals to alternative programs are not accepted.

**Assessment of Treatment Impact**

As stated previously, overall goals of the PACT program include the enhancement of the mental health and functioning of the parent and the child, strengthening of the parent–child dyad, and the stabilization of the family.

Since the PACT Nursery is an ongoing outpatient clinical service, mandated to treat all families meeting the criteria for program admission, our assessment procedure does not employ a control group against which we could compare our treated families on the various target variables. Instead, our evaluation procedure can be conceptualized as a series of single case (family) assessments in which each family serves as its own control. For each family we assess the status of the target variables at time of intake and following the intervention. The changes that occur between the pre- and post-intervention periods provide a measure of treatment impact.

The treatment goals have been operationalized into outcome variables as follows:

## For the Parent

Elimination of the need for hospitalization or reduction in the frequency and/or duration of hospitalizations; the amelioration of psychopathology or the reduction in the severity and pervasiveness of symptomatology; reduction in the need for major medications or enhancement of compliance with medication regimen; and when further post-nursery therapy is indicated, enhancement of the patient's ability to utilize a less intensive treatment modality.

## For the Child

Prevention of the onset, or the reduction in the severity and pervasiveness, of existing symptomatology; enhancement of social, emotional, and intellectual functioning to more age-appropriate developmental levels; and placement in an age-appropriate educational program.

## For the Mother–Child Dyad

Enhancement of the mother's attunement and responsiveness to the needs of her child; and, in turn, the achievement of a secure emotional mother–child attachment relationship.

Following is a summary, in part impressionistic, of the pre-intervention status and changes observed in those families who completed the program.

## Pre-Intervention Status of Children, Mothers, and Mother–Child Dyads

All of the parents treated in the nursery had a prior history of one or more psychiatric hospitalizations. Many of the mothers were, in fact, referred to our program by inpatient facilities as part of the mothers' discharge plan. At time of admission, all were on major medications, many presenting with histories of noncompliance. Often, noncompliance had been a factor in the need for hospitalization. At time of intake, all of the parents had diagnostic classifications indicative of severe psychopathology (i.e., mood, psychotic and major personality disorders). Their symptomatology also included significant functional impairment as measured by the Global Assessment of Functioning (GAF) Scale (*Diagnostic and Statistical Manual* 1994). The GAF scores for the parents ranged from 30 to 55 (indicating severe impairment in social and psychological functioning). The severity and chronicity of pathology and dysfunction that characterized these parents at time of admission to the program indicated the need for an intensive, long-term course of treatment.

The intake assessments of the children (from infants to preschoolers) revealed a profile of social, psychological, and developmental problems similar to that of the children of mentally ill mothers described in our literature review. The presenting symptoms among the children were sufficient to warrant diagnostic classifications (i.e. Reactive Attachment, Separation Anxiety, Dysthymic, and Oppositional Defiant Disorders and Parent–Child Relational Problem) reflecting social and emotional problems inherent in their relationships with their mothers. In addition to the social and emotional deficits, the children, as a group, were found to have delayed intellectual development, especially in the area of expressive language.

In terms of the mother–child dyad, our observation, based upon a theoretically informed assessment employing Stern's (1977, 1985) attunement criteria revealed that, as a group, the mothers were seriously misattuned (i.e., nonempathic) to the communications and needs of their children. In turn, applying Ainsworth's (Ainsworth et al. 1979) criteria for differentiating secure from insecure attachments, we found that all of the mother–child relationships were characterized by insecure (i.e., avoidant or resistant) attachments.

It should be noted that, at time of intake, a majority of the families were involved with Child Protective Services due to complaints of suspected child abuse or neglect. Thus, many of the children were at risk of foster placement.

## Post-Intervention Status and Follow-up of Mothers, Children, and Mother–Child Dyads

Four of the mothers required brief hospitalizations, all in the early stage of treatment. However, in follow-ups done between six months to one year after program completion, we found that only one mother had been hospitalized. As noted previously, all of the mothers had been hospitalized one or more times prior to admission, thus the program was effective in reducing the frequency of hospitalizations. This treatment outcome was achieved in part through the program's positive impact on two other target variables: compliance with medication and the parents' symptomatology. As noncompliance had been a pervasive problem, a major treatment focus in both individual and group modalities was on exploring and working through the issues underlying noncompliance and on enhancing both the mothers' understanding of the need for, and motivation to continue, their medication regimens. At time of program completion and in later follow-up, we found that, as a group, the mothers were in compliance with medication.

Our interventions also had appeared to have had an impact on the mothers' symptomatology as well as their overall level of functional impairment. While, in general, their diagnoses were unaltered, post-intervention mental status evaluations revealed a marked reduction in the severity, pervasiveness, and debilitating effect of the symptoms of the mothers as a group. There was also a noticeable improvement in overall functioning. This was reflected in an upward change in the GAF scores from a range of 30 to 55 at time of admission to a range of 55 to 70, indicating a general shift from the more severe to the more moderate or mild level of difficulty in psychological and social functioning. The overall lessening of the debilitating effects of their psychopathology and the corresponding enhancement of functioning was maintained at time of follow-up. Self-reports of the mothers' revealed that, as a group, they experienced greater self-esteem, perceived themselves as "good" mothers, and felt more confident and competent in their personal and social lives. A number of mothers were able to resume their education and/or obtain work, many for the first time.

While several of the mothers were able to complete the Nursery program without the need for further intervention, for the majority of mothers additional treatment was indicated. Their discharge plans included the goals that would serve as the outcome variables in post-Nursery therapy. Because of the gains they had made while in the Nursery all of the mothers continuing in therapy were able to utilize a less intensive program of treatment. For these mothers, post-Nursery treatment comprised weekly individual sessions with PACT therapists.

For the children, as a group, involvement in the therapeutic nursery had a positive effect on their social, emotional, and cognitive development. All exhibited improved object relations. On the one hand they were better able to negotiate conflict with peers and adults; on the other hand, greater reciprocity was observed when children were playing with peers or with their mothers and therapists. Overall, social interactions involved less physical aggression, less destructive behavior, and less withdrawal. Toward the end of the Nursery treatment, many of the 5- and 6-year-olds showed age-appropriate signs of the development of empathy.

In general, the children exhibited a greater range of affect. They not only expressed pleasure in their achievements but disappointment when frustrated. Inappropriate and intense anger was far less common at follow-up.

A reduction in the severity, and even amelioration, of symptoms resulted in many cases in alterations of diagnoses. Depressive symptomatology, withdrawal, and apathy were virtually absent and sleeping and eating disturbances subsided. Of special significance was the absence of reactive attachment symptomatology. Children in general showed a preference for their mothers, and more differentiated responses to others, post-treatment.

The program also seems to have had a positive impact on the cognitive lags present in most children at pre-intervention. Expressive language functioning for the group appeared to have caught up to age-appropriate norms. In addition, an enhancement of the group's capacity for symbolic play was noted. Most children were functioning intellectually at a higher level adjusted for age. They displayed greater curiosity and were eager to engage in educational activities (reading, writing letters, counting). They were able to focus on and attend to learning activities and showed pleasure in cognitive accomplishments. At follow-up, most children were mainstreamed into daycare, pre-kindergarten, or kindergarten programs.

Post-treatment observation showed substantial improvement in the quality of attachment of most mother–child dyads. The children showed less evidence of separation anxiety, more exploratory behavior, and increased ability to use the mother as a secure base for refueling, all parameters of the quality of attachment. The mothers were more responsive to their children, allowed their children to separate, and utilized more appropriate authoritative disciplinary measures accompanied by explanations. Simply put, after involvement in a corrective attachment milieu, maternal empathy and affective synchrony within the dyad grew, in turn enhancing the children's socioemotional functioning.

Finally, in relation to the goal of keeping families together, no child, either during the program or on follow-up had to be removed from parental care. It would appear from the above findings and impressions that the PACT program can enable mentally ill mothers to provide stable home environments and help reduce the transmission of mental illness from mother to child.

## SUMMARY AND CONCLUSIONS

Due to the demographic shift in the treatment of adults with severe mental illness from long-term hospitalization to community-based outpatient mental health services, more children are being parented by mentally ill mothers. While there is longstanding evidence concerning the potential negative developmental and psychological consequences of being raised by a mentally ill parent, at the time of the initial conceptualization of our program there was little agreement in the mental health field as to what should be done about it. A program of integrated services for SMI mothers and their children offered promising opportunities to protect these children from long-term maladjustment.

This chapter has described a program utilizing a multimodal intervention model to provide primary and secondary mental health services to both the children and their mentally ill mothers. It summarizes findings in the literature of the potential adverse effects of parental pathology on the development of their children.

We have stated the objectives of each of the nursery treatment modalities and identified what we believe to be the most important focus of intervention, namely the parent–child dyad and the enhancement of the mother's ability to attune and respond appropriately to the needs and communications of her child, resulting in the establishment of an emotionally secure attachment relationship between mother and child. A unique contribution of our therapeutic nursery model is the use of a group process (i.e., with multiple therapists and multiple parent–child dyads) to attenuate the impact of those aspects of the mother's pathology which interfere with the formation of a secure attachment. The importance of the dyadic work is predicated upon an awareness that a strong attachment relationship provides the basis for healthy social, psychological, and cognitive development during infancy, the preschool years, and beyond.

Dyadic therapy was also shown to be of potential benefit to the mentally ill mother by enhancing her sense of self efficiency in other life areas through increased experiences of success in the parenting role. We have presented treatment outcome data that we believe strongly support the efficacy of the Nursery model, both with the parents and with the children.

Future plans for the PACT Unit, as financial resources allow include: (1) increasing our advocacy efforts on behalf of these high-risk children. Within the adult mental health system there still exists a need for greater awareness of the rationale for, and the availability of, preventive services for these children. This need is readily demonstrated by the fact that in New York State, as recently as 1993, there was still no systematic procedure in place to ensure that inpatient facilities include the preventive needs of children in treatment and discharge planning for patients who are also parents (Blanch and Purcell 1993); (2) extending the PACT program to four or five days per week in an effort to maximize its impact and enhance its capacity to deal with acute parental illness; and (3) implementing a program of intervention services appropriate to the mental health and support needs of mentally ill parents with older children (i.e., ages 6 through 12 years).

## REFERENCES

Ainsworth, M. (1969). Object relations, dependency, and attachment: a theoretical review. *Child Development,* Dec., pp. 969–1025.

Ainsworth, M., Blehar, M., Waters, E., and Wall, S. (1979). *Patterns of Attachment.* Hillsdale, NJ: Erlbaum.

Blanch, A., and Purcell, J. (1993). *Task Force On Mentally Ill Parents With Young Children.* Albany, NY: New York State Office of Mental Health and New York State Department of Social Services, March 29.

Blanchard, M., and Main, M. (1979). Avoidance of the attachment figure and social-emotional adjustment in daycare infants. *Developmental Psychology* 15(4):445–446.

Bowlby, J. (1973). *Attachment and Loss: Vol. 2. Separation.* New York: Basic Books.

DeMulder, E., and Radke-Yarrow, M. (1991). Attachment with affectively ill and well mothers: concurrent behavioral correlates. *Development and Psychopathology* 3:227–242.

*Diagnostic and Statistical Manual of Mental Disorders,* 4th ed. (1994). Washington, DC: American Psychiatric Association.

Elkind, S. N. (1992). *Resolving Impasses in Therapeutic Relationships.* New York: Guilford.

Fendrich, M., Warner, V., and Weissman, M. (1990). Family risk factors, parental depression, and psychopathology in offspring. *Developmental Psychology* 26:40–50.

Field, T. (1992). Infants of depressed mothers. *Development and Psychopathology* 4:49–66.

Gochman, E. R. (1986). Preventive therapy for high-risk mothers and children. *Dynamic Psychotherapy* 4(1):34–39.

Goodman, S. H., and Brumley, E. (1990). Schizophrenic and depressed mothers: relational deficits in parenting. *Developmental Psychology* 26:31–39.

Goodman, S. H., and Isaacs, L. (1984). Primary prevention with children of severely disturbed mothers. *Journal of Preventive Psychiatry* 2(3,4):387–401.

Gross, D. (1984). Relationships at risk: issues and intervention with a disturbed mother–infant dyad. *Perspectives in Psychiatric Care* 21:159–164.

Guntrip, H. (1961). *Personality Structure and Human Interaction.* New York: International Universities Press.

Hammen, C., Burge, D., and Stansbury, K.(1990). Relationship of mother and child variables to child outcomes in a high-risk sample: a causal modeling analysis. *Developmental Psychology* 26:24–30.

Heston, L. L. (1966). Psychiatric disorders in foster home-reared children of schizophrenic mothers. *British Journal of Psychiatry* 112:819–825.

Jensen, P. S., Bloedau, L., DeGroot, J., et al. (1990). Children at risk. 1: Risk factors and child symptomatology. *Journal of the American Academy of Child and Adolescent Psychiatry* 29:51–59.

Kochanska, G. (1991). Patterns of inhibition to the unfamiliar in children of normal and affectively ill mothers. *Child Development* 62:250–263.

Landau, R., Harth, P., Othnay, M., and Sharfhertz, M. (1972). The influence of psychotic parents on their children's development. *American Journal of Psychiatry* 129(1):70–75.

Lewis, M., Feiring, C., McGuffog, C., and Jaskir, J. (1984). Predicting psychopathology in six-year-olds from early social relations. *Child Development* 55:123–136.

Lieberman, A., Weston, D., and Pawl, J. (1991). Preventive interventions and outcome with anxiously attached dyads. *Child Development* 62:199–209.

Lucas, L., Montgomery, S., Richardson, D., and Rivers, P. (1984). Impact project: reducing the risk of mental illness to children of distressed mothers. *New Directions for Mental Health Services*, Dec. (24):79–94.

Mahler, M., Pine, F., and Bergman, A. (1975). *The Psychological Birth of the Human Infant: Separation and Individuation.* New York: Basic Books.

Mowbray, C., Oyserman, D., Zemencuk, J., and Ross, S. (1995). Motherhood for women with serious mental illness: pregnancy, childbirth, and the postpartum period. *American Journal of Orthopsychiatry* 65(1):21–38.

Musick, J., Stott, F., Spencer, K., et al. (1987). Maternal factors related to vulnerability and resiliency in young children at risk. In *The Invulnerable Child*, ed. J. Anthony and B. Cohler, pp. 229–252. New York: Guilford.

Neale, J., and Weintraub, S. (1975). Children vulnerable to psychopathology: the Stony Brook High-Risk Project. *Journal of Abnormal Child Psychology* 3:95–113.

Oyserman, D., Mowbray, C., and Zemencuk, J. (1994). Resources and supports for mothers with severe mental illness. *Health and Social Work* 19(2):132–142.

Sachnow, J. (1987). Preventive intervention with children of hospitalized psychiatric patients. *American Journal of Orthopsychiatry* 57(1):66–77.

Sameroff, A.J., and Seifer, R. (1981). The Transmission of Incompetence: The Offspring of Mentally Ill Women. In M. Lewis and L. Rosenblum (Eds.), *The Uncommon Child* (pp. 259–280). New York: Plenum.

State Communities Aid Assoc., Citizens Committee for Children, Mental Health Assoc. of Orange County, Mental Health Assoc. of Westchester County (1991). *Parent Support/Family Preservation Services: Adults With Mental Illness and Their Minor Children.* Report of a Forum. October 3, Albany, NY.

Stern, D. (1977). *The First Relationship: Infant and Mother.* Cambridge, MA: Harvard University Press.

——— (1985). *The Interpersonal World of the Infant.* New York: Basic Books.

Stott, F., Musick, J., Clark, R., and Cohler, B. (1983). Developmental patterns in the infants and young children of mentally ill mothers. *Infant Mental Health Journal* 4(3):217–235.

Stott, F., Musick, J., Cohler, B., et al. (1984). Intervention for the severely disturbed mother. In *Intervention among Psychiatrically Impaired Parents and Their Children*, ed. B. Cohler and J. Musick, pp. 7–32. San Francisco: Jossey-Bass.

Tableman, B. (1981). Overview of programs to prevent mental health problems of children. *Public Health Reports* 96(1):38–44.

Waldo, M. C., Roath, M., Levine, W., and Freedman, R. (1987). A model program to teach parenting skills to schizophrenic mothers. *Hospital and Community Psychiatry* 38:1110–1112.

Zahn-Waxler, C., Cummings, E., McKnew, D., and Radke-Yarrow, M. (1984). Problem behaviors and peer interactions of young children with a manic-depressive parent. *American Journal of Psychiatry* 141:236–240.

# VI

# CHILDREN OF NEGLECT

# 12

# Sustaining Psychotherapy: A Long-Term Modality for Chronically Stressed Children*

*Arthur B. Zelman*
*Elizabeth Jacobson*

In 1974, Stein and Ronald (1974) described a therapeutic modality referred to as educational psychotherapy, which they taught to early childhood educators. The modality was based largely on the work of Augusta Alpert (1959), who in the 1950s had evolved a psychotherapeutic method called Corrective Object Relations (COR). "Working with children suffering from pathological fixations due to maternal deprivation, Alpert found that when children 2 to 5 years old were given the opportunity to regress in a warm mothering relationship, they were sometimes receptive to what became a restitutive mothering provided by their therapists" (p. 619).

Stein and Ronald mentioned several indications for the use of this modality, including "maternal deprivation, multi-problem families, chaotic family situations, drug addicted families, developmental lags of the children, lack of group readiness of the children and lack of self-observation of the children" (p. 622).

Techniques of the method were based on psychological understanding (mainly developmentally and psychoanalytically informed), translated into educational methods. Specific techniques included listening, the acknowledgment of emotionally charged issues, encouraging catharsis in word and play, making specific goal oriented developmental demands, putting wishes

---

*This chapter is based on a presentation to the American Orthopsychiatric Association 71st Annual Meeting, Washington, DC, April 29, 1994.

263

and feelings into words, and clarification of the child's ambiguous and chaotic environment.

Specific goals of treatment included enhancement of the following: increased capacity to learn, interest in others, ability to function in a group or classroom, communication skills in play and words, learning of boundaries (especially the deviant child), social reality testing, impulse control, and fuller participation in relationships and life events.

This modality, evolved at a time when classical psychoanalysis modified by ego psychologists such as Anna Freud, Hartman, Kris, and Lowenstein, was still holding sway. Accordingly these "corrective" and "supportive" modalities were seen as preparatory for a more psychoanalytically interpretive treatment. The use of psychoanalytic interpretation was discouraged and no mention was made of the transference and countertransference situation.

In fact children treated by educational psychotherapists at our clinic were rarely transferred to an analytically oriented therapist, even when they showed improvement. In practice, the ongoing relationship with the educational psychotherapist was felt to be more important than the interpretive skills of a psychoanalytic psychotherapist or child analyst, in light of the ongoing stressful realities most of these children continued to be subjected to.

Further theoretical underpinning for this decision was provided by Kohut (1971, 1974) in his approach to the treatment of narcissistic disorders. In simplest form, narcissistic patients were seen as not having experienced in their early years an adequate "selfobject" and that psychotherapy foundered with these patients unless the therapist fulfilled this role. Since most of the children receiving educational psychotherapy were observed to be lacking a sufficiency of real selfobjects it made abundant sense to view the children as needing the therapist to offer him/herself as an "auxiliary selfobject."

Kohut (1978) described this role in terms of the provision of "a set of functions which (the patient) had not acquired in early life" (p. 889), and therefore could not perform for himself. These functions included soothing, affirmation, admiration, and stimulation. The concept of the therapist as a corrective selfobject who could perform these functions for the child constituted for us the nucleus of the treatment modality around which the other techniques of educational psychotherapy revolved.

Informed by this concept, supervision of the work of educational psychotherapists revealed both their need and capacity for a deeper understanding of transference and countertransference phenomena in order to withstand the defenses that the children used to recreate their earlier negative interpersonal experiences.

Similarly it was found that the use of interpretations that focused on the linking of affects such as anxiety, rage, and guilt to separation and loss (Bowlby 1973, 1980), rather than to instinctual or intrapsychic conflict, facilitated the development of a positive transference (i.e., enhanced their capacity to perceive/construct and internalize a benign selfobject).

Among children living in high-risk situations are many whose well-meaning parents and other caretakers are sufficiently overwhelmed that they cannot provide adequate psychological care for them. They may be biological parents, extended family members, or foster parents. In the case of such biological parents, they may not even be able to take physical care of the child, yet the part of them that cares about the child is cherished and returned manyfold by the child. It is the task of the psychotherapist of children in such situations to sustain the child's capacity to hope and love by presenting herself as a person on whom the child can emotionally depend, by assisting the child to recognize and accept the hurt, disappointment, and anger generated in the relationships with their primary psychological objects, and to extend an ongoing hopeful but judicious invitation to the child's actual and potential primary caretakers to give what they can.

The case illustration presented here describes the treatment of a child over a long period of time (more than six years) so as to give a real sense of both the impact on the child of repeated disappointment and ongoing stress and the capacity of the modality to deal with it.

## CASE ILLUSTRATION—THE SEARCH FOR "A BLUE HOUSE WITH FLOWERS"

Sam was a stocky, 5-year-old African-American child. He had been placed in a foster home shortly before coming to the clinic because his alcoholic mother could not take care of him. His original home had been chaotic. When Sam was 3, his father had thrown a pot of boiling water on his mother, burning her badly. More recently, his mother had stabbed and seriously wounded a male friend in Sam's presence. She was admitted to a state hospital and Sam was placed in foster care.

Sam's elderly foster parents had difficulty controlling him. In school, his kindergarten teacher saw him as immature and disruptive and he was brought to the Clinic for help. Although his foster parents were willing to allow him to attend the clinic they themselves were inaccessible.

At our first meeting, Sam took the therapist's (E.J.) hand and walked to the therapy room accompanied by the CPS worker. He spontaneously began to play with toys in the room and readily answered questions. Separation issues quickly emerged, along with evidence of impaired reality testing. For example, Sam said his mother dreamed about him when he dreamed about her. Likewise striking ambivalence was expressed toward his absent mother. He called her on the toy telephone, but insisted that the therapist talk to her as he was "too busy" himself. Sam told stories of a reindeer who missed his mom and dad but didn't want to see them anymore, and of relatives who were "looking for him."

In early sessions Sam's play reflected the violence to which he had been exposed. For example, he repeatedly crashed cars and "killed" the people in them. The therapist linked this play to his father's attack on his mother as well as to his mother's violence. During this period he had outbursts of rage in his foster home during which he would tear up his bedspread and curtains. Alongside the theme of violence his play suggested damaged self-esteem, for example, he dumped small dolls out of a dump truck "like dirt."

One of Sam's first pictures was of "dangerous machines, ghosts, and little people hitting each other." The therapist suggested he might feel frightened and small as a result of the violence he had witnessed and worried about people who weren't there or who had died and couldn't take care of him. At another session shortly thereafter, Sam asked the therapist to call his mother and her male friend, Jimmy, on the toy telephone. The therapist was to tell them he was good and that he cries when he wants them. The next session he drew a picture of a "boy who didn't know where his daddy is." He imagined better days when his mother and father and he would go to live in a blue house with flowers, a picture of which he drew. The therapist empathized with his yearning for such a peaceful and happy place while regretting the reality that the blue house was not in his immediate future. Sam's response was to build adjoining houses of blocks—one for him and one for the therapist.

After five months of such work, Sam appeared less depressed. He seemed to accept his foster home and could say, "After all, somebody has to watch me." He continued to verbalize a wish that his mother would take him back, but added, "Sometimes I'm afraid something will scare me at Mother's house," and told the therapist that a man "from the world where my mother lives" had once hit him on the head and left a scar.

Sam's apparent adjustment to his foster home was short-lived. He began to have fights with his foster siblings as well as schoolmates. When the therapist commented that he seemed pretty upset, he said he was angry at his mother and "I don't see her no more." The therapist told Sam that his mother had come to see her once (although she had been drunk). "Tell her I love her," Sam said.

In a session soon afterwards he made a tower, placed a figure on it, and made the figure fall out of the tower. The therapist regretted that "the boy doesn't have a mother to protect him!" Sam answered "He did have a mother but she went away. He will get a bigger mommy." The therapist acknowledged his need to be protected by someone and his worry that his mother still couldn't do this. She added that she had to be sure that his mother could protect him before he went back to her. Sam started to play with the magnets, and the therapist wondered aloud whether Sam wasn't wishing to be held by his mother the way the magnet held the steel. He then drew a picture for his mother of birds flying to a black sun. Sam explained, "It's smoky—there's fire in it." The therapist reflected that maybe the birds were looking for a warm, happy sun but something was covering it, making it hard to find.

Sam did see his mother and her male friend at the office of the Department of Social Services months into treatment. After this brief visit Sam was visibly sad and became aggressive and destructive in his foster home. The foster family felt that Sam was getting worse and removed him from treatment. After four months without therapy his behavior had not improved. The foster family agreed to recommence treatment. When Sam came back the therapist engaged him in remembering things they had done together. Sam asked the therapist if she had a son. Once, when talking about where he should live, he gave the address of the Clinic.

The next week Sam built a block house for his mother, himself, and the therapist. In this house, Sam said, "there were no scary things." Nevertheless, a "bad truck" came and destroyed the house.

The theme of a safe but threatened house inhabited by his mother, his mother's male friend, the therapist, and himself persisted for some time. Once he stationed a toy police car near the house "to watch for something bad." The therapist recalled his previous statements about how police had been called when his father had thrown boiling water on his mother. She then asked where his father was. Sam answered, "He don't come to see me; he don't know where I am. We don't see him since he burned Mommy. I don't like Mommy getting burned. He called Mommy ugly and she called him ugly right back." Sam assumed responsibility for the fight. He said he had seen the shadow of his father coming up the stairs and hadn't warned his mother. Soon after this he revealed his notion that he had also caused his mother to abandon him. He said she had left him after he had crawled into her room one morning and "waked her up." He also said he remembered being a baby with a bottle and shaking milk on his mother. These ideas of guilt were explored and clarified.

In November, one year into treatment, when his mother didn't acknowledge his birthday, Sam said he was angry. He had expected a present. The therapist arranged a small celebration with a cupcake and a candle. Sam associated the candle with the burning of his mother. This was followed by other recollections of his mother, some positive, others negative.

Sam was able to elaborate on his intense longings for his mother. These elaborations not only reflected the intensity of his longings but an associated disorganization in his thinking and breakdown of reality testing. One day the therapist engaged Sam to reflect on why a mother wouldn't remember her son's birthday. He responded: "Every time I wake up I want my mommy. When I was little I used to cry and call for her. Now I close my eyes and go back to sleep." He wondered if his mother was "looking at the moon— it's the same moon I see." He said he would like "to be a bird and fly to her." He hoped she was not "in the swamps of Florida." He then drew a picture of "Space-Eyes"—eyes that could see everywhere, followed by a picture of a clown who had lost his job. When asked why the clown was smiling he said, "They have to keep smiling or else they get fired." It was clear that in the face of ongoing disappointment, Sam was still unable to speak of his mother with any objectivity or distance.

During the ensuing year his mother continued to disappoint Sam, making sporadic and unpredictable appearances. One day, after two years of treatment, Sam produced a graphic example of his struggle for self-esteem and its relation to his absent mother. "Some mothers never listen," Sam said. "I'm a pretty smart boy. People like me because I'm strong and smart." A moment later he added, "I feel like smacking myself." The therapist noted that it was hard to feel good about himself when his mother had left him. "What happens if everyone dies?" Sam responded. The therapist reassured him that she would make sure he would be taken care of, while noting that it can feel like everyone has died when someone has been separated from a person he loves.

Two months later, Sam's foster parents, citing his aggressiveness towards younger foster children in the home, requested his removal. Sam was placed with another foster family.

Just prior to the placement, Sam told the therapist (who is white) about a television program in which a black boy is adopted by a white family. Webster, the black boy, hits people, gets excited at school, and wets his bed. The therapist suggested that the boy might be wondering where his real parents are. Sam answered, "Maybe they are just waiting to get a house."

The therapist pointed out that some adults have so many worries of their own they can't take care of anyone else. Did Sam think it would be better to find out really whether his mother would ever be able to take care of him or not? (DSS was considering terminating parental rights at this point and freeing him for adoption.) Sam answered obliquely that the people would be nice who would keep him, but that he still gets sad and mad, bangs pillows at home, and that he can't stop thinking about his mother. He appeared unready to consider the possibility that his mother might not ever be able to take care of him.

Following the placement, Sam strove to maintain contact with his first foster family. Sometimes he telephoned them during sessions. He told them that the new foster family "gives me what I want." He also told his first foster father that he wanted to give him and his wife a Valentine card he had made for them. The man told him to mail it instead. Sam continued these telephone calls over the next months, inquiring about the other foster children, the parents' health, and the like. After one such call the therapist wondered how it felt to have lived in so many places. "I'm lucky. I'm a good doer. Kids like me," Sam replied while making war machines with Tinker Toys. In this play he had a "good" machine incorporate a "bad" machine and they both became "Good!" The therapist expressed her admiration for the strength of the good machine.

Simultaneously, Sam reported difficulties in the new school he attended due to the change of foster homes. He said the children were "bad," called him "ugly," and swore at him. "The move was too fast," he reflected. "I agree," said the therapist.

Sam's new teacher told the therapist he was "bizarre" in class. He was further described as being rude, using obscene language, and refusing to do his work. She felt that she couldn't give him the attention he needed.

At the next session, Sam admitted he had been suspended for a day for cursing. After some discussion Sam revealed that his mother and male friend had surfaced again and had been to see him. He said that they had brought presents and told him that he was a good boy. The therapist reflected how hard it must be for him to start hoping again that his mother would be able to care for him. He left the session acutely agitated.

The next month Sam had another visit with his mother at the DSS office. She was inebriated, assaulted the DSS worker, and required police intervention. In the ensuing session Sam talked about the visit. How did he feel? Mad, because "I don't like my mother when she gets that way." However, he denied that she had been drunk. He said he should take care of her. The therapist pointed out that it was parents who should take care of children, not the other way around. Sam's response was to reveal that he took things from children at school and had lit matches at his previous foster home. Having confessed his sins, Sam made an "oven" out of blocks and baked play dough cookies with the therapist in what seemed to be an attempt to both sublimate his rage and satisfy his longing for security.

Sam didn't see his mother until a few months later; this time with his aunt and uncle, cousin and half-brother. In one session, he said he had been happy to see her, but that he was worried about a foster sister, Natalie, whose mother hadn't shown up for planned visits. The therapist asked if he remembered past disappointments when his mother hadn't come as planned. She noted how hard it could be to think about unhappy things. Sam played with a car "driven by a fire setter" and carefully parked it in a garage. The therapist connected the impulse to set a fire with angry feelings about disappointments and pointed out how smart it was for the fire-setter to park in the garage until his fire setting feelings went away, so he couldn't hurt himself or anybody else.

Two and one-half years into therapy, Sam asked his new foster parents if they would adopt him. He told the therapist he thought his new foster mother would protect him and his real mother wouldn't, yet when the therapist agreed that it might be true that his mother could never take care of him, he said angrily, "If she doesn't, she'd better not call me 'son'." For the next two weeks Sam was flooded with anxiety and rage. These affects threatened the positive transference as well as his reality testing. "I'm Big Bad Sam, don't mess with me. I'm Mr. T. I'll break your neck. I'm acting like me, Mr. T. Don't bother me." He looked at the therapist menacingly and punched play dough. "My neighbor says I can't walk on her sidewalk. Is that fair? The devil lives under the sidewalk. The devil says to do bad things, but I don't." His play became aimless. The therapist worried that Sam's capacity to withstand disappointment may have been exceeded. These affects subsided, however, and the positive transferred survived.

At the start of third grade, an assistant principal took an interest in Sam and put him in a special class. During a session at this time, Sam said he felt in the therapist's office the way he felt in his second foster home. The therapist suggested it might be because people in both places cared for him. "It probably goes in me like that," he said. He said his mother had dumped him and didn't like him. He wondered why. The therapist suggested that sometimes mothers hadn't had good mothers themselves. Sam said, "Oh, no, my grandmother is good both to my mother and me." It was decided for the moment that the problem might be a result of his mother's drinking and smoking reefers plus not having a husband to help her.

Sam said he thought he would see his mother's picture in the newspaper some day and it would say she died. Then he wrote a story that began, "There was a boy named Sam. His mother dumped him in a garbage truck. The truck found out he was a boy and sent him to the Children's Department. The Children's Department gave him a foster home. The foster home gave him food, clothes, and everything nice. He thought his mother would not come again. The boy left the foster home because the foster parents were old and had canes and crutches. Then he went to another home. They let him stay. They gave him his own room. His sister gave him a digital watch. His mother would pick him up every day after school." ("Now I walk home by myself," he added, "because I said I could go by myself.") "My brother gave me a bracelet."

Sam, now age 8, began to verbalize reality-based anger toward his parents. He said he would punch his dad for burning his mother. He called his mother a "bad girl" not to take care of him and supposed he would just have to get adopted, yet he also revealed that he still sometimes cried for his mother. Sam and the therapist talked about how people change over the years and how he wasn't the same little boy who had had so many scary experiences, but had grown and could understand a lot more things now. He said he didn't feel "droopy" anymore.

It was November, the month of his birthday as well as his removal from his mother. One day Sam told the therapist he had to change his class because he couldn't read well enough. His class had actually been changed because he had assaulted another boy. The therapist confronted Sam with this information. Sam denied the assault and claimed that the other boy had said something bad about his mother. Alternative strategies of handling the situation such as walking away or telling the teacher were discussed.

Some weeks later, Sam came in wearing a hat that said "Captain." Expressing a combination of hope, denial, and defensive omnipotence he said he was captain of the school. He said he had been put in a new class. He said he would like to keep as friends not only the children in his old class but all his previous caretakers, including his parents.

The next session, after much hesitation, Sam acknowledged having gotten into trouble because he had dared another boy to stick a girl with a pencil. In the ensuing discussion, Sam became confused as to whether it was he or the other boy who had harassed the girl. He also acknowledged that he sometimes said other people did things that he himself had done.

Sam said he had told his teacher he was mad at his mother and that was why he had acted as he had. He went on to reveal that he sometimes pretended that his shirt was his mother and he bit it. Over the course of several sessions, both Sam's anger and his fear of admitting his wrongdoing were linked to his anger at his mother and his idea that it had caused the separation from her. His hostile acting out subsided and Sam received an award from the assistant principal for good work.

The therapist now encouraged Sam to think and talk about areas in which he said he now felt growing competence: reading, math, block-building, ballplaying, as well as remembering. He built an obstacle course and had his car negotiate it successfully. The therapist commented that this was like his life—that he was trying to get around a lot of obstacles successfully. In the next session, Sam was quiet and reflective. He talked about God, angels and the devil. He drew "God's eye" that watches over us and helps people be good (perhaps a further elaboration of "SpaceEyes" that he had months earlier associated with his mother).

By the end of his third year of treatment, Sam showed evidence of consciously trying to control his rage and elicit approval. He showed off for a new girl in his class. He complained about his short haircut and mused that he might wear a wig. He showed the therapist a note from an "enemy" classmate, full of swear words. He decided it was best just to tear it up. Sam said that if he had been his "old bad self" he would have hit the boy. "Maybe the boy needs therapy," Sam suggested. He recounted a dream in which he was a prince but no one believed him. He took a test and was elected prince.

One day Sam found out that a companion of his mother's, whom he had called "Dad," had died some time earlier. He said he was angry that no one had told him and "tore up his bed" at home. He was helped to do some remembering of this man, both good and bad things.

Due to the therapist's illness, treatment was interrupted for three months. When treatment resumed, Sam manifested surprisingly little ambivalence and was quite communicative. He said he had seen his mother. She now had a job driving a school bus, was living with his grandmother, and wanted him back. He also said that his mother was going to get him a "new father." Simultaneously, anger directed at himself reemerged. He called himself "a doo-doo head" and displayed an intensified uncritical readiness to rely on his mother. Using blocks, he constructed a "Hall of Justice" in which one prayed. Did he pray the court would return him to his mother, the therapist asked? Sam answered that she could read his mind.

After another visit with his mother Sam again talked about rejoining her. He recalled how he had felt the day his mother had given him up—how she had walked away from him at the DSS office saying she was going to the store, but had never come back. He cried.

Sam now expected to be imminently reunited with his mother. He said he was "embarrassed" to have been in foster care four years. "Four summers, four springs, four falls, and four winters." Simultaneously, his anxiety increased as his birthday and anniversary of his separation from his mother approached. He told the therapist he would hide in a coat closet at school so he could be by himself and worry about his mother. He also acknowledged a worry that she would drink again. During a session on his ninth birthday, Sam remembered previous birthdays during which he had been unable to see his mother.

Sam did not see his mother on this birthday either. He waited in vain for her at his grandmother's house. One day soon after, he called her during a session and talked for a long time in a small sad voice. He asked for a Transformer, gave her his shirt size, and asked when he could see her. After he hung up he said she sounded very "out of it." Still, he said, he felt better for having called her.

At home Sam decided to form his own therapy group with some friends. Sam said the group members talked about their feelings, like being mad and scared. They told secrets and had rules. One rule was "not to take the name of the Lord in vain."

Sam's mother did not contact him over Christmas. In January, over four years into therapy, he came into a session flushed with excitement. He had just seen his mother and had asked her to come to the session with them. She had agreed but had not kept her word. His play reflected his most recent disappointment. Using dolls, he elaborated a story in which a son helps a father. At one point the father and son, along with other family members, jump from a roof. The therapist ventured the interpretation that Sam wanted to help his parents but didn't know how because there are some things children can't help their parents with. The therapist decided to risk another invitation to Sam's mother to attend a session in order to help Sam with this issue; this time she came. During the session Sam, his mother and the therapist reviewed some of Sam's many past disappointments. His mother tried to assure Sam that it was not his fault that he had been placed in foster care. He drew a colorful picture for her.

Later Sam's mother was seen alone. She told the therapist that she had lost her job, her new husband had left her, and she was considering admitting herself to a hospital where she could "get some mental help." She said Sam would need the therapist "more than ever." Although she declared her intention to become a reliable support for Sam, she again disappeared. Once again Sam's anxiety intensified. He said he had two brains and would give one to his mother when she needed it. In a session soon after, he brought his foster brother, James, to treatment with him because "James is sad because his mother doesn't want him." Parallels were drawn between the two boys' experiences. Sam now seemed more or less consciously resigned to not seeing his mother and said he would like to visit his grandmother, whom he saw as more reliable.

A surprise visit to his foster home by his mother and grandmother, however, again raised Sam's hopes. Sam remained cheerful for several months. He hoped his mother would "get her act together," but he also expressed some doubt. For the first time he talked about his mother's drinking as a problem. "I wonder what's the matter with that woman," he said. The therapist pointed out that he used to say "I wonder what's the matter with me!"

Sam's grandmother saw him on his birthday and the idea of living with her or his aunt came up. His grandmother worked full-time and had not been able to cope with a young child. But now Sam was 9 years old and it might be a possibility. Sam's caseworker began to explore this idea with his grandmother, who decided to apply for custody of Sam. Sam was delighted, but work was done to fortify him in the event of a further disappointment. Still, he remained cheerful and increasingly affectionate in sessions. On his own initiative, he began to visit his grandmother on Saturdays.

One day he again brought his foster brother James to the session. James had become furious on finding out that his mother had taken back his sister but not him. Sam talked about his own mother and his anger at her. This anger could be clearly connected to his continuing longing for his mother and father figures.

As his eleventh birthday approached, Sam said he would rather grow younger than grow older. Would he like to go back and start all over again, the therapist wondered? He answered that he would like to be a baby and live with his mother and her deceased former male friend.

Sam came to a session following Career Day at school with the news that he didn't want to be a policeman or a soldier anymore. Instead, he wanted to be a psychologist. He would be a child psychologist on TV, and people would say, "How come that boy knows so much?" He was also proud that he got all As and Bs on his report card. "I am Einstein II," he said.

Around his eleventh birthday, nearly six years into therapy, Sam visited his grandmother and found his mother there as well. "She didn't smell of liquor," he said. His birthday was celebrated as usual in a session. He said he had never received presents from his family, "but maybe this year will be different." At the end of the session he attacked a punching bag, claiming it represented his foster brother's mother who wouldn't take her son back.

Sam saw his mother and grandmother on Christmas and did receive a watch and a game. His grandmother was pursuing her petition for custody of Sam. Sam reported that the principal at his school called him "the new Sam" because he didn't get into trouble there now. The therapist replied that she thought the "new Sam" was just the "real Sam" making his appearance.

Sam suffered intense anxiety concerning the reliability of his grandmother's intention to follow through and take custody of him. The therapist met with the grandmother to clarify this issue and was able to tell Sam that his transfer to his grandmother's custody was a realistic possibility. A few months later, Sam indeed moved to his grandmother's home.

Sam's grandmother felt all would be well now that Sam was with her. She now pushed for termination of treatment. Sam, too, indicated a wish to stop, as if he believed this might guarantee a happy ending to his troubles. Since Sam was now functioning well in school the therapist relented, with the understanding that she would be available if needed. Treatment, having spanned six and one-half years, stopped one month after Sam's arrival at his grandmother's house.

About one year later, following a fight in school, Sam returned for another round of treatment requiring an additional two years. During this period more work was done in relation to his previous losses and disappointments as well as new ones; including the death due to AIDS of his biological father and his mother's ongoing drinking and homelessness.

Psychological testing done at this time to assist in school placement yielded a full scale IQ on the WISC-R of 98, compared with a score of 82 obtained six years earlier.

## DISCUSSION

The case presented here in some detail is meant to provide an illustration of the ability of this treatment modality to sustain the development and maintenance of a viable sense of self (i.e., the establishment and integration of adequate self and object representations) via the identification with and internalization of the surrogate selfobject.

This case suggests the sustaining functions of this modality with the child's "psychological" parents as well. The child's mother and grandmother repeatedly inflicted disappointment and abandonment on the child, implying the inadequacy of their own object representations relative to Sam, yet the psychotherapy helped sustain the potential for a sufficiently positive representation of the child in their minds that the actual caretaking relationship could be renewed even after years of abandonment.

Specific goals of treatment, which we believe were achieved to varying degrees, were as follows: the construction and preservation of relatively positive self and object representations, and therefore a capacity to form more adequate relationships; a strengthened self-esteem system; an enhanced capacity to feel and fantasize on the one hand and to think and learn on the other; the reduction of anxiety and self-destructive guilt; decreased impulsivity and hostile aggression; and an enhanced capacity for empathy and even altruism. The achievement of such goals, to the extent that it occurred, should be viewed in the context of the many disappointments that occurred in this child's life during the course of treatment.

The case of Sam is representative of thousands of children in our society who are victims of neglect, abandonment or an emotionally inadequate environment. Their histories cannot be condensed to one terrible traumatic event. Rather they daily breathe the toxic air of deprivation and disappointment.

No easy cures or rescue operations are available or possible for these children. If their biological families cannot provide them with adequate care, neither do we have an alternative care system equipped to do so. Out-of-family placement, such as foster care or residential treatment, often constitutes valiant attempts to provide the best alternative care available. In many cases the quality of this care would be inadequate to nurture the potential of undisturbed children, let alone compensate for the devastation suffered by children such as Sam. A long-term emotionally sustaining relationship may prevent deterioration and allow the child's development to move forward.

Object relations theory helps us to understand the mechanisms whereby real interpersonal deprivation leads to the compromise of the child's capacity for relationships and later capacity for becoming a positively functioning member of society. It also helps us to understand better what it is the would-be healer, that is, the therapeutic selfobject must provide. Such an understanding is essential in order to sustain the therapist if he or she is to help the child. The literature on resilience suggests that one important variable that may enable a child to survive massive deprivation is a positive relationship with some adult. Other variables, such as intelligence and the possession of a special talent, have also been shown to be important. The importance of these latter two variables may be largely due to the fact that they make the child more appealing and thus more likely to attract the admiration and support from adults he so badly needs. We cannot rely on such special characteristics of deprived children to save them.

The dogged, psychologically informed persistence, over time, of empathic contact with the child in the face of both the child's cruelly inadequate environment on the one hand and the child's inevitable rage and withdrawal on the other is the essence of what we choose to call sustaining psychotherapy. Its employment with children such as Sam will rarely lead to the accomplishment of all we could wish, yet it is a practical and theoretically compelling endeavor that is almost certain to help.

## REFERENCES

Alpert, A. (1959). Reversibility of pathological fixations associated with maternal deprivation in infancy. In *Psychoanalytic Study of the Child* 14:169–185. New York: International Universities Press.

Bowlby, J. (1973). *Separation*. New York: Basic Books.

———— (1980). *Loss*. New York: Basic Books.

Kohut, H. (1971). *Analysis of the Self*. New York: International Universities Press.

———— (1974). *Restoration of the Self*. New York: International Universities Press.

———— (1978). Letters, 1961–1978. In *The Search for the Self*, vol. II, ed. P. Ornstein, pp. 851–929. New York: International Universities Press.

Stein, M., and Ronald, D. (1974). Educational psychotherapy of preschoolers. *Journal of the American Academy of Child Psychiatry* 13(4):618—634.

# VII

# HELPING INSTITUTIONS TO ASSIST HIGH-RISK CHILDREN

# 13

# Use of a Questionnaire to Compare Daycare Staff and Mental Health Staff Attitudes: An Aid to Mental Health Consultation to Daycare*

*Arthur B. Zelman*
*Murray J. Friedman*
*Bernard Pasquariella*

## DAYCARE CONSULTATION

In the Spring of 1979, our clinic received a small grant to provide services for a period of one year to three daycare centers in inner-city neighborhoods. The overall goals of the project were to enhance the child care knowledge and skills of day care workers, including early identification and improved management of children with emotional difficulties, and to enhance the overall functioning of the daycare programs so that their clients might be better served.

The contract with the agencies was sufficiently flexible to allow for client or consultee consultation as well as administrative consultation as needed (Caplan 1970). Similar programs have been described by Greenspan (1976) and Shrier and Lorman (1973).

It was anticipated that the major contributions of the project would be to impart a mental health point of view and to influence attitudes regarding (1) consultation itself, (2) need for utilization of mental health services,

---

*This chapter is reprinted from the *Journal of Preventive Psychiatry*, vol. 3, no. 1, 1986. Copyright © 1986 by Mary Ann Liebert, Inc., Publishers, New York. Used by permission.

(3) child development, (4) social learning, and (5) childrearing. In order to evaluate the extent to which the program was effective in achieving these goals, we constructed a questionnaire that was to be administered before and after the consultation period.

In reflecting on the pre- and post-consultation changes, as well as on the consultation experience itself, we realized that one factor that had limited our effectiveness was a lack of clarity as to precisely which attitudes, ideas, and aspects of child development should be focused on in a particular consultation. This information, we felt, could be useful in establishing more specific and measurable goals in future consultation efforts. Our basic idea was to pinpoint child development areas in which the daycare staff and mental health staff differed in their information and attitudes.

The questionnaire we had already constructed was therefore administered to the mental health staff of our clinic and then compared with the pre-consultation results obtained from the three original daycare staffs plus the staff of a fourth daycare center that had subsequently replaced one of the original three (see Table 13–1). A total of 40 daycare personnel and 20 mental health clinic staff completed the questionnaire. This represented 56 percent of the total daycare staff and 69 percent of the clinic staff.

This approach suggests a presumption that where differences occurred, the mental health point of view was necessarily "better." We are aware that this is not necessarily the case. Nevertheless, we believe it is appropriate that mental health programs be designed in accordance with explicitly stated mental health information and ideology.

## THE QUESTIONNAIRE

The questionnaire consisted of fifty-five items, some of which included sub-items. These items were arranged somewhat arbitrarily with respect to areas of child development. For purposes of analysis, the items have been rearranged and grouped together according to the specific topics to which they apply. Not every respondent answered every question so that the N varies among items.

One of the questions we had concerned the validity of combining two potential subgroups when considering daycare staff, namely the "professional" versus "nonprofessional" staff. Table 13–2 presents data identifying the location and professional status of the respondents.

**Table 13–1.** Number and Proportion of Respondents from Total Staffs of Day Care and Mental Health Centers

| Center | Total Staff | Number Responding | Percent Responding |
|---|---|---|---|
| Day Care I | 14 | 9 | (64) |
| Day Care II | 20 | 12 | (60) |
| Day Care III | 16 | 10 | (63) |
| Day Care IV | 20 | 9 | (45) |
| TOTAL DAY CARE | 70 | 40 | (57) |
| MENTAL HEALTH | 29 | 20 | (69) |

There were no statistically significant differences between these two subgroups on any of the items that later elicited significant differences between daycare and mental health workers. The highest t-value for any item was .72, indicating substantial agreement between professional and nonprofessional groups. This corroborates our assumption that the daycare staff comprised a homogeneous population with respect to the attitudes and knowledge sampled by the questionnaire.

**Table 13–2.** Day Care Respondents Grouped into "Professional" and "Paraprofessional" Categories

| Center | Professional Titles (N = 22) Director Asst. Director Educ. Coord. Social Worker Home Visitor Psychologist Therapist | Paraprofessionals Titles (N = 15) Teacher's Aide Asst. Teacher Home Base Secretary Nutritionist | Unknown (N = 3) |
|---|---|---|---|
| Day Care I | 4 | 4 | |
| Day Care II | 7 | 4 | |
| Day Care III | 6 | 4 | |
| Day Care IV | 5 | 3 | |

## RESULTS

Tables 13–3 through 13–8 compare the daycare staff to the clinic staff with respect to the responses of these groups to the questionnaire.

In some cases the respondents were asked to rate statements individually on a scale of agreement, from 1 to 4. T-tests, applied to the differences in the mean ratings on these items, were used as the basis for determining the significance of differences between the daycare and mental health groups. On other items, respondents were asked to choose from among several statements the one with which they most agreed. Chi-square was applied to evaluate the differences between the two groups on these items.

Table 13–3 includes various possible functions of daycare consultation. There were no significant differences between the two groups regarding the

**Table 13–3.** Value of Day Care Consultation Activities

(Based on a 5-point scale in which 1 signifies "very important" and 4 signifies "little or no help.")

|  | Mental Health Mean (N = 20) | Day Care Mean (N = 37) | t |
|---|---|---|---|
| Helping parents with referrals to appropriate agencies. | 1.25 | 1.38 | 1.00 |
| Identifying individual children in need of special help by conducting individual psychological, psychiatric and social examination. | 1.45 | 1.38 | .32 |
| Arranging seminars or workshops with staff around issues such as early childhood development, discipline, or promoting mental health in the classroom. | 1.55 | 1.68 | .65 |
| Identifying children with potential problems through classroom observations. | 1.03 | 1.51 | .60 |
| Participating with teachers in observation of total class for the purpose of gaining a better understanding of group dynamics and social interactions. | 1.95 | 1.75 | .57 |
| Conducting meetings with parents around mental health issues. | 1.80 | 1.68 | .67 |
| Meeting with Day Care directors to discuss ways to improve Day Care. | 1.70 | 1.92 | .66 |

importance they attributed to each of these approaches. Comparisons of the means within each population, however, shows that the mental health staff was almost unanimous in viewing classroom observation of individual children in order to identify problems as the most important consultation function.

Table 13–4 contains items pertaining to mental health service needs for preschool children. The only significant difference found was that the daycare group was less likely to disagree with the statement that "preschool children rarely have difficulties requiring evaluation by the mental health professionals."

Table 13–5 presents social learning items. Significant differences were found on several items. The daycare staff was in greater agreement, relative to the mental health staff: (1) that children need approximately equal amounts of rewards and punishment; (2) that up to age 4, children should always be expected to share their toys; (3) that young children should be taught never to express negative feelings about adults; (4) that children should start learning how to be independent as soon as possible; and (5) that young children should be taught to calm down before they express

## Table 13–4. Need for Special Help

(Based on a 5-point scale in which 1 signifies "you totally agree" and 4 signifies "you totally disagree.")

|  | Mental Health Mean | Day Care Mean | t |
|---|---|---|---|
| It is important to identify potential problems in pre-school children as early as possible in order to secure immediate help for them. | 1.36 (N=19) | 1.22 (N=36) | 1.00 |
| It is better to wait until children have had at least six months experience in Day Care before determining whether they have special problems requiring help. | 2.79 (N=19) | 2.58 (N=37) | .69 |
| All children should be screened soon after they enter Day Care to determine if they have special problems requiring special help. | 2.05 (N=19) | 2.08 (N=36) | .10 |
| Pre-school children rarely have difficulties requiring evaluation by Mental Health professionals. | 3.84 (N=19) | 3.12 (N=34) | 3.66* |

*p < .01

**Table 13–5.** Social Learning

(Based on a 5-point scale in which 1 signifies "you totally agree" and 4 signifies "you totally disagree.")

| | Mental Health Mean | Day Care Mean | t |
|---|---|---|---|
| Children need approximately equal amounts of rewards and punishment. | 3.50 (N=19) | 2.41 (N=36) | 4.28** |
| Children only need praise and rewards; punishment rarely does them any good. | 3.05 (N=19) | 3.22 (N=34) | .61 |
| Children need lots of rewards and praise but only occasional punishment. | 2.05 (N=19) | 2.29 (N=34) | .47 |
| Children do best when they are not given either a lot of praise or punishment. | 3.37 (N=19) | 3.17 (N=34) | .80 |
| Up to age 4, children should never be expected to share their toys. | 3.63 (N=19) | 3.66 (N=31) | .14 |
| Up to age 4, children should always be expected to share their toys. | 3.90 (N=20) | 2.66 (N=28) | 5.69** |
| Up to age 4, children should share their toys only if they want to. | 2.28 (N=18) | 2.67 (N=31) | 1.04 |
| Up to age 4, children should be encouraged not to share their toys unless other children share with them. | 3.11 (N=19) | 3.39 (N=30) | .64 |
| Young children should be taught never to express negative feelings about adults. | 3.95 (N=19) | 3.45 (N=39) | 2.67** |
| Young children should be taught to say whatever they think whenever they want. | 2.87 (N=16) | 2.97 (N=33) | .41 |
| Young children should be taught to calm down before they express feelings of anger. | 3.16 (N=19) | 2.21 (N=33) | 3.01** |
| Young children should be taught to express negative feelings towards adults in play activities but not directly to the adult. | 3.37 (N=19) | 3.00 (N=32) | 1.39 |
| Children should start learning how to be independent as soon as possible. | 2.84 (N=19) | 1.58 (N=35) | 4.58** |
| Children need to know they can be independent of their parents before they can learn to be independent. | 1.00 (N=19) | 1.89 (N=36) | 3.59** |
| Children best learn to behave well if they fear punishment. | 3.79 (N=19) | 3.32 (N=36) | 2.33* |
| Children best learn to behave because they fear losing the love of their parents. | 2.68 (N=19) | 3.29 (N=37) | 2.05* |

$*p < .05, **p < .01$

feelings of anger. They were more likely to disagree, however, with the propositions that children need to know they can be dependent on their parents before they can learn to be independent and that children best learn to behave because they fear losing the love of their parents.

Table 13–6 contains items pertaining to breastfeeding, thumbsucking and bedwetting. Daycare staff were more likely to agree that: (1) babies are better off being fed on a schedule than on demand; (2) thumbsucking is bad for children; (3) bedwetting after 4 years indicates a physical problem; (4) bedwetting after 4 years should be stopped as soon as possible. Mental health

**Table 13–6.** Psychological Function Development—Breastfeeding, Thumbsucking and Bedwetting

(Based on a 5-point scale in which 1 signifies "you totally agree" and 4 signifies "you totally disagree.")

|  | Mental Health Mean | Day Care Mean | t |
|---|---|---|---|
| Breastfeeding is usually the ideal way to nourish a baby for the first six months of life. | 1.42 (N=19) | 1.72 (N=36) | 1.11 |
| Breastfeeding is usually no better for a child than bottle feeding. | 3.21 (N=19) | 2.95 (N=37) | 1.00 |
| Breastfeeding is usually not advisable because of the demand it makes on the mother. | 3.68 (N=19) | 3.03 (N=36) | 1.45 |
| Babies are better off being on schedule than on demand. | 3.47 (N=19) | 2.41 (N=36) | 3.80** |
| Thumbsucking is bad for children. | 3.65 (N=17) | 2.35 (N=37) | 4.51** |
| Thumbsucking is good for children. | 2.68 (N=16) | 3.29 (N=37) | 2.86** |
| Thumbsucking usually indicates an emotional problem. | 3.08 (N=18) | 2.77 (N=34) | 1.15 |
| Thumbsucking may help a child to separate from his mother. | 1.91 (N=17) | 3.06 (N=36) | 4.11** |
| Bedwetting after 4 years indicates a physical problem. | 3.22 (N=18) | 2.52 (N=36) | 2.47* |
| Bedwetting after 4 years should be stopped as soon as possible. | 2.85 (N=18) | 2.03 (N=36) | 2.70** |
| Bedwetting after 4 years is a form of disobedience. | 3.41 (N=18) | 3.47 (N=36) | .25 |
| Bedwetting after 4 years indicates an emotional problem. | 1.80 (N=18) | 2.21 (N=32) | 1.45 |

*p < .05, **p < .01

staff were more likely to agree that thumbsucking is good for children and may help a child to separate from his mother.

Table 13–7 contains items referring to separation anxiety. Mental health staff agree that young children should be encouraged to view the body of the deceased. While they were unanimous in their disagreement with the idea that "for children under age 5, if someone in the family dies they should not be told what happened until after the adults have had a chance to get over their own feelings of mourning," a significant number of daycare staff agreed. The latter also agreed, relative to the clinic staff, that (1) the chil-

**Table 13–7.** Separation Anxiety

|  | Mental Health Mean | Day Care Mean | t |
| --- | --- | --- | --- |
| For children under the age of 5, if someone in the family dies: |  |  |  |
| they should be encouraged to view the body of the deceased | 2.50 (N=19) | 3.27 (N=33) | 2.54** |
| they should be told exactly what happened and then sent to stay with the person who is closest to them | 2.33 (N=18) | 1.87 (N=32) | 1.51 |
| they should not be told what happened until after the adults have had a chance to get over their own feelings of mourning | 4.00 (N=19) | 2.94 (N=33) | 3.37** |
| they should be told what happened but sent away from the household for a few days so that they will not be too upset seeing adults cry. | 3.89 (N=19) | 3.00 (N=32) | 3.25** |
| Most 1-year-olds can be expected to be unhappy when their mother leaves them to go to work. | 2.36 (N=17) | 2.46 (N=36) | 1.11 |
| A healthy 1-year-old won't care very much when mother leaves because the child knows the mother will be back. | 3.39 (N=18) | 2.67 (N=37) | 2.68** |
| Most 3-year-olds can be expected to be unhappy when their mother leaves them to go to work. | 2.36 (N=19) | 2.46 (N=37) | 1.04 |
| A healthy 3-year-old won't care very much when mother leaves because the child knows the mother will be back. | 2.47 (N=18) | 2.11 (N=37) | 1.15 |

*p < .05, **p < .01

dren should be "told what happened but sent away from the household for a few days so that they will not be too upset seeing adults cry" and that (2) a "healthy 1-year-old won't care very much when mother leaves because the child knows the mother will be back."

Table 13–8 contains items referring to attribution of differences between the sexes. The daycare staff was more likely to say that boys are either more

**Table 13–8.** Sex Differences

| Trait | Mental Health | Day Care | * Level of Significance |
|---|---|---|---|
| Activity | | | |
| Boys under 5 usually are: | | | |
| more (or less) active than girls | | | |
|   the same age | 10 | 20 | |
| as active as same aged girls | 10 | 18 | $X^2 = .03$, N.S. |
| Intelligence | | | |
| Boys under 5 usually are: | | | |
| smarter (or not as smart) than girls | | | |
|   the same age | 1 | 17 | |
| equally as smart as girls the same age | 18 | 20 | $X^2 = 7.75$, $p < .01$ |
| Need for Love | | | |
| Boys under 2 years usually require: | | | |
| more (or less) love than girls the same age | 0 | 17 | |
| same amount of love as girls the same age | 19 | 20 | $X^2 = 10.43$, $p < .01$ |
| Need for Discipline | | | |
| Boys under 2 usually require: | | | |
| more (or less) discipline than girls | | | |
|   the same age | 0 | 21 | |
| the same amount of discipline as girls | 19 | 15 | $X^2 = 15.43$, $p < .01$ |
| Use of Baby Bottle | | | |
| If given a chance a normal boy will: | | | |
| never suck on a baby bottle | 4 | 10 | |
| sometimes or often suck on a baby bottle | 16 | 24 | $*X^2 = .65$, N.S. |
| If given a chance a normal girl will: | | | |
| never suck on a baby bottle | 3 | 9 | |
| sometimes or often suck on a baby bottle | 17 | 26 | $X^2 = .34$, N.S. |
| Genital Play | | | |
| Boys under 5 - | | | |
| rarely or sometimes play with their penises | | | |
|   or testicles | 7 | 24 | |
| usually or often play with their penises | | | |
|   or testicles | 12 | 11 | $X^2 = 3.65$, $p < .05$ |
| Girls under 5 - | | | |
| rarely or sometimes play with their vaginas | | | |
|   or clitorides | 9 | 29 | |
| usually or often play with their vaginas | | | |
|   or clitorides | 11 | 7 | $X^2 = 5.91$, $p < .05$ |

* Chi-squares computed with Yates Correction

or less "smart," whereas the clinic staff said they were equal. Similarly, almost one-half of the daycare staff said one sex or another needed more love, while all of the clinic staff said the sexes needed the same amount of love. With regard to discipline, 59 percent of the daycare staff felt one of the sexes needed more discipline than the other (about equally divided over which sex) while the clinic staff all said the sexes required equal amounts of discipline. The daycare staff more often thought that pre-schoolers of both sexes "rarely" or "sometimes" played with their genitals while the clinic staff more often thought that both sexes "usually" or "often" played with their genitals.

## DISCUSSION

The results tended to corroborate some clinical preconceptions and miti-gate against others regarding daycare attitudes toward consultation, child rearing, and child development. While significant differences between the two groups were found on several items, it should be noted that these were relative differences and that, in general, intergroup similarities in attitudes and knowledge, as measured by the questionnaire, were greater than we had anticipated.

On the other hand, a profile does emerge of the ways in which the popu-lations differ. Daycare workers appear to place relatively more importance on punishment, while still appreciating the value of praise and positive re-ward. They also place relatively more value on the early development of in-dependence, seem less concerned about the need to meet dependency needs first, and thus expect the preschooler to be able to share more. Rela-tive to mental health workers, they have reservations about the children's expression of negative feelings about adults.

Daycare staff (not surprisingly) more often favor scheduled feeding over demand feeding compared to their clinical counterparts. They are more inclined to disapprove of thumbsucking and especially disagree with the clinicians' view that thumbsucking may help a child to separate from his mother. They are more inclined to view bedwetting after age 4 as a physical problem and to feel that it should be stopped as soon as possible. They also perceive young children as being less interested in their genitals.

Daycare workers are apparently not as convinced of the value of early in-volvement in rituals and communication regarding bereavement and are not as impressed with the degree to which 1-year-olds, at least, experience separation anxiety.

With regard to attributions of differences between the sexes, while clinic staff viewed boys and girls as equal, daycare staff viewed them as significantly different with regard to intelligence and their need for love and discipline. There was also an overall tendency, not mentioned above, for the daycare staff to view boys as being less intelligent and in need of more love than girls. It is not unlikely that these attitudes could lead to daycare staff behaviors reinforcing self-fulfilling prophecies regarding sex stereotyping, even if the direction of their stereotyping is not always in the same direction.

It is our impression that a questionnaire, such as that described here, can be useful in the following ways. First, it can help mental health consultants formulate concrete goals and objectives. This is often very difficult to do, given the complex and sometimes chaotic nature of inner-city daycare environments due largely to inadequate funding and staffing. It is also difficult because of failure of the mental health consultant to understand the classroom environment (Sarason 1966). Second, it can be useful in evaluating the degree to which these goals and objectives have been achieved. This is particularly important when political and economic pressures require increasingly concrete demonstrations of program effectiveness (Galbraith 1981).

Attitude change, such as that measured by questionnaires, can be viewed both as a process and an outcome variable. From the point of view of process, it is assumed that changing attitudes both precede and lead to changing behavior. In this sense the questionnaire is a more realistic way of evaluating the effectiveness of relatively short-term consultation or the early stages of long term consultation. One can also view attitude changes as an outcome measure per se. The assumption here is that the daycare consumers (children and their parents) pick up changing staff attitudes and benefit directly via more positive interactions and identifications with the staff and with each other. Such assumptions, of course, need to be evaluated in their own right.

Finally, our experience suggested the value of the questionnaire as a teaching tool. For example, the results of our questionnaire provided the focus of a discussion between the consultants and the daycare directors around the specific issue of the importance of meeting the dependency needs of young children. In the course of the discussion, one of the directors told the consultants that he had "never understood this before." He gave as an example his observations of the inability of seemingly "street-wise" and "mature" children to progress beyond a certain point. He said he now understood this phenomenon as an expression of unmet dependency needs. Similarly, a discussion of the results of the questionnaire with the entire staff of one of the daycare centers led to the staff's more engaged and frank participation in a dialogue with the consultant. It is our impression that the presentation of concrete data, such as that obtainable from a questionnaire, helps to "break the ice" in initiating and maintaining such involvement.

## REFERENCES

Caplan, G. (1970). *The Theory and Practice of Mental Health Consultation.* New York: Basic Books.

Galbraith, J. K. (1981). The conservative onslaught. *N.Y. Review of Books* 27:33.

Greenspan, S. I. (1976). The child psychiatrist and day care. *Journal of the American Academy of Child Psychiatry* 15(2):108–130.

Sarason, S., et al. (1966). *Psychology in Community Settings.* New York: Wiley.

Shrier, D. K., and Lorman, S. (1973). Psychiatric consultation at a day care center. *American Journal of Orthopsychiatry* 43(3):394–400.

# 14

# Comprehensive Mental Health Consultation to a Shelter for Battered Women: Preventive Implications*

*Rosetta M. Rhodes*
*Judith Brown Gordon*
*Arthur B. Zelman*

## INTRODUCTION AND CONCEPTUAL FRAMEWORK

Shelters for victims of domestic violence are a relatively recent phenomenon; few have been in operation for more than eight years. As newcomers to the human service field, such shelters are still defining their philosophies, establishing their ongoing services, and negotiating coordination of services with other community agencies. The purpose of this chapter is to describe a program of shelter-based clinical services to children and mothers, trace its implementation in one setting, and discuss implications for other domestic violence programs.

The functions of domestic violence shelters are many: to address immediate needs (both concrete and clinical), help clients plan for their futures, and facilitate clients' return to the community. It has become increasingly apparent that, in the context of providing direct services to victims, shelter staff must also preventively and actively address the problem of the cycle of

---

*This chapter is reprinted from the *Journal of Preventive Psychiatry and Allied Disciplines*, vol. 4, no. 1, 1990. Copyright © 1990 by Human Sciences Press, Inc., New York. Used by permission.

abuse whereby violent behavior is perpetuated in future generations. In the milieu of shelters, perpetuation of violent behavior by family members is more easily observed than in other settings, such as drop-in centers and outpatient clinics.

The family's tendency to perpetuate the cycle of abuse has underscored the need for effective clinical assessment and intervention. Using individual and family group work, a therapist can engage clients in problem solving, model appropriate methods of nonviolent conflict resolution, and offer parent guidance. Timely interventions can avert the continuation of abusive patterns.

For mothers and children residing in a shelter, the temporary breakup of the family and admission to the shelter constitute a crisis situation. Insofar as individuals and families are more amenable to intervention while in crisis, mental health intervention in a shelter may provide an unusual preventive opportunity.

Although the women who enter shelters do so in order to escape violent heterosexual relationships, the violence of which they were the target is often repeated in their relationships with their children. They often use verbal abuse as well as corporal punishment. This family problem needs to be addressed by both mothers and their children. The mothers must work through the violence in their own relationships with their partners, develop an awareness of the repetition of violence, and learn adaptive, nonviolent ways of coping with the stresses of parenting. The children need to work through the experience of violence between their parents as well as, in many cases, the violence perpetrated against them and sometimes by them. They too must learn adaptive, nonviolent ways of coping with siblings and peers and must be helped by shelter staff, and primarily their mothers, to reject violent responses to problem solving.

Living in the communal setting of a shelter is often experienced as safe and supportive. Regular routines evolve as staff expectations are made clear. The families begin to settle into their characteristic patterns of interaction. Both staff and clients become aware of conflicts around child-rearing issues such as punishment, discipline, limit setting, and verbal and physical abuse. As residents in a communal household, mothers are able to compare parenting practices. These may include limit setting, bedtime rituals, parentification of older children, corporal punishment, and feeding and nurturing styles. As participants in therapeutic family groups, they have the opportunity to share coping and problem-solving methods. They may gain strength as they recognize others experience problems similar to their own.

## Review of the Literature

The issue of family violence has received increased attention in recent years. Early studies focused on characteristics, dynamics, and treatment of victimized spouses. More recently, researchers have begun to investigate the characteristics, needs, and special concerns of children who are the unintended victims of violent familial relationships. In this context, the intergenerational effects of domestic violence as well as its impact on children's growth and development have been studied (Elbow 1982, Hershorn and Rosenbaum 1985, Hughes and Barad 1983, Jaffe et al. 1986, Rosenbaum and O'Leary 1981, Roy 1977). The literature reveals less material on program approaches to meet the needs of mothers and their children and to halt the perpetuation of violence. Services described include counseling, group therapy, supportive casework, play and art therapy, and evaluation, as well as referral to child and family agencies and to other community support systems. These diverse services may operate independent of or in conjunction with domestic violence shelters, and may be community-based or shelter-based. Auspices, location, mode of treatment, and service provider are all variables that affect impact (Alessi and Hearn 1984, Fleming 1979, Hughes 1982, Rhodes and Zelman 1986, Roy 1977).

Alessi and Hearn (1984) and Hughes and Barad (1983) have reported on the involvement of community agencies in the provision of services to children in shelters. They concluded that outside agencies can offer expertise in treating children in groups, which, when linked with shelter staff members' experience in working with children in a protected residential setting, produces an effective model of intervention. This chapter describes a more comprehensive array of services.

## Evolution of the Program and Services

The shelter described in this chapter is located in a city of 200,000 with a large inner-city population. The residence, a private house on a residential street, is a licensed special care facility that offers emergency housing and support services to up to twelve women and children. Clients stay an average of eleven days, though a ninety-day stay is permitted. Adult residents range in age from 18 to 45 and children range from birth to 14 years, with a predominance of preschool children. Family size averages four members. To the extent possible, families are assigned individual bedrooms. Other quarters—bathrooms, kitchen, dining, and living rooms—are communal. Household tasks are shared.

At the inception of this program, the shelter staff consisted of: a director, whose function was largely administrative; an assistant director, charged with the day-to-day management of the residence and supervision of workers; around-the-clock counseling staff of six; and support staff and volunteers. As the shelter evolved, it became evident that the victimized mothers and children in the residence needed not only concrete services and support but also clinical assessment and intervention. For example, there were a number of emergencies, such as suicidal threats, substance-abuse incidents, psychotic episodes, and on-site child abuse. The severity of clients' crises, as well as family members' ongoing behavioral manifestations of stress and pain, called for a level of clinical expertise unavailable from the shelter staff.

In response to this need, the shelter administrator decided to bring in a mental health consultant who could offer these clinical services as well as train shelter staff in appropriate interventions. The decision to seek outside consultation was not an easy one for the shelter's director and board to make. The shelter's grassroots origins and strongly feminist board dictated a stance of self-help and sisterhood, yet the staff's growing experiences with residents in crisis and recognition of unmet needs to which they could not respond prevailed.

In selecting a community mental health agency to provide the consultation, a number of criteria were deemed important. The agency needed to have: (1) a community orientation, evidenced by willingness to assign staff to the shelter site; (2) a propensity to coordinate with other community resources; (3) an availability of psychiatric back-up and psychological assessment; (4) an interest and expertise in crisis and abuse intervention; and (5) a physical presence in the community and the potential to provide follow-up services.

A mental health clinic and a consultant from that clinic were chosen who seemed to satisfy the above criteria. The specific form that the consultation would take was initially left open in order to allow for flexibility and to facilitate maximum involvement of participating staff from the shelter and the mental health clinic in the development of program and structure. During the 2½-year-period reviewed in this chapter, 162 families were admitted to the shelter, 100 of which, including 157 children, received services from the mental health consultant. These services ranged from one-time contacts to twice-weekly individual and group sessions.

## Description of Service Model

Services were provided by a female child psychotherapist with fluency in Spanish and Italian and experience with inner-city populations on a three-hour-per-day, two-day-per-week basis. Psychiatric back-up was arranged through the medical director of the mental health clinic. In addition to receiving services offered by the mental health consultant, adult residents also attended an ongoing battered women's support group sponsored by a community hospital.

It was agreed that the consultant would provide on-site direct service to the mothers and children as well as consultation to the staff. Direct services included: multifamily group sessions twice weekly for all residents (recently discharged residents were invited but attended infrequently); crisis intervention with women individually as needed, and with mothers and children when indicated or requested; individual contacts with children when indicated; and clinical assessment and referral when indicated. On-site consultation to shelter staff was also provided by the mental health consultant. Coordination between the shelter and the mental health consultant was achieved through her periodic attendance at shelter staff meetings. Regularly scheduled meetings between selected staff of the shelter and the consulting mental health clinic were also held.

## COMPONENT SERVICES

### Multifamily Group

The multifamily group was conceived as a vital tool to demonstrate the intergenerational manifestations of violence and to teach mothers and children new ways of relating to each other. Convened twice weekly, it was attended by all women and children in residence. The first 45 minutes of the group were devoted to *talking*, the last 15 minutes were devoted to *playing*. Frequently discussed themes included conflicts around the relationship between the woman and the batterer, and the long and complicated process of separation. This separation was a major issue raised not only by the women but also by their children. For example, it was a common occurrence for the children not to want to see their fathers at first. With the passage of time, however, this feeling often changed, and the children began to blame their mothers for the lack of contact they had with their fathers.

Group discussion further emphasized the complexity of familial relationships. Through their sharing of family experiences, participants were able to validate their feelings of stress and conflict and give and receive mutual aid in problem solving. For example, a woman who had left her spouse for the first time raised her concerns over the negative impact on her children. During group discussion, other women who had left their abusers multiple times and were further along in the resolution of ambivalence over separation helped her gain perspective on her actions and offered her support in her decision.

The talking portion also provided an opportunity for the development of constructive communication between mothers and their offspring. This component provided the children with a forum in which to express themselves through behavior and verbalization. In addition, specific family problems were often raised via symbolic communication. For example, on one occasion, three children decided to improvise a drama. A 10-year-old boy from one family and two sisters, ages 9 and 7, from another family, played the roles of husband, wife, and daughter respectively. As the drama unfolded, the boy became verbally abusive, lost his temper, and threatened the girls, who were unable to figure out what the boy wanted. The girls experienced the boy as "mean." Their choice of background music was taken from a record about a haunted house, perhaps a metaphor for the deprivation underlying much of the violence in their own homes. Additional recurrent themes which surfaced in discussion and play periods included separation and loss, problems with family communication, inclusion and exclusion of family members, and family fragmentation.

Nonverbal and verbal interaction between mothers and children were encouraged in the group. Such interactions constituted new experiences for some families, whose communication patterns were habitually chaotic and disorganized. Many of the mothers whose parenting styles did not include play with their children were helped to learn and participate in age-appropriate activities.

A number of shelter staff members attended and assisted with the group. During in-service training sessions with the consulting therapist, staff members were helped to explore material generated by the multifamily groups, such as the haunted house incident, which was explored on numerous levels. Staff had some difficulty comprehending the rationale for using family group time to play elementary games. The consultant helped them understand that the games enabled mothers to become familiar with developmentally appropriate activities they could share with their children, represented a nonthreatening way of dealing with parenting issues, and facilitated the consultant's modeling of ways staff could interact with the children while in the residence. (For a more detailed account of the multifamily group, see Rhodes and Zelman [1986].)

## Crisis Intervention With Individual Families

Crisis intervention was provided in the form of individual contacts with the women. These sessions were made available upon women's requests. Parents' complaints focused on chronic as well as reactive problems. Contacts were also initiated by the consultant when more serious symptomatology, such as suicidal ideation, severe despondency, or parental neglect was reported or observed. Themes raised during these contacts included concerns about children's symptoms (e. g., depression, aggressive behavior, withdrawal), reactions to separation from father, and adjustment to shelter milieu.

Children were included in the individual contacts with mothers according to the nature of the problem under discussion. For example, mother–child contacts might be arranged if multi-family group sessions or reports from shelter staff revealed physical or verbal abuse or an absence of parental empathy and/or understanding of children's needs. These sessions were particularly important as preventive measures to halt the perpetuation of violence.

Children were also involved in the individual contacts with the women when group sessions did not provide enough information for adequate assessment of a particular child's development or of a mother–child relationship. For example, the consultant might arrange a mother–child contact if she observed a withdrawn, nonverbal child with depressed affect whose mother reported that he or she was doing fine. Since mothers tended to find acting-out behavior more bothersome, they often did not perceive passivity as potentially pathological.

Finally, mother–child contact might be arranged if the group sessions were not adequately addressing the need for crisis intervention for a particular child. For example, in one session, a woman shared with the group the fact that her husband had shot her in her son's presence. In recounting the incident, she tended to minimize its severity and its impact on her child.

Most clients were eager to meet individually for the first one to three weeks. Beyond that time, the consultant was not sought out as much and appointments were frequently broken. This was most probably related to a decrease in the clients' anxiety levels as the initial crisis subsided. In addition, over time, relationships with shelter staff and other clients began to provide increased support.

It appeared that the clients who continued to seek individual contacts with the consultant beyond the initial crisis period were receptive to utilizing this experience as an opportunity for growth. Growth was evidenced with regard to development of insight and ability to solve problems, to function more independently and assertively, and to parent more constructively. This was particularly apparent with those women who stayed the full three-month limit at the shelter residence.

Clients, shelter staff, and consultant all had to deal with ambiguity regarding the function of the consultant as distinct from shelter staff. Initially, many requests from shelter residents involved their need for concrete services, legal advice, and other information more appropriate to the shelter staff's area of expertise. Clients often utilized defensive splitting, alternately viewing shelter staff or consultant as giving or withholding.

The chronological sequence of specific themes during individual crisis intervention was often similar to that noted in the multifamily group. Upon arrival, clients were eager to use sessions for ventilation and catharsis. They initially focused on recent incidents of domestic violence that prompted them to seek admission to the shelter. As the need-driven aspect of the marital relationship emerged, affect relating to separation and loss began to be revealed. As the women reviewed the history of their marital or common-law relationships, underlying conflicts emerged. Some clients were then able to appreciate the need for longer-term treatment.

At this juncture, many mothers expressed concern over their children's functioning. They sought advice and suggestions, became receptive to parent guidance and education, and sought assessment of and referral for treatment of their children when indicated.

Several factors probably converged leading to this shift of focus to the children. First, the mothers were less anxious about themselves and thus had an increased awareness of their children. Second, the initial stress of separation from the abuser and adaptation to the shelter had subsided. Third, the children frequently began manifesting more acting out behavior as the "honeymoon" period ended. Fourth, their presence in the shelter initially constrained some mothers from dealing with their children as they would at home, that is, by using withholding and physical punishment. This shift may have added to their experience of anxiety with regard to the children. However, as they became more comfortable in the shelter milieu, some mothers reverted to their former parenting styles, which conflicted with shelter norms and expectations. Finally, negative focus on the children often represented a displacement of conflicts previously exposed in the exploration of their spousal relationship.

As a client's departure approached, ambivalence toward the shelter was often expressed and acted out. This took the form of increased limit testing. In this context, clients tended to act out unresolved conflicts about separation through behaviors likely to provoke staff rejection. For example, a resident who was approaching the end of her stay might stay out past curfew several times during her last week at the shelter, as if wanting to be asked to leave. This pattern was most commonly noted among women who had stayed for periods of a month or longer.

## Direct Service to Children

Children in latency through adolescence were seen individually at their own or their mother's request or if the consultant identified a need for further assessment or intervention. Individual contacts helped work through problems related to the current crisis when group treatment was not sufficient. The most prevalent themes included: overwhelming fears that mother would be hurt or killed by father; ambivalence over separation, as father was increasingly missed and/or perceived as the aggressor; and feelings of helplessness and rage concerning changes and losses.

Children manifesting chronic pathology or developmental lags were referred to the consulting agency or other community service providers for further evaluation and/or long-term intervention. When working with school-aged children, contacts with school personnel were sometimes also initiated.

## On-Site Consultation to Shelter Staff

Consultation was provided to staff briefly before and after family group sessions, as well as at regularly scheduled weekly shelter staff meetings. The purpose of the pre- and post-group contacts was to apprise the consultant of developments in each case since her last visit to the residence and to process the group sessions. Supervision was provided around specific issues including management, assessment, referrals, and choice of intervention strategies. Sometimes staff chose to use this time to request consultation on case-related issues that had not surfaced during the groups but were evidenced in daily shelter life. Such issues might include the possible need for initiating a resident's referral to protective services or a psychiatric hospitalization.

Initial focus with shelter staff was on helping them to acknowledge and express feelings concerning shelter clients. Topics discussed during consultation included numerous issues which necessitated the development of understanding of mental health principles and crisis theory. Education in these two areas contributed to the staff's ability to understand such concepts as transference, acting out, repetition compulsion, and use of defense mechanisms. Staff often interpreted client apathy and rule violations as simple recalcitrance. Residents who watched too much television or used their emergency funds for "junk food" and cigarettes were frequently rebuked by staff.

Staff members were helped to view clients' behaviors as representing responses to deprivation (often chronic), stress and crisis. Staff were also helped to be more empathic and patient with clients, to have more realistic expectations, and to acknowledge the emergence of strengths following the working through the initial crisis. For example, the consultant emphasized the positive aspects of residents' assertiveness and lack of reliance on shelter staff.

The consultant sought to instill an appreciation of the relationship of some residents' behaviors to underlying conflicts, especially involving dependency needs that could not be quickly resolved. For example, she tried to explain the behavior of clients who habitually were not getting out of bed to care for their children or who were frequently missing medical and court appointments. In the occasional cases where severe pathology was manifested, staff sought the assistance of the clinical consultant for assessment and referral recommendations.

Increasingly, shelter staff members used the consultation time to bring up concerns about the quality of parenting they were observing. Simultaneously, staff became more aware of the need for preventive work on behalf of the children. Initially, staff members tended to respond to parental shortcomings with direct advice to mothers. However, they were helped to reflect on the results of this intervention and to see its limitations.

Over a six to eight month consultation period, as staff developed a more sophisticated awareness of the effectiveness of support and empathy for the women, the mothers with whom they interacted became better able to nurture their children. This was evident in all areas of parenting, from physical care to feeding to setting limits. In addition to "parenting" the women, the staff became better able to serve as role models through direct interventions with children, for example, helping contain children during tantrums and demonstrating appropriate adult–child meal-time interaction. They also became better able to serve as resources when mothers asked for guidance.

Consultation meetings with the staff also dealt with child-related issues, such as the development of a more informed perception regarding how experiences related to domestic violence, separation, and loss are perceived by children. Staff also developed insight into the child's need for adequate preparation upon entering new situations such as school and discharge from the shelter. As staff members learned to convert their preconscious awareness of these issues into conscious attitudes and words, they became better able to serve as models for the mothers.

Discussions with the shelter staff also included issues of assessment of children. Staff brought up concerns about observed symptoms and behavior patterns such as enuresis, passivity, assaultiveness, and withdrawal. The consultant helped differentiate which behaviors represented responses to situational crises and which were chronic. Staff members were also helped to develop skills such as history-taking and observation of the course of specific symptoms over time.

Indications for referral and treatment were also discussed in these meetings. In particular, the role and use of Child Protective Services proved to require clarification. Initially, staff had a tendency to view the use of these services as a betrayal of the mothers. A marked change in attitude came after a shelter mother who, with the consultant's help, had been referred to protective services, returned to the shelter to renew contact with the staff. This experience helped staff to view protective services as a supportive agency with which they could collaborate.

Management issues and policies were often discussed in these meetings. Shelter regulations covered a wide range of issues. Residents were prohibited from using drugs and alcohol, they were subject to a weekday and weekend curfew for returning to the residence, and all residents were expected to supervise their own children at all times. Violations of these established rules were a frequent topic at staff–consultant sessions. Staff members were helped to set limits in more therapeutic ways. During these meetings, staff members were also helped to acknowledge the anxiety created by certain kinds of situations, such as psychotic or physically threatening client behavior. This in turn led to decreased helplessness and earlier intervention. It also resulted in the establishment of more explicit and effective procedures, such as protocols for the use of local emergency resources, enabling staff to handle these situations with greater confidence.

## DISCUSSION

The provision of preventive mental health services to mothers and children may improve parenting sufficiently to diminish the likelihood of the perpetuation of the cycle of family violence in future generations. Whether or not this is so, the described services clearly provided much-needed crisis intervention with needy mothers and children and raised staff functioning to a higher level. Shelters for battered women present a unique opportunity for the provision of these services. Their milieu facilitates timely intervention. Shelters offer special preventive opportunities due to the following factors: the high-risk status of most of the mothers and children served; the low socioeconomic status of the majority of the population utilizing most shelters (this population does not characteristically seek professional help);

the physical accessibility of the clients in a residential setting; and the increased need for service generated by the crisis precipitating arrival at the shelter. The amount of time afforded by a 24-hour residential program facilitates the establishment of alliances, the assessment of need for intervention, and preparation of the client for further intervention as needed.

Our experience has corroborated both the need for and usefulness of a variety of mental health services in the inner-city spouse abuse shelter. Services should include assessment of children and parent–child relationships; crisis intervention for individual mothers and children; multifamily groups for shelter residents; groups for abused women; and consultation to shelter staff, with special emphasis on issues of children and parenting.

The very variety and complexity of these mental health needs and tasks, however, can prove threatening to a staff whose functions are primarily support and advocacy. The presence of a consultant-clinician can be viewed by shelter staff as turning the residence into a clinic whose approach does not coincide with their own. It is clearly evident, however, that in the shelter under discussion, the staff as well as the clients sought the consultant's help, despite initial reservations about her presence and periodic questioning of her role.

To further mitigate this problem, the authors suggest that the array of services herein described be included in a shelter's regular residential program. More specifically, we propose that a clinician with experience in domestic violence and expertise with children and families be included as an integral component of a shelter's staff. This individual's duties would include the provision of direct services as well as supervision of and consultation to shelter staff whose primary focus and training is not clinical.

The ongoing availability of specialized staff to work with sheltered children and mothers is vital in restoring and strengthening the adaptive capacities of the family in crisis. Moreover, in this kind of setting, such staff can play a pivotal role in interrupting the intergenerational cycle of violence.

Finally, we are aware of the need for the provision of services to the fathers and husbands of these families. The issue of how and by whom these services should be provided and coordinated with a shelter program is beyond the scope of this chapter.

## REFERENCES

Alessi, J., and Hearn, K. (1984). Group treatment of children in shelters for battered women. In *Battered Women and Their Families: Intervention Strategies and Treatment Programs*, ed. A. Roberts, pp. 49–61. New York: Springer.

Elbow, M. (1982). Children of violent marriages: the forgotten victims. *Journal of Contemporary Social Work* 63:465.

Fleming, J. (1979). *Stopping Wife Abuse.* Garden City, NY: Anchor.

Hershorn, M., and Rosenbaum, A. (1985). Children of violence: a closer look at the unintended victims. *American Journal of Orthopsychiatry* 55:260–266.

Hughes, M. (1982). Brief interventions with children in a battered women's shelter: a model preventive program. *Family Relations* 31:495–502.

Hughes, M., and Barad, S. (1983). Psychological functioning of children in a battered women's shelter: a preliminary investigation. *American Journal of Orthopsychiatry* 53:525–531.

Jaffe, P., Wolfe, D., and Wilson, S. (1986). Similarities in behavioral and social maladjustment among child victims and witnesses to family violence. *American Journal of Orthopsychiatry* 56:142–146.

Rhodes, R., and Zelman, A. (1986). An ongoing multifamily group in a women's shelter. *American Journal of Orthopsychiatry* 56:120–130.

Rosenbaum, A., and O'Leary, K. (1981). Children: the unintended victims of marital violence. *American Journal of Orthopsychiatry* 51:692–699.

Roy, M., ed. (1977). *Battered Women: A Psychosociological Study of Domestic Violence.* New York: Van Nostrand Reinhold.

# 15

## Group Intervention with Parents and Children Sexually Abused in an Unlicensed Daycare Center*

*Ann S. Kliman*
*Arthur B. Zelman*

The moment the initial disclosure of a severely injured, sodomized pre-school boy was made, Westchester County's Mount Vernon District Office Child Protective Services (CPS) Unit was called to investigate. By 1:00 A.M. the next morning, CPS had reason to believe that fourteen more children had been sexually abused at the same unlicensed daycare center. Within the next fifteen hours this number, in turn, had doubled.

As experienced as they were, the CPS workers were stunned and over-whelmed by the extent and severity of the abuse. Within thirty hours of the initial disclosure, Westchester County's Director of CPS called in the Direc-tor (A.S.K.) of the Situational Crisis Service of The Center for Preventive Psy-chiatry (CPP) to institute psychological intervention for the CPS workers.

The initial session with CPP staff included validation of the CPS work-ers' feelings of horror, exhaustion, outrage, and frustration, and the es-tablishment of an ongoing support system for the line workers on the case. Little resistance was evidenced, and a strong alliance between CPS and CPP was quickly formed. This alliance was facilitated by a history of collabora-tion between the two agencies.

---

*This chapter is based on a presentation to the American Orthopsychiatric As-sociation, San Francisco, CA, March 30, 1988.

The task of intervention, already formidable, was complicated by two facts. First, significant segments of the community refused to believe that the owner of the unlicensed daycare center, a powerful and respected "pillar of the community," could possibly be involved. Second, CPS, as an agency, historically had been viewed by the community as hostile, interfering, and intrusive (not at all an unusual perception of a child protective organization). Thus, the community tended to perceive CPS, the victimized children, and their parents as liars, villains, trouble-makers, and devils.

By the end of the first week, evidence was gathered suggesting that as many as sixty children had been abused. The list of possible victims included boys and girls, from 15 months to 14 years of age, but heavily weighted toward younger children. The alleged offenses ranged from fondling to seduction and rape, including oral, anal, and vaginal intercourse, physical and psychological abuse, and threats of further violence. The presence of the sexually transmitted diseases of chlamydia and gonorrhea was eventually documented in three of the girls.

The clinic (CPP) agreed to provide crisis intervention, assessment, and follow-up for all families who requested it. In addition, it was decided to offer groups for both the children and the parents.

This chapter will focus on the parents' group, since it was this modality that seemed to us pivotal in enabling us to help these families. The goals of the parents' group included: (1) support the parents in coping with their own feelings concerning the abuse; (2) educate the parents regarding issues of child abuse; (3) help the parents to support their children; and (4) help the parents to actively master the revelation of abuse, including participation in the prosecution of the perpetrators, should prosecution be deemed appropriate.

In addition to pressures from the community to suppress the investigation of the case, we were aware that many of the families served by the daycare center had severe preexisting problems (some, for example, were already known to CPS), and we expected to encounter much ambivalence and resistance to efforts to help them cope adaptively in their own interest and the interest of their children.

It took several meetings between CPP and CPS before either the parent or child groups could be set up. In the beginning, denial of the sexual abuse was as prevalent among the parents as it was in the community. Denial of abuse of the boys was stronger than that of the girls. It took many telephone calls, home visits, and time "beyond the call of duty" to get the parents together for the first scheduled meeting. Many parents initially declined to attend. Many others agreed to attend only if transportation was provided by a CPS worker.

The group was led by a clinician (A.S.K.), generally with the assistance of a CPS worker. However, in addition to parents and other family members, many other professionals from various agencies including the D.A.'s office, the clinic, community organizations, and CPS were periodically invited and attended. The group usually met weekly for about six months.

## THE GROUP—FIRST PHASE

Less than 25 percent of the parents, including two fathers, attended the first parent group. The majority of the group members were black and Hispanic. Parental socioeconomic and educational status ranged from college-educated middle class to grammar-school graduate on public assistance.

In the first weekly sessions, all the parents expressed shock, disbelief, denial, and strong ambivalence toward the daycare center owner. Their initial emphatic denial polarized families within the group as powerfully as within the community at large.

This phenomenon occurred as well within families, when one parent believed and the other denied the reality of the sexual abuse. Several of the parents had, as children, attended the same daycare center run by the same owner and many of their parents were friends of hers. In addition, several of the families belonged to the same church, choir group, and club to which the owner belonged.

The first therapeutic task was to acknowledge the difficulty of facing the possibility that a key member of the family's support system (and, to many parents, a parental figure) had failed them. It was necessary to empathize with the wish to disbelieve and deny, and to acknowledge and validate the pain involved in facing the reality of having a trusted friend exposed as someone who had, at the least, sanctioned abuse if not aided and participated in it, as many of the children alleged.

Other initial therapeutic interventions included counseling concerning predictable symptoms and behavior of sexually abused children, management of children's physical and emotional symptoms and behavior, and management of the parents' reactions. Many of the parents who were initially able to overcome their denial, viewed their children as "damaged for life." Helping them to correct this erroneous perception and to develop empathy for the children's victimization became an urgent task.

Equally urgent was the need to help the parents cope with, and control, their own rage and wish for vengeance. It was repeatedly pointed out that their children had been victimized by adults who were out of control, by adults who felt entitled to do whatever they wanted, whenever they wanted, and by adults who refused to think of the consequences of their actions. Thus, the children needed more than ever to have their parents demonstrate responsible adult behavior and in so doing provide the children with a measure of security.

The special need of the children for assurance of their parents' commitment to their ongoing safety was also stressed. For some of these parents the insistence on their importance to their children resulted in much needed support for their vulnerable self-esteem. Similarly, it helped counter the guilt and helplessness they felt at their failure to have protected their children.

Gradually, additional parents, including more fathers, attended the group. As the parents assumed more control over their own behavior they became increasingly able to sublimate their rage. Helped to resist the impulse to identify with the aggressor and act out impulsively or violently, their anger and aggression was harnessed in the interests of a common group task, namely to work together in the interests of their children.

Within weeks of the CPS and the Police Sex Crimes Squad investigation, it was found that the number of abused children had risen to 101. The ongoing revelations of new victims intensified the anxiety nascent in the community.

As anxiety increased so did the denial and paralysis. Resistance to the reality of the horror was not limited to the victims and their immediate community. It extended into the county, including the medical, legal, and political system. During this period, an assistant district attorney (ADA) came to the third group meeting to explain why no arrests had been made, and why no date had yet been set for the grand jury to convene. The parents were not reassured by the ADA's explanations.

After the ADA left the room, parents expressed heightened feelings of isolation, helplessness, and anger. This was followed by reports of increasing symptomatology of the children, including enuresis, nightmares, clinging, oppositional behavior, sexual provocativeness, and daytime fears. The group showed signs of increasing cohesiveness, however, in the process of providing mutual child guidance.

Meanwhile, harassment of the parents intensified. They received threatening and obscene telephone calls and letters, and were even followed by the perpetrators and their supporters. The parent group began to function as a bulwark against this intimidation. During the fifth weekly meeting, two new fathers came to the group. Led by one of them, himself a law enforcement officer, the group chose a letter written by another father to introduce a petition to the district attorney to pursue the investigation that they felt had been unnecessarily delayed. This letter, signed by the group members, was presented to him and given to the press (without signatures). The DA now publicly acknowledged the investigation for the first time and grand jury indictments were handed down within ten days.

The parent group, with the support of CPS and CPP, arranged meetings with legislative and legal representatives, school systems, and community action groups. Three experienced and skilled pediatricians finally diagnosed and treated those children infected with venereal disease. Previously, the virulent discharges caused by chlamydia and gonorrhea had been misdiagnosed as "poor hygiene."

The parents' anxiety lessened as they were helped to take action, for example, planning "safe places" for their children who were now without daycare. As appropriate medical, psychological, and daycare services were found, parental anxiety abated even more. The majority of parents allied more strongly and empathically with their children. Punishment of the children became less harsh and more appropriate as parents were educated to recognize that their children's often provocative and disturbing symptoms constituted predictable reactions to the stress to which they had been subjected.

Most children, according to their parents, showed symptoms of bedwetting, nightmares, fearfulness, forgetfulness, provocation of fights, overt and compulsive masturbation, crying "for no reason," clinging, and acting out of violent sexualized attacks. Parents were helped to understand that the basic wish of rapists is not sexual gratification but violence, intimidation, control, and humiliation of the victim. This distinction helped to prevent sex and the children's bodies from being implicated as the problem in parental communications to the children.

In parallel with the parents' group, weekly supportive and strategic planning meetings continued between Clinic staff and Child Protective Services. These meetings enhanced the ability of CPS to integrate the efforts, and to involve in the parent group representatives of the relevant agencies. A detective from the Mount Vernon Sex Crimes Squad, for example, became a valuable source for the group of both support and information concerning the work of the police in forwarding the investigation. Similarly, some community leaders attended occasional sessions at the request (or demand) of the parents.

The sixth group meeting proved especially encouraging to the parents. First a CPS worker reported on the testimony that CPS and the Police Department had given to the now convened grand jury. Then the ADA who was to prosecute the case introduced herself and respectfully described to the parents the sequence of legal proceedings that would occur. At the same time she warned the parents not to try to influence their children's testimony but to simply encourage them to tell the truth.

From the outset we were aware that the existence of groups of parents and children could increase the risk of the accusation attempting to influence and contaminate the children's testimony. This risk had to be weighed against the needs of the children and parents for support. Groups are generally the modality of choice for people who have been subjected in common to an external stress or crisis. Hence we elected, with the support of the DA's office, to provide these groups in spite of the legal risks. In fact, during the trial that ensued every parent who testified was asked about the group meetings. According to Barbara Egenhauser, the ADA who tried the case, it didn't hurt the case at all. In part for this reason Hechler (1988) regarded the Mt. Vernon intervention as "a model of what can be done" to assist families who need support and therapeutic intervention, without compromising the legal process. We believe that the reason the group did not damage the case was the emphasis we placed on the importance of observing and listening to the children.

At the same time that the group members were attempting and, to a great extent, succeeding in channeling much anxiety, rage, and guilt into adaptive modes, many symptoms of depression were reported and discussed in the parents' group. Parents reported sleep and eating disturbances, difficulty concentrating, extreme irritability, withdrawal, alcohol abuse, and sexual dysfunction (most frequently loss of interest) or even disgust related to any sexual activity.

The emergence of these symptoms seemed to relate to feelings of guilt for not knowing, not protecting, and putting their children in a "zone of danger" by having enrolled them in an unlicensed daycare center in the first place. (They had been forbidden to enter the basement room in which the children had spent most of their time.) Since they could not undo what had already happened, the parents began to distribute literature about the sexual abuse of children "so other parents won't make the same mistakes."

By the time of the grand jury hearing, eighteen children were accepted by the prosecuting attorney as reasonable witnesses, able to distinguish between right and wrong, reality and fantasy, and verbal enough to speak clearly to a group of strange adults. Sixteen of these children did in fact testify. A particularly poignant moment occurred when, following the testimony to the grand jury, one little girl ran from the room, tears streaming down her face, opened the door to the waiting room where she hugged her mother and said, "I told the truth, Mommy! I told them all the truth! I feel better."

Indictments were handed down on charges of rape, sodomy, reckless endangerment of children, and physical and emotional abuse, and two of the defendants were arrested. As a result, morale in the parent group ran high. At a meeting celebrating the indictments, attended by the principal detective on the case, a representative of the mayor's office, and CPS personnel, group cohesiveness was high and denial correspondingly low. For example two male group members revealed their own childhood victimization of abuse. This was, however, the beginning of another stressful period.

## THE GROUP—SECOND PHASE

The group was open to all parents and relatives who had had a relationship to the daycare center. During the second three months, a second wave of parents attended whose children had been in at the daycare center for years. They reported symptoms including severe learning problems, nightmares, oppositional or overly compliant behavior, stealing, fire-setting, and sexualized behavior. One of these mothers with a self-acknowledged history of poor impulse control described a struggle with bouts of murderous feelings. While support was provided for her feelings, the group leader pointed out the complexity of factors that could contribute to ongoing symptoms. A referral for individual help was immediately made for this mother, in addition to encouragement to continue attendance in the group.

During the fourth month, a mother who had earlier attended the group but had stopped coming returned. She took over the leadership of the meeting, reviewing for the newer group members what she had learned in the group about her children's reactions and needs as well as her own. Over the next two months, group process fluctuated between parent guidance issues and strategies of coping with the intensification of the defendants' efforts to generate community support and intimidate the parents who were cooperating with the district attorney's office. At one meeting it was reported that an earlier group member had acted as a "spy" for the defendant and had informed her of the proceedings of the group. The fear and rage generated by this revelation was addressed.

During the last month or two of the group, such examples of group cohesiveness alternated with expressions of despair regarding the victimization of the children and eruptions of rage at the defendants.

As the trial approached, the group proved useful in helping parents to prepare themselves and their children to testify. Parents expressed their fear

of the defendants and their supporters, including fantasies of violence occurring in the courtroom and even of voodoo being directed at them. The
group process worked to neutralize these fantasies with realistic reassurances.

Parents also expressed anxiety about their ability to testify effectively. One
father led a role-playing exercise in which first he, then a particularly anxious mother, "took the stand."

## TERMINATION OF THE GROUP

After much delay a trial date was set. This date was in turn twice postponed
before the trial actually got under way. Each delay constituted an additional
stress to the parents. The group continued to meet, but resistance mounted
and the group was interrupted by vacations, illnesses, and other plans.

Further evidence of the resistance of many parents to the group was manifested by what seemed, on the surface, to be a positive development. Pressure had been put on the parent group to find another space to hold meetings. A local community action agency offered both space and a trained
community activist who would work with the parents and join the group.
These offers were accepted without much discussion, and the community
activist attended the parents' peer group. Simultaneously, the ambiance of
the clinician-led parents' group changed. Activity was stressed at the expense
of reflection, and less attention was given to the children.

While previously, racial, religious, and ethnic issues had been openly discussed in the parents' group in terms of transference and countertransference, even including a joking characterization of the white therapist as a
"reverse Oreo cookie," ethnic and racial issues now went underground. We
speculated that the mostly black parents increasingly felt the need for the
support of respected members of the black community to counter the os-
tracism to which they had been subjected. Consistent with this interpretation was the relief felt by many of the group members when, almost four
months after the indictments, they succeeded in persuading the head of the
local Minister's Council to speak out against sexual abuse. While the need
of the group members to distance themselves from the representatives of
the outside agencies sponsoring the group may have been due in part to
fear, at the same time it reflected an increased sense of empowerment.

The group leader brought up in the group her increasing sense of isolation. Acknowledgment of the growing tensions was not sufficient to resolve
them. It was evident that the neighborhood parent group, now attended by
the community activist, had replaced the peer group. Since the trial was now

underway (with substantial participation of group members and their children), and many of the children had been successfully referred for individual and family treatment, it was felt that the goals of the parent group had been substantially met.

The last meeting of the parents' group with the therapist in attendance went smoothly, with appreciation expressed by all for what had already been accomplished. Acknowledgment of tensions was studiously avoided by the group.

A similar strain with the parents was experienced by CPS staff. It appeared that the collaboration between the parents and establishment agencies, resulting as it did in the ongoing prosecution of an informal leader of the community, was isolating the parents to an intolerable degree from that community. Further, it appeared that the clinic and social service agency would have to accept their status as the repositories of feelings inevitably directed to bearers of bad or unpleasant news. While the attempt to understand these dynamics was helpful, as was again accepting the realistic limits of what "outsiders" can facilitate or achieve, the staffs of CPS and CPP remained uncomfortable.

This discomfort was eased by the outcome of the trial. Two male perpetrators were convicted on all charges and sentenced to consecutive (nonconcurrent) terms of incarceration. The owner of the unlicensed daycare center was found guilty of criminal endangerment, although she had been charged with more serious offenses. The jury was not convinced that this woman could have knowingly allowed or participated in the exploitation of the children, although testimony was given to this effect. Subsequent appeals resulted in the upholding of six charges for rape and sodomy for one defendant, who is now serving time in prison on a multiterm sentence. The second defendant is still pursuing the appeals process. The reckless endangerment charges of the female owner of the daycare center were upheld and she served one year in prison.

## DISCUSSION

The allegation of the sexual abuse of children in daycare constitutes a trauma to the entire community. Daycare programs are given the responsibility, for long periods of time, of the care and safety of young children who are by definition defenseless. For this reason they are institutions in which the community puts a high degree of trust. The revelation that this trust has been betrayed thus constitutes a community crisis, resulting in a threat to community self-esteem and creating anxiety at all levels. This anxiety leads to a widening of natural fault lines, and an exacerbation of previous tensions.

As with individual victims, the trauma to the community created by such crises leads to maladaptive defense mechanisms including denial, splitting, projection, blaming, and scapegoating. Representatives of community agencies charged with the responsibility of assisting victims may themselves become the targets of such mechanisms.

The progressive discovery, over two or three days, by Child Protective Services of evidence suggesting a large number of victims created a situation of great stress for the workers. Since CPS was the pivotal agency responsible for the coordination of organized governmental and community efforts to identify, validate, and otherwise assist the victims, the clinic immediately responded to their request for intensive consultation.

This consultation first took the form of helping the CPS workers to anticipate expectable reactions to the stress to which they were exposed. Second, frequent meetings during the first few weeks following the charges of abuse enabled the workers to ventilate, clarify, and begin to master their reactions and feelings. Third, representatives from the clinic collaborated with their counterparts at CPS to plan services for the alleged victims.

The parent group was conceptualized as providing an opportunity and a venue not only for the participants to obtain mutual support, but as a focal point for the participation and collaboration of community agencies with the involved families. Hence, the group was attended at various times by representatives of the local mayor's office, the police department, the district attorney's office, and clinicians working with the children, in addition to the regular presence of a CPS worker. The group thus served a trouble-shooting function, for example, when it identified the slow pace of the prosecution of the case.

As is often (though not always) the case in human-made disasters, many of the families involved were already vulnerable. For example, several parents attending the group had already been known to CPS because of allegations of abuse or neglect. Others had preexisting drug or alcohol problems. Some of these problems were known to the alleged perpetrators and their supporters and were used against the parents, privately and publicly.

The vulnerability of many of the families was taken into account when the group was planned. It was understood from the beginning that many parents would be wary of working at such close quarters with agencies who they had reason to feel might judge them. Ideally, the parent group from the beginning should have been led by a professional who came from the ranks of the community. It is doubtful that such a person could have initially withstood community pressure to deny what had occurred. At the same time, it was felt that only through the power of a process generated by a group of their fellow victims could the parents mobilize their capacities to cope adaptively with the situation. This proved to be the case.

Unfortunately, the parents' vulnerability coupled with community dynamics limited the extent to which they could maintain an alliance with helpers about whom they were ambivalent to begin with. This was also true in relation to child therapists to whom they had been referred. Many parents either did not follow through or dropped out before any meaningful therapeutic process had occurred. These patterns were consistent with the high prevalence of severe pathology observed by clinicians who saw the children in groups or individually following the allegations of abuse.

While we were pleased with the result of our efforts to facilitate active mastery by the parents of a traumatic situation, we were deeply disturbed by the high prevalence of severe pathology observed by the clinicians who saw the children in groups or individually. The degree of denial and ambivalence that the larger community exhibited towards the families we worked with, as well as towards the Department of Social Services as they labored on behalf of the children, led us to suspect that the revelations of sexual abuse at this one daycare center represented only the tip of the iceberg with regard to the lack of protection that these and many other children in the community could count on.

We concluded with a larger question: Had we stumbled onto an epidemic that continues to rage? Further, is our view of the epidemic partially obscured by the diversion of all our attention and energy to the identification and prosecution of an external perpetrator rather than to the assumptions and conditions which permit the epidemic to thrive?

Unfortunately, no one is immune from succumbing to the need to oversimplify and scapegoat, including members of our own profession. In recent years, it appears that many clinicians, convinced of the fact of sexual abuse not only of children in daycare centers but in the childhoods of their adult patients, have proceeded to communicate their own agenda without being aware that they are doing so.

This is an occupational hazard for those in the helping professions, charged with the protection of others, especially where children are concerned. In part we must depend on the legal justice system to "keep us honest." Far more important, however, for our optimal functioning is our need to adhere closely to our knowledge base in such areas as child development and systems theory. When we do this, we have still more to contribute than the valuable functions described here of assisting in the bringing to justice the perpetrators of sexual abuse, and of helping the victims to cope. Our ultimate goal, as a profession, is to *prevent* the occurrence of such assaults on our children. We can only do this by maintaining our focus on the multiplicity of factors that must exist to allow such tragedies to occur in the first place.

## REFERENCE

Hechler, D. (1988). *The Battle and the Backlash: The Child Sexual Abuse War.* Lexington, MA: Lexington Books.

# VIII

# FOLLOW-UP STUDIES OF INTERVENTION FOR MULTIPLY STRESSED CHILDREN

# VIII

# FOLLOW-UP STUDIES
# OF INTERVENTION
# FOR MULTIPLY
# STRESSED CHILDREN

# 16

# IQ Changes in Young Children Following Intensive Long-Term Psychotherapy*

*Arthur B. Zelman*
*Shirley C. Samuels*
*David Abrams*

## LITERATURE REVIEW

It is generally accepted that negative social, educational, and physical environments lead to decreased academic performance and problematic social, educational or physical environments have shown changes in IQ as a results of intervention (Abelson et al. 1966, Beller 1973, Davis 1947, Gray and Klaus 1970, Heber and Gaber 1975, Julenville 1962, Karnes 1973, Karnes and Zehrbach 1977, Kirk 1958, Koluchova 1972, Levenstein 1970, 1977, Levenstein and Levenstein 1971, Miller and Dye 1975, Ramey and Campbell 1977, Skeels 1966, Skeels and Dye 1939, Sloan 1952, Strauzzula 1956, Tizard 1960, Tizard and Rees 1974).

A review of the psychoanalytic literature suggests that what is variously referred to as "pseudobackwardness," "pseudoimbecility," or "pseudostupidity" may represent a defense against knowing, understanding, or seeing, pertaining especially to sexual matters, or may represent aggression used

*This chapter is reprinted from the *American Journal of Psychotherapy*, vol. 39, no. 2, April 1985. Copyright © 1985 by the Association for the Advancement of Psychotherapy, New York. Used by permission.

to defend against feelings of rage (Berger and Kennedy 1975, Bornstein 1930, Buxbaum 1964, Hellman 1954, Klein 1949, Mahler 1942, Oberndorf 1939, Sprince 1967, Staver 1953). The emphasis in the studies of children by these clinicians has been on the inhibition of curiosity resulting from the children's unconscious need not to know their own instinctual feelings, since this would result in anxiety and guilt. In her study of schizophrenic children and adolescents, Bender (1970) found that for most of these children, IQ's dropped with age. For those who made an adult adjustment, the IQ increased. The findings that emotional problems are associated with IQ are not always consistent in studies of adults (Bloom and Entin 1975, Martin et al. 1977). In a review of research on schizophrenic adults, however, it was concluded that they tend to score at an average about 10 IQ points below the normal mean (Winder 1960). Findings such as these have led to much discussion as to whether lower IQ leads to a psychiatric disorder or occurs as a consequence of this disorder (Beitchman et al. 1982, Rutter 1964, Rutter et al. 1970).

Exactly what constitutes the negative social environment leading to the impairment of social, intellectual, and emotional development of the child is also not clear. A broad range of studies has provided evidence that social class by itself does not lead to greater disturbance (Beitchman et al. 1982, Rutter et al. 1970, Schoonouer and Heitel 1970). It seems that the tendency for lower socioeconomic children to have a higher incidence of social and intellectual problems results from family disruption and its associated disadvantages, rather than from poverty per se.

The apparently close relationship between family disruption and impaired child development makes it logical to hypothesize emotional disturbance as an intervening variable between poor social environment and impaired social behavior and intellectual performance. If this assumption is valid we would expect effective treatment of emotional problems to lead to enhanced social and intellectual skills including IQ changes even if the environment is not actually changed.

One method of testing this hypothesis would be to provide psychotherapy to a group of environmentally stressed or deprived children with poor social and intellectual functioning and to measure IQ changes prior to and after treatment. To make such a study more convincing, one would use a control group of matched children who received no treatment. The use of such a control group, however, raises ethical questions.

A review of the literature has revealed surprisingly few examples of IQ testing before and after psychotherapy for young children. Axline (1949) presented some short-term pre- and post-therapy IQ results in a group of 5- to 7-year-olds who had received brief psychotherapy. Five of fifteen children receiving the intervention showed IQ gains. Bernstein and Menolascino (1970) reported on a 7-year-old boy who after two and one-half years of intensive psychotherapy showed a change of IQ from 76 to 100. Woodward and colleagues (1960) provided a specialized psychiatric nursery program for children with retarded functioning. Specific gains were reported in only two cases.

In reviewing these studies our search of the literature revealed positive pre- and post-psychotherapy IQs for eight children. Only three of these cases, however, involved long-term treatment, and only two involved long-term follow-up.

This paucity of pre-treatment versus post-treatment IQ data encouraged us to pool some of our own clinic experiences retrospectively, since we have treated many environmentally deprived children whose environment has not materially changed, yet who have shown marked improvement intellectually as well as socially and emotionally.

## METHOD

The ten cases presented here were selected from the clinic population at The Center for Preventive Psychiatry. Clinicians were asked for past or current cases of children in long-term intensive treatment who they felt had made significant intellectual gains as part of their overall progress.

A total of fourteen cases were referred to the investigators. One of the cases showed no gain in IQ. Another three had had only one IQ test and were unavailable for a follow-up IQ test.

Three major modalities employed with children at our clinic during the years from which this sample was drawn were the Cornerstone Therapeutic Nursery, psychoanalytic psychotherapy, and corrective object relations psychotherapy. In addition, some of the graduates of the Cornerstone Therapeutic Nursery received small group psychotherapy, usually weekly.

The Cornerstone Therapeutic Nursery has been described elsewhere (Kliman 1975; see also Chapter 2). Briefly, it consists of an interpretive approach by an analytic therapist who works with the child individually in the classroom in collaboration with the teachers. Indications for this form of treatment include an ability to make use of interpretation, a need for socialization and demonstrated difficulties in this area, some minimal ability to function with other children, and at least partial resolution of the separation process. More recently the Nursery has been used for deprivation syndromes.

Psychoanalytic psychotherapy is a traditional psychoanalytically based, intensive, interpretive treatment modality. Corrective object relations psychotherapy has also been described elsewhere (Stein 1970). Briefly, it consists of a one-to-one therapist–child intensive, corrective supportive relationship. Since children who receive this treatment are often more regressed than those who receive psychoanalytic psychotherapy, their parents often require similar treatment along with the parent guidance that all parents of the children received to varying degrees. In addition to these modalities, some parents also received group therapy utilizing a mixture of parent guidance, analytically oriented group, and supportive techniques.

## RESULTS

Table 16–1 summarizes data characterizing the children. Seven of the 10 children were male. Mean age on admission was 44 months, with a range of 20 months to 66 months.

Diagnoses are also presented in Table 16–1. Five of the 10 children received a primary Axis I *DSM-III* diagnosis of Oppositional Disorder of Childhood. There were two Pervasive Developmental Disorders and one Attention Deficit Disorder with Hyperactivity. On Axis II of the *DSM-III* system, 7 of the 10 children suffered from developmental delays of expressive speech or language. While not constituting a *DSM-III* diagnosis, depression was found in all the children. We also noticed that over time oppositional symptomatology often alternated with depressive symptomatology.

Table 16–1 also summarizes the caretaking circumstances of the children. On admission, 4 of the children were living with their biological parents, 2 were living with their biological mother alone, 3 were living with their biological grandmothers, and 1 was in foster care. Only two caretaking changes occurred during the period between pre- and post-testing.

Since IQ tests were not generally given immediately upon admission, treatment had already commenced to one degree or another in each of the 10 cases. Table 16–2 shows the number of visits with children and with caretakers prior to and after the first IQ test. A mean of 117.4 visits with the children and 37.4 visits with caretakers had already occurred prior to the first IQ test. An additional 404.4 visits with the children and 74.0 visits with the caretakers took place between the first and final IQ tests. Thus, a mean of 521.8 visits with each child and 111.4 visits with each primary caretaker were provided between the time of admission and the final IQ test. The mean time between initial and final IQ tests was 54 months, with a range of 20 to 132 months.

**Table 16–1.** Sex, Age, Diagnosis, and Family Structure of Subjects

| Case | Sex | Age on Admission (Months) | Primary DMS-III Diag. on Admission | Caretaking on Admission | Change in Caretaking Prior to Post Testing |
|------|-----|------|------|------|------|
| 1* | M | 20 | Developmental language disorder— Multiple URI's | | |
| 2* | M | 20 | Developmental language disorder— Multiple URI's | Biological parents | |
| 3 | M | 35 | Oppositional disorder (depression) | Biological parents | Marital separation. Lived with mother, regular visits with father |
| 4 | F | 36 | Pervasive dev. delay (speech) | Biological parents | |
| 5 | M | 37 | Oppositional disorder (depression) Dev. delay (speech) | Foster mother | |
| 6 | M | 37 | Pervasive dev. disorder (depression) Dev. delay (speech) | Grand- mother | |
| 7 | M | 42 | Oppositional disorder (depression) Dev. delay (speech) | Grand- mother | |
| 8 | M | 54 | Oppositional disorder (depression) Dev. delay (speech) | Biological mother | |
| 9 | M | 57 | Oppositional disorder epilepsy (depression) Dev. delay (speech) | Biological mother | |
| 10 | F | 66 | Atten. def. disorder with hyperactivity | Grand- mother | Grand- mother died |
| Mean | | 44 | (depression) | | |

*Twins

Table 16–3 presents data on treatment modality and IQ changes. The major treatment modality utilized in 9 out of the 10 cases was the Cornerstone Therapeutic Nursery. The tenth case utilized a psychoanalytic psychotherapeutic approach with the mother as well as the child. In this case, the ratio of caretaker visits to child visits was highest. Several visits tabulated here as child visits also included the mother.

**Table 16–2.** No. of Pre- and Posttreatment Visits and Time between IQ Tests

| Case | Number of Visits before Initial IQ | | Number of Visits between 1st and Final IQ Tests | | Time between Initial and Final IQ Test |
| | Child | Primary Caretaker | Child | Primary Caretaker | |
|------|-------|-----------|-------|-----------|-----------------------|
| 1 | 229 | 15 | 216 | 88 | 46 months |
| 2 | 215 | 15 | 211 | 88 | 29 months |
| 3 | 55 | 14 | 850 | 179 | 132 months |
| 4 | 34 | 21 | 165 | 20 | 98 months |
| 5 | 210 | 80 | 815 | 59 | 70 months |
| 6 | 50 | 18 | 614 | 57 | 25 months |
| 7 | 111 | 8 | 500 | 19 | 20 months |
| 8 | 38 | 28 | 293 | 77 | 55 months |
| 9 | 232 | 175 | 233 | 111 | 21 months |
| 10 | -0- | -0- | 147 | 42 | 30 months |
| Mean | 117.4 | 37.4 | 404.4 | 74.0 | 52.6 months |

A treatment was considered to be significant if it occurred regularly over a period of at least ten months. Parent guidance was not included as a separate significant treatment modality, although it was provided for all caretakers. Mean initial IQ was 84.9; mean final IQ was 112.8, indicating a mean IQ change of 27.9 with a range of 10 to 53 points.

## CLINICAL NARRATIVE

Mrs. S. brought her 2-year, 11-month-old son Dennis (Case 3) to our clinic after her psychotherapist had allegedly advised her to place him in foster care. She did not want to give up Dennis, yet she bitterly complained about him. She said that Dennis became easily upset, whined much of the time, had frequent tantrums, and was generally "negativistic." For example, when offered something that his mother had first withheld, he would say, "I don't want it." He screamed when his mother returned from work and Mrs. S. felt she could not satisfy him.

Dennis initially presented in the Nursery as a thin, pale, unkempt, waiflike child. He had a pathetic and unattractive manner. According to one observer, "he exuded a feeling of helplessness." His communications were vague and diffuse and he presented few opportunities for the staff to comfort him.

Almost three months after treatment began, Dennis obtained a full scale score of 90 on his first IQ test (Stanford-Binet). In spite of his score, the testing psychologist felt Dennis possessed at least average intelligence. The

**Table 16–3.** Treatment Modalities and IQ Change

| Case | Maj. Treatment Modality | Other Significant Treatment Modality | Initial IQ | Final IQ | Gain in IQ |
|------|------------------------|--------------------------------------|------------|----------|------------|
| 1* | Cornerstone (3x/wk) | COR† for Child Group for Parents | 70 (Stan.Binet) | 99 (WISC-R) | 29 |
| 2* | Cornerstone (3x/wk) | | 70 (Stan.Binet) | 99 (WISC-R) | 29 |
| 3 | Cornerstone (5x/wk) | P.P.†† for child Group for mo. boy-friend | 90 (Stan. Binet) | 143 (WISC-R) | 53 |
| 4 | Cornerstone (5x/wk) | P.P. for child | 107 (Stan.Binet) | 149 (WISC-R) | 42 |
| 5 | Cornerstone (5x/wk) | COR for child Small group for child | 75 (Stan.Binet) | 101 (WISC-R) | 26 |
| 6 | Cornerstone (5x/wk) | P.P. for child | 72** | 97 (WISC-R) | 25 |
| 7 | Cornerstone (5x/wk) | — | 92 (WPPSI) | 111 (WISC-R) | 19 |
| 8 | Cornerstone (5x/wk) | P.P. for child Small group for child | 86 (WPPSI) | 117 (WISC-R) | 31 |
| 9 | Analy. Treat. (2–4x/wk) incl. some tripartite | P.P. for Parent | 102 (WISC-R) | 112 (WISC-R) | 10 |
| 10 | Cornerstone (5x/wk) | COR for child | 85 (WPPSI) | 100 (WISC-R) | 15 |
| Mean | | | 84.9 | 112.8 | 27.9 |

*Twins
**This figure represents the mean of two IQ tests given at the same time. 61 IQ on Stanford-Binet, 83 IQ on Merritt Palmer
† – Cornerstone
†† – Psychoanalytic Psychotherapeutic

psychologist added the following: "There is evidence for a precocious and traumatic separation and ensuing oral and anal fixations. He remains strongly object-seeking, albeit by negative means."

From the beginning, Dennis proved capable of much symbolic play. Early themes included drowning, falling, and getting lost. During the seventh month of treatment Dennis said pathetically, "I am nobody . . . don't say my name." Later themes to emerge included castration, confusion, and ambivalence concerning sexual identity. The early themes were generally worked through toward positive resolutions. For example, his initial helplessness gave way to a jubilant "I did it" upon completing a task. His vagueness gave way to more focused expressions of rage, which appeared simultaneously with the consistent use of the pronoun "I." By the fifteenth month, he said, "I need to be a big man now," and further amended that to a more realistic and accepting if somewhat sad statement, "I'm just Dennis S————."

Early in treatment Dennis had eagerly responded to the teacher's suggestion that an outline be made of his body. He asked her to include the "tushy" and the "penis." During the thirteenth month he introduced Bugs Bunny and his carrot to express his concerns. This carrot repeatedly got red or black paint on it and Dennis readily responded to the therapist's interpretations concerning his oral, anal, and phallic fantasies connected with the carrot. Interpretations were made concerning Dennis' equation of having a penis with being dirty, bad, and humiliated, as well as his fear of being vulnerable to bloody mutilation.

Very rich material emerged in connection with his work. One day he told the teacher he did not want to change his wet pants because he was afraid she would laugh at his penis. He then told her he also had a vagina. He drew a vagina which contained a circular "button" which turns it on, "then it gets long and it hurts." A few days later he said that a Donald Duck puppet had died because "he didn't have a beak no more. His beak changed into a nose because he didn't listen to me. But Mickey Mouse listens because his nose will never grow to a big long one because he listens to me."

One month later, Dennis asked the teacher to draw him "peeing on the floor and making a puddle." Next to him was to be his mother, who he decided should "also have a penis and be peeing and making a very large puddle." Two days after this experience, he asked a girl in the Nursery if he could see her vagina. He offered to return the favor by pulling down his pants so she could see his penis. He then said, "Isn't it cute, isn't my penis cute? Look at my little tiny penis."

In parallel with the aforementioned sexual preoccupation and concerns we were able to observe shifts in Dennis's handling of aggression. He initially presented as apathetic. This was followed by episodes of self-deprecatory behavior in which he dumped water and paint on himself. Alternating with this behavior he began to exhibit temper tantrums manifested by indiscriminate destructiveness, for example, knocking down shelves and throwing objects. His repertoire of aggressive behavior expanded to include attempted attacks on other children and the staff, especially the therapist. At the same time, however, he began to frankly seek out the laps of the teachers.

After one and one-half years of treatment, Dennis was given his second Stanford-Binet (Form L-M) IQ test. His score was 122, hence a 32 point increase had occurred within a fifteen month period.

The psychologist doing the test added, "Dennis showed some major ups and downs in his overall adjustment." He showed much "assertive, aggressive, and notably exhibitionistic behavior," was described as "lusty and fun-loving," but "a mournful expression would sometimes cross his face." He appeared at each testing session wearing costumes representing various animals (e.g., a rabbit and a bird). He was seen as a predominantly phallic-oedipal child with a vulnerability, particularly around issues of aggression.

Seventeen more months of treatment in the Therapeutic Nursery and about five years of intermittent once or twice weekly individual psychoanalytic psychotherapy were provided to help Dennis to consolidate his gains and further enhance his development. His home life continued to be turbulent. His parents, after a brief separation and reconciliation, separated permanently at the end of the first year of treatment. His mother, who suffered from a Narcissistic Personality Disorder, became more deeply involved with an even more disturbed man and an intensely sadomasochistic, very unstable relationship ensued that included many separations and reconciliations over the next several years. During these years, Dennis's biological father, a passive and chronically depressed man, nevertheless faithfully visited with Dennis on a twice-weekly basis and brought him to therapy.

Dennis was tested for the third time at the age of 14, eleven years after his first IQ test. His overall score was 143. At the end of the eighth grade he had a 97 average in his subjects. He was described by his teachers as pleasant and cooperative.

To his therapist (A.Z.), whom he continues to see about every two months, he presents as lucid, in possession of a good sense of humor, and as having considerable insight into himself and his family. He is aware of the emotional limitations of his mother and consciously, at least, can separate himself from them. He is aware that he is vulnerable to feeling humiliated by others. While sensitive to slights from the therapist, for example, starting a visit late, he can verbalize and control his anger to the extent that he consistently projects and takes in warm feelings to and from the therapist.

## DISCUSSION

Reflection upon the data leads to the often-asked question of what the IQ measure represents. Is it a fixed, genetically determined entity, variations of which can be ascribed mainly to artifacts such as unreliable testing? The current consensus would appear to reject this view in the light of a greater appreciation of the interaction of genetic and environmental variables.

Granted then that we might expect IQ changes for environmental (including effective treatment) and developmental reasons, what is it that is changing? Briefly, we would submit that a key variable is anxiety. We think that the children in our series were helped to be less anxious. Due to the age of these children, anxiety has an especially powerful effect on structural aspects of personality. Hence we are not merely talking about "test anxiety," which could alter test results from day to day. Rather, we are referring to the interaction between intensity of anxiety and the development of increasingly reliable and sophisticated mechanisms to regulate anxiety. We believe that the treatment, by reducing anxiety in these children, provides them in turn with the opportunity to internalize anxiety-reducing mechanisms of a more adaptive nature. Berrini and Tommazzolli (1972) found that half the children they studied had overwhelming anxiety connected to depression. Additionally, in this study an inhibition of the wish for knowledge in all the pseudo-retarded children was found.

In doing this study we had not a priori chosen to focus on any particular treatment modality. As has been described above three major modalities have been employed for treating preschool children at our clinic: (1) analytically oriented individual treatment, (2) corrective object relations, and (3) the Cornerstone method.

As it turns out, 9 of the 10 cases reported here involved the Cornerstone method as the primary therapeutic modality. It is possible that some of this is artifact. For example, the Cornerstone children may have received more systematic pre- and post-treatment testing. It is our impression, however, that this is a real finding that will hold up after further analysis. It seemed to us that the more intensive and extensive involvement with the children necessitated by the Cornerstone Therapeutic Nursery method provided the opportunity for them to internalize a sufficiently positive object world to counteract the catastrophic anxiety responsible for the development and overuse of defenses such as projection, denial, psychic numbing, and cognitive inhibition. Such a sequence provides us with a possible explanation of their apparent increased ability to learn, concurrent with and following the treatment they received.

In addition, the course of Dennis's treatment would seem to corroborate, in a general way, psychoanalytic hypotheses summarized earlier concerning the cause of pseudo-retardation and cognitive inhibition. Hence we could observe a dramatic increase in IQ concomitant with the expression of vivid sexual fantasies and anxieties, as well as more frank expression (and presumably decreased fear) of aggression.

The IQ changes reported here are theoretically even more dramatic when we consider that pre-treatment IQs on the whole actually represented testing done while treatment was already well under way. We believe that some positive IQ changes had probably already occurred prior to the first testing.

In addition to the Cornerstone Therapeutic Nursery, other modalities were generally used to consolidate and extend gains already made in the primary modality. These modalities were usually less intensive, but seem as necessary in the light of the ongoing stress from external sources with which these children had to cope.

The case narrative presented here was meant, among other things, to illustrate the characteristic interpersonal environment of the children in our series. The IQ gains are especially encouraging since we would expect IQs to decrease in such a home environment—an environment that we believe is unfortunately frequently found in child psychiatric clinic populations. By and large, we are not speaking of psychotic families but of chaotic, disorganized, acting-out, or isolated and withdrawn families and parents. These include many children, who like the one described here might, without preventive intervention, require foster care or child protective services. We are encouraged to be able to present data suggesting that much can be accomplished without removing children from their caretaking environments.

However, this is no easy task. The IQ changes presented here occurred in the context of long-term and intensive treatment entailing the provision of hundreds of clinic visits. We are not surprised at this. An earlier study (Zelman and Byrne 1978) at our clinic suggested that the longer the treatment of the preschool child, the better the result. This finding is consistent with psychoanalytic-developmental theory and clinical experience concerning the damage that can be done to developing psychological structures, by an inadequate parent–child relationship over the first three or four years of a child's life. Shorter effective treatment would certainly be desirable. One possible model we have been finding very powerful involves an application of Margaret Mahler's tripartite method to the nonpsychotic but seriously disturbed child population (Mahler et al. 1975).

The thrust of the present study was to help to fill a gap in the literature by providing data suggesting that early intervention may bring about major long-term positive results. We are aware, of course, of the limited conclusions that can be drawn from this uncontrolled study. We are hopeful that these findings will stimulate more refined and controlled outcome studies with young children. Such studies are noticeably lacking compared to analo-

gous studies with adults even though intensive treatment of young children
may yield more dramatic results.

## REFERENCES

Abelson, W. D., Zigler, E., and De Blasi, C. L. (1966). Effects of a four-year follow-
through program on economically disadvantaged children. *Journal of Educational Psychology*, pp. 756–771.
Axline, V. (1949). Mental deficiency: symptoms or disease. *Journal of Counseling Psychology* 13:313–327.
Beitchman, J. H., Patterson, P., Gelfand, B., and Minty, G. (1982). I.Q. and psychiatric disorder. *Canadian Journal of Psychiatry* 27:23–28.
Beller, E. K. (1973). Research on organized programs of early education. In *Hand-
book of Research on Teaching*, ed. R. M. Travers, pp. 530–600. Chicago: Rand
McNally.
Bender, L. (1970). The life course of children with autism. In *Psychiatric Approaches
to Mental Retardation*, pp. 149–189. New York: Basic Books.
Berger, M., and Kennedy, H. (1975). Pseudobackwardness in children: maternal
attitudes as an etiological factor. In *Psychoanalytic Study of the Child* 30:279–306.
New Haven, CT: Yale University Press.
Bernstein, N. R., and Menolascino, F. J. (1970). Apparent and relative mental retardation: their challenge to psychiatric treatment. In *Psychiatric Approaches
to Mental Health*, pp. 91–114. New York: Basic Books.
Berrini, M. E., and Tommazzolli, C. M. (1972). Depressive aspects of mental inhi-
bition and pseudoretardation. In *Depressive States in Childhood and Adolescence*,
pp. 273–280. Stockholm: Almqvist and Wiksell.
Bloom, R. B., and Entin, A. D. (1975). Intellectual functioning and psychopathol-
ogy: a canonical analysis of WAIS and MMPI relationships. *Journal of Clinical
Psychology* 31:697–698.
Bornstein, B. (1930). Zur psychogenese de pseudodebilität. *International Journal of
Psycho-Analysis* 16:378–399.
Buxbaum, E. (1964). The parents' role in the etiology of learning disabilities. In
*Psychoanalytic Study of the Child* 19:421–447. New York: International Univer-
sities Press.
Davis, F. (1947). Final note on a case of extreme isolation. *American Journal of Soci-
ology* 52:432–457.
Gray, S., and Klaus, R. A. (1970). The early training project: a seventh year report.
*Child Development* 41:909–924.
Heber, R. F., and Gaber, H. (1975). The Milwaukee project: a study of the use of
family intervention to prevent cultural-familial mental retardation. In *Excep-
tional Infant*, ed. B. Friedlander, E. Sterritt, and G. Kirk. New York: Brunner/
Mazel.

The authors gratefully acknowledge the assistance of Dr. Hope Conte in evaluating the data.

Hellman, I. (1954). Some observations on mothers of children with intellectual inhibitions. In *Psychoanalytic Study of the Child* 9:259–273. New York: International Universities Press.

Julenville, C. P. (1962). A state program of day care for severely retarded children. *American Journal of Mental Deficiency* 66:829–837.

Karnes, M. B. (1973). Evaluation and implications of research with young handicapped and low-income children. In *Compensatory Education for Children Ages 2–8. Recent Studies of Educational Intervention*, ed. J. C. Stanley. Baltimore: Johns Hopkins University Press.

Karnes, M. B., and Zehrbach, R. R. (1977). Educational intervention at home. In *The Preschool in Action. Exploring Early Childhood Programs*, ed. M. C. Day and R. K. Parker, pp. 75–94. Boston: Allyn & Bacon.

Kirk, S. A. (1958). *Early Education of the Mentally Retarded.* Urbana, IL: University of Illinois Press.

Klein, E. (1949). Psychoanalytic Aspects of School Problems. In *Psychoanalytic Study of the Child* 3/4:369–390.

Kliman, G. (1975). Analyst in the nursery: experimental application of child analytic technique in a therapeutic nursery: the Cornerstone method. In *Psychoanalytic Study of the Child* 30:477–510.

Koluchova, J. (1972). Severe deprivation in twins: a case study. *Journal of Child Psychology and Psychiatry* 13:107–114.

Levenstein, P. (1970). Cognitive Growth in Preschoolers Through Verbal Interaction with Mothers. *American Journal of Orthopsychiatry* 40:3–17.

——— (1977). The mother–child home program. In *The Preschool in Action. Exploring Early Childhood Programs*, ed. M. C. Day and R. K. Parker. Boston: Allyn & Bacon.

Levenstein, P., and Levenstein, S. (1971). Fostering learning potential in preschoolers. *Social Casework* 52:74–78.

Mahler, M. (1942). Pseudoimbecility: a magic cap of invisibility. *Psychoanalytic Quarterly* 11:149–164.

Mahler, M., Pine, F., and Bergman, A. (1975). *The Psychological Birth of the Human Infant.* New York: Basic Books.

Martin, P. J., Friedmeye, M. H., and Sterne, A. L. (1977). I.Q. deficit in schizophrenia: a test of competing theories. *Journal of Clinical Psychology* 33:667–672.

Miller, L. B., and Dye, J. L. (1975). Four preschool programs: their dimensions and effects. *Monograph of the Society for Research in Child Development* 40:162.

Oberndorf, C. P. (1939). The feeling of stupidity. *International Journal of Psycho-Analysis* 20:443–451.

Ramey, C., and Campbell, F. (1977). Prevention of developmental retardation in high-risk children. In *Research to Practice in Mental Retardation. Care and Intervention*, ed. P. Mittler, pp. 157–164. Baltimore, MD: University Park Press.

Rutter, M. (1964). Intelligence and psychiatric disorder. *British Journal of Social and Clinical Psychology* 3:120–129.

Rutter, M., Tizard, J., and Whitmore, K. (1970). *Education, Health and Behavior.* London: Longman Group, Ltd.

Schoonouer, S. M., and Heitel, R. K. (1970). Diagnosis implications of WISC scores. *Psychological Reports* 26:967–973.

Skeels, H. M. (1966). Adult status of children with contrasting early life experiences. *Monographs of the Society for Research in Child Development* 31.

Skeels, H. M., and Dye, H. B. (1939). A study of the effects of differential stimulation on mentally retarded children. *Proceedings and Addresses of the Sixty-Third Annual Session of the American Association on Mental Deficiency* 44:114–130.

Sloan, W. (1952). Preschool class at Lincoln State school and colony. *American Journal of Mental Deficiency* 56:755–759.

Sprince, M. P. (1967). The psychoanalytic handling of pseudo-stupidity and grossly abnormal behavior in a highly intelligent boy. In *The Child Analyst at Work*, ed. E. R. Geleerd, pp. 85–114. New York: International Universities Press.

Staver, H. (1953). The child's learning difficulty as related to the emotional problems of the mother. *American Journal of Orthopsychiatry* 23:131–141.

Stein, M. (1970). The function of ambiguity in child crises. *Journal of the American Academy of Child Psychiatry* 9:462–475.

Strauzzula, M. (1956). Nursery school training for retarded children. *American Journal of Mental Deficiency* 61:141–149.

Tizard, B., and Rees, J. (1974). A comparison of the effects of adoption restoration to the natural mother and continued institutionalization on the cognitive development of four-year-old children. *Child Development* 45:92–99.

Tizard, J. (1960). The residential care of mentally handicapped children. London conference of the scientific aspects of mental deficiency. *British Medical Journal* 5178:1041–1046.

Winder, C. L. (1960). Some psychological studies of schizophrenics. In *The Etiology of Schizophrenia*, ed. D. D. Jackson, pp. 191–247. New York: Basic Books.

Woodward, K. E., Brown, D., and Bird, D. (1960). Psychiatric study of mentally retarded preschool children. *Archives of General Psychiatry* 2:156–170.

Zelman, A. B., and Byrne, J. (1978). *Treatment of 100 Preschoolers in a Multi-Modality Clinic*. White Plains, NY: The Center for Preventive Psychiatry.

# 17

# Children's IQ Changes and Long-Term Psychotherapy: A Follow-up Study*

*Arthur B. Zelman*
*Shirley C. Samuels*

The present authors have published a study (Zelman et al. 1985), reprinted here as Chapter 16, that described long-term IQ gains averaging 27.9 points in 10 children who had received one or more varieties of long-term psychotherapy. A review of the literature presented in that chapter revealed only three studies of long-term psychotherapy of children in which pre- and post-treatment IQ scores were reported. Subsequently, one study has appeared demonstrating significant IQ gains in a group of 19 autistic children who were treated intensively for up to six years (Lovaas 1987).

One obvious limitation of our first study was that it represented a selected series of cases chosen for positive outcomes. We recognized that a controlled prospective study in which two groups of children, one treated, one un-treated, would provide the most reliable kind of data bearing on the question of IQ change and psychotherapy. However, the ethics of deliberately not treating children in obvious need of help, as well as other methodological difficulties, precluded this approach.

A second approach, which was the one followed in the study reported here, was to review our clinic records and report all cases of long-term psychotherapy in which pre- and post-treatment IQ tests were performed, thus expanding the original sample into a nonselected series.

---

*The assistance of Stanley Samuels, Ph.D., Department of Neurology, New York University Medical Center, is gratefully acknowledged.

## METHODOLOGY

The records of all children receiving psychotherapy at the Center for Preventive Psychiatry (CPP) from 1970 through 1983 were reviewed. Fifty-two children, 20 to 83 months of age, had had pre-treatment and post-treatment IQ tests and were included in the present study. The 10 cases in the 1985 study were also included in this group. As in the original study, many of the children had already undergone a significant amount of treatment when the "pre-treatment" IQ tests were given. Similarly, many of the subjects received further treatment after the "post-treatment" IQ tests were administered. Several of the subjects received more than two IQ tests. Where this was the case, the first and last IQ test were used.

The children were tested by a series of clinicians using the Peabody, Stanford-Binet, WPPSI, WISC, or the revised form of the WISC. Within-subject IQ score changes were examined by means of the paired t-test. This was done for the entire sample and for subjects grouped according to what were determined to be possibly relevant variables (e.g., socioeconomic status). When appropriate, group mean differences were assessed using the t-test for unequal groups. The correlation of IQ test score difference ($\Delta$ IQ) with quantitative data (e.g., time between the IQ tests) was measured using Pearson's coefficient. The relationship of $\Delta$ IQ with the severity of an associated condition (e.g., parental pathology) was examined by means of the Kendall Rank Correlation Coefficient. All diagnoses of children and parents were made using *DSM-III* categories. One tail t-tests were used throughout since the results were expected to be consistent with those in the initial study.

## RESULTS

Table 17–1 shows initial IQ, final IQ, and IQ change ($\Delta$ IQ) of the children. Within-subject comparisons were made using the paired t-test. The change in IQ between the initial and final test was significant at $p < 0.001$. Mean IQ in the 34 subjects whose IQ increased was 18.7. Mean IQ change in the 12 subjects whose IQ decreased was 9.7. Six of the subjects IQs remained the same.

The relationship between the time separating the initial and final IQ tests (in months) and the IQ change was correlated using the Pearson correlation method. The mean number of months between initial and final IQ test was 32.8 with a range of 6 to 119. The correlation of 0.298 is weak but statistically significant at $p < 0.025$.

**Table 17–1.** Initial IQ, Final IQ, and IQ Changes of the Children

| Case No. | $IQ_i$ | $IQ_f$ | $\Delta IQ$ |
|:---:|:---:|:---:|:---:|
| 1. | 83 (WP) | 93 (WI) | +10 |
| 2. | 111(WP) | 132 (WI) | +21 |
| 3. | 72 (S-B) | 88 (S-B) | +16 |
| 4. | 100 (WP) | 118 (WP) | +18 |
| 5. | 103 (WP) | 117 (WI) | +14 |
| 6. | 101 (WP) | 121 (S-B, PPV) | +20 |
| 7. | 79 (S-B) | 94 (WI-R) | +15 |
| 8. | 96 (S-B) | 116 (WP) | +20 |
| 9. | 91 (S-B) | 109 (S-B) | +18 |
| 10. | 75 (PPV) | 80 (PPV) | + 5 |
| 11. | 102 (S-B) | 112 (WI) | +10 |
| 12. | 100 (WP) | 126 (WI) | +26 |
| 13. | 93 (S-B) | 103 (S-B) | +10 |
| 14. | 90 (S-B) | 94 (S-B) | + 4 |
| 15. | 102 (S-B) | 114 (WI) | +12 |
| 16. | 86 (S-B) | 86 (WI-R) | 0 |
| 17. | 89 (WI-R) | 105 (WI-R) | +16 |
| 18. | 83 (S-B) | 107 (PPV) | +24 |
| 19. | 72 (S-B) | 101 (WI-R) | +29 |
| 20. | 80 (S-B) | 84 (WP) | + 4 |
| 21. | 73 (WP) | 97 (S-B) | +24 |
| 22. | 97 (PPV) | 102 (PPV) | + 5 |
| 23. | 92 (WP) | 107 (WP) | +15 |
| 24. | 83 (S-B) | 109 (WP) | +26 |
| 25. | 124 (WI) | 130 (WI) | + 6 |
| 26. | 70 (S-B) | 99 (WI-R) | +29 |
| 27. | 70 (S-B) | 99 (WI-R) | +29 |
| * 28. | 90 (S-B) | 143 (WI-R) | +53 |
| * 29. | 107 (W-I) | 149 (WI-R) | +42 |
| * 30. | 75 (S-B) | 101 (WI-R) | +26 |
| * 31. | 72 (S-B) | 97 (WI-R) | +25 |
| * 32. | 92 (WP) | 111 (WI-R) | +19 |
| * 33. | 86 (WP) | 117 (WI) | +31 |
| * 34. | 102 (WI-R) | 112 (WI-R) | +10 |
| * 35. | 85 (WP) | 100 (WI-R) | +15 |
| 36. | 65 (WP) | 65 (WI-R) | 0 |
| 37. | 104 (WP) | 104 (WP) | 0 |
| 38. | 71 (WP) | 71 (WP) | 0 |
| 39. | 85 (WP) | 85 (WP) | 0 |

(*Continued*)

**Table 17–1.** (Continued)

| | | | |
|---|---|---|---|
| 40. | 91 (WP) | 84 (WP) | −7 |
| 41. | 102 (WI-R) | 89 (WI-R) | −13 |
| 42. | 112 (S-B) | 100 (WI-R) | −12 |
| 43. | 109 (S-B) | 99 (WI-R) | −10 |
| 44. | 82 (S-B) | 70 (S-B) | −12 |
| 45. | 97 (S-B) | 85 (WI-R) | −12 |
| 46. | 76 (WP) | 69 (WI-R) | −7 |
| 47. | 88 (WP) | 85 (WI) | −3 |
| 48. | 99 (S-B) | 92 (WI-R) | −7 |
| 49. | 67 (S-B) | 58 (S-B) | −9 |
| 50. | 90 (S-B) | 77 (S-B) | −13 |
| 51. | 93 (WP) | 83 (WI-R) | −10 |
| 52. | 104 (WP) | 104 (WP) | 0 |

*Original Series
** Twin
WP = WPPSI, SB = Stanford-Binet, WI = WISC, WI-R = WISC-R, PPV = Peabody
Mean IQ Change = 10. 1 ± 2.25
Paired-t = 4.4809 df = 51
p< 0.001

It was found that a considerable amount of treatment was often provided before the initial or "pre-treatment" IQ test: a mean of 30 visits with the parents and 83 visits with the child. Between the two IQ tests, the caretakers had an average of 77 visits and the children averaged 316. The high number of children's visits reflects, in part, the participation for one to two years of many of the children in the five-day-per-week Cornerstone Nursery School (CNS) nursery (Kliman 1975; see also Chapter 2). The time in months and the number of visits are correlated with r = 0.332 and t (of r) = 2.491, corresponding to p < 0.02.

The mean age on admission was 45 months. Three-quarters of the sample were boys. Almost three-quarters of the children were receiving Medicaid and an additional one-fifth lived with families on incomes less than $15,000 per year. Twenty-eight percent of the biological parents had attended or graduated from college, while over 65 percent had not. About two-thirds of the sample were in the care of their biological mother alone and more than three-quarters of the children were not living with their fathers. Neither age, sex, economic status, parental education, or separation from parents were found to correlate significantly with IQ change.

From observation or history, global ratings of the mother's pathology were made. Well over one-quarter of the mothers had "extreme" pathology, while well over half had "severe" pathology. The pathology of three mothers was unknown. Even assuring that these three mothers had mild or no pathology, less than 10 percent of the sample had mothers whose pathology was judged as "moderate" or less severe. There was no statistically significant difference in IQ change of children whose mothers had lesser pathology as compared to those whose mothers had severe pathology.

Table 17–2 provides information on the pathology of the primary caretakers. Each primary caretaker's diagnostic category (usually the mother, foster mother, or female relative) was ascertained according to *DSM-III* criteria from clinical or historical information. In some cases, more than one primary diagnosis was made. Over 70 percent of the primary caretakers (over two-thirds of whom represented the biological mothers of the children) had a personality disorder as the primary diagnosis. About one-fifth had a primary diagnosis of affective disorder and another one-fifth were rated as psychotic. Another 7.7 percent were classified as having an anxiety disorder. The 37 children whose primary caretakers were found to have a personality disorder showed a mean IQ change of $10.9 \pm 2.63$. The paired t was 4.1569 with $p < 0.005$. No significance was found for caretakers with affective disorders, anxiety disorders, or psychoses.

Due to lack of information about many of the fathers, almost 54 percent could not be rated as to severity of pathology. However, of those fathers whose pathology could be rated, three-quarters were judged as having severe pathology or worse. Severity of the father's pathology was significantly associated with the child's IQ change ($p < 0.01$). The 6 children whose fathers were rated as having only "moderate" pathology showed a mean IQ

**Table 17–2.** Psychological Diagnosis of Primary Caretaker

| Diagnosis | N | Mean IQ | ± S.E.M. | Paired-t | P |
|---|---|---|---|---|---|
| Personality Disorder | 37 | 10.9 | 2.62 | 4.1569 | <0.0005 |
| Affective Disorder | 11 | 20 | 4.16 | 0.4812 | NS |
| Psychosis | 8 | 10.5 | 7.44 | 1.4108 | NS |
| Anxiety Disorder | 4 | 16.5 | 9.73 | 1.6951 | NS |
| Other | 4 | 10.5 | 7.31 | 1.4366 | NS |

change of 26.3 compared with mean IQ changes of 5.9, 3, and 2.1 for the other two groups.

Table 17–3 compares the effects of the primary treatment modalities of the sample. Forty-two children received therapeutic nursery treatment (CNS) (Kliman 1975), either alone or with other modalities ($\Delta$ IQ = 11.7), and 21 percent received analytic psychotherapy, alone or with CNS ($\Delta$ IQ = 11.4). As can be seen from the table, there was no significant effect of educational psychotherapy on IQ ($\Delta$ IQ = 4.22). Any combination of the more intensive therapeutic modalities were highly significant at $p < 0.001$. The 4 children whose parents attended an adult group had IQs that increased significantly ($p < 0.0005$).

Twenty-two (42.3 percent) of the sample were still in treatment at the time of the data collection. Ten children, whose terminations were planned, averaged IQ increases of 12.5. In contrast, the 9 children who were withdrawn from treatment because they moved or for other reasons had an average $\Delta$ IQ of 5.2. These findings did not reach statistical significance.

A total of 105 *DSM-III* diagnoses were made of the children, reflecting an average of about two per child. Almost half of the sample had developmental disorders; more than a quarter had pervasive developmental disorders; more than one-third had oppositional disorders; almost one-fifth had attention deficit disorders; 15 percent had psychotic disorders; and more than one-tenth had an adjustment disorder. There was no relationship between the children's diagnoses and IQ change.

On admission, the level of psychosocial stress and global functioning during the year preceding admission was ascertained. Almost one-fifth of the

**Table 17–3.** Treatment Modalities and IQ Change

| Treatment | N | Mean IQ Change | ± S.E.M. | Paired t | p (1-tail) |
|---|---|---|---|---|---|
| Educational Psychotherapy Only | 9 | 4.22 | 4.57 | 0.9246 | NS |
| Cornerstone Nursery (CNS) Only | 13 | 11.5 | 4.22 | 2.7366 | <0.02 |
| CNS &/or Analysis Only | 21 | 11.4 | 3.76 | 3.0377 | <0.005 |
| CNS &/or Analysis with or without any other treatment | 42 | 11.7 | 2.54 | 4.6063 | <0.001 |
| Child Group | 6* | 22.0 | 7.23 | 3.0431 | <0.02 |
| Adult Group | 4* | 32.8 | 3.54 | 9.2573 | <0.0005 |
| Medication | 4* | −4.25 | 3.59 | −1.1835 | |

*All the children were also receiving other therapies.

children were judged on admission to be "grossly impaired," more than two-thirds were functioning "very poorly," and about one-seventh were functioning "poorly." All of the children in the sample were judged to have been subjected to intense environmental stress as defined by *DSM-III* in the year preceding admission. More than two-thirds had been subjected to extreme or catastrophic stress and the remainder to moderate to severe stress.

The relationship between global outcome of the children and their IQ change was examined. Global clinical outcome was rated by the psychiatrist on a 7 point scale ranging from "major deterioration" to "asymptomatic or cured," with the midpoint of the scale at "no change." None of the cases was rated as worse (the three lower points of the scale) and none were rated as "asymptomatic or cured." The cases were combined, leaving three groups: "no change," "some improvement," and "much or major improvement." The 30 children rated as having undergone "much or major improvement" had a mean IQ change of 12.2. The "some improvement" group mean IQ change was 5.3, and the "no change" group's mean IQ change was 2.7. These differences did not reach statistical significance.

## DISCUSSION

The primary purpose of this study was to see to what extent the IQ gains reported in a previous study would persist if the original selected samples were expanded without prior selection.

A highly significant mean IQ change was found in this cohort of nonselected cases. The findings in this study support the strength of the effectiveness of therapeutic intervention. As expected, the change was less than that found in the original sample (Zelman et al. 1985). The possibility that the observed IQ changes were due to initial low IQ scores has been ruled out.

There were two different IQ test instruments used for the same individual about half the time. This might be considered a problem in terms of controlling this important variable. However, the Stanford-Binet was the first test 18 times and the second test only 2 times. The Stanford-Binet has been reported to give consistently higher scores relative to the WISC (Moriarity 1966). The elevation of scores would have inflated the initial IQ, making it more difficult to obtain significant IQ changes in the present study. As far as the other instruments that differed from test one to test two (13 cases), it is suggested that the results would not be significantly affected. For the most part, it is felt the different order of the tests would lead to the canceling out of error in the results.

The fact that, on the average, a significant amount of treatment had already been provided prior to the first IQ tests may also have decreased the observed IQ change. It may be that had the entire sample been tested prior to therapy, lower initial (i.e., pre-treatment) IQs would have been seen and, therefore, greater IQ changes would have been obtained.

The second objective of this study was to explore some of the variables that might correlate with the IQ gain. Unfortunately, it was hard to achieve statistical significance with the relatively small number of subjects. It is likely that with a greater number of subjects the differences would have reached statistical significance. This is supported by the finding that with many of the variables, there were nonsignificant trends in a predictable direction: (1) intergroup differences in mean IQ change tended to decrease with increasing global impairment (12.3, 10.6, and 2.4); (2) mean positive IQ change for the group with severe stress was 14.9, while the extreme-catastrophic stress group had a mean IQ change of 6.8; (3) greater gains in IQ were made by 10 children whose terminations were planned (average gain was 12.5) than by those who were removed from treatment (an average gain of 5.2); (4) the mean Δ IQ of the children increased as the global pathology improved (12.2 for those children who made major improvement versus a 2.7 point IQ change for those children where there was no change).

Kazdin (1985) has pointed out that change in a specific target behavior, as measured in a particular manner, may not correlate with the achievement of major clinical objectives. It was our assumption that improvement in cognitive functioning, as measured by IQ tests in these multiply stressed children, would be likely to result in better function elsewhere and might protect them from worsening of pathology. The nonsignificant but strong trend toward a correlation between global improvement and IQ gain supports this assumption.

The significant results of an increase in IQ appeared to be due, in part, to the relatively young age (mean of 45 months) of the entire cohort on admission. This remains to be tested further by comparing IQ changes in treated school-age children with preschool children. Money and colleagues (1983), in a study of IQ changes in children "rescued" from abuse, found that the younger the child when rescued the greater the IQ gain.

It is also worth noting that 37 primary caretakers (70 percent) who had personality disorders had children whose IQ changed significantly. Since some of the diagnoses were made primarily from history, it is possible that the category of personality disorder was overrepresented to the detriment of the other categories. In spite of this reservation, it appears that personality disorder is a common pathological entity for parents of multiply stressed children. The results bode well for our potential ability to help such children increase their IQs and their ability to learn.

Of special note is the finding that the presence of fathers in the family unit, particularly in instances of relatively low severity of paternal pathology, was associated with positive IQ change. This observation, suggestive of the importance of fathers, is consistent with Wallerstein's (1987) finding that children of divorce whose fathers remain involved do better than those who lose touch with their fathers.

The present cohort represented a highly stressed group of children, whose parents and other caretakers demonstrated pervasive disturbances. The fact that these children nevertheless managed to show IQ gains strengthens the impression of the power of intensive psychotherapeutic modalities to preserve as well as improve cognitive function.

This study supports the authors' earlier report (Zelman et al. 1985) of the unique value of the therapeutic nursery modality (compared with educational psychotherapy). The later conclusion may not be justified, however, since educational psychotherapy was generally prescribed for children with more stressors and greater pathology (Stein and Ronald 1974). Also, they generally had fewer sessions early in therapy than did those children who were receiving analytic psychotherapy in the five-day-a-week Cornerstone program or those children who were in analytic treatment four or five times a week.

Of further note is the finding that the 4 children whose parents were in an adult therapeutic group had significant IQ changes ($p < 0.0005$). In looking at the original data, it was found that: all of the mothers in the adult group had personality disorders; their children were all in the five-day-a-week Cornerstone Nursery; all 4 fathers were living in the home; and 3 of the 4 fathers had only moderate pathology. The significance of these four cases ($p < 0.0005$) is greater than that found for the whole group of children in the CNS therapeutic program ($p < 0.005$). Therefore, even when the mother has pathology as severe as a personality disorder intensive child therapy, parent guidance, an intact family (which includes fathers with only moderate pathology), and adult group therapy may significantly increase a child's IQ.

It is not surprising that the combined group of children whose terminations were planned and those still in treatment at the time of the study showed greater positive IQ changes than did those whose treatment stopped for other reasons. The literature on psychotherapy generally indicates that a positive result correlates with the presence of a good therapeutic alliance and/or positive transference. Generally when terminations are planned, there is a good alliance and transferential relationship between parents and therapist.

This study provides evidence for the effectiveness of intensive psychotherapy with children. Unfortunately, the retrospective nature of the data, coupled with the limited size of the sample, precluded identification of additional variables that might help predict and enhance IQ gains obtained from psychotherapy. Large and more systematic prospective studies will have to be done to answer these important questions.

## REFERENCES

Kazdin, A. E. (1985). Selection of target behaviors: the relationship of the treatment focus to clinical dysfunction. *Behavioral Assessment* 7:33–47.

Kliman, G. (1975). Analyst in the nursery: experimental application of child analytic-technique in a therapeutic nursery: the Cornerstone method. In *Psychoanalytic Study of the Child* 30:477–510. New Haven, CT: Yale University Press.

Lovaas, O. I. (1987). Behavioral treatment and normal educational and intellectual functioning in young autistic children. *Journal of Consulting and Clinical Psychology* 55:3–9.

Money, J., Annecillo, C., and Kelley, J. F. (1983). Growth of intelligence: failure and catchup associated respectively with abuse and rescue in the syndrome of abuse dwarfism. *Psychoneuroendocrinology* 8:309–319.

Moriarity, A. E. (1966). *Constancy and the IQ Change: A Clinical View of Relationships between Tested Intelligence and Personality.* Springfield, IL: Charles C Thomas.

Stein, M., and Ronald, D. (1974). Educational psychotherapy of preschoolers. *Journal of the American Academy of Child Psychiatry* 13:618–634.

Wallerstein, J. S. (1987). Children of divorce: a report of a ten-year follow-up of early latency-age children. *American Journal of Orthopsychiatry* 57:199–211.

Zelman, A. B., Samuels, S., and Abrams, D. (1985). IQ changes in young children following intensive long-term psychotherapy. *American Journal of Psychotherapy* 39:215–227.

# Epilogue

*Arthur B. Zelman*

The twentieth century has provided terrible evidence to refute the idea of moral, as opposed to technological, progress. For many of us who nevertheless choose to cling to this idea, the ongoing raising of consciousness of the ways in which we do harm to each other helps to sustain hope.

Within the past fifty years, for example, the evils of colonialism, racism, totalitarianism, and sexism have been recognized. This recognition has led, often with astonishing rapidity, to dramatic social change in each of these domains that had been deemed impossible only a few years, if not months, before the changes occurred. Desegregation is one example and the sudden and unanticipated collapse of Communism is another.

I would like to believe that we are on the verge of a further expansion of our consciousness. This time the issue concerns human development and the problem of hate and violence. Bombarded as we have been by individual acts of hatred, either because of its increased frequency or because of our increased exposure through the mass media, the subject has come to center stage. Various explanations have been brought to bear, some old, some new. There is, on the one hand, rekindled interest in the idea of the devil and demonic possession; on the other is the modern medicalization of evil, as reflected in the renewed search for genetic and organic causes of·criminality. In my opinion, neither the religious nor the medical explanation will do. We are almost as unlikely to discover a gene for hatred as we are to provide scientific evidence of the devil.

Hate (as opposed to aggression) is a social phenomenon and can only occur in a social context. A child may have a genetic loading for aggression; still, he has to acquire not the capacity for hatred, which is universal, but the readiness to do its bidding. This is something he learns from his experience and the meaning he derives from it. If he is abused, he is likely to feel he is an object of hate and will hate others in return. If he is neglected, he learns that he is of no importance, nor are others.

The issue is admittedly more complicated than this, for it is not always easy to discern what constitutes neglect or abuse. Nor is it always possible, given the inherent creativity of the human mind, to foresee the meaning the child will give to his experience. Nevertheless, the more negative the realities to which he is exposed, the more predictable and intense will be his negative response. The well-documented incidence of childhood neglect and abuse in the histories of adolescents and adults with severe antisocial personality disorders is but one example from a mountain of evidence for this assertion. But such evidence, while scientifically significant, does not have the force of experience to which early interventionists are exposed. It is difficult, for example, to experience the fear, mistrust, and rage of a 4-year-old homeless child who, like his mother and father before him, has been abused or neglected without concluding that one is observing a criminal or mentally ill person in the making. Without intensive clinical, educational, or familial help over a long period of time in a corrective environment, this child will be at high risk to do hateful things to himself or others.

Work at close range with severely environmentally stressed young children not only provides a perspective on risks to their well-being, but also on principles regarding their protection. These principles highlight the fundamental importance of a "good enough" social environment with which the child can identify. At this writing, institutions such as Welfare, Medicaid, Public Housing, and Public Education, which were designed to support and protect children, are under attack. Presumably this attack reflects not only their cost but the judgment that they are insufficiently effective.

This crisis might prove a good thing so long as our attempt to change these institutions is driven by our ongoing awareness of the minimal needs of these children, their dependence on the adult world to meet them, and the consequences to society if we don't. We must inform our decisions concerning the care we provide our children with the understanding that children who are not cared about will not grow up to care about themselves or others. This awareness will surely help us to close the increasingly dangerous gap between the technological and moral accomplishments of our society.

# Index

Limit setting
  Cornerstone Therapeutic Nursery,
     26–27
  as therapy, 54–56
Lindeman, E., xiv
Lindholmand, B., 125
Loewald, H. W., 141
Lopez, T., 27, 28, 30, 66, 127, 157
Lorman, S., 281
Lovaas, O. I., 335
Lucas, L., 232
Lush, D., 128

Madonna, J. M., Jr., 174
Mahler, M., 9, 11, 192, 201, 202, 207,
     208, 230, 322, 331
Martin, P. J., 322
Masterman, S. H., 175
Masterson, J. F., 201
Mayes, L. C., 126
Medical model, prevention and, 1–18
Medication, Attention Deficit Disorder
     (ADD), 89–90
Meisels, S. J., 17
Mendik, L., 13
Menolascino, F. J., 323
Mental health consultation
  daycare questionnaire, 281–292
  early intervention, 14–15
  homeless children, 151–170
  women's shelter, 293–305. See also
     Women's shelter
Mental illness, prevention and, 1
Miller, J., 24
Miller, L. B., 321
Milrod, D., 126, 141
Minuchin, S., 92
Miringoff, M., 16
Modell, A. H., 60
Molnar, J. M., 151, 152
Money, J., 342
Moriarity, A. E., 341
Mowbray, C., 230
Musick, J., 229, 232

National Committee for Adoption, 125
Neale, J., 229

Neglected children, 263–277
  case discussion, 275–277
  case illustration, 265–275
  overview of, 263–265
Neubauer, P., xiv
Nickman, S. L., 141

Oberndorf, C. P., 322
Object relations theory
  bereavement, 201–203
  early intervention and, 9
  neglected children, 264
O'Leary, K., 295
Osofsky, J. D., 16
Outcomes
  bereavement, surviving parent–child
     relationship, 190–191
  early intervention, risk factors,
     severity of, 12–14
  foster care placement, personal life
     history book, 122–123
  PACT Therapeutic Unit, 251–256
Overstreet, H., 106
Oyserman, D., 233

PACT Therapeutic Unit, 227–260
  case illustrations, 241–251
  future plans, 257–258
  literature review, 229–234
  overview of, 227–228
  program description, 234–239
  program evaluation, 251–256
  therapeutic nursery, 239–241
Parental bereavement. See
     Bereavement
Parental psychopathology, PACT
     Therapeutic Unit, 227–260. See
     also PACT Therapeutic Unit
Parents, Cornerstone Therapeutic
     Nursery, 48–54
Parents of sexually abused children,
     307–318
  discussed, 315–318
  first phase, 307–313
  overview of, 307–309
  second phase, 313–314
  termination, 314–315